# Correspondence: 1919–1973

# New Heidegger Research

**Series Editors:** Gregory Fried, Professor of Philosophy, Boston College, USA; and Richard Polt, Professor of Philosophy, Xavier University, USA

The *New Heidegger Research* series promotes informed and critical dialogue that breaks new philosophical ground by taking into account the full range of Heidegger's thought, as well as the enduring questions raised by his work.

## Titles in the Series

*Heidegger's Gods: An Ecofeminist Perspective*
    Susanne Claxton
*Making Sense of Heidegger*
    Thomas Sheehan
*Proto-Phenomenology and the Nature of Language*
    Lawrence J. Hatab
*Heidegger in the Islamicate World*
    Edited by Kata Moser, Urs Gösken and Josh Michael Hayes
*Time and Trauma: Thinking Through Heidegger in the Thirties*
    Richard Polt
*Contexts of Suffering: A Heideggerian Approach to Psychopathology*
    Kevin Aho
*Heidegger's Phenomenology of Perception: An Introduction, Volume I*
    David Kleinberg-Levin
*Confronting Heidegger: A Critical Dialogue on Politics and Philosophy*
    Edited by Gregory Fried
*Proto-Phenomenology, Language Acquisition, Orality and Literacy: Dwelling in Speech II*
    Lawrence J. Hatab
*Transcending Reason: Heidegger on Rationality*
    Edited by Matthew Burch and Irene McMullin
*The Fate of Phenomenology: Heidegger's Legacy*
    William McNeill
*Agency, Freedom, and Responsibility in the Early Heidegger*
    Hans Pedersen
*Heidegger's Phenomenology of Perception: Learning to See and Hear Hermeneutically, Volume II*
    David Kleinberg-Levin
*Towards a Polemical Ethics: Between Heidegger and Plato*
    Gregory Fried
*Thought Poems: A Translation of Heidegger's Verse*
    By Martin Heidegger - Translated by Eoghan Walls
*Correspondence: 1919–1973*
        By Martin Heidegger and Karl Löwith - Translated by J. Goesser Assaiante and S. Montgomery Ewegen

# Correspondence: 1919–1973

Martin Heidegger and Karl Löwith

Translated by J. Goesser Assaiante and
S. Montgomery Ewegen

ROWMAN & LITTLEFIELD
*Lanham • Boulder • New York • London*

Published by Rowman & Littlefield
An imprint of The Rowman & Littlefield Publishing Group, Inc.
4501 Forbes Boulevard, Suite 200, Lanham, Maryland 20706
www.rowman.com

Martin Heidegger / Karl Löwith, Briefwechsel 1919–1973 edited by Aldred Denker
© 2015 Verlag Karl Alber part of Verlag Herder GmbH, Freiburg im Breisgau

English translation copyright © 2021 by The Rowman & Littlefield Publishing Group, Inc.

*All rights reserved.* No part of this book may be reproduced in any form or by any electronic or mechanical means, including information storage and retrieval systems, without written permission from the publisher, except by a reviewer who may quote passages in a review.

British Library Cataloguing in Publication Information Available

**Library of Congress Cataloging-in-Publication Data**

Names: Heidegger, Martin, 1889-1976, author. | Löwith, Karl, 1897-1973 author. | Goesser Assaiante, Julia, translator. | Ewegen, S. Montgomery, translator.
Title: Correspondence : 1919-1973 / by Martin Heidegger and Karl Löwith ; translated by J. Goesser Assaiante and S. Montgomery Ewegen.
Description: Lanham : Rowman & Littlefield, [2021] | Includes bibliographical references.
Identifiers: LCCN 2021027734 (print) | LCCN 2021027735 (ebook) | ISBN 9781786607225 (cloth) | ISBN 9781538188125 (paper) | ISBN 9781786607232 (epub)
Subjects: LCSH: Heidegger, Martin, 1889-1976—Correspondence. | Löwith, Karl, 1897-1973—Correspondence. | Philosophers—Germany—Correspondence.
Classification: LCC B3279 .H485 2021 (print) | LCC B3279 (ebook) | DDC 193—dc23
LC record available at https://lccn.loc.gov/2021027734
LC ebook record available at https://lccn.loc.gov/2021027735

*This volume was made possible through the kind support of the Martin Heidegger Archive in Messkirch and the Martin Heidegger Foundation at the German Literary Archive in Marbach, as well as the Gerda Henkel Foundation.*

# Contents

| | |
|---|---|
| Translators' Foreword | ix |
| Editors' Foreword | xvii |
| Correspondence | 1 |
| **APPENDIX** | 157 |
| Supplement 1: Letter from Elisabeth Förster-Nietzsche to Karl Löwith | 159 |
| Supplement 2: Martin Heidegger's Assessment of Karl Löwith's Habilitation Thesis (1928) | 161 |
| Supplement 3: Excerpt from Karl Löwith's Italian Diary (1934–1936) | 165 |
| Supplement 4: Letter from Ada Löwith to Elfride Heidegger-Petri (1976) | 167 |
| Supplement 5: Entry from Karl Löwith in the Heidegger Family Guestbook at the Hut in Todtnauberg (1924) | 169 |
| Supplement 6: List of Martin Heidegger's Courses in which Karl Löwith Participated | 171 |
| Annotations | 173 |
| Annotations to the Supplements | 281 |
| Editor's Afterword | 287 |

| | |
|---|---:|
| Abbreviations | 293 |
| Biographies | 295 |
| Selected Writings of Karl Löwith | 299 |
| List of Documents | 303 |
| Image Credits | 307 |
| Index of Names | 309 |

# Translators' Foreword

Translation is conversation. To translate entails bringing one language into conversation with another, and in such a way as to let the one turn about (*conversare*) with the other, as if in a dance. Through that dance, traces and movements of the animating spirit of one language work their way into the other; and it is the ardent hope of translators—or, at the very least, of *these* translators—to let the original language take the lead by showing the target language where to go, how to move. As conversation, translation should be a responsive and sympathetic partner, and at its very best it intuits and anticipates the guiding moves of the source language—that is, the language that *initiates* the dance.

In the present case, the translation/conversation was concerned with translating nothing other than a conversation: namely, the written conversation that took place between Martin Heidegger and Karl Löwith between 1919 and 1973. In this way, we the translators *conversed with a conversation*, one which lasted for fifty-four years, years that saw promise and success, frustration and failure, love and hate, war and reconciliation. Life and death, in other words: the conversation between Martin Heidegger and Karl Löwith—their intellectual dance—spanned over five decades of life and death, with all of the existential facticity that such life and death entails.

Like all conversations, the one presented here is incomplete. It is incomplete owing to the fact that occasionally letters or postcards are referenced by Heidegger or Löwith to which our eyes are not privy—documents which, as the annotations say time and again, "are not in the possession of the estate." The conversation is also incomplete because those who were engaged in it died before they finished saying everything they had to say to one another. (This is, of course, the way in which nearly all conversations remain unfinished.) But most crucially, the conversation presented herein is incomplete because it is held up and sustained by an entire universe of thought that remains *unsaid* within the documents themselves—or, indeed, perhaps *two* universes of thought. Behind every word of every letter, there is the mind of a great thinker, a mind only some of whose inner workings made their way onto the printed pages that they shared with one another. The documents presented herein are *intimations* or *indications* of the lives and spirits of two leading figures in the intellectual history of the west, lives that turned about with each other for their entire adult lives and were all the richer for it.

Although the editors' extensive Foreword and Afterword relieve us of the duty of preparing an expansive introduction, a few words should be said regarding some of (what we take to be) the most important terms that occur during the course of their written correspondence. (We urge the readers to make their own determinations of what is "most important," and to take our determinations with a grain of salt.) For the most part, the conversation between them is casual and friendly, even relaxed and vulgar at times; as a result, the letters are largely lacking in the kind of specialized language that one finds in, for example, Heidegger's lecture courses. However, there are a few letters, especially early on in their relationship, where the discourse becomes dense and technical; as a result, some ink must be spent in the explanation of some of their vocabulary.

One of the more interesting terms that comes up through the course of their correspondence is *Eigendestruktion*, a word that occurs a single time within the volume and, as far we were able to determine, never occurs in Heidegger's work itself. The word appears within a letter from April 1921 (Document 22), the same semester that Heidegger was delivering his lecture course "Augustinus und der Neuplatonismus" (now in *The Phenomenology of Religious Life*), a crucial course regarding the development of the notion and practice of *Destruktion* (destructuring). Owing to the context in which it appears, one is tempted to understand *Eigendestruktion* as a conceptual equivalent (and perhaps terminological precursor) to *Destruktion*, one that sheds interesting and revealing light upon the process of destructuring. Like *Destruktion*, *Eigendestruktion* entails a critical stance toward the cultural and intellectual tradition to which one owes one's own factical self—a tradition that, through the operation of *Eigendestruktion*, is not only confronted and assessed, but also grasped and taken up anew. In order to capture the way in which one's tradition is always *one's own*, we have translated the term as "destructuring one's own."

One of the reasons for the above rendering is the fact that the perhaps more concise "self-destructuring" could not be used, owing to the appearance in Document 35 (from 1922) of the term *Selbst-Destruktion* (self-destructuring), whose meaning is evidently equivalent to *Eigendestruktion*. Both terms point to the highly personal and situated character of destructuring, the manner in which its backward facing critical operation always proceeds from out of *one's own* factical situation of thrown projection. It is owing to this personal character that Heidegger can write in a letter from 1920 (Document 8) that "[a]t the moment I am destructuring myself {*destruiere ich mich selbst*}, which takes the most effort." One's own self is always already implicated in the operation of destructuring, at least when it is done correctly. In short, an individual destructures herself even as she destructures her own tradition and history—and, indeed, precisely then.

Given the presence of the notions of "destructuring," "self-destructuring," and "destructuring one's own," it is perhaps not surprising to find that *history (Historie)* plays an important role in the correspondence. In many of the letters, the notion of the historical character of factical existence, as well as the historical character of philosophy itself as it seeks to understand factical existence, is discussed. In almost all cases in this volume, *Historie* refers to the lived experience of factical *Dasein*, and is thus to be understood as more-or-less equivalent in meaning to *Geschichte* (as Document 20 makes clear), the term Heidegger will later use to distinguish authentic history from the reckoning and assessing of historical events (i.e., *historiography*). (Indeed, in Document 44 from 1923, one can already see Heidegger beginning to draw a critical distance between *das Geschichtliche* and *das Historische*.) Owing largely to the paucity of terms within the English language that adequately capture the differences between *Historie* and *Geschichte*, we have translated both as "history" (or "the historical"), and have included the German when doing so was necessary to indicate the intended sense.

As suggested above, the operation of destructuring never consists in the bare rejection of a tradition, but rather entails both critical assessment *and* informed appropriation of one's own history, a dual structure that can be adequately captured with the term *Auseinandersetzung*. This term occurs somewhat regularly throughout the correspondence, and Löwith even uses it numerous times (in Documents 73 and 76) to refer to his own engagement with Heidegger's work. It marks both a respectful engagement with, but also a decisive setting apart from, another's conceptual framework, an engagement through which the limitations of that framework, but also the indebtedness of one's one position to it, come to light. In the hope of catching these nuances, we have rendered it as "critical engagement," except in those few cases where its meaning is utterly nonphilosophical.

Perhaps one of the more conceptually difficult terms that arises in the correspondence is *Vollzug*, here translated as "enactment." Already finding frequent use in Heidegger's lecture courses from the early 1920s, this term plays an important role in Heidegger's (and thus also the younger Löwith's) understanding of phenomenology. Integral to the way in which one accesses one's own genuine *Dasein*, enactment has to do with the realization or actualization of the structures of possibility that belong to oneself. Because of this, and as the letters make clear, enactment always operates in relation to one's own factical situation, and thus to one's own historical tradition. Genuine enactment as the authentic realization of the possibilities belonging to one's own *Dasein* is, thus, only possible on the basis of a critical engagement with—which is to say, a destructuring or self-destructuring of—one's own tradition and history.

The term *Dasein* appears numerous times throughout the volume, especially in Document 74 (from 1927, the year that *Sein und Zeit* was published) and in Document 98 (from 1929, the year that *Kant und das Problem der Metaphysik* was published). In almost every case, it carries the meaning that Heidegger assigned to it in *Being and Time* and the texts leading up to it: namely, it refers to that entity for whom being is an issue, the entity who exists in the "there" of being and in such a way as to comport itself toward beings and concern itself with them and their being. As has become somewhat customary, we have left the term untranslated. In the few occasions when "existence" in a more general sense is meant, we have rendered it as such, and have included the German (so as to differentiate it from *Existenz*, which occurs in the letters with great frequency).

The German word *existenziell* occurs a few times in the text, and we have transposed it as "existentiell." As in *Being and Time*, the word here refers to the ontic (or lived) side of existence and the self-understanding that characterizes it, in distinction to the ontological structures that constitute and make possible such lived existence. (This is true even in the letters from the early 1920s that predate *Being and Time*.) The latter structures are described by Heidegger with the neologism *existenzial*, which occurs in this volume only in Document 77 (from 1927). We have rendered it as "existential," and have provided the German in curly brackets.

The term *Mitwelt*, which Heidegger had employed in multiple lecture courses in the early 1920s in which Löwith participated, occurs in numerous letters. Although the notion was structurally important to Heidegger in *Being and Time*, it becomes absolutely integral to Löwith's habilitation thesis (which was submitted in 1928). As Heidegger himself explains in his assessment of that document (which is included in this volume as Supplement 2), the term *Mitwelt* refers to the manner in which the human always already shares a world with others, a sharing that bears an ontologically primary and existentially determinative role in the constitution of the individual. In other words, the world of one's own *Dasein* is foundationally co-determined through the world of the *Dasein* of others. We have translated it accordingly as "shared world."

The common but problematic word *Wissenschaft* occurs in the letters with some regularity. In almost all cases, what is meant is the practice or institution of rigorous, formalized knowledge (i.e., "science" in the broadest and most literal sense). In order to avoid confusing it with particular academic or "hard" scientific disciplines, we have rendered it as "scholarly knowledge" and "academic knowledge," depending on the context. However, as the reader will see, the meaning of the term shifts between rigorous scholarly knowledge in a positive sense, and overly rigidified and stuffy pedantic knowledge that risks losing touch with the ontic world of lived existence. In other words, the meaning and value of "scholarly knowledge" is at issue in the letters, especially to the younger Löwith as he grapples with his decision to, and uncertainties about, pursuing a life of academic philosophy.

During their discussions of academic life, and especially in the annotations, various words for academic appointments at German universities are used (e.g., *Dozent, Privatdozent, Außerplanmäßig, Extraordinarius, Ordinarius*, and *Professor*, listed here in ascending rank). Because the system of appointments in Germany does not correspond to those used in the United States or the United Kingdom, we have left the various terms untranslated.

And now for some housekeeping.

As mentioned in the Editors' Afterword, in preparing the German volume the editors deliberately avoided standardizing dates and greetings in order to allow for the personal character of the individual letters (and their authors) to be preserved. We have followed that practice here. As a result, some letters use Roman numerals for months, and some use Arabic; sometimes the name of the city is abbreviated, and sometimes it is spelled out; sometimes the entire year is given, and sometimes just the last two numbers. In Document 14 (from 1920), Löwith mentions an acquaintance of his, a graphologist, to whom he gave a handwritten manuscript of Heidegger's in order to have it analyzed. It would perhaps be worthwhile to have the idiosyncrasies of Löwith's and Heidegger's letters analyzed in such a way; in any case, the preservation of such subtleties lends a touch of authenticity to the otherwise uniform printed page.

Despite having made this particular allowance, the editors did standardize punctuation. We have done the same, and have in fact altered it in certain cases where not doing so would have muddied the sense. In some of Löwith's letters to Heidegger—especially those in which his enthusiasm or frustration supersedes his desire for clarity—rearranging the punctuation was an absolute necessity, at least when bringing the ideas into English. However, we have tried to be as sparing as possible in our shuffling about of dashes, semicolons, and the like, in order to preserve the mood and character of the letters.

To further allow the idiosyncrasies of the letters to shine forth, the editors also reproduced Heidegger's and Löwith's use of the *Eszett* (ß), owing to the fact that the letters were written prior to the German orthographic reforms of 1996. Although this practice does indeed lend a sense of authenticity and historicity to the letters, it is not achievable in English translation. (For example, it doesn't matter, when translating the German word *Gruss* (greeting) into English, whether it is spelled *Gruß*.) For the sake of our projected readership, we have Americanized the spellings of proper names (e.g., *Meßkirch* has become *Messkirch*); however, when a word with the *Eszett* occurs within the title of a seminar, article, or book, we have let it stand.

Because the editors employed standard brackets while making their various editorial insertions (as described in the Editors' Afterword), we have used curly brackets (i.e., { }) when inserting German words or expressions. That being said, for the purposes of eloquence and flow, we have tried to keep our insertions to an absolute minimum. We encourage readers of this translation to acquire the German volume as well so that they may expose themselves to the full richness of the German vocabulary that animates this correspondence.

As they mention in their Foreword, the editors have provided abundant annotations relating to the letters and the supplements. (Indeed, they make up almost one-third of the volume's total length.) As they are performing their ampliative and clarificatory functions, many of the annotations provide bibliographic information regarding Heidegger's and Löwith's works, as well as the works of people to whom Heidegger and Löwith refer during the course of their nearly lifelong conversation. Because the focus of this volume is that conversation itself, we have only translated the names of works authored by Heidegger and Löwith; the rest, even for thinkers of such rank as Friedrich Nietzsche, Edmund Husserl, Karl Jaspers, Hans-Georg Gadamer, and Søren Kierkegaard, we have left in the German. When an annotation refers to a text of Heidegger's or Löwith's that has been translated into English, we have provided the English bibliographical information as well. Occasionally, an annotation *quotes* one of Heidegger's or Löwith's published texts; in those cases where a published English translation exists, we have quoted from those editions rather than translating the passages ourselves.

A precious few grammatical and citational errors have been silently corrected.

We offer our gratitude to Richard Polt and Gregory Fried for their assistance in preparing this translation, and to Frankie Mace and Arun Rajakumar for their hard work and patience. We also extend our thanks to the editors, Alfred Denker and Holger Zaborowski, and especially to the former for his help in answering questions regarding the German volume. We offer additional thanks to Trinity College for providing us with a research grant to aid in the completion of this work. Finally, we would like to thank LEG for their generous and enthusiastic support.

Our translation of this volume serves as our contribution to the scholarly conversation underway concerning the relationship between Martin Heidegger and Karl Löwith and the many conversations regarding the intricacies of their respective works. We hope that it provokes many conversations to come, and we look forward to the dance.

J. Goesser Assaiante and S. Montgomery Ewegen

# Editors' Foreword

Martin Heidegger has decisively determined the contemporary philosophical landscape. His work is the subject of countless scholarly investigations, and the literature regarding his writings is so vast that a comprehensive overview is close to impossible. He belongs without a doubt among the most significant thinkers of the twentieth century. Thus, his influence is felt not only within philosophy, but also within many other cultural and intellectual areas as well, such as Catholic and Protestant theology, literary studies, classical philology, psychology, and medicine, as well as art and literature. Martin Heidegger's collected works (the so-called *Gesamtausgabe*), which is comprised of some one-hundred volumes, continually provokes new critical engagements with his thinking. Above all, Heidegger was a philosopher whose thinking developed from out of his particular life experiences, specific conversations, and extensive correspondences.

For these reasons, it is of great significance—not only for Heidegger research, but for twentieth-century intellectual history as well—that his various correspondences be made available to the public in a scholarly collection. Heidegger's letters are scattered throughout the world, and *The Collected Letters of Martin Heidegger* will bring them together for the first time.

*The Collected Letters of Martin Heidegger* combines letters of significance to and from Martin Heidegger into a single, unified collection. In addition to varied correspondences with scholars from all disciplines, this collection publishes—comprehensively and for the first time—"private" and "institutional" correspondences. This collection not only helps fill in the overall picture of Heidegger, it also makes possible new emphases and distinctions regarding Heidegger's work and Heidegger himself. However, this collection of letters is not an historical-critical one, as it does not contain all letters and drafts. From an editorial standpoint, the present correspondence is a continuation of the already published volumes of Martin Heidegger's correspondences with Hannah Arendt, Imma von Bodmershof, Max Müller, Ludwig von Ficker, Karl Jaspers, and Kurt Bauch, among others. To date, over 200 people with whom Heidegger corresponded have been determined. At this time, there is evidence of some 10,000 letters written to and by Heidegger, the first originating from the year 1910, the last having been written shortly before his death in 1976. A great number of these correspondences can be found in the German Literary Archive in Marbach, as well as in various other public archives. The present edition was made possible by the Martin Heidegger Archive in the city of Messkirch, with additional support from the Heidegger family.

The work of the editorial directors, Dr. Alfred Denker and Prof. Holger Zaborowski, was supported by an international academic advisory board, which consists of Prof. Günter Figal (Freiburg in Breisgau), Prof. Marion Heinz (Siegen), Dr. Matthias Flatscher (Vienna), and Dr. Ulrich von Bülow (Germany Literary Archive, Marbach). For the publication of future volumes, additional editors will be consulted.

In preparing the collected letters of Martin Heidegger, the original source material is used whenever possible. If copies are employed instead of originals, at least one direct comparison is carried out using the original. As a rule, the letters are ordered chronologically within the perimeters of the correspondence, and are numbered sequentially using Arabic numerals. Minor spelling and punctuation issues are corrected and standardized for ease of understanding. More idiosyncratic linguistic usages are reproduced as they appear in the original. Any necessary additions in this volume, apart from customary abbreviations, have been placed within square brackets, and italics have been used to represent underlining. In addition to the letters, certain texts that are important for understanding the letters are included, as well as supplemental documents originating from the correspondents' estates.

All letters that appear in the volume are published in full, and for the sake of reference all letters are listed in the appendix. Specific details and additional connections between particular letters are outlined in the annotations. In the Afterword, the editors provide additional information about the relationship between Martin Heidegger and his correspondents. Each volume contains a registry of persons, a chronological overview of the life of Martin Heidegger and the correspondent, as well as an abridged bibliography of their most significant works.

*The Collected Letters of Martin Heidegger* is divided into three sections:

I. Private correspondences
II. Scholarly correspondences
III. Correspondences with publishers and institutions

The following correspondence between Martin Heidegger and Karl Löwith appears as Volume 2 of Section II.

Alfred Denker                                     Holger Zaborowski

# Correspondence

Figure 1  Karl Löwith (circa 1950).

**1.** *Martin Heidegger to Karl Löwith*
[Freiburg] VIII.22.19

Dear Herr Löwith,

Many thanks for the postcard, and also for the one from Munich. I will be here until Wednesday. My holiday plans have changed. Please come visit me tomorrow (Saturday) evening at 8:30.
   With kind regards,
      Your
         Martin Heidegger

**2.** *Karl Löwith to Martin Heidegger*
Sternwaldstr. 10/2 Freiburg
9.8.19

Dear Herr Doctor Heidegger,

I see from a card sent by Prof. Pfänder to Fräulein Walther that you all have gotten together a few times to philosophize. Was it fruitful?!
   I must admit that I am curious to hear what *you* will have to say! I will be visiting a friend in Tettnang on Lake Constance around the 20th. Will you still be there around this time? At the moment [I] am reading Spengler's droll book *Untergang des Abendlandes* with great interest. Fräulein W. is here again.
   Have a good rest, and best greetings from
      Your loyal
         Karl Löwith

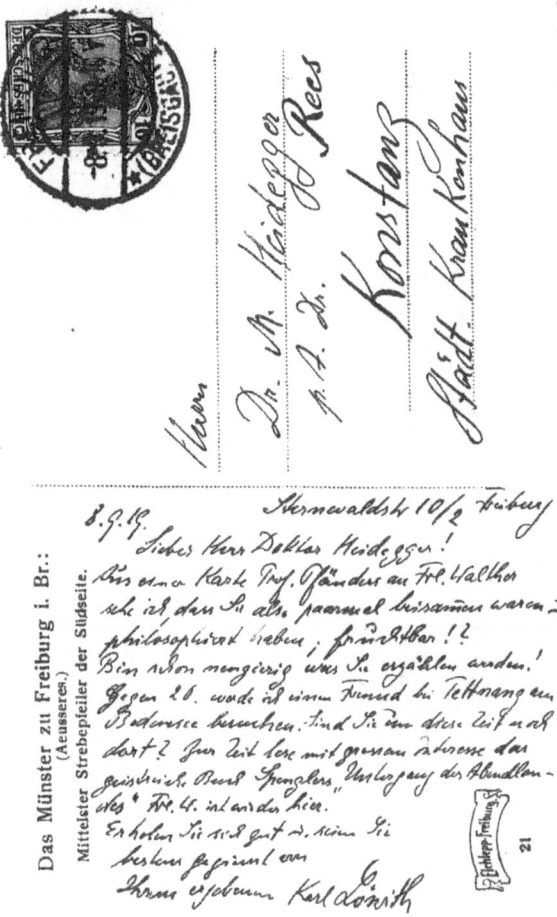

Figure 2  Facsimile of Löwith's Postcard to Heidegger from 9.8.19 (Document 2).

**3.** *Martin Heidegger to Karl Löwith*
Const.[ance] IX.10.19

Dear Herr Löwith,

Thank you for your card. The days with Professor Pfänder were very interesting for me, and I now have a much clearer understanding of the sort of phenomenology being practiced in Munich. However, in the next few days,

I will be leaving here to travel home, where I will spend the rest of the month. The coming semester will probably be very difficult. But I can trust in a few people to make some genuine contributions.
   Kindest regards,
      Your
         Martin Heidegger

My regards to Fräulein Walther as well.

**4.** *Martin Heidegger to Karl Löwith*
[Freiburg] XII.14.19

Dear Herr Löwith,

Please get me a ticket—I would prefer Gallery II, Row 4; I don't want to spend more than 40 {marks}—perhaps you could arrange it that we go together.
   Could you also tell Fräulein Gerling to come to the Natorp seminar, should she have the interest and the inclination? I forgot to mention this yesterday evening.
   Warm regards,
      Your
         Martin Heidegger

**5.** *Martin Heidegger to Karl Löwith*
[Freiburg] 1.24.20

Dear Herr Löwith,

I am traveling today in wonderful weather to the Black Forest and I won't return until Monday evening. I leave it to your instincts to dig out the questions that are most valuable to me.
   I would like to thank you again personally for that excellent presentation of yours, in which I detected actual intellectual spirit without adherence to a specific scholarly dogmatism (which is the death of all philosophy).
   Warmly,
      Your
         Martin Heidegger

**6.** *Martin Heidegger to Karl Löwith*
Freiburg Br. II.15.20

Dear Herr Löwith,

Thank you so much for your card. There was not much skiing to be had here; there were two days with very little snow. I have been working so hard that I have been completely laid up for the past few days.

I have nixed the entire summer lecture course and am now reworking it anew. Ideally, one could hold three simultaneous lectures all oriented toward the same topic of "phenomenology." Perhaps I will dare to try this experiment in the coming semesters after all. Even we in philosophy are so weighed down by tradition, so unhistorical {*unhistorisch*}, that we no longer know ourselves.

I have again thought about the Hegel seminar, and must say that there is no way that he could have chosen a more inappropriate text than the *Encyclopedia of Logic*; it is evidence of the absolute innocuousness of everything when compared to Hegel, and also of the sort of dallying with philosophy that is so often practiced here.

I hope you have success with your Hegel studies. One needs a long time to immerse oneself in it. Have I already referred you to Dilthey's book *Die Jugendgeschichte Hegels* (Academic Essays, Berlin, 1905)?

Please write again, and please extend my greetings to the "Munich circle."
Warm regards,
  Your
    Martin Heidegger

**7.** *Martin Heidegger to Karl Löwith*
[Freiburg] III.23.20

Dear Herr Löwith,

Besseler was just here and invited me to a musical afternoon; it appears Curjel has resurfaced. I was very happy to receive your letter. I do believe, however, that you take Lask too literally—for if one asks what he is after and how he sees things without oneself moving beyond Kantian formulations, then he gives a grand impression. In such a case, I would be inclined to see him as the most important philosophical mind we have been *unfortunate* enough to have in the current era.

Hey.[?] offers up good, individual analyses—I only remember him vaguely—but they are not comprehensively worked through.

When subjected to a lengthier engagement, Jaspers' book begins to wilt. What is actually new in it lies more in the structure and arrangement, in the "catalogue," and is, therefore, ultimately unphilosophical. Besseler tells me that the "Society" intends to take Bergson as a focus. I am very much in favor of that. Of course, care must be taken that he is not merely taken literally, or only superficially confronted with the *Ideas*. However, this requires intense philosophical work. If it were not in conflict with the underlying principle of the society and also "improper," I myself would like to take the lead in this work. I know the new translator—he is a senior teacher in Berlin and an "intellectual grandchild" of Dilthey. The translation appears to be much better, but it needs to be more grounded in the French.

Some time ago, I was invited to Wiesbaden to speak for two hours about Spengler as part of a "research week"; Born (Frankfurt) will also deliver a talk on Einstein's laws, Oncken (Heidelberg) on modern history, and Wolzendorff (Halle) on some juridical issue. "Spenglerizing" seems to be subsiding, and it is now finally time for one to engage these ideas philosophically. Perhaps I could repeat the lectures here in the summer. After Easter, I will travel to Wiesbaden for 14 days.

Stern is also writing to me. He would like to listen in on Scheler, who will be lecturing on Bergson. By the way, a while ago I read Scheler's *Idole* and I see how *strongly* he is influenced by Bergson—and, indeed, what a positive force he possesses.

You are still in those pleasant years during which one has time to read; only rarely do I have occasion to do so, and when I do read, it is always "with a particular purpose."

In working through my lecture troubles I have found myself heading in entirely new directions, which means that once again economy goes out the window—I am not sure how I am to manage given the short semester, especially if I would still like to present things of importance from the prior semester.

Nevertheless, and regardless of all results (which themselves could always appear different), what remains most decisive is a vibrant, active guidance, and an ever-intensifying transporting into a perspective: for we do not practice philosophy in order to stockpile bits of knowledge and propositions, but rather to shape life. And your rejoinder will surely be: Is this not *Weltanschauungsphilosophie*?! Now, it is the case that this word is also one link in the sort of misguided alternating chain of idealism/realism, rationalism/irrationalism, and so on, to which we traditionally cling because of our desperately held belief that "the truth" must lie either somewhere in the middle, or at one of the ends.

It is my hope that this summer is rather lively, and that our circle, notwithstanding all its freedom and independence of opinions and convictions and interests, nevertheless represents a true cell from out of which university life and intellectual spirit experience a continuous and genuine rejuvenation. The world begins in the human, precisely because it is not a "representation."

I plan to leave on April 7th or 8th, and will return at the end of the month.

With warm regards,
Your
Martin Heidegger

**8.** *Martin Heidegger to Karl Löwith*
[Freiburg] IX.1.20

Dear Herr Löwith,

The second lad has arrived, and all is well. If you would like to speak with me, come before Saturday (this week), as that is the day on which I will travel back to Messkirch, where I have my manuscripts and can work undisturbed. Perhaps you could come to tea on Friday (4:30 p.m.).

At the moment I am destructuring myself {*destruiere ich mich selbst*}, which takes the most effort.

Warm regards,
Your
Martin Heidegger

**9.** *Martin Heidegger to Karl Löwith*
Messkirch, IX.13.20

Dear Herr Löwith,

Has it been precisely determined who actually belongs to the private phenomenological society? I do not want to be preemptive regarding the topic to be discussed—in principle, I am very much in agreement with it, but would only caution against the "danger" of making "relativism" into a standpoint: for by virtue of an explicit defense of it, relativism has already sacrificed what is best about itself. By inquiring among Dozents, one is sure to get enough "Simmel." I do not own Dilthey's essays, but only very exhaustive excerpts, some of which are transcriptions that I made myself in 1909/1910 as a theologian and which are only of value if one knows the whole. Husserl has a few essays, I think—at the moment they are with Szilasi; I was in possession of them this summer.

In regard to the "cogito," for me the entirety of Christian philosophy comes up for consideration—and this because I want to see it all backward. It is just important that you have some "knowledge" of the other two metaphysical treatises and the *Regulae*, so that the incorrectness of epistemological detachment can then be studied. I have many disappointments regarding the seminar—without a good theological foundation it is all dilettantism; and theology, above all that of the two Christian denominations, cannot be mastered sufficiently in one or two semesters to allow for a true, scholarly engagement. At first, I considered splitting it up, focusing only on the philosophical, but that is not possible. Also, Kierkegaard can only be taken apart at the hinges theologically (the way I understand it, and am developing during the winter semester). I fear that, over and against him, you fall into the same error that you always expose so well in refutations of idealism. But it is indeed a tall order when one attempts not to be bewitched by Kierkegaard. I have a different conception of a relationship to him. Above all, it is incorrect to exploit him psychologically (as, for example, Jaspers does), for it results in a confused syncretism. Worse still is to give oneself over to him completely in a Christian way, which is not difficult to do but, for me, is a sign that one has not really confronted Christianity but has instead confused it with Kierkegaard himself. To become a Hegelian is only half as bad as becoming a Kierkegaardian. The importance of what Kierkegaard said must be taken up and appropriated anew, but by way of a criticism that arises strictly from out of one's own situation. Blind appropriation is the greatest temptation, to create a cheap novel out of one's own inwardness and to give the characters within it the creeps. Not everyone who speaks of existence is necessarily a Kierkegaardian—my own formulations have been misunderstood in this way; I am after no less than something else. And this is not much, but only what I, as living in today's situation of factical upheaval, experience as "necessary," without so much as a glance toward whether a "culture" will arise from out of it, or, rather, the acceleration of its demise. Because I myself would like to learn something in these seminars—by way of opposition and difficulties, which themselves only arise in their necessary clarity when the participants measure up to the matter at hand—I have preliminarily decided to forgo my seminar on the phenomenology of religion, for it could only result in precisely the religious–philosophical prattle that I would like to stamp out in philosophy: namely, chattering on about the religious based on what one has read in an encyclopedia. Perhaps we can dare to do it next summer. I then considered Plotinus, but this poses many of the same difficulties. That is why I decided on the *Metaphysics* of Aristotle. The Luther edition is by Otto Clemen—four volumes published by Marcus and Weber in Bonn, 1912 (the so-called little "Bonn" edition). You will most likely take fright if you work through it—and practically speaking, it is perhaps an unnecessary diversion, especially because I am not yet engaging Luther in the lecture. Husserl has written to me again, saying that he is in "heartfelt agreement" with my suggestions regarding teaching activity and the approach to the doctorate (all with express reference to you). If I may give you some advice: refrain from addressing it yourself until you are past the beginning. I am in grave danger of overworking myself here, and thereby becoming useless for the rest of the semester. Could you please send me the Kahler, or perhaps get me a copy through the publisher? I am too poor at the moment to buy books.

I send my warm greetings,
   Your
     Martin Heidegger

Greetings to Dr. Becker and the other phenomenologists from the right and left wings.

**10.** *Martin Heidegger to Karl Löwith*
Frbg, IX.19.20

Dear Herr Löwith,

Many thanks for the shipment. It is difficult for me to read Kahler; it is in an exaggerated and turgid style that nevertheless originates from out of rather thin air. He strikes me as an academic who is pondering something he has never experienced in his own life. If M. Scheler had confronted the problem of scholarly knowledge, he would have surely had more to say than in his little, informal speech. Nevertheless, one will have to pay attention to Kahler's work—not by writing against it, but by taking the lead and working against it—and only a manifesto-hungry age such as our own could think that this can be achieved like a change in parliamentary government. For such purposes Kahler is ideal, but the horizon of such an endeavor also appears weak to me! I would not have allowed the religious to become a topic of "conversation"—however, it would probably have been unavoidable. For it is an erroneous assumption about my lectures that I engage in that; it is, therefore, probably good if I am clear about it from the outset.

Regarding the private phenomenological society, I would not like to interfere; however, I would prefer it if I were a proper member and not just an honorary one, which should be possible given the current composition of the society. (I agree with your suggestions about purgation.) As a Dozent, I am already lecturing enough as it is, and as an honorary member all one does is lecture. Whether Ebbinghaus should be admitted is a matter I leave up to the society. I would only like to say that internally he stands in opposition to the issue, and that he is allied with Kroner and so on in ways very different from what most know about. He must simply focus on the factical "situation," rather than the genuine one, in his habilitation. Personally, I value him as a solid, clear-thinking person whose facility and precision of comprehension and formulation far exceeds ours. And yet, he is missing something, and it is this that hinders me from really philosophizing with him wholeheartedly—he remains in another world. And I have some concern that he would be a hindrance to the free and unrestrained working out of independently guiding phenomenological tendencies. However, in no way am I making my participation dependent upon his presence—or rather, absence. I only mention it because, if I see it correctly, the private phenomenological society is only separating itself off in order to work in a clean, although not at all univocal, phenomenological sphere. After my return, I will once again engage with Husserl on Dr. Becker's behalf. When courses and other obligations arise again, which is not to be avoided, we must take care not to allow our hands to be taken off the wheel. It does not matter what others say about the practice of phenomenology; yet, and for the sake of the matter itself, it must not come to a ghetto-like closing-off, and one should not desire to create proselytizers. However, these days especially one must not fail the determinative, intellectual influence of the university, if one is able to carry it out. Dr. Metzger will eventually minster to the phenomenological proletariat. Regarding this matter, I am an "Ostelbien aristocrat." Unfortunately, I will not be in Freiburg early enough to speak with your parents. Did you not say before that they are coming on October 19th? If they are indeed coming earlier, please give them my best.

I am sending you my warm regards. Please also send my regards to Dr. Becker and whoever else is there.

**11.** *Martin Heidegger to Karl Löwith*
[Messkirch] X.9.20

Dear Herr Löwith,

I will be arriving on the 18th of this month, and Husserl on the 17th. I have no idea when he [Husserl] will actually start. This time, I would like to start a bit earlier; it is not as though I am particularly enthusiastic about my lecture; I have the feeling that it comes apart at the seams over the course of the semester, owing to the fact that I myself have moved much farther ahead, and thus the lecture is already somewhat dated in parts. Quick fixes are always difficult in such situations.

In the Descartes seminar—about whose "beginner" character I am not yet totally sure—I have a very nice presentation for you.

I am looking forward to this winter, and hope above all that we manage to bring together a circle on the intellectual plane that has a uniform style and character—not in order to philosophize, but in order to be together in a human, social way, in which philosophy is unpretentious.

I think often, and fondly, about the evenings at Besseler's (and not only because of the cakes!), and I think that we could expand upon them a bit by reading aloud, or by delivering informal reports on new books—not an imitation of the Schlegel–Schleiermacher circle, but a taking up of their initiative, independence, and passion for things. We do not need to take ourselves for geniuses, but everyone has something to contribute—perhaps Thust will then also show up with something. Greetings to all.

Warmly,
   Your
      Martin Heidegger

It seems that I must abandon the Gurlitt seminar, for it is getting to be too much for me and I am in full swing with my own work.

Dear Herr Löwith,

As you can see, I addressed the card incorrectly, and it remained lying here. I already arrived here yesterday, the 16th. Husserl will start on the 28th, and I the day after. Would you like to come Wednesday evening? Or in the afternoon? We could take a little walk with Besseler and Afra Geiger. In any case, I will be home.

**12.** *Martin Heidegger to Karl Löwith*
[Freiburg] X.20.20

Dear Herr Löwith,

Frau Szilasi has asked me to ask Besseler if he would perhaps be inclined to accompany a visiting Hungarian violinist next week at the Szilasi's (the violinist is on a concert tour).

I am to let her know by early Saturday, and am also to send Besseler's address (Dreikönig 28?). Please write me a postcard.

I would like to ask your little club to come by for a walk at the beginning of next week, around 3:30.

Please give Dr. Becker a hint that he is not to ruin the whole matter. Of course, Metzger is "absolutely brilliant" and "first-rate," but he is "unfortunately a Jew"; and among the candidates, Becker is still clearly more promising (and this is also true in a practical sense regarding the habilation). Husserl has the highest opinion; and while it might sound petty, I would advise you to report his marriage to Husserl. If the old man gets miffed, things will be over for him before they even get started. "Academic freedom

{*freien Wissenschaft*}" is in a sorry state, but I only mean well in regard to Becker. I myself am not even seen as a "philosopher" anymore, for I am "in fact only still a theologian."
   Warm regards,
     Your
       Martin Heidegger

Please tell Wilke that he should come over on Friday evening a bit *before* 8 o'clock.

**13.** *Karl Löwith to Martin Heidegger*
[1920]

Dear Herr Doctor,

The decision on Baden-Baden ended positively. That is why I wanted to ask quickly about the 400 marks in advance and to [???]—hear Scheler. He is really something—he looks quite the opposite of decadent; more brutal, like a grifter. I will come back Thursday.
   Looking forward to seeing you again,
     Your thankful
       Karl Löwith

Leyendecker is also here.

[Addendum by Wilke]
Rudolf Wilke is taking the liberty of attaching his own warm greetings.

**14.** *Karl Löwith to Martin Heidegger*
XI.29.20
Baden-Baden
Haus Adler

Dear Herr Doctor Heidegger,

I would now finally like to write to you in more detail. Besseler was here yesterday, and I am sure that if he has had the opportunity, he has already told you about my feudal and monotonous surroundings; the feudal is pleasant, and I don't care about the monotony. At the moment I am an absolute autocrat anyway, as both of my parents are in Berlin. Regarding the war-profiteering predilections of my students, this I would rather relay in person, as writing about it would only be a waste of paper. I gave Rickert's tearjerker to Besseler to take with him, along with a thoroughly delightful newspaper excerpt. My sadness at taking a leave is abating, and I am already feeling the benefits that come with distance from the university atmosphere; I have not yet seriously gotten down to work, but it will happen soon enough. I have read many nice things: the superb Nietzsche–Rohde correspondence; the Hölderlin letters in Dilthey's *Teubner* edition; *Passions of the Soul* by Descartes; Kierkegaard's *Fear and Trembling* and *Repetition*; G. Keller's *Sinngedicht*, and so on. On a personal level, I have been very preoccupied with my fairly exclusive disposition toward friendship, and therefore the abovementioned letters speak to me in an oddly clear and scrutable way. Everything that I have up to now experienced as a person, everything decisive and expansive along with everything joyful and painful, all of it is rooted in such relationships, and I don't regret it.

I am not merely being polite when I admit to you quite readily that it is solely your lectures that I miss. Besseler read some of his notes to me, and I was once again impassioned. I can't wait to see where you go with "formal indication"! At the moment I am indeed destructuring {*destruierend*}, but only in a practical sense, namely, in regard to the laughably spoiled habits of the boys I am tutoring. For example, the ten-year-old could come up with nothing better for his Christmas list than having H.G.H (his monogram) imprinted on a suitcase, a pencil, and a watch, and so on!!! I often feel myself to be more nanny than tutor. In the absence of intellectual interests, I am at least teaching him chess, stenography, and how to play the violin.

We will have to speak in person about the Descartes presentation, for, to be honest, after a first read-through of the "passions" I don't know what can be done with it, without imposing a rather bold interpretation upon Descartes. It now also appears to me that an interpretation from the perspective of the medieval era is exceedingly bold (especially given Dilthey's illuminating contribution regarding the medieval doctrine of affect and its connection to the renaissance of the Stoa). Of course, what is seen with phenomenological discernment is scattered throughout in various comments, but the so-called physiological explanation takes up most of the space. The foundational category of "wonder" is of interest. But as I said, we will have to talk about it.

With the exception of Becker's course, all else I heard from F. was pretty depressing. It appears that the phenomenological society has completely fallen apart; there is such a lack of people with initiative, insight, and ambition. In the absence of the abundantly and thoroughly learned Dr. Becker, precious little would remain. Cleverness in the style of Neumann will not cut it; and precisely in the realm of philosophy, deficiency of character bothers me so much that in the long run I would not want to have a discussion with such people. Or has new greatness revealed itself in the seminar?

It just occurs to me: Have you heard anything about Husserl getting an offer from Leipzig? I myself hardly believe it—I wish for you, and also for me, that something changes. How is it going, anyway, with the Husserl seminars? Will there be anything new and different beyond what was in the second investigation, and how is the time-seminar going for the "initiates"? Is Metzger still vehemently agreeing with everything? Did anything come of it?

It is through a distancing from university business that I subsequently sense, once again, the corrupting influence of its atmosphere.

It is a relief to open Nietzsche or Kierkegaard, and so on, once again, and to refresh myself through substantive concentration on the rich and lively wealth of ideas, all in contrast to the tedious and dull kneading out of what is already a damned thin dough. For surely, such kneading does little to shore up one's respect for scholarly rigor and exhaustiveness, and little to cultivate an intellectual respect for the necessity of refuting and criticizing a superficial, incorrect, and vapid engagement with things. In reaction to this, there always quickly arises within me the hidden wish that the intellectual conscience would allow us to philosophize in the aphoristic, distilled Romantic way, thereby allowing our intellectual energy to serve personal issues and problems, rather than the production of scholarly literature. Today, one must sacrifice so much in order to satisfy, in order to be of value, in order to be heard. Indeed, how could it be otherwise: for that other approach I have in view relies entirely upon a more originary and more original productivity, one that is intensely inflected by the personal, and it is only out of this that I can derive my right to philosophize over and above the heads of philosophical scholars. In this, one inches close to the threshold of an artistic existence. If one does not feel strong enough for it, there really only remains the other approach, and one is burdened from the outset by such a conflict and is full of inhibitions. Nevertheless, it offers one the possibility of creating something already dignified, without it needing to be based solely and alone upon the gift of an ingenious wealth of ideas in which the utter or even passionate dedication to philosophical scholarship no longer occurs. For as much as I agree with you about the separation of philosophy and scholarship, the problem nevertheless remains unsolved, given that today one cannot allow oneself to posit philosophical claims in the manner of Schelling or even Hegel. It is, fundamentally, a question of one's subjective digestive powers in regard to existing scholarly material. Who today is able to master it—assimilate it—in a critical and thought-through way, without either being destroyed by it or lugging it along like a heavy burden? Someone with the intellectual vitality and energy of M. Weber was able to do it—but who else? And why shouldn't one allow oneself to assimilate what "concerns" oneself! It is the same old and yet new problem that I am once again addressing here, albeit in a clumsy way, although I am sure that you will fill in the missing links correctly. I have yet to experience a semester in which, after a few weeks, I didn't feel the urge to jettison the whole thing. Not only due to such oppositional motives, but also due to entirely personal stresses that continually make it necessary for me to "catch myself" through self-reflection. Given such doubts and such hesitancies regarding scholarly activity, it is difficult to justify making philosophy into a career. An entire world separates one from the little literary prophets, and an equally wide chasm separates one from the scholarly philosophical day-laborers and manufacturers of editions. It is often the case that even after one day I regret virtually every sentence that I've written (e.g., the critique of the Rickert text) and flee into the epistolary communication of what is essential—into letters to my friends.

I cannot quite say to what degree the above was written while being momentarily hung over, but I don't think so—for such reflections, arising out of weakness and honesty, overcome me too frequently and powerfully.

I send you my heartfelt greetings. It is almost becoming difficult to write to you—I have the feeling that you are living under too much "pressure" to bear it in inner (and not rational) *freedom*. May I speak frankly? After all, we know one another quite well: if it is still the case today that you are not able *to reach* the students in your lectures in a manner befitting your intellectual efforts, it is due to this weak point. One senses a certain unease and humane insecurity within you, whose consequence is a slightly overcomposed acerbity and mistrust, and one seeks in you that indefinable inner freedom and ability to be in control of oneself. I am sure you yourself are suffering the most from this, and I would never mention it if I myself were not able to empathize all too well.

    Your
        Karl Löwith

M. Weber was of a "demonic nature" and unconsciously despairing in Kierkegaard's sense. Others are often conscious of it. Where is the person who can elevate himself to that ethical height upon which, for example, Alexei Karamazov stands?! I am on principle unable to affront anyone or anything, unable to offend—and this without resignation or resentment. Lastly, a confession: before I knew you personally—during my first semester—I gave your writing to an acquaintance for analysis; I think it is very good—if you like, I am happy to give it to you.

**15.** *Martin Heidegger to Karl Löwith*
[Freiburg] 12.17.20

Dear Herr Löwith,

Many thanks for your card. Of course you will come to our house on Christmas Eve. You are not a bother. And please come early, if possible: around 5 p.m.

From last Saturday through Monday I was skiing; it was wonderful, but I overdid it and overnight I caught a cold. On Tuesday, I was still able to lecture and run my tutorial. However, on Wednesday while with Husserl, I came down with a fever and took to bed. But I think that by Sunday I will be back on top of things.

The graphological essay is excellent in some respects, while in others it is—if not incorrect, *per se*—at least too general.

According to the Leipzig list, it is Driesch who appears to have the best chance. However, in these matters, one always encounters the greatest surprises.

A new volume of the *Kant Studien* arrived a few days ago—it is worthless from beginning to end. There is an advertisement for a 29-page system of religious philosophy by Scholz; then a discourse on Hegel. Also, the second edition of Spengler. As you can see, anything is possible, even if one is not yet capable of truly understanding Vol. I of the *Logical Investigations*.

Scheler is to speak here around this time; I actually don't know whether it hasn't already happened.

Warm greetings to you,
    Your
        Martin Heidegger

**16.** *Karl Löwith to Martin Heidegger*
[Baden-Baden] I.22.21

Dear Herr Doctor Heidegger,

It is too bad that I did not meet up with you this time in Freiburg. How are you doing? Does Husserl (or we ourselves!) have any prospect of moving on? According to a rumor out of Munich, Pfänder appears to have prospects in Erlangen. But I should probably stop with such gossiping.

Despite all conceivable conveniences, I will soon be sick of this place. The boys I am tutoring are such pitifully vacuous creatures that it is a wasted effort to drum up any enthusiasm for them. I am thinking of finishing on March 15th, and then coming to Freiburg for fourteen days, after which I have to go home for a few weeks. I don't have any concrete plans yet for the summer semester; I would most like to be near Freiburg, somewhere out in the country so that I could quickly reach Freiburg from there. I am hoping for an intensive collaboration; aside from Dr. Becker, it is possible that Schapiro, and perhaps also Thust, will be there again. Then, there will surely be an "unconscious" discussion!! And you are planning to offer a seminar on the history of medieval history and Aristotle?!

If it doesn't take up too much of my time, I would also like to fabricate zoological misbirths with Spemann once again. Regarding my own philosophical "births," there is not much I can report to you; however, I have gathered together some thoughts in connection to my preoccupation with the problem of expression in Croce. I believe that these thoughts allow me to see the problem of the concept as central, and I am thereby able to strip off all of that rationalistic Platonism. I find what you have delivered in your lectures since the vacation very interesting and consequential.

Will Ebbinghaus give a Hegel seminar??

Regarding Jaspers, it is probably best, and easier, to talk in person; Jaspers impelled me to read the big edition of Van Gogh's letters—dreadful and shocking. A devastating confluence of our human and spiritual distress.

For a few months now, and more than ever, my entire disposition toward philosophy and more important things is one of skepticism and ambivalence, a disposition out of which I have not yet really emerged; that is the reason why I have not been able to work in a sustained manner. Nevertheless, in no way do I regret having made a pause this semester; it was a necessity.

I have expended my entire power of reflection upon myself, and sit here as though in a wasp's nest. In times of weakened self-confidence, one is unable to perform productive work. But now things appear to be looking up, and I hope this continues without me succumbing to resentment and resignation.

The path of an inner and complete self-reflection (in the Kierkegaardian sense) is covered in thorns, for all the means of such a self-contemplation and critique all-too-easily turn against one, and their effect is only positive and fruitful when this kind of self-illumination arises out of concealed strength.

Tell me, how do things stand with the Descartes seminar? The entire complex of questions that revolves around self-observation is so expansive, difficult, and fundamental that I would rather omit the presentation (i.e., postpone it until the Aristotle seminar). Indeed, perhaps Aristotle's *De anima* is a more fruitful point of attack than the largely meager *Passions*?! Would this be very inconvenient for you? In any case: should this audacious attempt be made at all, then only at the very end of the semester (i.e., the end of February). What do you think?

At any rate, I will give the Croce presentation on February 10th; I will stay in Freiburg then for two to three days—I hope I will be able to speak with you then.

With my best regards to you, and also to your wife,
 Your
  Karl Löwith

N.B.: If you find a Hegel advertised in a catalogue, please let me know!

**17.** *Martin Heidegger to Karl Löwith*
Frbg, I.25.21

Dear Herr Löwith,

I also regret that we did not see each other. It seems that I will be here for the entire vacation. I recently organized my summer lectures somewhat and saw that it will be impossible for me to manage, even if I restrict myself to mere delineation. That is why I will only lecture on Augustine and Neo-Platonism for three hours a week. Ebbinghaus will address Hegel's essay on natural law in the seminar. You should feel free to postpone your presentation until the summer. The participants are very sluggish, and the Stern–Neumann clique is totally failing; I am testing them without them even noticing it. I am glad that Becker and Besseler are there; otherwise, it would be like talking to a brick wall. In my lectures, the whole thing feels even stranger.

It is not a bad thing if you feel yourself to be in inner turmoil—in that state, one gets an entirely different grasp of oneself. I "read" the Van Gogh letters too much during the war. And what even is art history when measured against documents such as these!!

I am looking forward to the summer, although I am growing ever-more skeptical of those who are now clamoring to study at the university. Also appearing in the annual edition containing Pfänder's logic is the paper by Ingarden about the danger of a *Petitio principii* in epistemology. I haven't seen it yet. Once again, Fräulein Stein has a new book on the philosophy of the state. It seems likely that Metzger will become Husserl's personal assistant. Dr. Schwartz will easily be admitted to the seminar on time—he speaks solely in platitudes, always about "opining."

When measured against Becker, Metzger is totally falling off in the seminar, but Husserl doesn't notice it, and instead thinks that Becker "is not yet far enough along" (i.e., far enough along to agree with everything that Husserl says).

I still hope that we can do a ski tour together. At the moment, I am living much like a hermit and working intensely.

I hope that you will have a strong start to the summer after your break. If I have the time, I would like to come to your presentation.

With warm regards,
    Your
        Martin Heidegger

My wife sends her best wishes.

**18.** *Karl Löwith to Martin Heidegger*
[Baden-Baden] 2.18.21

Dear Herr Dr. Heidegger,

I hope that you were not displeased that on Sunday I absconded at 1:30; I really wanted to be in Freiburg by 4, and I did indeed arrive on time—it is scandalous how I let my tongue get tied here. I hope that in mid-March there is still some good snow up there, for I could [come] up again for a few days then. Regarding the notion of the historical {*das Historische*}, which was orbiting around and was then so suddenly cut off—will you still make it accessible to us? (I would rather not enumerate who "we" are—the list would be short.) *Will Afra Geiger be assigned the Romantics?* That would make me very happy for her.

Tell me: What was your impression of my reflection? I imagined that it contained a few good and essential formulations—the whole problem of concept and actuality must surely be graspable by means of this approach?! It seemed to me that you were very disappointed this time.

What do you think overall? Do I have what it takes to be a philosopher—that is, what kind of philosopher does what I have make me? These are all ultimately vain and childish questions that only I alone can answer; nevertheless, the judgment of people who think critically and who know me is not worthless to me. I am *not* experiencing an inner, *overflowing productivity of thought*. I am also not sure how I should confront that so-called sober *vigor* of thinking that is demanded—I also do not philosophize with a hammer. With what then? Perhaps it is best described as an inner *discontentment*, and a need for *clarity* and *curiosity*—the compulsion *to think* is part of my life, and yet it does not drive me forward with an overpowering sense of determination. At the moment I am reading *Aus Schellings Leben in Briefen*—how pitiful this [???] makes my so-called talent appear to me. From out of a greater abundance, Besseler is also [more] talented than I.

Best regards,
    Your
        Karl Löwith

**19.** *Martin Heidegger to Karl Löwith*
[Freiburg, February 1921]

Dear Herr Löwith,

In no way did I resent that you left early. I was up there three days last Sunday and I feel absolutely outstanding.

I would have told you that I was disappointed by your presentation, but I did not want to do that in the evening in front of Walther.

I was disappointed only because you drilled down into it too little and wanted to bring in too much—to me this seems to be a mistake you make generally—at this point you know enough so that you could do more to approach the actual work. Someday you will have the experience of needing to re-read everything that you are reading now, and to read it properly. Of course, this initial orientation is not to be avoided, but it must not be allowed to take the upper hand, and I have the impression that this is the case with you. It is my ideal that one's mastery of things arises out of the clearest and most stringent expertise—but in the philosophy itself, one should not notice this.

These days, it is particularly difficult to advance toward a vibrant and enlivened philosophizing and to accomplish what it demands. And that is why you must not work at half strength, but must rather fuse reflection into, and with, philosophizing. Philosophy is not fun—one can be destroyed by it; and he who does not risk this will never come to it.

Rothacker gave a talk here yesterday. I have never encountered anything like it—shallow-mindedness personified and thereby possessing only quasi-knowledge—he only knows what others have already done—there is no trace of an actual grasp. He does not even have an inkling of the problem of the humanities—if such a thing even exists. In exchange for that he cites the entirety of world literature. Ebbinghaus is very impressed by him. You have to know that in the coming years, more than ever before, such people will be running the show.

A critical engagement is impossible, because the means for it are missing. What's more, these people partake of such intellectual filthiness that they reach out and grab everything, snatching up things as they hear them, and then peddle them without ever really having entered into them.

I do not wish to make the world better—even less so university philosophers; everyone should say what they want to say, and then apply themselves accordingly.

You must also know that scholarly existence is very difficult for the philosopher—and I am not referring to professional advancement and career.

I am not judging you in accordance with the schema of what is usually "done"—there is no question you can do it as well as many others—I am using a different yardstick—and I have come to the following judgment: you must become more disciplined in your work—not in regard to quantity, but in regard to quality.

The meaning and sense of philosophizing is itself historical {*historisch*}, and what matters is to find one's own—and to leave aside all the yardsticks of earlier philosophers. This has been utterly neglected.

I now resist being discussed more than before; and I resist providing the occasion for it. You will not be happy with what I have to say about the historical {*das Historische*}.

During the next semester, and in the future to come, the air will clear up a bit—I am filled with dread at the thought of how these stalwarts, dispersed to other universities with their half-digested thoughts and lecture transcripts, indulge in self-importance.

Finke will first travel to Münster again. It is also possible that Schmitz-Kallenberg will only allow the work to be done with him.

Apart from that, you should not fret too much about the failure of the presentation—it happens to everyone, and most of all to those who truly dare something. One should not unduly hasten the formation of one's thoughts.

Warm regards,
   Your
     Martin Heidegger

We will see each other in mid-March.

**20.** *Karl Löwith to Martin Heidegger*
II.26.21

Dear Herr Dr. Heidegger,

I had planned to write you in more detail today, and was therefore happy when your letter arrived. I am very thankful for your genuine and frank critique, all the more so because I myself agree with your justification for it. That is why I am in no hurry now to embrace those so-called "good intentions" with which the way to hell is paved. Beginning with my first semester in Freiburg, what attracted me and held me was precisely the awareness that here I was being grasped and impelled more stridently—by you—than by the Munich crowd, or even by Jaspers. And I cannot deny that I *need* to be grasped in such a way. Despite the high expectations that he had, Husserl himself was, from the outset, not a consideration for me, and you will remember how already during my second semester I often expressed to you my vehement resistance to his philosophical cast of mind. Today, it is absolutely clear to me that Husserl, on the deepest level, is not a great philosopher, and that it is a massive delusion to put him on the same pedestal as Kant; his whole disposition is infinitely far removed from reality—it is without life and is doctrinally logical. It would be a waste of time and energy if I were to penetrate into his way of thinking, all from out of a misguided intellectual conscience. Unequivocal and strident rejection is preferable to carrying along this argumentative ballast. In contrast, I need not tell you what I find so positive in you. A simplistic existence, such as Husserl has, simply does not see essential problems. From personal experience, you certainly know the oppressive gravity of the temporal situatedness of spirit (in the inner, individual sense), and you will thus understand my conflictual stance regarding the erroneous but nevertheless factual alternative: namely, the more *scholarly philosopher*, whose work is purely objective (in the higher sense), and the so-called *philosophical literati*; and to the latter I ascribe the latest of what is now being philosophized at universities—for it is mostly literature practiced academically, but I am thinking also of Lask and Spengler, as well as Keyserling, Kahler, and so on, and also of someone like Jaspers. For example, at the moment I am looking at Vaihinger—wretched, weak, and cheap. But the Nietzsche book isn't totally without substance. Vaihinger's preface is scandalously typical—a tepid stew made out of the most varied ingredients. But as ridiculous and dubious as Kerler's pamphlet is, he nonetheless feels something that is both correct and deeply problematic: namely, that the good, proper philosophical instinct that grows out of vibrant, personal experience is today largely only found amongst the philosophical literati, and not among those who are strong, resistant to decadence, and spiritually disciplined. Motived by this trivial tendency, and also by a conversation with Jaspers—who, oddly, is in the middle of all of this—I read Keyserling's *Philosophie als Kunst* a few days ago, with the sole purpose of retroactively justifying my instinctive and objective rejection of such things. Of course, nothing changed, but the problem reformulated itself: there is much in the way of a keen, philosophical instinct for the essential issues, but little more is accomplished than an elegant sniffing around the edges. To say it spitefully: to me, he seems like an optimistically urbane *epicure* of *"that which is necessary!"* To be sure, the Husserls, and so on, are no epicures of that which is necessary, but this is because they are totally missing any sense for it, or because they themselves do not "do what is necessary" but write one superfluous book after another. However, with this I in no way wish to justify my position and weaken your concerns regarding my presentation. There is no doubt that I *read* much too much in relation to actual appropriation and digestion. It was not for nothing that, as a fourteen-year-old, I underlined the lines in Schopenhauer regarding the balefulness of too much reading—only then to continue reading and accumulating more and more. It then happens that from time to time there comes a powerful shift and I just want to throw it all away; I curse my ever-expanding library, and desire to ramble and rove with at most two or three books, with open eyes and a clear head. Whether or not this means that the "Dr." title is thereby achieved a few years later is a matter of utter indifference to *me*, but not to my parents, and thus this summer I will turn toward "actual" work. The fact that I am now writing to you, and that I now know enough to work and think in a more principled way—all of that is true in some sense; nevertheless, I still intensely feel my *vast* historical gaps, and thereby find myself always in the dilemma of already knowing too much and yet also too little; although I am now able to differentiate instinctively and correctly what does and does not matter in the whole philosophical jumble, and from the outset I always read critically and underline as I go. But it is only now that I sense the necessity of a certain asceticism regarding my studies, in order to avoid a suffocating excess of knowledge.

It should be obvious that with this I am not referring to the Husserlian notion of "phenomenological cloistering." For I share your conviction that the meaning of the "historical {*Historische*}," when understood correctly and systematically applied to oneself, turns into its opposite: namely, what is commonly designated as "historicism {*Historismus*}." The danger of unilaterally circumscribing philosophy by way of such a self-evident point of departure does indeed exist, but in my opinion this is only an argument for someone who understands philosophy in "object-like" terms. Whether or not a philosophy will ultimately be relevant depends upon the seriousness of personal difficulties and concern, and also upon the depth and essentiality of subjective thinking; and certainly an honest, intensive meaningfulness is more valuable than an expansive and peripheral one. Whether or not I "have something to say" is something that I cannot quite make clear to myself today; I only know that whatever it is, its content will be, in the widest sense, "psychological," that is, its origin will arise out of self-reflection; it is not possible for me to contain the dominant nature of my naivety, and therefore Nietzsche, Dostoevsky, Van Gogh, Kierkegaard, and so on, are dearer to me than the great Hegel and Goethe. I will work on qualitative disciplining. (It is a secret agenda of mine that, when among those Freiburg students who are under the sway of Husserl and other sterile tendencies, I would rather evince a greater proximity to so-called imprecise philosophy than to the alternative. Perhaps this is why it came off as weaker than necessary in my presentation.) My personal gain from this was above all: to capture some thoughts, albeit too aphoristically and unmethodically, regarding the problem of the concept, as well as acquiring some knowledge of modern *aesthetic* literature.

My own, specific topic, which is near and dear to my heart, is increasingly focused on the problem of *life and concept*; and while this is very broad, it does nevertheless allow itself to be more stringently pared down, and it contains within it almost all essential issues:

| | |
|---|---|
| Actuality—Concept | "Subjective Thought" |
| Experience—Theoretical Thought | "Relativism" |
| Philosophy—Science | |

Your lectures, as well as the work of Dilthey, Simmel, Bergson, Scheler, Jaspers, and so on, come to mind.

I will be in Freiburg for roughly one week after March 15th, and we can speak about it then; after that [I] have to be in Munich for a month, making a guest appearance.

It is really too bad that precisely this issue rubs Husserl the wrong way, and I hope that he does not end up causing any difficulties; for all of "my" topics would be most suspect to him, along with all of my philosophical reading matter. I am sure that he takes Nietzsche, for example, to be little more than a witty depressive.

N.B. I do, however, have a *positive* partial critique *in mente*, when I unconditionally refuse to accept the manner in which you think about working through things in a *principally methodical* way. To be honest, you "drill" down on me *at times too much* and too often in the same place. Certainly, I defended you fiercely in front of Jaspers, for Jaspers has a largely superficial grasp of principally philosophical and methodical modes of questioning; but sometimes it seems to me that a last bit of that perspicacity with which Husserl infected you misleads you to drill down so persistently in a spot where your drilling has already reached bedrock, and that this drilling itself can become an obsession. This was also the originary motive of my rather far-fetched criticism of "formal-indication"—while I did indeed know that you only meant this as a methodological means of representation, and I read this explanation umpteen times (in Becker's dependable transcription), I was still vacillating over whether perhaps a great profundity is behind all of these complicated things, only to come to the conclusion that all of it is actually much simpler and could be said with fewer words. I will now wait for our reunion to see whether I will be forced to reverse this "conclusion" regarding formal indication.

I send my warm regards,
    Your
        Karl Löwith

What has plagued me during the entirety of my time here, much more than these "problems," is the "problem" of friendship, well-nigh the most disastrous problem for me.

N.B. A little while ago I met a certain Herr Bury (he introduced himself here as a devoted disciple), who has been attending your lecture courses for two semesters and is already working independently (he would like to earn his doctorate with Jaspers). It appears that he has really digested your lectures with great engagement and gain. Thus, there are unknown people running around, of whose existence one is unaware, but who nevertheless understand matters and follow them ardently. It would be interesting to get to know him—it shows me once again how certain issues and problems are simply in the air, and that there does indeed exist a kind of invisible church of philosophy, whose members, at the very least, are united in that they are equally concerned with, and with the same, *nothing*!

**21.** *Karl Löwith to Martin Heidegger*
III.19.[21]

Dear Herr Doctor Heidegger,

Please come over after 8 p.m. on *Tuesday* evening. Becker will also be here. We had quite an argument yesterday! My "discipline": conscience embarrassingly asleep and rebellious.
    Your
        Karl Löwith

Was able to sell off Vaihinger for 50 marks. Could you perhaps please bring me *Monrad, Balzac,* and *Gundolf* (the Archipelagus essay)?

**22.** *Martin Heidegger to Karl Löwith*
[Freiburg, 4.2.21]

Dear Herr Löwith,

Many thanks for your postcard. It really is too bad that we did not manage to get together.
    I was able to secure a spot for Afra with Finke (the Hamann thing will not work out, as a legal dispute has broken out regarding the letters). Finke plans to give Afra some work over the course of the summer, and I believe that he is now actually interested in her. In the beginning he was a bit reserved.
    Through Afra I was able to get a volume of the *Historische Zeitschrift*. I will ultimately move my lecture to June–July. I anticipate much in regard to the semester.
    At the moment, however, I would most like to continue working as proficiently as possible for the next few months, the way I have been up to now.
    After several different approaches, the issue of destructuring one's own has finally begun to take off, and in conjunction with it I am getting closer to a new explication of life; such experiences show me the original meaning of the term "method"—the word is a bad one, but as an aggressive, polemical device, it remains suitable.

I experience ever more clearly all that escapes one in regard to the possibilities of explication, but also how these are not something that can be forced but only open themselves through the very process of enacting them. Thereby, the inner obligations to oneself grow, not in the sense of an orientation toward some a priori ethic, but as the enactment of one's own historical {*historischen*} providence, which proceeds in fits and starts and must be grasped radically, and which comes not from an empty racking of one's brain but rather through a critical engagement with, and examination of, the richest intellectual history whose themes have occupied us, and which is thereby made new.

In the course of this, I am increasingly losing any desire and aspiration to publish, and I think too highly of myself to be spoken about and discussed in places where philosophy is merely a pleasant pastime, or an occasion to showcase one's talent. And at 30 years of age, one really is still too young; one has one's hands full making sure that one's own life doesn't get away from oneself in such a way that it can't be retrieved later—one then arrives at the system—put in philosophical terms: it's a search made in vain.

Warm regards to you and Besseler,
 Your
  Martin Heidegger

**23.** *Karl Löwith to Martin Heidegger*
[Freiburg] 8.15.21
Faulerstrasse 2/II

Dear Herr Dr. Heidegger,

Have you returned? For my part, the first week was spent in the company of Besseler, and the second at Lake Constance, staying with the Walthers, and so on. I moved today—devilish work. When is it possible for me to visit you? I have a nice new acquisition: Augustine's *Sermones* 1521—a huge tome. Becker is annoying me with the theory of relativity.

You will have to see my new room—I quite like it.

Afra wrote from Florence, she is now in Rome and will soon be in Naples.

What is Husserl doing in St. Märgen? Well—why do I even ask! It is a matter of indifference to me. I prefer your lectures.

A new book by W. Haas (Cologne) came out: *Die psychische Dingwelt*—a repellent title, but I will nevertheless take a look at it.

Until we meet again. This postcard reflects the enacting synthesis [?] of moving into a new room.

With fond regards,
 Your
  Karl Löwith

[I] met young Bauer only at the end of the semester: a fine bloke—"bloke" meant here as the opposite of a wimp.

**24.** *Karl Löwith to Martin Heidegger*
8.17.21, evening

Dear Herr Doctor Heidegger,

Dr. Becker told me about your latest conversation; I had asked him (to tell me), and I find it too bad, both that you mostly prefer to find out about me via Becker's opinions, and that I only ever hear anything specific coming from you about me in a very parenthetical way. (Even getting information "indirectly" would be more substantial.) Today, Becker wishes to show me that the essential differences between you and me are much greater than those between the two of you, and that given a common ground of scholarly methodological thoroughness, rigor, attentiveness to things, and seriousness, [you] both have a dismissive attitude toward what Becker decries as my subjectivism, my inattentiveness to things (at least for Thust such inattentiveness was grounded in "religion," according to Becker), and my worrisome proximity to syncretic dilettantism, which makes it possible for me to take people like Blüher, Keyserling, Spengler, and so on, seriously and be receptive to them—even though academic interest in them did not even last ten years, and their books are unnecessarily long and perhaps simply unnecessary, as long and unnecessary as most other scholarly works.

Furthermore, it appears my grasp of your philosophy is ultimately a big misunderstanding, as it overlooks the essentially logical (even if not in a traditional formal-logical sense) "concerns" of your work and your desire: in short, it overlooks the analytical and objective scholar in the philosopher. Be that as it may, at the moment I am not concerned with justifying my "personal" position—nor do I even desire the personal and private dimension (nor to become a beloved, second Becker)—for in your university lecture courses this dimension played an entirely subordinate role to the "attentiveness to things" as the sole, binding link of a scholarly philosophical community!! While on the other hand, the "I am"—an identifying feature of the person thought solely in terms of the private dimension—is *the* theme and *the* point of orientation in the Jaspers critique, a theme that cannot, nor desires to, obviate the fact that the human is not irrelevant in philosophy—as little irrelevant as the problem of anticipation {*Vorgriffsproblematik*}. I write these lines because it is important for me to tell you why, for the time being, I am *not* convinced that I am misunderstanding you, and above all to make clear in what way and why I have the attitude toward philosophy that I do.

The part of spirit that pertains to conscience is conscientious, and the intellectual conscience is, first and foremost, a *conscience*; that is why any philosophy that takes up the phenomena of existence in the broad sense, and that occupies itself with them owing to an inner necessity, is most especially and from the outset *also personal*, precisely in the real, philosophical sense and appropriate to its specific matter: namely, the self. The question even arises whether it is not contradictory to the meaning of the self to explain itself in a philosophical / theoretical manner (despite the scope of historical facticity). (Kierkegaard's manner of explication is very particular, and is Socratic and indirect in form.) By making use of somewhat clever intellectual resources, it is now always possible to secure, assess, and justify one's own position from all sides, and to erect a wall around oneself, a porcupine-like fortification that arms one against all people and philosophers who are so tactless and so embarrassingly direct as to approach one with questions (philosophical questions no less) utterly lacking in objectivity—questions that even get under one's skin with *ad hominem* argumentation—thereby shaking the foundations of that artfully constructed spider's web. I say: this is not only possible today, but also probable—however, to me this nevertheless appears irreconcilable with the free disposition of a philosopher who really understands himself, a philosopher who must, in the decisive moment, have the courage not to veil the self-insight gained through self-criticism for personal, pedagogical, and material reasons. He must rather be open to discussion and allow precisely that sore point to be prodded where every critical engagement {*Auseinandersetzung*} so easily increasingly critiques and thus sets apart {*aus-einander-sezt*}, thereby preventing, or, alternatively, eventually forcing the revision of his fundamental concepts and ideas. If one does not do this, then one is comfortably immune to all attacks on the part of the spiritually—or better yet, intellectually—weak. However, such a stance forces the intellectually equal opponent to undertake the laborious task of destructuring their judgments, to undertake the tedious and often futile digging out of that Achilles' heel that exists for everyone, always!—all of this insofar as it is akin to the biblical "last things" (among which I count the problem of today's youth in its stance toward scholarship). Among people who are free, the detour of a thorough and methodological explication of this Achilles' heel is generally not necessary, for everyone knows about it well enough without needing to lean on this crutch of intellectual circumspection and human hiddenness. I am of the view that the highest degree of conceptual clarity and methodological fastidiousness does not always guarantee the seriousness and the so-called rigor of the critical engagement with a particular phenomenon—on the other hand, I often wonder, even in regard to myself, how quickly and easily a sort of descent into the scholarly explication of the phenomena of existence comes to pass, and that the theoretical interest and objective concern (?!)—akin to the "*temptations*" or the "stages of despair"—take the place of a "lively life" (see the end of Dostoevsky's novel *Notes from the Underground*).

Real life, in its existence, is always at a never quite bridgeable distance from philosophizing; and the conceptual, even as phenomenological expression, nevertheless remains in a very problematic situation *vis a vis* lively life. (For a strange movement of thoughtful philosophical expression into the aesthetic–artistic realm, see Kierkegaard, Nietzsche, and a few of the Romantics). Then again, a critical encounter that appears dilettantish to the analytical perspective, one that takes up all manner of useless, syncretic categories, does not guarantee existentiality; in the same way, being unscholarly does not guarantee genius, and being scholarly does not guarantee a serious character. (Nietzsche speaks of scholarliness in terms of the German housewife and her family values: upright, industrious, honest, capable, thrifty, thorough, and so on.)

All the same, impatience, fleetingness, and immature fragmentariness can be more and something other to such people and their work than just a sign of lazy Romantic idleness, lack of character, weakness, superficiality, lack of depth and seriousness, and things related to it. Intellectuality is not identical with scholarliness, and a man such as Gustav Landauer has more intellectuality in his little finger (and of greater intensity) than many of the professors at the university in Munich combined. Given the typical presumptuousness of the scholarly attitude, one can also, regrettably, write off the all too typical Blüher with the following: "The *Wandervogel* no longer attracts—now he'll try Christianity."

For example, I would even go so far as to speak of a "genuine disingenuousness." It is equally a misunderstanding—and the understanding public should be able to understand people of its own historical situation above all—to condemn what everyone has already been crowing about, namely, the "sloppiness" of Scheler. Everything depends upon knowing what someone has to fight against within himself—this is necessary in order to "understand" the contents of the result. Measured by current philosophical conditions, even just his essays and papers contain a truly estimable richness of thought and incisiveness, and I do not take his character to lack seriousness—the reckoning from which all of this proceeds is one that we of the 1920s might better provide to ourselves. I stand in defense of these "types," and also others who are quite different (ones whom you don't know—I was just thinking of Percy Gothein, but also of Thust), because I have the will to defend myself—also *to* myself; not out of vanity, but because it is a necessity for me. From day one, I have regarded my own stance toward scholarly, philosophical work with great suspicion, and I am not lacking in self-criticism; on the contrary, I often carry with me a measure of reflection that is too great, owing to the fact that it is unfruitful. Just one example. With this, however, I am not conceding to the admittedly healthy, positive, and capable way out taken by the objectively inclined scholar (who finds purchase in his work and his understanding, as long as it does not become a purchase within the infinite . . . card catalogue?!); those who, like Dilthey, for example (in the latest volume), pass an ill-informed judgment on Nietzsche's empty brain-racking through the observation that the individual does not hit upon the essence of the human through introspective reflection, but rather "human spirit" is only revealed to historical consciousness. The fact that Nietzsche—insofar as he was an existential {*existentieller*} thinker—was not concerned with (Hegelian) human spirit, but rather with the "I-am," is overlooked by Dilthey, who cringes before the danger and sterility of such an undertaking.

However, it was necessary for Nietzsche to justify his existence {*Dasein*}—he speaks objectively about an existence {*Dasein*} that needs justification. That says it all! Even M. Weber, whose significance we must not underestimate (unless one were to think of an M. Weber coming after Jaspers and with philosophical aspirations), was perhaps (?!) more of a "reluctant scholar" than he let on. Concerning his relativism, however—in my view it is on the same level as "historical facticity," which steps in at decisive moments and not only overcomes, de-hypothesizes, and leaves behind formal indications in the most-pointed concretion of a determination of fundamental meaning, but actually leads the explication from the beginning. After all, your way of proceeding in the historical seminar—and by this I mean carrying out the process of formalizing the categories of history—also had the positive purpose of once again clearing a path to determinations seen in different, new, more originary and "proper" ways. I would not call such anticipatory determinateness {*Vorgriffsbestimmtheit*} "subjectivism," but rather an honest philosophy of actuality! It is of significance that, among others, Knut Hamsun's *Mysterien,* Dostoevsky's *Notes from the Underground,* and "Ein Gespräch mit dem jungen Bauer," and so on, give me more of the *philosophical* than Reinach's collected works and the complete writings of Rickert combined (the latter of which you once treated like a "worthy opponent" in your lecture on the transcendental). And this is not only owed to a "personal impulse," "on a personal level," and owing to my "world view"—for I am not able to set these three things apart from scholarly philosophy, and it always gives me pleasure to see that those who are "analytical" and "objective," *à la* Becker, are unable to separate these things in *actuality*—thank God!—such people who, due to a lack of self-insight, never really admit such things to themselves; that is to say, it does not really announce itself so clearly when the person in question is *in and of himself* in fact objective—including in the manner of his attitude toward himself. The type of historicism and relativism that is present in you is also too little for me—for you still have the tendency to supplant the authentic self-understanding *of the other* with your own authenticity. In distinction to Dr. Becker (and you??), I do not place any value on an objectively valid standardization and definition of what philosophy is; I would also not fall apart if someday a philosopher—one who knows what philosophy is—were to assure me that what I am engaged in is no longer, or not yet, philosophy. One thing is certain for me: the philosopher is something other and something more than a scholarly, cognitive theoretician, and he is different from a scholar of the individual sciences, due not only to content, but to particular modes of questioning (about "οὐσία") that delve into the background (second level!) and are principal, deep, encompassing, and foundational; he is different from scholars not only due to his more foundation methodological problems, but also to the inner quality of his problems, his ability to see deeply into them, and the entirety of his inner way of life, the *how* of his enactment. As central as the posing of methodological problems may be for the work of philosophy, what is *philosophical* in the *philosopher* cannot be determined from out of the theoretical content; nevertheless, this becomes a methodological tendency. Or do you understand method to be something else and more? A proposition such as "*what is decisive* in Kierkegaard is the methodological consciousness" is still not entirely clear to me! Of course, he knows what is decisive in the Christian problematics of the book, and to this he applies the Hegelian dialectic, but he also knows exactly what is decisive in the enactment of access, of the "how" obtaining to having-one's-self, and so on (see *Christian Discourses* with its transparent method and manner of representation, and so on); and while it is true that he executes his methodology in an often monotonous, stiff, and repetitive way, it does little damage, because not only does he see the *difficulty* of the "how" pertaining to a concernful self-appropriation of the self in an infinitely concentrated and deep philosophical way, but because he also sees and experiences the *self*! A proposition like the one partly cited above (pg. 28 of the Jaspers critique) seems typical to me of the scholarly decline regarding the *problematics of the self*. You speak of the historically enacting{*vollzugs geschichtlichen*} life in the "how" of the problematics of . . . and you say it originally belongs to the meaning of the *factical* "I am." It is my presumption that the problematic self (*quaestio mihi factus sum*) and the problem of the self undertake a doomed permutation—doomed and unavoidable, as doomed and unavoidable as the philosophical life!!—and as a result, the theoretical, philosophical explication of the "I am" takes the place of the factical "I am" of facticity. Elsewhere you say, in opposition to Jaspers—and in my opinion correctly, albeit exaggeratedly—that whatever method is used to understand the psychical is itself something that belongs to the psychical; however, from this I only understand the following: what belongs to the soul and the historically enacting enactment {*vollzugsgeschichtlicher Vollzugszugang*} of access are nothing separate, and the manner of having-oneself also determines this self (though not without remainder—I think there is a certain justification to Jaspers' objective concept of substance, which in its deepest depth remains untouched by a self-reflective stance that arises from itself—similar to the way in which a psychical disorder "persists," even in the absence of discoverable disease—and therefore, it is possible to speak, as Kierkegaard does, of a "latent" despair, or to speak with you yourself about someone who "does not understand himself" in his facticity). To me, there seems to be a long journey of theoretical molding and formation stretching from this seemingly actual method (which then represents a more precise explication of self-reflection) to the methodological apparatus as expressed, for example, in your Jaspers critique! For me, another unseemly expansion—which does not concede anything to those who think along with Jaspers—is to be found in the concepts of existence, although it is risky to say anything about this, because the intimations of it in [the] Jaspers critique are insufficient to allow for certainty.

To put it in a provisional way: the concept of existence, as formally posed, leaves (to be sure, only apparently so) the substantive determination of existence to historical facticity. Given this, however, a fundamental tendency of your philosophizing (or perhaps one of many such tendencies) remains hypothetical in a way (for the listener), namely, a tendency that only poorly coincides with your content-heavy concept of existence at all decisive moments of interpreting, such as in the critique. Also, I do not believe that one can exist in the proper sense within just any and all sorts of scholarly philosophical questioning (the way your department at the university allowed itself to be understood?!). One can only exist in a true and complete way when asking questions about existence, and existence does not coincide with scholarly fanaticism. In actuality, the material/authentic/anticipating—that is, the historical/personal/genuine—slips into your formal concept (and justifiably so); as a result, your formal concept then makes some suppositions which, from the outside, cannot be dismissed as "prior"—they are instead subject to authenticity; as with, for example, spontaneous, conscious, self-worldly concernful enactment/anticipation, which every artistic person would reject—but not me!

It all depends on how, and if, one is able to endure it in one way or another. On that point, I am in complete agreement with you; "what is necessary" and "genuineness" can never be objectively standardized. It is true that the danger of a lazy subjectivism is present in such a self-reflection of the individual, but this is not an objection—except perhaps by the standards of the kind of pseudo-councils that warn against "dangerous books." If we lived in an intellectual situation of unshaken, naively believed and experienced cultural and traditional bonds, valuations, and desires—not Alexandrian, but rather young, trusting, and constructive: *youthful*, but not like the youth of today, who are corroded by thousands of hesitations, half-measures, and ambiguities—(in the best case scenario, today's youth will only turn young at a more advanced age)—full of honesty (i.e., often, although not always, sterile) and critical reflection (i.e., not constructive) about the common world and in regard to the self. Without all this, the life of today's youth would be more analytically oriented, more positive, more achieving, more apparent, and naturally more alive in a "something" (i.e., thing, problem, task, and so on).

I can think of two typical mottos for a paper on Nietzsche: "I have no need for someone to refute me, I can do that well enough on my own," and something along the lines of: these days, the only thing that can be accomplished is thoroughness in insignificant things; the days of greatness when great men built things are over—we need most of our strength just to hold ourselves together. Perhaps there is something more important now, and the time for building up has passed. (Side note: in some sense, even you have a kind of "system"—albeit a "methodical" one.) On the one hand, a concept such as "that which concerns us" is unilaterally limiting, but it also inhibits the *defluxus in multa*: it makes one resigned; and truly, honestly (and sometimes despairingly so) desperate, because critical honesty is incongruous with our dubious substantiality. For me it is here, among other places, that the sticking points regarding your positive and negative possibilities lie: Luther will probably always remain distant to me, as for him it was not a question of believing *robustus in existential sua*—he *was* it fundamentally. This is also why Nietzsche (and so on) concerns me, and this not only since 1921, which is why I will probably muster the scholarly tenacity of so-called methodical and principled working-through—but without thereby believing that explicit explication is necessarily a more thorough approach to reaching a more profound and deeper ground. It is not *always* my impression that your manner of "boring down" and explicating exhaustively really does bring about a delving deeper and a moving ahead. I could show you entire pages—not only in Geiger's *Unbewußte*, but also in your Jaspers critique, as well as in most phenomenological *Jahrbuch* contributions—that speak to me not one whit more than a single sentence that is analyzed to breadth and death over the course of a page, in which the operative question long ago hit land; and one's understanding at such points is more likely to be damaged because one simply can't get enough of that manner of Husserlian logical thoroughness, and one—with humble pride (albeit by the sweat of one's brow)—is still warmed by the thought of "very crude distinctions." On this point, all phenomenologists should allow themselves at least a little bit of a knowing smile!

The spirit and meaning of these lines is not one of *confessiones*; I neither want to foist my personal side upon you, nor do I wish to force you into saying something if you don't want to; I also do not want to be up in arms regarding a skepticism (experienced here not for the first time) over and against my own stance toward scholarly philosophy—perhaps this letter only underscores this skepticism. But it is important to me that I am not misunderstanding you, and that I am not being misunderstood by you. To speak with Becker is easier and more free-flowing; nevertheless, I always have the feeling that I fundamentally remain at a greater remove from him than from you; in unimportant matters he takes himself too seriously, and in important ones he is too flippant, and he has cast me as a crazy romantic—I allow him this view because it's not important enough to me to be understood by him on a "personal" level.

I hope it goes without saying that in you I am not looking for religious edification, and the fact that a continuation of the Augustine lectures or some lectures (a seminar?!) on Kierkegaard would interest me more than Aristotle (already on account of the Greek!) does not contradict that. Your suspicion that you are being misunderstood, with its attendant mistrust, appears a bit exaggerated to me. Of course, one can always cause damage without meaning to, and this danger decreases in correlation with the superficiality and stupidity of your students and increases in correlation with the way that they enact and realize the interpretation of your philosophy. I don't think you can deny an historically enacted {*vollzugsgeschichtliche*} understanding of the content of your philosophy; and, for my part, I can openly admit that it was *you* and your *how* (in distinction to Husserl, for example) that attracted me right from the first semester, and which made me value your objectivity, though I also found it problematic and eventually became critical of it—in your work, it is not *primarily* an effort toward a logic of expression that I (along with Becker) see, but rather a concern born out of what is necessary in life today. But there is [one] point that still remains, somehow, *theoretically* ungraspable and thus confusing to me (and presumably also others—and not only "presumably"): namely, the coincidence of theoretical–philosophical objectivity and existentiell/pedagogic/maieutic tendencies, along with certain demands to awaken awareness of methodology and thereby advance a bit further. (I do not agree with Becker that your fundamental tendency is of a purely scholarly sort.) For my part, I adhere more to the conclusion of your Jaspers critique, in which you speak of a different anteriority in "reflection," and also of "self-reflection" and "what necessity demands." But with this, one has moved beyond the immanent cognitive-sense of knowledge and has taken up a problematizing stance toward scholarship. I resist the easy dissolution of the contradiction I sense here by way of "historical facticity" (as in the scholarly man). For example, I do not see it as irreconcilable that one could, despite being "engaged" with the "I am," also be interested in it in a *theoretical–philosophical way* and work on it; I just see it to be a self-deception when one takes this possibly theoretical–philosophical "also" (here I mean "theoretical" not in the sense of detachment [???]) and posit it to be as originary, genuine, and full as a lively life, thereby expanding the concept of historical-facticity to such a degree that it encompasses each and every enactment (thus, the theoretical, cognizing, and explicating enactment as well)—and in this expansion precisely that moment of facticity is lost that you emphasized in the Augustine lectures!

Given the manner in which Becker inhabits the typology of an analytic and objective scholar, he is not particularly interested in *his* self—at most perhaps the *problematics of the* self; having-one's-self and self-understanding are to him unseemly and a sign of hubris, which nevertheless, as a philosophical "problem" (along with thousands of other things) is interesting to him, and in a certain way he is perhaps also passionately, polemically, and critically interested in *opposition* to it. I am unable to see your manner of scholarly "analyticity and objectivity" in such a clear way.

For obvious reasons—and this is something I spoke recently about with Besseler and Rieniets (Rieniets has more extensive experience concerning it than I do from my vantage point in Munich)—it cannot be a matter of indifference to me that so many young people today split off or are driven into the quagmire when facing that dark something (or any something, for that matter) that cannot be dispatched by such hulking concepts as "dilettantish, weak-willed, playfully undisciplined," and so on—which is something that the young Nietzsche must have experienced in heightened form, otherwise he would not have been able to deliver those lectures on the future of German educational institutions. The "music-making Socrates" is also *our* vexing problem!! In relation to students and Dozents! If you will, these lectures are the idle musical program of a genius individual; if you will—or better yet, you *must* agree that it is so—these lectures are the most vital expression of our times and its attendant "individualness."

N.B. for example: speaking of the method concretely—I would like to ask you to be patient until the end of the break, for at that point I hope to be able to give you an outline of the paper and you will then have something in hand that can be discussed; I wish that you will speak to me stridently, in the same way that I have spoken today regarding those particular questions with which I am engaged. Please forgive me if I have taken too much advantage of the adage "in German one lies when being polite."

As always, I remain your thankful
    Karl Löwith

[Slip of paper]
11:20. Dear Herr Dr. Heidegger

I am traveling to Munich tomorrow for a few weeks and wanted to visit you before leaving. Best wishes
    Your
    Karl Löwith

Figure 3   Karl Löwith (circa 1920).

**25.** *Martin Heidegger to Karl Löwith*
Aug.19.21

Dear Herr Löwith,

In your letter you address two things: (1) a justification of yourself, and (2) the "correct" interpretation of "my philosophy." Writing to you a year ago from Messkirch I told you what it is that I miss—and I told Becker the same (and I would *never* have opened up about this to anyone else)—motivated only by this: you are on track to attain a "doctorate" at the university. How one judges this title—how others do so, and so on—is of no consequence—but I take the matter very seriously.

To what degree *this* course of yours stands in a relation of existential possibility to your position (to which I make no claim) regarding "scholarly philosophy" (more on this later), I am not able to judge. I must take you in the way you present yourself to me—with this I am not saying that I had viewed you primarily and actually as being my "doctoral student." I feel a *certain* assessment regarding your academic work is necessary (because I worry more about you than others). And the "scholarly way of life" is also different from that of the other "academic disciplines." I don't care about a definition of philosophy primarily and in isolation—it only matters to me insofar as it belongs to the existentiell interpretation of facticity.

A discussion about the term philosophy in this isolated sense is pointless—and therefore also the consideration of "scholarliness."

I must now turn the conversation to myself.

First of all, the discussion suffers from the following foundational error: namely, that you and Becker measure me (hypothetically or not) by such yardsticks as Nietzsche, Kierkegaard, Scheler, and other creative and profound philosophers. You are free to do so—but then it must be said that I am not a philosopher. I do not imagine myself to be doing something even remotely comparable, nor is it my intention.

I merely do what I must and what I feel is necessary, and I do so only in the manner I can; I do not tailor my philosophical work to suit the cultural tasks of the "common man." I also don't have Kierkegaard's inclination.

I work by proceeding concretely and factically from out of my "I am"—from out of my spiritual and altogether factical background/milieu/life context; I work from out of that which is accessible to me as the lived experience in which I live. This facticity is, as existentiell, no mere blind *Dasein*; it lies there amidst existence; that means, however, that I live it—the "I must" about which no one speaks. On account of this factical being-such {*Soseins-Faktizität*}, and on account of the historical, existence rages; this means, however, that I live the inner obligations of my facticity, and I do this as radically as I understand them. It belongs to my facticity that I am a "Christian theo*logist*" (which I mention in passing). In this lies a certain radical concern about the self, a certain radical scholarliness, a strict objectivity in facticity; in all of this lies the historical consciousness determined by "intellectual history"—and I am all of this within the context of the university.

For me, philosophizing is tied to the university in a factical and existentiell way; however, I am not hereby asserting that philosophy only exists within the university, but rather that philosophizing, precisely because of its foundational purpose at the university (understood in an existentiell way), therein has the facticity of its own enactment, and with that, its own limits and restrictions.

This does not rule out that a "great philosopher," one who is creative, may come from the university, nor does it rule out the possibility that philosophizing at the university is nothing other than *pseudo-scholarship* (i.e., neither philosophy nor scholarship). What university philosophy is, then, can only be demonstrated through one's own life.

It is, therefore, not possible to decide which one of you two understands me correctly, nor to whose side I belong; and what I say is not to be taken as a lazy equivocation of your positions. On the contrary, while you and Becker are both equidistant from me, it is in opposite directions. It was always clear to me that you are as little involved with the Christian as Becker is, and I never understood you as attaching importance to agreement on this point—as in Becker's case, I have not sought to influence you. You both take something different to be essential in regard to me, something which I do not separate but which, in turn, is not such that it keeps its own balance; namely, on the one hand, conducting research conceptually and in a scholarly theoretical way, and on the other hand, my own life. The essential manner of the existentiell articulation of my facticity is scholarly research, in the way I practice it. In doing so, the motive and goal I ascribe to philosophizing is never to increase the reserve of objective truths, because the objectivity of philosophy—insofar as I understand it and factically proceed out of it—is something separate in its own right. This does not rule out the most rigorous objectivity regarding explication; on the contrary, I see it to be in line with my existence. Objective rigor does not pertain to any one particular matter, but rather to historical facticity.

I can emphasize research, but from a position of concern principally different from Becker's. I take the person to be of decisive importance, but regarding the possibilities of enactment that are, in all honesty, at my disposal (without taking creativity into account), I run the risk of spouting empty phrases when measured against the greats if I now only issue phrases from out of *myself*. That this also often ends in failure, I know only too well.

I can easily believe that you are not able to bring the how of my philosophizing together "theoretically" with the position of its concern. Such a bringing together is not a topic of theoretical consideration. I cannot change my "I am"; I can only grasp it in one way or another and be.

Also, in destructuring, I neither wish for nor dream about an intrinsic objectivity, because it is one's own facticity that is "implied," if you will. The only thing that matters is whether an all-knowing, seemingly impersonal approach accomplishes more than a simple, direct diving into things (in which one must of course be personally present, otherwise it is not a true hands-on approach). One is then objectively one-sidedly dogmatic, but philosophically one is "absolutely" objectively rigorous.

Jaspers wrote to me and said that I am doing him an injustice in several ways. My reply: Husserl and others have also postulated this—but to me it is only a sign that at least I have attempted to grasp things in a hands-on manner, rather than to record the "results" of some book in an imaginary storehouse of knowledge.

To me it only matters that everyone does that which he is able to do; ultimately this happens in the moment of "doing"—unreflectively—even when one has a thoroughly reflective "philosophy."

Perhaps I am much less objective than you. You are, insofar as these labels signify something, an objective relativist; by contrast, I am a dogmatic subjective relativist—that is, I "fight" for my position and am "unfair" toward others in recognizing that I am "relative." But this interpretation does not interest me at all, as I do not wish to introduce a new direction into the history of philosophy.

The goal of my teaching at the university is that people grasp things hands-on. One cannot move beyond the old university strictures by making the "intellectualism" of sclerotic lecturers into an object of ridicule, and by taking oneself to be more expansive, more lively, and more profoundly passionate than such individuals. Rather, one must return to the origins of enactment of what survives within today's facticity and decide for oneself what one is capable of. What is to come—whether or not we will still have universities in fifty years—who knows; for they are not eternal institutions. However, there is one thing over which we do hold sway: whether we torture ourselves with varied feelings and endlessly ponder possible new cultures, or whether we sacrifice ourselves and return to, and find ourselves in, existentiell limitation and facticity, rather than projecting ourselves to programs and universal problems. The majority of young people today have it too good, most of all in an intellectual sense: from early on everything is handed to them (travel, literature, art, and so on). I would not wish my time as a student upon anyone; however, I could never wish it away.

You have not misunderstood me, but there is something that you do not understand, and you yourself have formulated it well. To that I can say: I cannot do otherwise without surrendering myself. That should, I think, suffice for you.

Becker has misunderstood me, because he grasped the same thing out of context, and only too well. Both sides of this are unimportant. Only this one thing is decisive: that we understand that each of us would radically commit ourselves absolutely to what we take to be the *unum necessarium*. According to "system," "doctrine," and "position," we are perhaps far removed from one another—but we are all together in the manner that the human alone can genuinely be together: in existence.

It is good that you were piqued and then let off some steam in your letter. I only wish to object to one thing: that in relation to the great detail with which you interpret and measure me, you still take me to be too important.

But you yourself must decide to what degree I "harm" you or am of use to you.

I am not good at dealing with people. And "leading" always becomes awkward; moreover, I am not in a position to lecture you; what I mentioned to Becker about you is something that you yourself have heard once before from me; not, however, with the immediate effect of your spontaneous self-defense.

Would you and Becker like to come on Sunday evening?

Warm regards,
    Your
        Martin Heidegger

**26.** *Karl Löwith to Martin Heidegger*
[Munich] Rosenstr. 6
X.1.21

Dear Herr Doctor Heidegger,

All of the hubbub is over, and despite the massive throngs of people (oh, what joy for the profiteers of currency exchange), Munich is really beautiful, with an air much fresher and clearer than that of Freiburg. I have not yet sought out Geiger and Pfänder. I have only visited various galleries, and so on, rummaged through antiquarian bookshops, and looked for a room for Gerling. *When will you begin lecturing*? I would be very happy if you were to conduct the small seminar you've planned—*"The Idols of Self-Knowledge"*!! I did some work over the final weeks of the break on self-reflection and the experience of the self. Have you already taken a look at the new Augustine book by W. Achelis? Do you reject such an approach *completely*, or just *partially*? How are things with you? Those few days in Heilbronn were nice. Besseler is now back in Vienna again. Maybe we will come to Freiburg occasionally in the winter, provided that something like that can be organized. I am disinclined to forgo university and student communality entirely. I do not like it when everyone just yokes themselves exclusively to their work.

With warm regards,
    Your
        Karl Löwith

**27.** *Martin Heidegger to Karl Löwith*
[10.3.21]

Dear Herr Löwith,

Many thanks for your postcards from Heilbronn and Munich. I am sorry that I was not home at the time of your departure.

Husserl will not lecture in the winter; he will only hold a 2-hour tutorial for wider circles.

I am having great difficulties with the planning of my lectures; I could easily give a 4-hour a week lecture and still not be finished. I have decided that this time I will approach the matter from two sides—I will give a principled but substantially shortened methodological observation, which will perhaps be more comprehensible if I simply deliver it like an excerpt from the last, extended treatment, with a focus on particular issues; I have not yet decided which of these I will take up, for it is all equally valuable and beneficial and, for my philosophical purposes, fruitful: rhetoric, logic, ethics, or physics—they are all more or less inaccurate terms. I don't want to waste my time lecturing more, as this tires me out too much to be productive, and in the winter there is just more in the way of sport and socializing. I also wish for a few capable people—tenacious go-getters like Bauer—who are just better equipped.

I will begin the lectures on November 2nd, and the preliminary discussion for the tutorials will be on October 25th; I cannot spend too much time on the latter, the emphasis being on the lectures which are, so to speak, *privatissimum*. If I were to do a small seminar, it would probably be on Aristotle (i.e., if you could get ahold of his biological investigations).

I have not yet seen the Augustine book, and there is surely little that I could learn from it: from a philosophical perspective the formulation of the question is completely worthless. For the bloodhounds following the tracks of the spiritual, it might be a feast, and for the next few decades certain people will have a new field of study that will keep them busy psychoanalyzing the affairs of the world; when it is isolated and turned into an "operation," destructuring is also not worth very much, despite its belonging to a more radical level of questioning.

You will surely learn all manner of things in working with Ebbinghaus. He is still away; I do not know how he will structure things.

I would like to organize my lecture course to be very exclusive; it will, in any case, be very difficult, and that always proves to be unduly arduous on those who are just sitting in.

Even still, such people can sometimes learn something, even if not everything is understood.

Greetings to Fräulein Gerling. Why not come here? Ah, but our faculty is worthless.

Warm regards,
    Your
        Martin Heidegger

**28.** *Karl Löwith to Martin Heidegger*
[Munich]
Rosenstra. 6/III
X.17.21

Dear Herr Dr. Heidegger,

I am gradually beginning to look forward to leaving Munich, although I do not wish to give up the refreshing abundance of my role as a guest here. To see new things and people is a need for me from time to time, and I see it as belonging to what I would like to call inner expanse and freedom, without me thereby taking the often merely voluminous fullness of Jaspers as a model. [I] had a few quite animated meetings with Geiger; there isn't much of a backbone to him, but it is so nice to discuss things with him, and I see his humane and decent loyalty in a largely positive way. [I] had no time to visit Pfänder, and also no reason; it is not fun for me to play the Freiburg "name-game," and in substance I am far removed from him. Recently, Fräulein Walther was [here]. Gerling will come in the next few days. Also, a delightful coincidence: yesterday I attended a wonderful evening of Beethoven (featuring Lamond), and there I happened to meet Marseille. All semester we had been watching each other, all without finding the courage to bridge the cautious distance between us. But yesterday evening it was as though we had known each other forever; he came home with me and we sat together until 1 o'clock—something commonplace for a night owl like myself! At the end of the month he will come back to Freiburg. It is indeed a strange thing, the collective spiritual "situation" (in the "collegiate-philosophical" sense) in which we find ourselves today. What each person wants, expects for themselves, negates, and seeks, and what each person is—is fundamentally always the same. And I see that in my letter to you from Freiburg I could have just as well written "we" instead of "I."

A while ago, an old teacher and friend was in Elmau to visit Johannes Müller, and he shared his enthusiasm for this man with me. Do you know his writings? I am, of course, very prejudiced when it comes to all of these holy apostles; it is mostly a gospel interpretation right on the edge of pastoral, optimistic, transfigured bourgeois culture. How much grander, by contrast, is Nietzsche's anti-Christianity—and perhaps, indeed, also more "Christian." What plagues me is the absolute de-objectification and de-ontologizing of the concept of God, this protestant (?) and Kierkegaardian emphasis on enactment and the concomitant emphasis on the *Tentatio* in your work! Why such great mistrust (even if it is pedagogical) regarding the "good news," Christian joy, comfort, security, and devoted piousness? Only now am I slowly beginning to understand why Becker spoke to me of Kierkegaard's "hubris." I sense in the "self" and the "I am"—in the way that you understand it—something of the air of Fichtean German idealism, as well as something atomistic. I come to such thoughts primarily via Nietzsche—P. Gothein said something very profound to me when the conversation turned to Nietzsche: namely, that he often takes fright at Nietzsche's *mercilessness*. He defended a "metaphysical realism," if you will—a belief in *Da-sein* (which for him, as

for all of Gundolf's students, precedes *Dasein* as existence). Do you know Gundolf's essay "Wesen und Beziehung" (from around 1910s, in *Jahrbuch für die geistige Bewegung*)? I have read it several times. It is indeed very good, and it would be too easy to shrug it off along with "*Der Teppich des Lebens.*" Here also lies the secret reason why I do not underestimate W. Achelis' interpretation of Augustine or even Blüher's Christology. It may be that there is nothing "philosophical" to be learned from it—but in the end, neither Augustine nor Christ were "philosophers." Because they are "psychological," such interpretations may be superficial; but a theological interpretation of Augustine is not everyone's thing, although it *is* in this case, because the "thing" in question concerns everyone. It is also the case that almost everything depends upon how profoundly or superficially one takes the "psychological"; at the very least, one can grasp and implement psychoanalysis in such a way that it leads to the core; perhaps then it no longer has anything to do with Freud's intentions, but that doesn't matter. It could be that our interest in Blüher, Freud, Keyserling, Wyneken?, etc., etc., belongs to those indirect-paths without which we today could hardly reach the true path at all; for the situation out of which our sort grew was the blessed age of all platitudes. Today, one is inclined to reach more pure and absolute sources in art, philosophy, and all else; and to that end it is often the *beginners*—that is, those who still stand with one leg back behind them, and with the other in new territory (or in good, old territory)—who are of more use to us than those who are whole and substantial. I read the letters of Franz Marc, who fell in the war. They are among the most beautiful things I know. There is also a big Lehmbruck exhibit here at the moment. Hoping to get together soon,
    Your
       Karl Löwith

**29.** *Karl Löwith to Martin Heidegger*
[Munich]
8.17.22

Dear Herr Doctor Heidegger,

It turns out that I left sooner than I had planned. It still seems completely implausible to me that this time I have left Freiburg for more than just a break. But that isn't saying enough. I cannot imagine myself without having had those 2.5 years in Freiburg, and I am terrified by the thought that, due to mere happenstance, I could have gone without ever having attended your lectures. I also cannot imagine the "fabric of my life" without Besseler and Becker, Afra, Marseille, and von Rohden. Regarding Husserl—I picked up what was valuable in his work *within and through* your work, in which it was already reformulated and improved. (From the very beginning—indeed, from the very first semester—it was clear to me that *you*, and not Husserl, are my teacher, and that I arrived in Freiburg so pared down that I did not need to make a detour via Husserl to get to you.) On a personal level—and also from the very beginning—I found Husserl entirely disagreeable, and he seemed to me to be at heart an extremely unphilosophical person and thinker. At that time, the *Logos* article was devastating for me—no intellectually vibrant person could write like that today. The unambiguous clarity with which the end of my relationship with Husserl came about is beneficial for me—and I have always felt badly that you and Becker cannot always live and breathe freely in Freiburg. Hopefully something will work out this summer regarding Göttingen?! (I have not yet looked up Geiger here.)

In the next few days I will apply myself intensely on the completion of my work. I now have the Nietzsche volume with his (hitherto unpublished) early writings; I will then incorporate what turns out to be of consideration—they are very important for the issue of the starting-point, and in Nietzsche's typical manner, the philosophical "starting point" is also chronologically intelligible. For all intents and purposes, Schopenhauer was also "done" at 25, and it is the richness of Nietzsche's thought that deceives in many ways; he has more in common with the monomaniacal mode of questioning characteristic of Kierkegaard, though the latter is much richer and more thorough—Nietzsche is always starting over again at the same old spot. During the last few weeks in Freiburg, I was unable to do anything substantial or proper—Becker, Besseler, and I were just rattling around like ghosts—we were unable to understand each other or reach common ground. In such a situation, it is better to part ways thankful for what we have given one another, instead of fruitlessly bothering and torturing each other; that is itself the highest torture, because one wants the exact opposite! Relationships with other people—more precisely, "friendship"—is for me the other thorn in my flesh, the first being philosophy. Becker told me that you two once had a long talk—regarding the manner and way in which one can meaningfully carry out facticity on an existentiell level. I am likely of a different opinion, although (and precisely because!) up to now I myself have almost always failed at it with people.

I have one regret: namely, that you (explicitly in your letter from one year ago, almost every word of which was essential to me) so quickly refused to engage the question of the "Christian." (In that regard, my stance is very different from Becker's.) Before it was clear that I would not be able to cope with Husserl, I considered that perhaps some commonality might be found via the detour through Overbeck and Nietzsche, a concrete point of contact that, on the one hand, connects to my work on (and justification of) the "Nietzsche" problem and, on the other hand, to what I (for my own reasons) am working out as your "negative theology," in which I see or intuit a structural similarity with Overbeck's position. Perhaps something will come of it later, if not already this winter: after all, the impulses, stimuli, impact, as well as the entire intellectual bearing and philosophical content which I experienced through you, is much too great for it to be the case that my time in Freiburg should be recorded only chronologically and theoretically as 2.5 years—and through such calculating be annulled.

For the first little while it will be very nice for me here in Munich, because I am entirely alone in the apartment—my parents are traveling, and the housekeeper is as well. I am, therefore, able to continue my familiar and beloved student-dormitory existence. I also sense how important the air of a place is. I am much fresher here and need less sleep—I found the climate in Freiburg to be less than invigorating. [I] will look up Marseille tomorrow. [I] met Walther in the city—he was once again buying things for the household. Ach—these married students: "students" might be a *lucus a non lucendo*.

The catalog for the philosophy department here has turned out to be extremely pathetic.

I will make a decision as soon as I find out whether [I] will get [a] room in Heidelberg.

Are you sure that you will come to Feldafing in September? Then I will show you Munich, and my parents have already written to me that you are to stay with us then. That would work well and would make me *very* happy! You must finally see my books. Will Becker visit you in Todtnauberg? Are you not planning to discuss the "pros and cons" of the assistant position at Gurlitt and Co.?

So much for today. I would have liked to come up to Todtnauberg—but I did not want to fritter away any more lost weeks in Freiburg, and my autocratic situation was a positive provocation for me. I hope that over time I will be able to demonstrate more adequately my gratitude for all of your efforts on my behalf, and to do so in the only meaningful way: namely, through a complete working-through and appropriation, itself a result of my learning ever more, and ever more insistently, from you.

Whether or not this learning and what is thereby learned can ever be expressed in a scholarly (and then, in turn, professional) way, I am not in a position to decide. At any rate, it is there—it exists within me. With wishes for nice days in Todtnauberg,
    Your
      Karl Löwith

I did not visit Husserl. Fräulein Walther arrived one day before my departure. Please extend my heartfelt greetings to W. Bauer.

**30.** *Martin Heidegger to Karl Löwith*
[prior to September; 1922]

Dear Herr Löwith,

Thank you for your kind procurement. Please buy everything.

The days in Munich were very rewarding for me. Admittedly, we did not philosophize much, but I am of the opinion that it is much better if everyone does their own thing: for in that case, one never finds oneself in the awkward situation of perhaps arriving "too late" or "not early enough" for something important.

I would be very happy if you were to approach the Renaissance anthropology, and then later Montaigne.

The old man told me (through my wife) that I should pay a visit to Pfänder—it appears that he has written him, alerting him that I am in Munich.

I really have no desire to play the part of the traveling phenomenologist; please stick the enclosed card for Pfänder to his door.

Regarding the other things by Ritschl, Sulpicius Severus, and Sedulius, I have not yet figured out the finances. Perhaps one can reserve them.

Warm greetings to you,
    Your
        Martin Heidegger

**31.** *Martin Heidegger to Karl Löwith*
Frbg, IX.20.22

Dear Herr Löwith,

I started a letter to you while up at the hut. But then a registered letter including travel money arrived from Jaspers, in which he fervently bade me to come for a few days, offering me the opportunity to work and to converse to our mutual contentment.

I immediately decided to go, for I had in any case already planned to be down here a few weeks working alone; I will now write an "introduction" after all (though a very condensed and propaedeutic one). The weather was terrible, and the children were constantly indoors. In August, I had a few good days—at the beginning I was very tired—a reaction to the semester.

The eight days with Jaspers were nice; other than him I did not see or visit anyone—in the mornings I focused on my own work. I have come away with an even stronger impression of Jaspers. He has a certain philosophical instinct but is completely helpless and naïve; he possesses a thorough, scholarly education only in psychiatry and psychology, but in that regard he is very independent; he now has a strong drive toward philosophy. Whether he will even get to it, I do not know; he said that on a purely physical and intellectual level, he is incapable of working in such an intently conceptual way as I do; after half an hour, he becomes tired and remains useless for the rest of the day.

We became quite close on a personal level. We spoke about the critique once again; regarding content there is nothing I would take back, but there are some things I still need to express in a more positive way. In all of our conversations, I noticed how the critique affected him. I also tried to prepare him to have a more stringent academic presence, but due to psychological reasons he is also not able to undertake much in that regard.

Jaspers is eagerly awaiting your work, but he would like for me to look it over one more time beforehand; he will not allow any further changes to be made. He either accepts or rejects; it is, therefore, best that you have it typed up now.

However, there is one difficulty: it is policy that you must have studied two semesters in Heidelberg, which means that the earliest you could take your degree would be at the end of the summer semester '23.

If you are in a hurry, Munich is all that remains. I don't know anything about Göttingen. I remain skeptical that I could compete with Geiger—especially if it all comes down to seniority!

In the event that Göttingen becomes tenable, you could take your degree with me over the course of the summer semester. Regarding the final editing of the work, please keep in mind what I have always told you about your presentations: don't cram too much into it; structure it in a transparent way and don't add too many "extraneous thoughts"—have ideas, but work through them; one should not encounter too many of them.

Thank you so much for your letter—the possibilities open to a "Dozent of philosophy" are not great these days, and are not great in general owing to the way that the contemporary world lives under completely different expectations. I am under no illusions regarding my work. The one thing that could unsettle me, however, is the possibility of turning into a passing fad; but the Aristotle essay is written in such a way that this particular danger is unlikely. I don't know when it will come to print; perhaps I will use this opportunity to bring the whole thing into even greater focus. The quasi-introduction is a lot of work for me. I have absolutely no capacity to imagine what a normal person knows about the issue. I read some things out loud to Jaspers, and he finds it much too difficult; he thinks I have a totally "dull, stubborn style." If I finish with the "introduction"—which is the focus of my entire "existence"—I will come to Feldafing before the beginning of the semester. I really should find some time to recover. Besseler is traveling to Karlsruhe tomorrow; it seems he sees the fleeting nature of the business and wants something else, but I can't say to what extent he has mastered the influences of the milieu. It really is incredible what Gurlitt is up to. I will not lecture in the winter; I don't know what will become of the semester. I need to catch my breath before the next attempt; it is one that makes me a bit anxious, because sometimes it overcomes me like a delirium. I had a conversation with Jaspers about it: "one isn't always aware of what one is actually doing"; what actually is accomplished is something other, which speaks to one over one's head and from behind.

The hut is wonderful, my wife and boys blissful, and I am looking forward to the winter and the coming vacation.

I live here all alone in my cell. Jaspers has many books, but no library, only a psychiatric and psychological one. On the final evening, I met Marianne Weber; unfortunately, she is a little too "cerebral"—as is the Heidelberg milieu in general (according to Jaspers' descriptions)! One evening he spoke to me of Max Weber. With that I once again saw what it means when an extraordinary person crosses one's path during a decisive point in one's life.

The second edition has come out; very few changes were made. The heading for Part III is now the more fitting "Leben des Geistes"! The print and configuration are completely different—more pleasant. Jaspers gave me a copy; for now he is not considering publication.

During those eight days, I was able to breathe freely; with Jaspers, there is that sort of philosophical existence that Husserl does not even remotely possess; it often became clear to me in what sort of environment I must live, and I now no longer wonder about the expenditure of energy this demands, also in relation to the students.

Please write to me and let me know what you have decided. I send my heartfelt thanks for the invitation extended by your parents. It will surely be quite lonely in the winter. Come with Marseille up to the hut to ski—in January!

Warmly,
> Your
> > Martin Heidegger

Rohden wrote a letter today; sounded pretty insecure.

**32.** *Karl Löwith to Martin Heidegger*
Munich
Rosenstr. 6/3
9.22.22

Dear Herr Doctor Heidegger,

I just heard from Besseler that you are back in Freiburg, and that you are diving into your work intensely. Yesterday, I wrote a card to Szilasi to ask what was happening with you, and if you were planning to come here. I had been counting on it and would have been very glad. Besseler wrote that you were with Jaspers. If you have the time and inclination, please do write and tell me what, if anything, resulted from it. From the beginning, Jaspers has seemed to me to be the only person whose intentions actually point in approximately the same directions as yours. Indeed, he conceives of things; and while he may not have things in his grasp, he does have them within his sights. Is he planning something more substantial? I wrote to him a few weeks ago to ask if he knew of any students whose rooms would be opening up. Jaspers wrote back with a friendly reply and sent me some addresses. Unfortunately, everything was already rented out. I will figure something out. But damn—how expensive everything has gotten! More importantly, though—how strict is the implementation of the two-semester guideline?! I would much rather submit it to Jaspers than here. Moreover, the air at home is too stifling for me. I am emancipating myself completely, to the greatest extent possible for me, and I live here almost like an old-fashioned "lodger." And I can no longer stand the many comforts of home: they are bothersome, stultifying, and dull the mind. Such a self-aggrandizing student-dorm existence in a small, unfamiliar city is much nicer—more fruitful. I have not committed myself to Jaspers in either a positive or negative way. [I] await what Jaspers will write to me regarding the two semesters. Of course, I don't feel like doing *that*, as I now want to finish as quickly as possible, and Heidelberg University with its attendant student crowd is simply too dumb to make a year there worthwhile.

I am now almost solidly in the revision phase, and today my manuscript became illegible even to me owing to the many cross-outs, changes, and additions. Marseille will begin typing it up next week. By happenstance, I was able to secure a position for him as a private tutor. He sends his warmest greetings, and still lives off his memories of Freiburg. His broken leg is still not quite healed. Apart from him, I saw that older student on the street the other day, the one who went to Pfänder from Freiburg. He will take his degree in the winter under Pfänder with his work on a "phenomenology of race." Well—still better, I suppose, than a description of the essence of the devil. I have not yet sought out Pfänder. In fact, I have not visited a single one of my local acquaintances—it doesn't bring anything, the boring gossip, the wasting of time. Good old Walther has become thoroughly stupefied by his marriage—he only talks about various cooking-utensils, linens, and how high the prices are. I can have all of that at home for cheaper. [I] only really spend time with Marseille. He is an outstanding, decent guy; considerate. I have also gotten sick of P. Gothein's passion for George. By the way, did Bauer visit you?? Has he changed? But now I am writing to you about a colorful mishmash of people whom you only know by my descriptions, and even then only fleetingly.

There are a few matters regarding books that I would like to share with you. The two volumes by Gratry ("Erkenntnis Gottes") that you are still missing, and of which there are definitely no used copies here, *are still available* at Manz in Regensburg. And, surprisingly, something else is also available there: "Der Monat Mariä: 31 Betrachtungen." In Lesemeister's French book store, I also got ahold of one more by Gratry—*Les sources conseils pour la conduite de l'esprit.* They now [???] cost around 60 marks. And when I was looking for it in a Catholic antiquarian bookshop here, something interesting happened. There were four volumes of Gratry lying on the table, and they had been ordered on behalf of "a certain Herr Dr. Scheler and a certain Dr. Hildebrandt"!! Hildebrandt opened a publishing house here. Of course, it is for texts pertaining to reform-Catholicism . . . and saintly icons! Seriously! Additionally: Fr. Overbeck's *Vorgeschichte und Jugend der mittelalterlichen Scholastik* is still available for 150 marks at Basel publishing. Also, an antiquarian bookshop here has something absolutely magnificent, and it makes me very angry to think that it will probably be bought by some stupid American, if it doesn't land in better hands before then. I told the gentleman there that I would write to you about it right away. In case the department has enough money (or maybe Jacobi, for the library), please write immediately to the antiquarian bookshop *Mittler München Finkenstrasse* (with reference to me): for they have the first edition of Luther's 12 volumes in parchment by H. Lufft Wittenberg (1552–1559), very well preserved. Later, five volumes appeared, but this edition is complete; it costs 20,000 marks—not so much for such a work *these* days!

Of course, I would very much like to hear from you, what you are currently working on and plan to publish. If you so wish, I will not share it with anyone. Will you skip Sextus Empiricus? The old Pappenheim translation doesn't seem too bad to me. With great effort I was able to hunt down a few other good things: for example, Overbeck's *Über die Christlichkeit der heutigen Theologie*, 2nd edition; Vinet and Cousin's *Études sur Pascal*; Schleiermacher's *Einleitung in das Neue Testament*; F. Schlegel's *Briefe*; Winckelmann's *Schriften*; F. von Baader's *Religionsphilosophie*; and a few good Latin things—for example, the complete Seneca (Teubner), and the complete letters of Cicero along with the *Manutius Commentary*. Together with Marseille I am reading Cicero's letters to Atticus; he is doing it because he wants to learn Latin, and I am doing it to freshen up mine, and because Cicero's letters are important for my psychological specialties. They are not easy to read. The M-C is interesting.

I have tacked an overstuffed introduction onto my paper—it was one of the more difficult things to write, a kind of pre-recapitulation of the thought processes in all four chapters. Right now, I am still working on a concluding chapter, in which I will retract the moments of "overfocus." If it wouldn't take up too much of your time, I would be very happy if you were to write to me! Has v. Rohden been in touch? You have probably received the letter I sent to Todtnauberg.

I will only write to Husserl "for decency's sake," and only once I know for sure whether I can take my degree with Jaspers, or whether, like it or not, I will have to stay here.

With many warm regards,
    Your thankful
        Karl Löwith

As soon as I have it all typed up, I will send you a copy.

N.B. By the way—In case you need me to proofread, or anything else, as you prepare your works for print, I would be *very happy* to assist.

**33.** *Karl Löwith to Martin Heidegger*
[Munich; 9.22.22]
{Salutation missing}

[???] The very moment I posted my letter, yours arrived. Thank you. I will then just wait for Jaspers' answer (the regulation states: should . . . no fewer than two semesters). *I* am not in a hurry—but my parents! Perhaps you will still come here after all, at the beginning of October. Then you will stay with us a few days; that would be nice. I am very happy that you felt comfortable and at ease while with Jaspers. From the first, he was also important to me—whereas Husserl is a petty, utterly insignificant person.

Please give me *Rohden's address*. I apologize that everything is so scattered. Next time I will send a letter more sensible than this Italian salad.

Warm regards,
    Your
        Karl Löwith

**34.** *Karl Löwith to Martin Heidegger*
[Munich, 9.30.22]

Dear Herr Doctor Heidegger,

Given Jaspers' uncertainty that a request to be freed of the two-semester obligation would be approved (*he* would speak in support of it, but the department decides by a majority of votes), I have decided—also under pressure from the financial situation as it now stands—to stay *here*. We have been typing it up for five days now. It is moving forward slowly. As soon as a larger part [is] done, I'll send it to you.

On Tuesday I spoke with Geiger—I will let you know in detail how things stand here. Still hoping that you will come in October. Too bad—I would have rather gone to Heidelberg and to Jaspers. But one can't always do what one would like. I am deep into my work, and after all, I left my skis in Freiburg! It would be really nice if I could visit you at the hut in January! Marseille sends his best greetings to you. [I] got a pretty disconsolate letter from Becker; he is worn down by the whining about finances at home.

Warm regards to you,
    Your thankful
        Karl Löwith

**35.** *Karl Löwith to Martin Heidegger*
Munich, Rosenstr. 6/3
XI.20.22

Dear Herr Doctor Heidegger,

How are you? Are things moving along? And how are the prospects of breaking free from Freiburg? My life here is not at all "established"—everything that happens is calculated to drive one away from Munich. I often have to ask myself whether or not I have enough life-force in me to make it through the crushing situation I'm currently in. Much of my strength fizzles out fruitlessly in the both silent and clamorous battle with "home"—a complex of close-minded, close-hearted, bourgeois calcification. Even passive resistance, not reacting, consumes me. A further blow for me is that Marseille left ten days ago. He got a very nice position as a private tutor for Dr. Müller's boys in Elmau. He was also not able to stand the industrious aura of our big, dead cities; and the university is a ridiculous, overly enlightened [?] grave; most especially the philosophy department *facultas—lucus a non lucendo*. The lecture courses and seminars given by Baeumker, Becher, Geiger, and also Pfänder are dismal, although Pfänder's primitive explanations still give one the sense of a real personality, at least more so than the others. If Wölfflin were no longer in Munich—well, then the whole *facultas* could let itself be interred. Even E. Schwartz is a big disappointment. I am thinking again of M. Weber—how high he towered [over] these more or less erudite larvae. Geiger's seminar on Plato's "theory of knowledge"(!)—based on whatever random translations—is fruitless and weak. At least Baeumker knows historical facts—he is a storehouse of memory—but in all else he is senile. Just yesterday, while dictating, he arrived at "§3": "truth." This truth lasted all of 10 minutes. He invoked his cherished colleagues Geyser, Hagemann, and Mercier. "You can also read this in print in my essay in *Deutsche Philosophie der Gegenwart*." I get together with practically no one except for Bösemann, whom you also know from Freiburg; lots of stupid exam candidates—theological ones in the seminars—even worse than in Geyser's lecture course. Cohn, for example, is way above the standard of what the Dozents deliver here. L. Klages spoke once during a lecture—not bad. The student-corps commands the field, inviting Tirpitz and Ludendorff, and so on, and practicing rightist politics. It's horrible, this predatory movement in Bavaria! Everyone is hustling, of course—some in order to get rich, some out of necessity in order to keep their heads above water. Walther also has to withdraw from his studies. But, then, he was never really a "student." Geiger is familiar with every last bit of hastily published modern shit, but with nothing decent. He is interested in my dissertation. A few days ago, I gave him a fully corrected and typed copy. He is somewhat amazed by the fact that one can learn quite a bit more in Freiburg than here. Regarding the content, nothing substantial will come of it. As soon as he sends it back to me, I would very much like to send it to you, in the event that you have the time and inclination to read it. I won't submit it until February. In any case, given just a few months, it will take some pressure and much effort for me to prepare for the minor subjects and oral examination with Baeumker and Becher. A ton of useless things have to be read up on—and I don't have enough time to read this stuff in a thorough and critical way, such that I could profit from the experience. I thus find myself in a state of haste and impatience, and I am fidgety and explosive due to tensions at home. But all that is possible has, through "self-destructuring," begun to flow within me, and in lighter moments I do have the courage and hope that I need in order to get through all of what Nietzsche designates as "nihilism" and "modernity." I am a bit curious to hear what you will have to say about the conclusion of my dissertation. As far as is possible today without engaging in intellectual dishonesty, I have distilled concepts and have only said what I can answer for. *For me*, Nietzsche is "principally" the beginning—the source—in the way that Aristotle is for you (both in a different but also quite similar way). You will see what I mean. I have tried to prevent it from being too overloaded by appending a big supplement with "annotations" (200 of them!).

Have you seen the latest scam in the bookstore? A so-called *collectanea* by Harnack: *Reflexionen und Maximen* by Augustine! He is trying to make Augustine palatable with that gussied-up French moralist title. It should be a supplement to Overbeck's Harnack encyclopedia! Also, another one of those philosophies of religion (a monologue, of course) by Herr O. Gründler—with a preface by Scheler! Some weak stuff by Haas, a botched book by Troeltsch, and so on. Geiger hosted once, and Utitz talked about F. Brentano. He must have been a very strong philosophical presence {*Existenz*}! Even just the few anecdotes that Utitz shared from his own experience show that Husserl (Brentano's student) appears much weaker when considered as a philosopher in the stricter sense.

How did things turn out with Ebbinghaus? And with Becker? He is so lazy about writing, I never hear from him. And here are two typical reminiscences of Scheler: once, when someone accused him of not living very "ethically," he is said to have replied: "Indeed, for I am a guide post, and such a post cannot also go whence it guides." And when someone confronted him about his "presuppositions," he said: "I don't wish to know my final presuppositions."

I recently got a long letter from Rohden. Insecure, but nevertheless "on the way." If it can be managed practically, he would also like to come to Freiburg—that is, to Todtnauberg—during the Christmas vacation. I say "also," for I too would like to leave here during the vacation, and once again want to ask if it would indeed be a pleasure for you and your wife if I were to come in the beginning of January; my skis are still in Freiburg, anyway. One can surely get something to eat at the inn; and if your wife is fine with it, I could also bring something to eat, cook, and so on, and you would then only need to calculate what the provisions would cost. I could then also secretly concoct a little swindle, and possibly settle the expenses for Rhoden with my father. It would certainly be very nice if we could spend some time together this way.

Do you see Besseler on occasion? Is he doing alright? And are the children well?

One more thing: the Englishman to whom I gave lessons in Freiburg wrote to me from England and said that he might have use for the Russell. I asked him about it back then, because I knew you wanted to sell it. Please write to me and let me know how much you want for it (of course, it would have to be a little less than the book presumably costs in England; otherwise, he won't take it)—in case he wants the volume (which one? the *first*?), I will let you know—it could be sent as a parcel post.

With many regards,
 Your thankful
  Karl Löwith

**36.** *Martin Heidegger to Karl Löwith*
Freibg, Nov. 22. 22

Dear Herr Löwith,

Many thanks for your letter. Today one really has to muster the requisite strength to bear the sight of how our universities are decaying. One can hardly fathom how irresponsible and lazy today's university lecturers are.

At the beginning of the semester, I took a more focused look at all the detritus that washes up in my introductory tutorials, and it is awful: mostly people in the fourth–seventh semester (i.e., regular ones, not war semesters); in addition, the likes of Alpheus, Mertens, Wiesemann, and Elken. It is indeed disgusting to see these corpses sitting around oneself. Regarding the Aristotle tutorial: Fräulein Bondi handed in a nine-page "interpretation" of the first third of the first chapter of Book II of the *Physics*—and that was it!

Because I am not lecturing, I cannot suspend these tutorials. And in order that the tutorial even take place, I had to give up the requirements—that's how all the detritus got in, as you know. There is a new habilitation candidate from Amsterdam (classical philology)—there is also a Jesuit (in his eleventh semester), and also a "Marburger"—he is supposed to be a "guiding light"; on a personal level he gives a more modest impression—there won't be much to him.

Kaufmann and Becker are also here; it's like pulling teeth with these people; and it seems like my summer lecture was spent talking to a brick wall. Not a single decent question gets posed; of course, everyone starts scribbling away when I say something; when I myself pose a question, a big guessing game ensues, and one can tell by their faces that they would be equally good at solving a crossword puzzle. Amongst all this I then hear mutterings of "taking care of things {*Umgang*}" and "caring {*Sorgen*}," but always in ways that don't at all fit. Becker is very disappointing, lacking all momentum in my tutorials; Besseler says the lecture course is wan and dull, leaving no lasting impression, but is pedagogically adept. But maybe he'll still come around.

Ebbinghaus read my Aristotle introduction, and his wife typed it up. His whole habilitation is thus silently turned on its head; he is critical of Hegel, and very much so of Fichte, but in all that is essential he is not independent and simply puts my things into his desk drawer; nevertheless, I enjoy him—he approaches things with a certain vehemence, albeit perhaps a superficial one.

One evening a week I interpret important passages from early Luther and Melanchthon for him, so that he gains a few concrete perspectives when it comes to his interpretation of Hegel.

I have no one from whom I could learn anything decisive. And so I keep to my work and my books.

In the summer I would like to give my "logic" lecture (over 3 hours per week); I am sure you are surprised by this, but I am ready.

However, given my experiences during the last semester, I am asking myself whether to cast this pearl to the swine. After all, the lecture won't perish if it remains in my desk. And why should I commit such a folly and squander my strength when the whole world is taking it easy and faring much better for it; perhaps it is better if one only works on what is the most necessary—people can then do what they want with what I leave behind. In this way, one is able to stay respectable in one's own eyes.

As you well know, Göttingen is finished for me. Geiger is in first place; he is older, after all, and has written more. If I also wait that long and put that much ink to paper, perhaps I will also be taken in somewhere out of pity. It is only that right now, and in general, the practical circumstances of waiting for this while having a family are different for me than for Geiger. But that is just how it is.

I am also being talked about in Marburg. Natorp, who has the introduction and translation of the *Aristotle*, is "smitten," and he says that it goes far beyond what any Ordinarius Professor in Germany today could do. Of course, the old man is proud of me now.

But this is all just Platonic gossip; at most they will put me in second place, and Kroner in first—"he is older, after all, and has written more."

Such a suggestion—and in this location—is for me neither an honor nor a success, but rather the most embarrassing humiliation that could happen to me. Given his lack of critical discernment, Natorp's enthusiasm is meaningless to me.

Also, Hartmann, Scheler, and Geiger will surely table any concrete prospect I might have in Marburg; if they are sufficiently clever and egoistic they won't miss out on doing so; I can understand it and don't fault them for it. It cannot be expected of anyone to feed their own executioner. In case you haven't already been informed by Geiger about the strategic situation, don't speak about it. If Geiger gets the appointment, he will surely notify you. Please let me know then, as I don't read newspapers and am otherwise also out of the loop.

I would rather read your dissertation after your exams, for you will surely need it immediately if Geiger is only there until February. I am also too busy with my own things. In any case, don't make any more revisions; when I read it, I will do so with a critical eye.

We would be delighted if you came with Rohden in January. There is talk that the semester will end here on January 31st. February would thus be more favorable, and the snow conditions more certain. In any case, you can anticipate that after Christmas you will be able to duck out.

My wife will let you know about the finances.

I have Vol. I of the Russell; I don't know the English price. I would like to get 60 percent of whatever the English price is for a new volume.

The Japanese donated 10 English pounds to the department. The French Academy edition of Descartes is to be acquired! Throw in a Hume, for all I care! I have given up trying to make the library respectable. All three new volumes of Dilthey's collected works are gone, as well as *Schleiermachers Leben*.

The old man is writing contributions to a Japanese newspaper. Rickert arranged it over the summer. The title of these contributions is "Renewal"!

According to him, it is completely "humanities-oriented and socially ethical." He also wanted to publish it in German in the *Jahrbuch*. You would not be able to imagine in your wildest dreams how disastrous it is. In order to prevent the worst, I told his wife that something like this could never be published in Germany—it is too elementary.

Some guy named Wasmund is here—he is from Kiel, and says that in the past he attended my lectures over the course of several semesters; one of Ephraim's friends, I can't remember—and it really doesn't matter; the latter has submitted his Kierkegaard thesis to Jaspers and will earn his doctorate under Hans Freyer, Ordinarius Professor in Kiel.

And now you have a letter full of gossip. But this is the only way that one can write about one's "situation"; to speak of other matters in between would be a shame, it's better to do that in person.

On his own initiative, Cohn has ordered Harnack's edition of Augustine for the department. The old man is excited that he still has the chance to learn Augustine. There is so much useless stuff in the department library that one more page-turner will not tip the scales.

For Todtnauberg you should bring a blanket, pillow, bedding, towels, something to snack on, and something to cook.

I am very much looking forward to you coming. Do you have Afra's address?

Warm regards,
    Your
        Martin Heidegger

**37.** *Karl Löwith to Martin Heidegger*
[Munich] XII.7.22

Dear Herr Doctor Heidegger,

Many thanks for your letter. In comparison to the "situation" here (the students in the department, and so on), you would surely designate the "corpses" you mentioned at least as the *living* dead, whereas here it really is a case of mindless automatons, ones that don't even perform when one drops 10 cents into them. It is simply absurd what off-the-mark presentations Geiger is content with. They are not proper presentations or discussions at all, but rather mostly just the transcriptions of whatever kernels of wisdom arose during the course of the previous lecture. Also, and frighteningly, hidebound nationalism and anti-Semitism (fueled by Bavarian beer) are spreading. Campaign posters are being hung in the lecture halls [?]—it's hair-raising. They demand, for example, that the university should only be allowed to have 1 percent Jewish professors, because this correlates to the percentage of the population at large.

And yet, all of these student "masters" are delighted to be living here, etc. Almost daily there is some evening presentation or lecture—in short, always the prattle of some academic association—and at virtually all of these events (and by invitation of the senate) there appear various decommissioned royal dignitaries and excellencies, above all Ludendorff, who, by the way, looks disastrous when seen up close, a complete *poseur*, brutal, sententiously vain and vacuous.

There, now you see how one ineluctably ends up gossiping. I held back my reply because I wanted to wait for an answer from Mr. Cuckow regarding the Russell. But the guy just isn't writing back, and probably fancies that he will simply be given the book for 1,000 marks. Afra's address is probably still: Berlin-Wilmersdorf, Paderbornerstrasse 2. It's been two months since I have heard anything from her.

I am very much looking forward to Todtnauberg. It will not work in *February*, however, because of the exam—I will submit in January or February. So far I haven't really crammed for the exam; those seminars and lectures take up a lot of time, and I would rather take up what remains to be "crammed" two months before the exam. By virtue of my education in Freiburg, my mind has no patience for cramming together a seemingly random assemblage of various philosophies all at the same time, and according to what I see and hear no *reasonable* examining is happening here at all. However, it is difficult for me to attend a Kant seminar (Baeumker) and a Plato seminar simultaneously—for the *Charmides* alone demands a few months of rigorous engagement—and Geiger checks it off in *one* lecture, based on some random translation! It's just stupid, all this cramming for exams—it's stupid, because as I have finished with the Nietzsche paper, I am so eager to try my hand at something new—albeit in connection with what has come before—most of all in regard to the works of Freud. I am (still) not getting to the bottom of what brilliant and methodologically aware research exists in these analyses; and as for *me*, I can grasp "facticity" in a more unmediated way in the realm of psychology than I can through an orientation toward intellectual history. However, what I mean by this, and why I say it, is better discussed in person.

Yet another Nietzsche volume has been published—two essays by E. Gundolf and K. Hildebrandt. As with all things coming from this circle: relatively cultured, clever, never pedantic—but one quickly tires of these stereotypical, arrogant, smug, canonized, univocal results; they are not archaic, but rather archaistic, and thereby, in reality, simply an outline of that all too modern-impressionism. It amounts to an intellectual corset, "priestly knowledge of path and destination"! For both of them (explicitly!) poor Nietzsche remained stuck halfway to George. George—the standard, the fulfillment, the consummation, the form, the orienting center, and so on—and Nietzsche as the guide to getting there. How stupid!—these know-it-alls.

Some time ago I even sold off my copy of Gundolf's *Goethe*. I kept only the Shakespeare. By the way, his *Kleist* is not uninteresting, absolutely symptomatic of our time and of the George Circle—this engagement with Kleist. As always, there is much of Klages in his books, much that is instinctually certain, and also a relatively clear position and opposition—however, when taken together, each of Kleist's little stories (and letters) are more substantial than any of this. I have engaged with Steiner—he is not nearly as dull as the Nietzsche apologists always make him out to be (in distinction to Nietzsche himself). There is much that would surely interest you—he rubbed elbows with Bruno Bauer!

Please write back to me as quickly as possible and let me know if you would like the following by Bruno Bauer (I had it laid away today, it only costs 700 marks): *Kritik der evangelischen Geschichte der Synoptiker* (1841, bound in three volumes). I could perhaps also get his: *Kritik der Evangelien und Geschichte ihrer Ursprünge* (1850, three volumes; also around 600–700 marks).

And please also let me know when you will be in Todtnauberg, as well as the exact address (perhaps that of the farmer) so that I can send some food there; it would be best to send it before XII.15. I don't know anything concrete yet regarding Rohden.

N.B. I was not informed about the "strategic chapters" regarding Göttingen—but he did make it apparent that he is pretty secure in counting on it. I didn't speak about anything else with him. The only assurance he made me regarding the paper due on May 10th is this: he is slowly moving forward; the paper is "so difficult." I cannot then reply: his lecture course is "so easy."

With many warm regards and thanks, also to your wife,
    Your
        Karl Löwith

Please also send my regards to Ebbinghaus; why hasn't he responded to me about the publisher's request?

**38.** *Martin Heidegger to Karl Löwith*
[Freiburg] XII.9.22

Dear Herr Löwith,

Many thanks for your kind letter. At the moment, my wife is sick with an infection of the middle ear—I am, therefore, unable to work or write; if possible, I would still like to write you a real letter this year. Please get me both things by Bauer. For Jaspers, I got Overbeck's *Christentum und Kultur*—he hadn't read it—he recently wrote to me about it; his interpretation is typical; I will show it to you when you come.

Our vacation only lasts until January 2nd. But my lectures are at the end of the week, so there remains time for the hut; at the moment it is lovely, but I can't take advantage of it.

The address of the farmer: Master Carpenter Pius Schweitzer, Todtnauberg (Rütte), the Black Forest of Baden. I will let him know so that he does not mistake the package as a Christmas gift for himself. Bring with you: bed sheets and a towel.

"No news from the Paris front." I am in a very good position; it's just annoying that the whole publishing business is still ahead of me—half a year will be lost with it.

Rudolf Unger should also bring a "Kleist."

Warm regards, also from my wife,
    Your
        Martin Heidegger

Can you please let me know exactly when, and for how long, you will be coming?

**39.** *Karl Löwith to Martin Heidegger*
[Munich, December 1922]

Dear Herr Doctor Heidegger,

Thanks so much for your card. The two "Bauers" have been secured; I will bring them to Freiburg myself. I am thinking of coming on the 30th, if that works for you. Today, I can't manage more than just this card. If you would still like to write me a "real letter" this year, you must know how happy this would make me; I am actually already waiting for one (and as a result am getting some insight into the "time-consciousness" of waiting). There is always too much in my head, and too much that is disconnected, to allow for me to write real letters; and I can no longer afford to write those spontaneous, and in a certain sense irresponsibly and eruptively emotive, letters, at which I have surely too often caused friends to take umbrage. This is what one usually calls life experience! These days such life experience is almost identical with earning money—and sadly lacking in foundation for most people. To work out everything in silence and alone, and then settle it—I cannot allow this to be the norm, though it might be necessary—due to necessity; it would be more natural to have a reciprocal, vibrant enrichment and communication.

And it has always seemed to me a characteristic and limitation of scholarly life that—if it is honest, and only making one attentive to oneself—it communicates *indirectly*. Not all direct approaches have been avalanched. If I take stock of my way of living, thinking, and working, along with those utilized by Besseler, the possibility of a comparison is ultimately missing—because an existence {*Dasein*} that is unbroken in its core misunderstands what is decisive for others—and most often where seemingly similar demands and necessities appear to hold sway. I do not know to what degree I overextend my strength in following up on misinterpretations, but this is not really what is decisive, if what *is* decisive is the "how"—only, the "how" is also not everything. "Please forgive these abrupt sentences." They flowed out of me on their own, into my pen.

Warm greetings,
Your
Karl Löwith

Hopefully the situation with the middle-ear infection is not too severe. I will certainly still be here until XII.25.

**40.** *Karl Löwith to Martin Heidegger*
II.15.23

Dear Herr Doctor Heidegger,

I got a letter today from Mr. Cuckow, the Englishman—it was the reply to my inquiry regarding *Russell*—which I sent before Christmas! He needed a long time to come to his decision—but the important thing is that he will take the volume for *1 English £* (now approx. 100,000 marks). But you would have to send the book off immediately and at your own risk (in case [it] is lost by the post). The postage is worth it for the 1 £; it would be best to send it by *registered* post. Once he hears from me that it [has] been sent, he will send the money via *check*. If it gets lost, he will pay the postage costs. If you [are] in agreement with all of this, send it right away; he is only there until March 10th! Please let me know whether you [have] sent the book so that I can write to him.

Haven't you heard anything yet? How are things going in general? Has the semester already come to an end? Here it runs until IV.10. As soon as I [am] finished, I will have to seriously consider what to do in order that (1) I can do that to which I am most suited, and (2) do this in such a way that therewith (or thereby) I can earn enough money in order to be independent of my parents. If philosophy were an "exact science," there would surely be paid institutional assistantship positions. In case you are still in Freiburg during the summer after all, do you think I could find something there? As a private tutor, perhaps, or for one of the Japanese "stragglers," and so on, or something else that's not too beneath me? (How is the *Volkshochschule* doing? Is it still headed by *Spemann*?) Have you heard anything from Jaspers? Is he still pondering Berlin? I would also be open to going to Italy or Spain as a private tutor for two years. But that is hard to find. I cannot make any concrete plans regarding career or interim-career possibilities in advance, for [I] am in the midst of cramming. This high school approach is really childish. I have never memorized all the various syllogism formulas, but it is possible that Baeumker would ask even about those. He liked my Kant presentation—it was splendid, and [he] made several references in front of the "Husserl contingent." Husserl himself would have thrown up his hands at this presentation, and would have entirely given up on me as unsalvageable back-[???]. Baeumker's every other word is: Külpe's "critical realism."

My cramming has only gotten up to Petrarch—so yet another 600 years of philosophy to go!! From time to time I revive myself with the Dilthey volumes. I now see that I must study this wonderful Dilthey much more extensively. I also feel like engaging more with the Stoics and their psychology. A forbidden little book on Nietzsche by Schrempf has come out.

Rittelmeyer recently spoke here—well-intentioned hogwash. By contrast, *Schweitzer* is a very respectable, well-rounded guy.

How do things stand with the Aristotle?? It would be a shame if you had to split it up; what you gave me to read was so compact and taut and yet still clear (if one only thinks through it in a similarly taut manner) that I can hardly imagine a change. I will have to speak with you in greater detail regarding one point—namely, the paragraph regarding "death" as "the how of life." I don't believe that it amounts to not wanting to think about it or putting it out of mind when the human does *not* include a thinking of death in its life, excepting the general sense of the temporality of life. To me the passive occurrence {*vollzugslose*} of merely being born has always seemed more essential—through the necessity that arises out of it later to "take up" this fact and its consequences, to choose that which cannot be chosen (in Kierkegaard's sense); and one point of departure for these questions and all other such facts would be illuminating for me: namely, in the specifically *human* possibility of suicide; the voluntary and free exiting from out of an entrance whose "whence" is not up for discussion. I don't know if these few sentences suffice to make clear in what way I mean this.

It is terrible to see only lots of shriveled up and phony people in the seminars, people on whose faces only the dismal annual debris of so-called studying deposits like rings that indicate entombment rather than growth. And among them, here and there, is a carefully wary squinting at the light. It is a disgrace how Plato is being curtailed. And as for the rest, it all revolves around questions of money as the nervus rerum, and it has indeed become the *rerum* nervus. It is grotesque how much effort must be expended in order to get some breathing room for oneself. Do you see Besseler sometimes?

I send you my warm regards.
Your
Karl Löwith

**41.** *Martin Heidegger to Karl Löwith*
Freiburg Br., Febr. 20. 23

Dear Herr Löwith,

Many thanks for your letters and your assiduities. It was very interesting to study the Gsellius catalogue—beautiful things, and cheap: the Calvin commentary; *De Wette*, the Apostle story (the edition that Overbeck published). I wrote immediately—but I didn't get any of the most valuable things. Did you ultimately snatch up the Overbeck?

I will not send the Russell—it is very inconvenient to send it, and by the time I would be able to, Cuckow will be long gone.

I have added in four Aristotle sessions—but I have only just now finished with the preliminary interpretations. The momentum of the participants was a bit better after Christmas. At any rate, they are all making a tremendous effort. Fräulein Victorius is by far the best—completely emancipated from Schelerism. She would like to work on Aquinas' Aristotle commentaries.

I don't have much hope for the rest of the lot. But the whole "bevy" wants to "relocate" with me. Despite my pointed, almost impolite refusal, Rothacker has already written me two long, business-like letters saying that I should still submit my work to his journal. In the last seminar session, I publicly scorched and destructured {*destruiert*} Husserl's *Ideas* in such a way that I can now say that its essential foundations all lie prominently exposed. If I now look back on the *Logical Investigations* from this vantage point, I come to the following conclusion: never in his life, not even for a second, was Husserl a philosopher. He is becoming increasingly ridiculous. What you say about "death" is also my view, insofar as death is not what is decisive for the problem of the historical {*Historische*}—which should, nevertheless, be "indicated." But death is the easiest way by which anything of what I mean may become visible. Nonetheless, what I designate as "derivativeness" (being-from somewhere) hits upon something of the uncanniness and properly existentiell difficulty of our facticity—this is to say nothing other than that the interpretation is itself subject to the same difficulty. I am not in the remotest sense "finished" with this "question"—thus my withholding of the "historical [*Historische*]."

An "elaboration" of the Aristotle introduction will only unfold through an expansion of content—that is, through the integration of foundational aspects of the interpretation of facticity, provided that the ensuing interpretation of Aristotle is related to it. Of course, I realize that in response to this critique the world will also find a way to take recourse to platitudes, that is, to "make something out of it." But at the same time, I am also convinced that even I myself cannot know what the actual effect might be. In any case, it will be subterranean. I think that the real Dilthey nonsense and hype about "intellectual history" is yet to come—and the time is not yet here to allow oneself to be "triggered" by Dilthey. My wife brought Jörg to Feldafing today. I will

**Figure 4**  Martin Heidegger (circa 1925).

most likely go there for a few weeks at the beginning of March. Tomorrow I will go to the hut for a few days. The matter of the "practical" is better discussed in person. Stay strong while cramming. Just got a letter from Rohden!
Warm regards
  Your
    Martin Heidegger

**42.** *Martin Heidegger to Karl Löwith*
Freibg, April 21, 23

Dear Herr Löwith,

Thank you for the letter and cards. I stayed a little longer in Messkirch and roamed around a lot in the woods that are still familiar to me from my childhood. I wanted to take something with me of the ground, air, landscape, and light—looking back, I think this was because, while back in my *Heimat*, I was assailed in an "unimaginably" strong way by the loneliness of what one carries along with oneself.

I was not here for even two hours when Becker came running up; then Husserl wanted to know when I was coming; Ebbinghaus was also in approach—I had to ask myself whether I am perhaps a clerk at a bank.

And when I came to the department to fix the library, Elken was sitting there—the whole apathy and lazy clinginess of my department then overcame me.

I immediately decided in favor of "reductions"—I will only lecture on "ontology" for one hour, only what is needed for the Aristotle seminar—the "essential" I will keep to myself—I will only offer two hours a week of the Aristotle tutorial in order to complete the required workload for the winter. The tutorial with Ebbinghaus will hopefully "shrivel up." The only things to which I will apply myself are the beginning tutorials on Aristotle's *Nicomachean Ethics*. Maybe there will be one or two among the fresh youngsters sitting there who will be gripped by it. My seminar for the more veteran students seems like the sea voyage of old leaking tugboats that were too defective from the beginning as to have had an engine built in for self-propulsion.

The fact that Becker attends my lectures, as well as the beginners' tutorials, reduces my already low estimation of him by a few more rungs. Ebbinghaus is now contorting himself with his Kant; I don't think he even knows what he wants to do with it. Tellingly, a few days ago, he said to me—"You know, we are still thinking too much instead of simply interpreting from out of the material." I believe we are still thinking much too little—given his mindset, a forty-hour a week seminar wouldn't help any more than a one-hour seminar.

Husserl is running a campaign of well-intentioned impotence. It is now patently clear that Scheler is scheming against me in all possible ways. And Natorp is apparently sitting harmlessly at his desk, just like the old man. I have asked him not to speak of questions relating to appointments when we meet in the future. Perhaps at least common decency will still win out in Berlin. By August, there really should have been time to consider various possibilities of shuffling jobs about.

I will "review" your thesis over the course of the summer—I will just add in the slips of paper with my notes on them at the corresponding points. Publishing it with Rothacker and Co. will surely be possible. I am absolutely in favor of it.

I think next time I will also be able give you the "Introduction."

It would be best if Marseille worked from home. From the library, it's Schlatter that would be important for me—if it's the commentary.

Finke and Göller are not yet here—Finke is traveling again—lectures don't begin until next week. The Japanese students are also gone—one is in Greece—but they should be back at the beginning of May. I have not yet been able to reach Kiba. I will try to drill out some information from Tanabe; he is a Dozent at a state university. Unfortunately, Große [?] is completely unreliable. Besseler, it appears, is "feeding" off of Becker. And Müller-Blattau is already the editor of a new collection: the publications of the musicology department at the University of Königsberg. Issue 1, Müller-Blattau: "Zur Geschichte der Fuge." The editor's own dissertation!

When Nietzsche was writing his *Untimely Meditations*, there was still work being done in philology and history {*Geschichte*}—today one is only doing busywork. That insipid phoniness of which Scheler is the chorus leader will surely continue to spread for a few more generations, given that it is only now beginning to "establish" itself under the banners of the "ascent to metaphysics" and "religious renewal." As soon as I know and have something of its substance, I will write to you about it.

Young Baumgarten is hopeless—he is helplessly "Georgine" and swears by the philosopher "Gerda Walther." There seems to be an enlivening atmosphere in Heidelberg. It's better, though, if there is nothing going on, like here.

Warm greetings to you
    Your
        Martin Heidegger

Friendly regards to your parents.

Please leave out the "Dr." in your future addresses to me—I always forget to mention it.

**43.** *Martin Heidegger to Karl Löwith*
Frbg—May 8, 1923

Dear Herr Löwith,

Many thanks for your letter. I got the little book a few days ago. I only just finished the second essay. The money will be sent to you after the holiday.

I received word from Finke and Göller yesterday. Finke had nothing to report concerning the Spanish lecturer who used to be here and is now in Hamburg; Finke himself advised against going to Spain or Italy in the absence of having found a highly recommended position. He came across several young Germans in Barcelona who had also been teachers for a time—and now they are literally lying in the gutters and barely earning what they need to live by shoveling coal.

Prof. Tanabe (Japan) has announced his visit with me today—I will drill him a bit—Kiba wrote from Florence but left no address.

I would like to suggest that you just take the next somewhat favorable opportunity in Germany.

There are a few among the young people who are making a very good impression. There are eighty in the beginner tutorials (on Aristotle's *Nicomachean Ethics*)! About 70% of them "know" Greek—I had a lot of fun in the first two sessions—although ideally it would be the case that I could be completely free to apply myself fully to these tutorials. But my "ontology" continues to slide off the rails—although it is clearly improving. It contains devastating attacks against phenomenology—I am now standing completely on my own two feet. But communicating these things sometimes drives me to despair—and yet, over and over again I experience how new ideas are literally just popping up.

I am undergoing a period of confident creativity; I am awake almost constantly—I sleep only a little—hopefully I can bear it all physically. But I have always moved forward best when I simply allowed myself to be hounded by the work—it is all so uncanny sometimes—to the extent that I am literally dizzy at times.

There are six here from Marburg—quality unknown.

The tutorial with Ebbinghaus has begun—he is certainly very formalistic and lives hand to mouth—in essence, Berlin street smarts—but he really does put in a lot of effort. A female licentiate from Berlin has arrived among the usual participants; she wishes to earn her doctorate with Troeltsch on Kant's writings.

Fräulein Walther sent off a pretty stupid insult-letter to Husserl about Jaspers. Husserl gave it to me to read: it says that Jaspers understands nothing regarding phenomenology—he is a relativist—and during the lectures he even said that a thick annual volume appears in which literally nothing is said; phenomenology has no future; the only phenomenologist worth his salt is Heidegger, and he stands completely offside; and so on.

The worst thing is not the letter itself, but rather that it is possible for such a shrew to write such things to Husserl (i.e., it shows that Husserl is in agreement). It has now come out that Fräulein Stein has already reserved a place for herself in the next volume.

I am seriously considering withdrawing my Aristotle. It does not seem like anything will come of the "appointments." And once I have it published, I will have no prospects whatsoever.

For presumably the old man will then truly see that I am wringing his neck—and then any possibility of succession is over. But I can't help myself.

For a few semesters now, I have been accompanied by a statement Van Gogh made to his brother: "I feel with full force that the history {*Geschichte*} of man is exactly like that of wheat. What good is it that one is planted into the earth to blossom, if one is then simply ground up to make bread. [N.592] Beware to those who are not ground up!" To be sure, as a theologian I was already between the millstones—but precisely today, existence {*Dasein*} is so incredibly harmless—I do not, however, wish to be presumptuous.

That Afra is really something—Besseler is attending my lectures.

All Dozents for philosophy have full courses. In my ontology seminar, the content of which I myself don't even fully understand, there are ninety students (!).

The whole family is going up to the hut for Pentecost. The wife and kids will then stay up there—Besseler also wants to come up for Pentecost. Give v. Rohden my greetings. Write to me about what you are up to.

Friendly greetings to your parents.

Heartfelt greetings to you,

    Your

        Martin Heidegger.

**44.** *Karl Löwith to Martin Heidegger*
[Munich] 5.10.23

Dear Herr Heidegger,

Why is it so difficult to find a fitting address in German—our "Herr" sounds so empty and insignificant—we are missing the many registers between "most honorable Herr privy councilor" and "dear friend," and for a long time now

I have been searching for a word that expresses the natural unity of teacher and friend. Today, I will tell you a little bit about Söderblom's guest lecture.

The *auditorium maximum* is completely packed—but tellingly not by students (not a *single* student corps cap is to be seen!), but rather by the public; pretty much all of Protestant Munich with its councilors, as well as its many old ladies and well-meaning citizens.

The *Rektor Magnificus*—that Bavarian Pfeilschifter, brutal and falsely solemn—delivered a scandalous introduction. This already gave Söderblom quite an advantage. Pfeilschifter: "Your Grace, archbishop...most esteemed pro-chancellor of the University of Uppsala...etc., etc. After last semester, prelate Mausbach as representative of the *Catholic* church...it gives me particular pleasure to now also introduce one of the most renowned representatives of the Protestant church, the researcher of comparative religion...." Short and of poor quality: Pfeilschifter gave Söderblom a passing grade. A particularly amusing blunder: "Döllinger, the crown of Munich's theology faculty."

Then Söderblom ascended to the podium, wonderfully supple and youthful given his age, with a distinguished stature; full of character; a large, angular head like Strindberg but without Strindberg's uncanniness; a large, broad forehead; friendly eyes; a mouth slightly broad yet still subtle; energetic and self-contained features; well-maintained, wooly, golden-blond hair. Most impressive was his sonorous voice, rich in modulation; a bit like a preacher, and due to an impassioned seriousness, all too easily morphing into indifferent, studied, and quickly encapsulated explanations. People who have heard Harnack lecture say there is a good bit of Harnack in him; perhaps also a conventional education in homiletics. He spoke for three hours.

His introductory remarks were genial to the superior—yet not at all ambiguous—freedom from European nationalism, and if it hadn't been for an instinctive respect for the "theologian," the "esteemed" students would have surely shuffled their feet in protest to the quotes in French and English. (Parenthetically, when he once remarked with satisfaction that such quoting in French would be nearly impossible today at a *French* university, the people almost fell all over themselves!) Söderblom has a brilliant command of the German language. The international scholar, the Swede, and the church dignitary with the golden chancellor's necklace all alternated with one another in a strange way. Regarding content, the lecture had such little organization that it is difficult to say much about it. Following some remarks on Erasmus, Luther, and Ignatius of Loyola, the core of it seems to have been a characterization of the difference between Protestant and Catholic "assurance of salvation," piety. At no point did he shy away from illuminating the touchiest points, but he did have an odd way of speaking ironically—in a significant way—at difficult moments. The third lecture brought his actual orientation to light—his union efforts—"Protestant Catholicism" (Heiler!).

He did not justify his observations transparently enough in terms of the current, European *world*-state; if he had simply said that we, as at least *superficially* united Christian churches and federations, must all attempt to create a *social-political* mouthpiece and counterweight to the lunacy of European nationalism—then everything would have been clear. That is how things progressed *factically*, although they were meant to arise from out of the idea of the "pure doctrine" of "practical Christianity." A paltry attempt at *"civitas dei"* here on earth. Only when taken in light of its opposing front, that of the protestant war preachers, does it take on meaning.

He addressed pretty much everything in a cursory way, but no mention was made of the Barth–Gogarten Movement. And, of course, not a word about Kierkegaard. When a Swedish bishop "shows up" to give a lecture, one automatically thinks of Kierkegaard, and is thus totally disappointed. Seen from this perspective, Söderblom is nothing other than the little Bishop Martensen!

I also don't know of a way in accordance with which such a Christianity of the individual—he made specific mention of Luther (Large Catechism, etc.)—could "organize" itself without seceding. The possibility and necessity of a true organization is Söderblom's premise, which explains the numerous and surely sincerely intended attestations of respect for the Catholic institution. However, he does himself raise the objection that the most active Christians today—the Quakers—are not organized (in this sense). He believes in the power of today's "Christian world," and has that typical liberal Protestant optimism.

By contrast, how much more clear-cut did Schweitzer appear, who admits to the meaninglessness of *world*-process from the beginning, to then derive its consequences for the active, effectual *life* of the individual in *its* own domain. A quote from Luther's text against usurious interest and reward does not convey much about his public efficaciousness. However, I have a great deal of respect for anyone who honestly perceives his efficacy as that of a usurer on behalf of humans and human*kind,* and who does not allow himself to be scared off by the terrible effort it takes to be "universally" efficacious. And I do not conceal from myself the great X lying within that very "existenziell constraint," insofar as I think that such necessary limiting of oneself to what is accessible is a *positive* negation of all industriousness, but one which still cannot prevent its neglecting of the *factically universal* powers of a public life gone mad—nor is it able to prevent someday being objectively crushed by it. Positive universalities that are "not" opposed to the most objective universalities clear the air for life, as well as free one *from* something (though I often have my doubts whether they are sufficient to free one *for* something)! The nonoriginality of all regulatory organizations does not disprove their necessity, and even in the private life of the individual, the mechanically-violent "anonymous" plays a large factical role today. (Think of Kierkegaard's diaries on the *press,* for example). Said in absolutely concrete terms: for me it would become a decisive situation (not merely a "condition") if this condition—a revolution, a war, etc.—would simply force one to take a position, precisely because it is more than a mere condition. And I don't know if I could continue to watch the shameful politicization, etc., of today's state of affairs passively if I were to come into contact with it professionally. For not everything that is encountered lets itself be fused into the "how of enactment" obtaining to philosophical work; today we constantly encounter difficult, indigestible things on "our way"—a way that can be properly ours in only a very contingent way. Perhaps there exist politicians who, as people, are "politicians" through and through, passionate characters about whom it would be wrong to say that they are sacrificing themselves for some universal "matter"—for they truly live as the expression of *their* matter. This is most blatant with "musicians"—and here I don't mean those who are only musicians in a post hoc and overly serious way, but rather those who are musicians through and through, like Bruckner. In philosophy, it is neither entirely this way nor that; presumably, it is somewhat difficult to find a clear-cut form of existence in philosophy, not like in theology, on whose cloak Söderblom wishes "to restore torn seams"(?!).

You can see how it all revolves around questions concerning the "historical {*Geschichtliche*}" and the "historical {*Historische*}" and their factical incongruity, despite their "syngenetic" entanglement.

A calm, disciplined, and vigorous development in the formation of one's own abilities has not been granted to us. I mean not only an "overenlightenment" due to the haphazard effects of a literary metropolis. More important than this, we have also been prematurely and rashly swept up into the current of a "life" that had already senselessly pulled us into its orbit even as high school students, only then to find out that it was, and remains, a moribund hurtling-about of ungoverned powers.

In Bischofstein, near Marseille's school, the youth see, hear, and read nothing about Germany, politics, the Ruhr occupation, etc. They are thus able to avoid the baseness of Protestant influences in the nicest of ways. But what will happen when they, at 17 or 18, have to enter into that other pandemonium, when they must unspool their path within it, unknowingly prejudicial like any other citizen of the older generation, reading their father's newspaper and remaining within their own tight social circle? No teacher in Bischofstein cares a whit about the telling pictures that the boys hang up in their rooms: German Kaisers, Hindenburgs, daddies in their fancy uniforms, battle ships, etc. It doesn't bother anyone and it comes to no effect—but it is also not snuffed out, not even by way of a critical engagement with those of a different opinion. Thus, they remain only *apparently* apolitical; and when it comes to it, they will march into the next war with the same lack of memory, the same catch phrases, and the same absolute ignorance regarding the dirty tactics of a tenacious press and the formation of public opinion.

To be sure: what can be done should be done fully! But it is the case today that "time" does not allow us the peace and quiet *to be*—most of all with what one "properly" is.

I don't know whether you will be able to make sense of this letter; it is not a regression back into a *diffluxus* of "reflections." It's just hard not to allow oneself to become confused within the general confusion, and to bring oneself into accord with the disparate and competing demands of the situation. That's it for today.

Do you know when Becker will earn his doctorate? I never hear from him.

With warm regards,
   Your
      Karl Löwith

Did the seminar with Ebbinghaus fizzle out?

P.S. Characteristic of Söderblom: the *apologia* of Luther's concept of faith as not "antimetaphysical"—the weakening of *creare* in the "belief in God," of "subjectivism"—because good old Söderblom is also overmatched by the venerable opposition: subjective–objective.

The latest: a Luther . . . film! Some famous actor is "playing Luther."

If by Pentecost I don't have anything better, I will have to take a position as a private tutor in Mecklenburg (it has been guaranteed to me) for a fourteen-year-old boy (von Flotow).

**45.** *Karl Löwith to Martin Heidegger*
Kogel [June, 1923]

Dear Herr Heidegger,

I did not have the time in Munich to answer your letter; I came here on Pentecost as the private tutor of a fourteen year old. You will hear from me as soon as I get settled. I spent 1 day in Berlin, with Afra and Ch. Grosser. It is not easy for either of them regarding the tiresome necessity of earning money. I took a lot of books with me—hopefully there will be time for them.

The air here is humid and oppressive (the elevation is only 100 meters), and coming from Munich, I need time to adjust to it. Many thanks again for your efforts regarding Fink-Göller! I would suggest to Fräulein Walther that the title be reversed: "Mystische Phänomenologie." Is your Aristotle finally in print?! Marseille wrote that Nohl visited the school and told him that

Geiger would be going to Göttingen, and you to Marburg. Do you know of any profitable prizes to be won? I only know the *Kant-Studien* one. Could you get Stern's address for me (for this purpose)? Or do you yourself have W. Stern, *Person und Seele* (or something like that—a psychological study)? I am in dire need of it (it now costs over 50,000) and I couldn't find it in Munich. Not even Geiger had it! I would also need Litt, *Leben und Erkennen* (Teubner, 1923). In case these two books cross your path, I would like to borrow them for a short while. I send you my kind greetings,
    Your
        Karl Löwith

**46.** *Martin Heidegger to Karl Löwith*
[Freiburg] VI.18.23

Dear Herr Löwith,

I have obtained an appointment in Marburg with the rights and status of an Ordinarius Professor beginning on October 1st. At the same time, there is the possibility that a Japanese student who is in Heidelberg at the moment, and who studies with my current one, will join me in Marburg in the winter. Things are looking up. Please write to Marseille and v. Rohden.

In the winter, we will take a big ski trip up to the hut.

I made such productive use of my wakefulness that I have now been laid up for a couple of days, but I have it all under control. Jaeger's book on Aristotle has been published, all 430 pages—worthwhile in the same vein as the earlier one, if a bit more garrulous. It is without philosophical significance and makes no such pretense, in the manner of Reinhardt's *Poseidonius*—it deals with "inner form."

Fräulein Walther's opus has come out: in a single footnote she cites (1) Ricarda Huch, (2) Kierkegaard, and (3) Hedwig Conrad-Martius. She should be thrown out for such tastelessness. Jaspers is sending me the third edition of the *Psychopathologie*, which is important and fresh!

I don't have the Litt—abominable—Simmel-like.

Stern's address is Sternwaldstr. 6.

My relationship with the old man has gotten very tense, because I proceeded so ruthlessly.

Becker is a disappointment. It has to do with personal difficulties, I think. I will respond to your letter, for which I am very grateful, at another time.
Warmly,
    Your
        Martin Heidegger

**47.** *Karl Löwith to Martin Heidegger*
[Kogel] 6.21.23

Dear Herr Heidegger,

I have to write a few lines to you right away in response to the good news. It is a great joy for me that wretchedness did not win out, after all. And Ordinarius no less—this is all the nicer, for you will always remain, in principle and in the end, "Extraordinarius." I am sure you don't expect the usual congratulations from me; I just wish, with all my heart, that you will feel well and at ease in Marburg, and that the more advantageous "conditions" are also of benefit to the overall situation. For one never emerges entirely unscathed from a scandalous setback. And the pressure of a forced cohabitation with Husserl has now also come to an end. I am already anxious to hear what you will begin with in Marburg. Augustine? Does Besseler already have concrete plans for the winter? Has he obtained the doctorate? Marseille will be very happy. V. Rohden's parents recently moved to Halle. I am still subject to the oppressive climate here; 100-meters above sea-level are too few for my constitution, and I have constant headaches. Have Göttingen and Königsberg also been decided? Fräulein Walther sent me her book. It also angered me—in ways beyond its tastelessness—for example, this marriage of Husserl to St. Therese, with Pfänder serving as witness. I am reading it entirely from the psychological perspective, in relation to what I know about her. There is no serious scholarship here, and on a personal level she is remarkably clueless about how much her theoretical thinking suffers as a result of her dissatisfied, cranky feminine existence. The book contains a lot of revealing pages. It is a painful read for me, but one that, after all, I owe her. It would also not be helpful for her to know that her supposed insight is merely a bad interpretation, and her metaphysics and George obsession a sad imitation.

In our first history lesson, I asked my pupil what he understands "history {*Geschichte*}" to be. He gave an honest answer: "History {*Geschichte*} is when one has to learn something about the old Teutons in school." When I told him that his family, Kogel, and he himself all have a history {*Geschichte*}, he was very surprised. I remembered the determination of the "hat" in our seminar ("extended thing of…").

It would be wonderful if something were to work out with "the Japanese student"!!

Until we see each other in Marburg!
I send you my warm greetings,
    Your
        Karl Löwith

**48.** *Karl Löwith to Martin Heidegger*
[Kogel] 7.9.23

Dear Herr Heidegger,

It looks like it will be a wonderful exodus to Marburg, then; Marseille is very happy. V. Rohden wrote to me that he would like to send you a short paper on Romans 5–8 instead of, and I quote,

> the *Nicomachean Ethics* and a few nebulous letters that I would rather omit. If this works out for me, I will move heaven and hell to get to Marburg for the winter semester. I will not go until I have the assent of Heidegger himself.

Even though I wrote to my father that I would only go to Marburg *if* I am able to support myself there, either by way of the Japanese student or something else, one of those patented finance letters arrived today containing the categorical declaration that I am not to expect any money from him, and that he feels free of any fault and obligation for the fact that I have chosen to take up such an unprofitable study as that of philosophy. This is nothing new or unexpected. But I would like to ask you once more to try, if at all possible, to think of a way for me to earn money in Marburg, and to let me know as soon as there are some concrete prospects. Some random position as assistant is out of the question—I would feel like risking a "seminar," but leaving aside whether that is even possible, I still wouldn't even gain a proper foothold by doing so. The little bit of money that [I] earn here doesn't go very far given this ever-rising inflation. There won't be many other opportunities for earning money in a small city like Marburg. If I could know something concrete about the Japanese student by August or mid-September, that would be great, for I can't just leave here on a moment's notice.

The very second that the dismal rainy weather abates here, we are already languishing in the heat. I am swimming a lot in the lake and am angry that the good, early hours of the day are taken up by the teaching of my not-overly gifted employer. I will have to try a different daily rhythm; sleeping in the afternoons and remaining awake at night.

Please excuse these tiresome financial matters, but unfortunately, nothing is possible without them.

Hopefully everything will work out for the fall.

May I still count on your letter?

With kind regards,
    Your
        Karl Löwith

**49.** *Karl Löwith to Martin Heidegger*
[Kogel] 7.27.23

Dear Herr Heidegger,

The prospects regarding Marburg appear brighter. I just got a letter from Marseille that Natorp was visiting your school (one of his sons is an art teacher there), and it turns out that Natorp himself *might* (in case he is lecturing, etc.) need someone to help with stenography for the department (for foreigners). It appears that there is quite a lot happening culturally in Marburg—just like in Heidelberg! The George enthusiast Wolters seems to be at the helm!

Do you already have [an] apartment? Will you move without your family, for the time being? And *when*? The appointment Husserl got at the O3 [?] level doesn't change anything, does it?! If it does, please let me know! I sent a rather blunt critique of her *Mystik* to G. Walther, to which I got a rather insightful response, saying that given certain, different circumstances, she would leave philosophy "with pleasure" (even underlined!).

Around here, one mindless celebration follows another. I gave my students a few days of vacation just so I could get some peace and quiet!

I saw an advertisement for a little work on *"Augustine's* inner development" by K. Holl. Do you know it already? Shocking things are apparently happening in the economic world—during our meal someone told a joke, namely that a canoness, after not having traveled to Berlin for years, came with 2,000 marks in order to buy herself a dress, and instead she returned home with two steel springs.

I send you warm greetings and see more and more that [I] am only suited to being a "faithful servant" to my mistress.
    Your
        Karl Löwith

Should the Natorp opportunity actually happen, it would be a pleasant way to earn additional income—it seems that Natorp, like Husserl, has many connections with foreigners. I wanted to share this story with you in any case, despite some uncertainty regarding its veracity. Positions for private tutors, as Natorp told Marseille, are nonexistent in Marburg. The whole thing is hopeless. Did von Rohden send anything?

**50.** *Martin Heidegger to Karl Löwith*
[Freigburg] 7.30.23

Dear Herr Löwith,

Many thanks for your postcard. Unfortunately, I cannot yet report any concrete prospects regarding the Japanese students; then there is the further question of whether the Japanese students in question would even take lessons—they are younger, not yet Dozents, and therefore not here with state support. As soon as there is something certain, I will write to you.

I am not responsible for assistantships, as I am not the co-director of the department—only Jaensch and Hartmann are. Karsch is with the latter and has meanwhile earned his doctorate with Hartmann; there is also a student of Hartmann's, Dr. Gadamer, who is here for only one semester, and both of them are also trying to get something along those lines. The prospects for you are, therefore, quite slim. Wouldn't it be possible to find a position as a private tutor near Marburg? Wilke was here a few days ago—through Driesch he has some very good connections to China and Japan, and he is planning a paid stint at universities there. I told him that you would also not be disinclined toward such things, for a time at least—he will surely write to you. Wilke looked exhausted—very tense—he is working at the German bookstore in Japan. I will try, at all costs, to keep Herr Stern and his ilk away from me—I fear in general that too much of a fuss will be made—I prefer not to have any "hustle and bustle" around me. It seems Husserl will remain here—the organization is to be expanded. Jaspers published an eighty-page booklet, *Die Idee der Universität* (Springer)—he sent it to me a few days ago—he is retaliating against relativism by way of an "existential absolutism {*existenziellen Absolutismus*}"—it contains many good observations, but is without the energy of positive "reflection."

My "Introduction" is really exhausting me—I will not expend an inordinate amount of energy this winter, and instead will already work on the summer, preparing for the four-hour a week Augustine lecture. I have heard from Fabricius that von Rohden is not doing well health-wise.

Ebbinghaus' Hegel is still very broad.

The summer with him was a big disappointment for me, much empty energy—but everything composed of slick formulas and results, all very juridical—without discernment—my students were continually dumbfounded. Becker doesn't seem to be getting through to the students—he will never get an assistantship. I think that over the course of the winter in Marburg it will be much easier to see what can be done for you—it would, thus, be best if you wouldn't come until summer—I will also be more "established" then—the first semester will really only be provisional. I will be here for the next few weeks—I hope that I will have occasion to get to the "letter."

Kind regards,
    Your
        Martin Heidegger

**51.** *Karl Löwith to Martin Heidegger*
[Kogel] 8.6.23

Dear Herr Heidegger,

Many thanks for your card which, thanks to one of those well-known happy coincidences, arrived at the same time as a letter by v. Rohden and the transcript of your lecture by von Bröcker. (Haven't heard anything from Becker the whole semester.) Before that I was in Rügen for a week of vacation; I crisscrossed this big, wonderful Baltic island on foot, particularly along the coast, and did lots of trekking and bathing. It is through the ocean that nature has always spoken most clearly for me: *solus ipsus*, but not alone in the sense of abandoned.

V. Rohden will do various things for his health during the vacation—in this regard, Marburg would also be more advantageous than the awful climate of Halle (much worse than Berlin). Anyway, he has probably already written to you himself.

And since we are speaking of Marburg, there is one more thing. Charlotte Grosser also wrote to Friedländer (in Marburg) about possible accommodations for his wife, with whom she is befriended, and she just replied to me. There is one more option: "The emergency assistance program is distributing grants to such individuals who would like to become Dozents and wish to work in peace. For example, in May the amount came to ½ million. Friedländer justifiably secured such a grant for his student, Dr. Klingner. Friedländer also thinks that it would be granted to you if there is support; one can't do anything about it oneself." Of course, such a thing could only be attempted over the course of the semester, when you are there. If you find the idea of supporting my desire to become a Dozent agreeable, I would ask you to please do so! For the time being, I am being as patient as possible in waiting for the fall, and am doing nothing to imperil my current position before [I] have other prospects. Here, at least, I have half the day free, and if the inflation does not continue to increase, I now also have a salary that allows [me] to save a little—at least enough to get me from here to Marburg! It is not really possible for me to say anything positive and definite about a "resolution" to attempt a habilitation in a few years; not even the ready comparison with other dissertations tells me anything—for, among other things, their authors have had different teachers than I have. Only one thing can be said: while the thought of "professional scholarship" used to be highly problematic for me (because I saw myself as too problematic within it), I now believe that I could fully effect my existence within that particular problematic, after all. "Passion" is such a pretentious word; but I missed it in regard to Becker; the way he does it, it appeared to me like the cultivated fostering of a garden, the occasional refined and deliberate breeding of modified plant species—he never truly tilled the soil, he just had better fertilizer. I myself cannot judge my own capacity for scholarly work; I only feel strongly the distance from what you achieve. Whether settling the question of my becoming a Dozent is a necessary condition of the question regarding the grant, I can only leave to you. As soon as I once again have a little cohesive work finished, I will, of course, send it to you, provided we don't meet before then.

Unfortunately, Jaspers still hasn't read the dissertation, and he also hasn't replied to my wish to get the new edition of his *Psychopathologie* more cheaply (than in the bookstore). Given that, I don't want to pester him further with a new entreaty regarding his *Idee der Universität*. If you don't have use for your copy later, perhaps it could be sent to me then.

I am very happy about your plan to give the four-hour Augustine lecture over the summer. Please write and tell me on which works you plan to focus, and give me a few, further pointers for a fully engaged A-level course of study! (I can't track down Holl's little work from here, it seems already to be out of stock at the publisher). I was barely back from Rügen when the pastor from Gatow called and asked me to come by, for Pastor Slotty was also there—the same one who had given a talk on Schleich a few weeks ago. At least the evening spent in these environs was less vacuous than the chamber hall dinners at which a middle-class private tutor feels exceedingly awkward. All the Protestant country parsons around here have a touching "educational desire" and maneuver around the critical-historical biblical scholarship with great effort; otherwise, they are capably social people, they write their sermons, work their pretty little parcel of land, confirm, baptize, bury, bless— whatever is needed in the locality. Pastor Slotty earned his doctorate in 1915 under Falckenberg with a dissertation on Kierkegaard (I was ignorant of "Schleich und Kierkegaard"); he gave me his dissertation—a clean extract and not that compromising, because it contains only "propositions." But through this all I was lent a work of Kierkegaard's that was unfamiliar to me: *Leben und Walten der Liebe* (Leipzig 1890, Richter), translated by Donner. It was written before the *Training* and is similar, but less rigorous. Its chapters are not of consistent value, but its manner of interpretation is often just as methodologically clear and pure of style as the Christian discourses and the *Training*.

As of yet, I have only glanced at your summer lectures in order to familiarize myself with Bröcker's work: among all of yours with which I am familiar, they are the most self-contained—lots of concise directives, each word carefully considered, but not such tiresome directives and empty pockets for the expansion of the "system" as one gets with Husserl. After these lectures there should hardly be any possibility of misunderstanding, excepting if someone were to ask once again what his "factical *Dasein*" is! (Has Metzger habilitated? And how are Kaufmann's reserves?) Seen from the perspective of their efficacy, it would be good if such lectures would alternate with a detailed analysis that proceeds in a destructuring way—if one sticks only with the lectures, the students will grow accustomed to the thesis-like style and will just accept the demonstration of everydayness in an everyday way. What I mean is this: the anatomist who already knows the construction of the skeleton is continually reminded by his students that each individual must learn to clear away the skin and muscle on his own.

In leafing through it, I noticed many clear indications, unencumbered by an "idealistic past," an absolute clarity within which it does not pay to want to answer certain questions—the further development of old categories, which the "philosopher" would probably not accept as such because they result in such simple facts instead of those nice juggling balls—my joy at how vigorously and clearly you are enacting the break with conventional philosophy was boundless—for what is desired is, after all, universally similar, but those on the upper floors just yell down to those below them, and neither a simple song together in the open air nor an artistic smoking out of the other renters is achieved—all one does is write up new rental agreements with an up-to-date market index.

*You* really don't need to be afraid of creating a "sensation" in Marburg. I don't know anyone more gifted at making *repelling* attractive.

The great and silent power of foreboding seashores bathed in sunlight cannot be accommodated "categorically"; it is more meaningful if this and much else remains outside of "critical" philosophy. Also: three months in the country and one's focus shifts. Does two weeks up at the hut remain bound to a tumultuous before and after?

I send you my warm greetings as your thankful Karl Löwith

**52.** *Martin Heidegger to Karl Löwith*
[Todtnauberg] The Hut, VIII.23.23

Dear Herr Löwith,

Many thanks for your letter. Two days ago, a relocation opportunity suddenly came up and that threw things into disarray. I will only write you briefly. Dr. Klinger did habilitate this semester. Once things become concrete for you, I will, of course, be ready to assist you. At the moment, I am not sure whether you will feel at home as a scholar, or whether you may not someday angrily claw your way out of that milieu. In any case, I am in support of you taking some time with it. I will also hit the brakes regarding a student of Hartmann—a certain Dr. Gadamer, who was here this semester—and who is now up at the hut for a few days with his wife. With him it was first Hönigswald—then Natorp—and now he is an impassioned Hartmann-adherent, affiliated with me this semester—very well-versed, full of academic gossip, very impressionable—his father is an Ordinarius Professor in Marburg; he would like to habilitate under Hartmann with a work on Aristotle; for now, I don't see anything positive in regard to him. He repeats concepts and propositions—but he is just as helpless as his "Meister." I will absolutely insert myself if it should come to a quick habilitation. He is now writing a critique of Hartmann's *Metaphysik*—he gets his thoughts on it from me; up to now, he does not have the faintest clue concerning philosophy.

It seems that things generally look pretty desolate in Marburg, and yet the gentlemen there take themselves to be great prophets. Therefore, I hope all the more that you can fortify yourself and can register fully armed. I don't know whether or not it is of much use for you to be close to me—you should become independent—and I don't want to train "philosophers," but rather truly scholarly people—initially in the humanities and theology. I am still not sure, but given your opportunities, perhaps you could break into biology. I asked von Rohden to come to Marburg—what he sent to me is extremely straightforward—without conjectures and well understood. He has what is essential for becoming a theologian—but he is slow, although that doesn't matter.

I have been named director of the department—a novelty—perhaps something can be done regarding an assistantship—but surely not until the summer. Less pleasing are the prospects regarding the high number of final university examinations—Marburg is the hub for that. I will, therefore, have to deny myself quite a bit during this first semester, and I will, most likely, only give beginner tutorials. I should almost think it were better for you to prepare yourself for summer semester '24: (1) you will have more of me when I am established and settled in, and (2) I will then have more of a sense of what is to be done.

I would already now like to invite you up here for a few weeks of skiing at the end of the winter semester (in March). We can then discuss all manner of things. I brought in a lot of wood this week. Perhaps we can also invite Afra. On my way to Marburg I will spend a few days in Heidelberg—I will meet up with Jaspers. I can give you his work soon—I just need to take another, closer look at it.

Do you have your current position only for a limited time? I don't know anything definite yet regarding the Japanese gentleman, other than that he is coming.

I don't wish to create a precarious situation for you this winter—and that could very well happen, as for the time being I have to evaluate everything from afar.

You can surely count on one thing, though, and that is my help, whenever you have decided concretely in favor of scholarship—in whatever discipline that may be.

Most importantly, write and tell me how things stand with your current position—perhaps we could already take action during the course of the winter semester.

Warm greetings,
   Your
      Martin Heidegger

**53.** *Martin Heidegger to Karl Löwith*
Feldafing, 9.27.23

Dear Herr Löwith,

I have been here for some time—for the duration of the move. But now the whole plan regarding the move has come to nothing for the time being, as the wife of a link in the chain of the whole process has died suddenly. A final decision on how to proceed has yet to be made. Most likely, I will have to move by myself.

I am happy that you are able to come now, after all. Jaensch himself has a permanent assistant.

I will be lecturing two hours on an introduction to phenomenology, and two hours on Aristotle—I have yet to decide on what exactly; it will depend on what I have to do. I would like to orient the lecture more directly toward the coming course of lectures on Augustine, so that I will be able to work on something new beyond my manuscript; at the moment I am occupied with it. For weeks now, Niemeyer has shelved all publications. But since I am not quite settled yet with my "Introduction," which was slated to appear separately, I am not unhappy.

In my seminars—I have two—I am doing the *Logical Investigations* for beginners in one, and the other is on Aristotle and the Middle Ages—exactly what that entails will depend on what's in the library. The prerequisite texts for a tutorial on Augustine are missing. Regarding Aristotle, the *Metaphysics* will be a focus, so that you should have no difficulties—for the purposes of these exercises, I place the most emphasis on the handling of the phenomena themselves, so Marseille will be able to participate fully. Hartmann has tutorials on Hegel (advanced) and Kant (beginner).

I will travel to Marburg via Heidelberg.

Warm regards, farewell,
   Your
      Martin Heidegger

**54.** *Martin Heidegger to Karl Löwith*
Feldafing, 10.1.[1923]

Dear Herr Löwith,

I am sending you a letter once more from here to Kogel. It is all over with our move. I will thus have to go to Marburg provisionally as a "furnished gentleman." I will leave the day-after tomorrow for Messkirch (my father is in very bad shape) and then travel to Freiburg again, from which I had a (very difficult) departure, as the plan had been for me to leave directly from here for Marburg. I am not sure I can still make it to Heidelberg under these conditions. Rieniets came to see me and I liked him very much. Let's talk in person about your letter. I don't hear anything from Becker. By harnessing the entirety of his juridical abilities and through a hundred machinations and difficulties, Ebbinghaus was able to grind out a new and larger apartment for himself. The whole thing gives him exactly the same "pleasure" as one of his interpretations of "Hegel," from whom is he is distancing himself more and more in favor of Kant. Six of one, half-dozen of the other! I often think of the two girls Grosser and Geiger—one can't compare Walther to them. If only she could borrow Fräulein Grosser's Greek. If possible, I will be helpful as you arrange your financing.

Because you will have a decisive influence on my "devotees" in Marburg, I would like to ask that you present yourself in such a way that nothing that could be called an academic conflict or a "different direction" arises. I like this even less than treading lightly, and I wish that by way of straightforward work and sober presentation my people will participate in the renaissance of scholarly existence at the university.

When it comes to what is decisive, Jaspers is very naïve and primitive—almost a step backward since the *Psychologie der Weltanschauungen*. I see that I will be on my own, and that all help from outside is merely "temptation." So good luck regarding new work, and don't allow yourself to get down.

Your
Martin Heidegger

**55.** *Martin Heidegger to Karl Löwith*
M[esskirch] III.19.24

Dear Herr Löwith,

First off, I would like to thank you very much for the bellows—this addition to the furnishings in the hut gave me great joy. We left for the valley on the 14th, as my wife was no longer able to get any rest because of the little one. I came here on the 16th, and will stay until the 23rd.

The Überweg book is reliable—although by now outdated by ten years—but it is the best of its kind.

I have looked previously for the Seidmann edition and never found it. The lectures have now also come out in the Weimar edition. If it's not too expensive, I would suggest you acquire it.

I have now definitively decided to publish the Aristotle—to the extent possible. I have to get it off my desk, most likely by writing the whole thing anew during the publication process.

But this squeezes out Augustine; I am lecturing on Aristotle and only giving the one medieval seminar. In accordance with my capacities, I will hold a *privatissimum* on Augustine every fourteen days. All this publishing business is causing me to lose out on one of the nicest years—but at some point I just have to get to it.

I still have a lot to do on the *Introduction*; one recent evening up at the hut I even wrote down an entirely new structure for it—and for the time being, it's good enough. I don't know how long I will stay with Jaspers. In any case, I will be in Marburg at the end of the month.

According to a report from Gadamer, Marseille has alighted in Marburg. My wife is still in Freiburg with the little one. V. Rohden stayed up at the hut, as he twisted his leg practicing the Christiania turn. Freiburg is giving off a rather listless and helpless impression.

Goodbye. Warm regards
    Your
        Martin Heidegger

Friendly greetings to your parents.

**56.** *Martin Heidegger to Karl Löwith*
Hdlbg, III.26.24

Dear Herr Löwith,

Many thanks for your letter. You would have fun with Jaspers, as I do—he has his own kind of security in taking risks—the whole is what is decisive—the whole of today: he has the stomach for taking everything in, in his way, and using it.

My way is different, my goal more limited—you also reach too high regarding your expectations, as do all who know my works. That it comes to this is simply the result of the stance, the role, and the intellectual milieu (philosophy: philosopher). I have never had to force myself up to the lectern the way I had to this past semester. The curse of my work, the work I must do, is that it has to move about in the region of the old philosophy and theology, and it must do so critically when it comes to certain irrelevances such as "categories." Thus, an illusion arises, as though what has been negated should be confronted with what corresponds to it, with content. And it is as though the work were something for school; direction, continuance, supplementation. This work is inimitably circumscribed and can only be done by me, from out of the singularity of this constellation of conditions. This work is always antiquated, and grows out of a form of existence that perhaps remains completely untouched by "today."

I can never prove to a broader audience that this work must be done—but within certain boundaries I can make it scrutable as to its possibilities.

Whether or not it achieves something is all the more irrelevant. I don't know how its effect might look. I am only clear about this, namely, that as long as I regard it in an immediate sense, there is no effect. But these are just reflections, and they don't move things forward.

I have thought about your inquiry regarding the tutorials. I am against it, and first of all for your sake. Should you have plans to habilitate, which I assume you do, then the only thing that matters is to submit a solid work; apart from that, do not let the intention become explicit in any way. On this occasion, I must tell you once again that the prospects of a position as a professor in the next decades are poorer than ever, owing to the fact that chairs in philosophy will most likely be reduced (i.e., in places where there is more than one, the second or third will no longer be filled). The career track is a matter of luck. If you put effort into it, you will have my help. However, beyond that, I don't want the aggravation of having to lead you by the hand.

Lastly, the whole thing isn't technically possible; even if I were in agreement with it, I would not be able to make the decision that you would be the one to hold my summer tutorials at the university. Jaspers is of the same opinion. And I have previously said to Husserl that the whole Metzger way of doing things really isn't permissible.

If you end up doing something privately, I only wish that it is done quite independently.

Warm regards from
   Your
      Martin Heidegger

Jaspers sends his greetings, as well.

**57.** *Karl Löwith to Martin Heidegger*

Sunday
Rosenstr. 6/III
Munich, 8.17.24

NB: This is *not* the promised letter.

Dear Herr Heidegger,

I arrived yesterday evening. On the final evening in Freiburg, von Rohden just barely made it; he was very cheerful, and we chatted for a long time; he wants to head up to the hut tomorrow. The drive through the Danube valley with open windows in wonderful weather was very beautiful. In the apartment here, [I] am an autocrat; my parents [are] in the Bavarian mountains for [the month of] August.

[I] came upon a letter from my father, for whose sake I must now, unfortunately, importune you with things that I otherwise would not have brought up. I would rather not comingle my "philosophical letter" with these tiresome worries, and with the—tried and true—insurmountable incongruity between parents and son. Today, this seems to be a truly "typically sociological" phenomenon (generation?)—for it repeats itself verbatim with frightening tediousness; I observed this in others (Becker, and also Gadamer with your habilitation). *You* will already have understood everything essential in my postcard; at the same time, my parents have completely misunderstood a letter already tailored precisely to their capacities of understanding. Their response to it consists of well-meaning, though totally misguided, reproaches regarding my alleged "self-sacrifice" in *friendship*—a much too flattering prejudice concerning me, and a resentful one concerning Marseille. But mainly: you went to Marburg a year ago in order to *habilitate* yourself "*as quickly as possible*"! and thereby to get a "*real*" position. "The seriousness of the times," and so forth. I know I am innocent regarding the existence of these two expectations of my father. The only concern that I could rectify, if you are also of my opinion, would thus be the following: whether I am in Marburg for the winter or somewhere else does not change anything regarding the prospect of a habilitation; for this depends upon (1) if I produce a work that meets your expectations and that leads you to advocate for me, and (2) on the faculty. Besides, not many people have starved to death yet. If you share my view, I would be very happy if you could send me this in your reply, in "black and white"—not for me, of course, but for my father's peace of mind. I can't ask for a grade regarding effort and participation for the sake of my father, as I am, unfortunately, no longer a high school student and you haven't seen anything from me since the Humboldt presentation—actually, we have spoken about something philosophical only once, on the final evening.

Of course, the matter is clear to *me*: I can now get to work anywhere rather than in Marburg or here at home, and I know what I owe Marseille and myself. However, I would understand it very well if you also, despite all patient waiting, were gradually to become skeptical regarding the repeated disruptions of our work by personal matters. But please don't think of "Besseler"—this time it was about something else entirely—or, said differently, it was about the same thing, but with the big difference that Marseille and I ourselves conceded that we would have to follow a path to its end that actually brought us together in the first place; there is no one I have more to thank than him, but it was a torturous fight for both of us. Perhaps I only now understand what you once, long ago, meant when you wrote in a letter: "the way in which people can be together"—and are allowed to be together—"in existence."

Now we must allow ourselves some peace and quiet and allow things to heal in their due course. If I were to swear off Marburg for now, it would not be some kind of romantic adventure. However, the following is uncertain, and I would have rather waited to write to you about it once it is more concrete, but now I can send it along in this letter. While in Freiburg, [I] got a letter from Charlotte Grosser; it would probably be possible for me to be employed in her bookstore in Rome, half days, earning enough money to live there. I am now in correspondence with her regarding this. At first this seemed to me as if right on cue, but then came some doubts as to whether I would remain fresh and focused enough in my free time there in order to continue my work. What do you think? In any case, it's not my style to simply throw down a *phenomenological* work at a hurried pace, but I don't really feel certain regarding "Rome," even though, on the other hand, this half a year has rubbed me so raw that I am also a bit afraid of a circumstantially determined, dogged, and isolated desire to just tear through it—in Freiburg, for example. Concerning the latter, there remains the vexing question of finances—Becker needs his two Japanese students (by the way, is Miki staying?), and I won't undertake a Canossa pilgrimage to Husserl; I am sick and tired of begging. At most, I would see if the *3-Masken Verlag* (here) has any work for me; I will go see tomorrow.

I would be grateful if you were to resist shaking your head about me, even though this would be understandable—and it isn't even necessary for you to have my father's specifically narrow "tunnel vision" to react this way—however, I can't prevent such a reaction—and I myself would have been glad if I would have been able to give you a written work in the summer. (Note: Perhaps sometime you will get the chance to tell me something about "Nietzsche"?).

Naturally, I am not in good spirits right now, but I am also not without hope, for I believe myself not to be in error when I take the two weeks—alone in Freiburg—to be a sign that nothing was in vain, that I have not been given a burden too heavy to shoulder, and that my philosophical-scholarly abilities have continued to grow silently along with me, despite, and because, of everything—in a subterranean way, as it were. Concerning Marseille, I also trust that he will make it through, despite his compromised constitution.

I send my heartfelt greetings,
    Your
        Karl Löwith

Please address as follows: Herr Pharmacist Braun
            For K.L.
            Munich, Rosenstr. 6/III

(otherwise the post office readdresses it all to my parents)

**58.** *Martin Heidegger to Karl Löwith*
Marbg, Aug. 21. 24

Dear Herr Löwith,

The Rome opportunity is right on cue. You would not be the first person to prepare for the habilitation in Italy. Whether what you do on the side is the book trade, or the collating of handwritten manuscripts on behalf of the academy, makes no difference as I see it.

I would jump in with both feet. To sit here is torture; one attends lectures in some manner and is interested in the current hustle and bustle. If something were to compel me to go to Japan—which is rather assuredly out of the question—then it would be the desire to withdraw from my students: for it never occurs to them to study somewhere else. In any case, everything is clannish here.

You will not be too late regarding the habilitation. According to the statutes, it would be impossible to do it before the spring; the earliest, therefore, is summer semester '25. But with such a thing there is no setting of deadlines. The first thing that is needed, which I mentioned to you in a letter in March, is a work that meets my expectations. Once I have that in hand, the faculty must then be won over. It is unfortunate that imponderables, graft, and intrigues play a big role, but that cannot be helped. There are many faculty members who make a career for themselves out of such things—even in fields far removed from their expertise. And I don't think it is impossible that such work could be done via detours from the philosophical side. But presumably Hartmann will no longer be here by then. However, the habilitation does not *ipso facto* secure a solid existence—it cannot be predicted what stance the government will take on the subsistence level of the Privatdozent.

Because the government has taken on a certain responsibility regarding the universities, it now urges that only those with the potential for really making it are habilitated. Position and provisions should no longer be of primary importance when deciding on an academic career. I come from a very poor family—all that my parents scrimped and saved, without ever understanding what I was studying or what I planned to do—all of that was still so meager that I had to endure my time as a student with far greater privation then is the case today among "poor" students. And it worked out because I never gave up. And what's more, I had such "luck" that it still seems uncanny to me today.

I don't need to write more about it to you—I only wanted to point out, so that you are clear on it, that this track, when in correspondence with existential risk, is something all its own—of course, there are people whose position as Ordinarius Professor is assured already in the cradle (by their father's hands), but I know of no such people who could have produced anything great.

You will not starve to death, but life is not pleasant; not even when one is an Ordinarius Professor. One must first have come far enough so as to experience how much strength one uses up in order to fortify oneself over and against one's career.

Natorp has died. I have thereby lost the one person here who gave me the invaluable opportunity to venerate.

Miki left yesterday. I assume that he will not be returning.

When you get to Rome, please give my regards to Fräulein Grosser.

With warm regards
    Your
        Martin Heidegger

PS: Unfortunately, I have to write in bed, as for a few days now I have had a stomach issue and am unable to work—plans versus facticity.

Please give your parents my best.

At some point, please visit the below named gentleman in Rome—a Franciscan—whom I know from Freiburg and who visited me recently here in Marburg; he won't be back in Rome until November: Dott. P. Bruno Katterbach OFM. *Archivista nell'archivio segreto della Santa Sede. Roma/3. via del S. Uffizio 1.*

And keep an eye out for the soon to be published *Festschrift* for P. Franz Ehrle S. C. in five volumes! *Miscellanea Ehrle*. I am interested in the content of the volume dealing with the history of philosophy and theology.

**59.** *Karl Löwith to Martin Heidegger*
Rome, Borgo Pio 105 [9.13.1924]

Dear Herr Heidegger,

[I] didn't write from Munich, because [I] departed quickly; am here already one week. I start in the bookstore the day after tomorrow. For today, only my kind regards from the "Freiburg in Rome"!
    Your
        Karl Löwith

[Added by Charlotte Grosser: Best greetings, your Charlotte Grosser]

Many thanks for the letter you sent to Munich!

**60.** *Karl Löwith to Martin Heidegger*
Rome, Borgo Pio 105 [9.22.1924]

Dear Herr Heidegger,

By the 26th you should also have gotten a postcard from here—it is the church whose steps will be familiar to you from the Luther biography!
 Yesterday, I was deep under the earth—in the Callixtus *catacombs*, and then I walked along the Via Appia. I have to make use of my Sundays. Hopefully I won't need to be the order clerk at the bookstore much longer! In this, one learns once again to value the freedom of one's own intellectual "work"; and that thing with the "pots and bowls" is easier said than done! Rome is full of beauty and vitality. I've also already been to the ocean. I hope that you are enjoying Aristotle/Luther and the Kierkegaard picture. I send my heartfelt greetings.
  Your
   Karl Löwith

Charlotte Grosser is already in Arosa, in Switzerland—her body was doing very poorly.

**61.** *Karl Löwith to Martin Heidegger*
[Rome] 10.18. [1924]

Dear Herr Heidegger,

The peace and quiet I need in order to write you what I wish to report is still missing; I must now look around for something *half*-day. It is unbelievable all that can unfold in one month—truly, a new "world"—and all the more so for me here, as I don't know anyone well; I only see academics by chance, on the tram or in the catacombs (e.g., Hildebrandt in the former, Lietzmann in the latter). I also met up with Tillich. For today, I only wish to send a quick report on some books, and to ask for a *speedy* reply should you want anything. I saw the following in antiquarian form, 90 lire per volume: *opera varia* A. Maii: *Nova Patrum Bibliothecae* Vol. I–VII (available separately). Volume I contains: *Augustinus Sermones CCI ex codice vaticanis* with five paleographic tables, etc. (*S. Cyrrilli alexandrine adlocutio et fragmenta commentarium in Matheam et Lucam*) and many *summari* and *vetera* of works by Augustine. And an old (1590, Bergamo) complete *Summa* with the *Cajetan*

*Commentary*—in five bound volumes, all together 150 lire (about 30 marks), but a poorer quality, smaller print—maybe someone you know wants it. If you could give me a list of your most important theological interests now and again, I can take a look in the large Catholic–theological antiquarian bookstores here. I myself have no money for books right now. I visited Katterbach and am to send you his greetings. I am very happy to be here. I would like to have von Rohden's address. Are you lecturing on Plato, then? And Thomas [in] the seminar? And what, pray tell, is happening or not happening in Marburg?

Will you see Gadamer and Marseille more often?

Here in "Rome" I am living much more like an immigrant than I did in the "garden bower."

The archeologists here "construe" that the most serious metaphysics is an orphan in comparison to their field. Amelung is the wary high priest, who always prophesizes that a "profane" construing and interpreting is *eo ipso* already more cautious!

Warm greetings to you, your wife, and the boys
    From your
        Karl Löwith

**62.** *Karl Löwith to Martin Heidegger*
X.28.24 Rome Borgo Pio 105
Presso Sartori

Dear Herr Heidegger,

I would very much like to write you one more letter as the semester begins. Right now, a fascist crowd is shouting on the street; they are celebrating some random anniversary at the moment, as currently there is no new assassination to commemorate. This makes me think of Munich, of when you and I saw the Hitler guard, narrow-minded and fanatical, and right after we went into a nice old Catholic church.

I already know my way around here much better than I do in Munich, and it is easy to feel at home in Rome—Rome is not a metropolis in the usual sense; here one never drowns in an undifferentiated sea of houses—each corner has its own, true style, and the most heterogeneous joins with its surroundings most naturally, tenaciously cemented together by the power of a continual history. Everywhere one senses that the conservative preserving tie is the Catholic Church. And the numerous daily masses in the countless churches of Rome, which themselves simultaneously contain all forms of architecture from the fourth to the twentieth centuries, get along splendidly with all the precious remains of bygone Roman imperial glory. Egyptian medicinal bathtubs, which some Roman emperor had dragged into his thermal baths; as altars, the seven Roman hills, on top of which sits the cross, itself on the top point of the obelisks; churches with three more underneath them; a bourse with the columns of a Jupiter temple; a temple of Bacchus in which stands a painted cardboard statue of Mary; another Mary (mounted on a Corinthian column) whose halo glows with electric light bulbs in the national colors; an infant Jesus carved of wood in Arcadi that is slated to perform some miracles on January 6th; catacombs in which nonsilent Trappists sell eucalyptus liqueur; at least five graves for Paul and so many mortal remains of Peter that an entire anatomy school could be supplied; an infallible pope who grants audiences on a daily basis to, for example, the actor Jacki Coogan (from the Chaplin movie!), after which the twelve-year-old J. C. has a "manifesto" distributed in which he thanks the "*Kaiser*"; speeches by a Jesuit on something concerning a saint that lasts for hours, delivered with such great rhetorical effort and gestures that the most audacious baroque saints couldn't hold a candle to it—and kneeling in one of the foremost rows are Herr Dr. Grünling and Professor von Hildebrandt!! If one descends into the catacombs, one is assured of coming upon archeologists from all German universities, with Amelung as the high priest; by way of his daring combinations, Lietzmann, unscathed, is able to hold fast to his miscellaneous, unscientific field-specific asceticism. The eyes of the young German Catholic clergy who come here for a visit begin to shine when they—along with me—suddenly arrive way up high (140 meters) at the top of the dome of St. Peter's and come face-to-face with the visible power of their popes, their church, organization, and world-prestige. And they continue to kiss the big toes of the bronze statue of St. Peter in the basilica until they are totally worn down (this particular St. Peter was once the statue of a Roman consul).

It always becomes clear here, as well, that "Europe" is a reality, and not only because you can, for example, see Dürer's *Hare* in Rome, while the Italians look for their Botticelli in Berlin. A few lower level Italian civil servants live in my (so-called!) boardinghouse, as well as a Polish authoress and a lady from Berlin who has been living in Rome for four years already and has created a position for herself as secretary for various cardinals and secular greats—she has a big, friendly child, a bad marriage, her husband is a (Calvinist) minster in Berlin, and she has a true Berlin temperament: a female cuirassier, she snows all of the cardinals and gladly allows them to snow her in return, and someday she will be a willing oblation—a convert. She has already collected a library of over 100 little Catholic tracts, all gifts, and 10 alone by Lippert! Of course, it's all of an admittedly lower standard—but the same kind of bustle as in Winckelmann's time! Good old Tillich was here. He wants to gather up "impressions" in order to be able to withstand the winter in Marburg. It is too bad that someone of such a well-meaning nature had to undergo such a confused "scientific" schooling—Troeltsch's legacy! By contrast, how refreshingly clear does such a conservative, "positive" pastor seem, like the one that is staying here right now for eight days and with whom I often go for a walk—his name is Klein, and Tillich spent a lot of time with him as a student. In Rome, one gets a general, and most likely also correct, "impression" of the unbelievable merging of Christianity into antiquity—as Catholicism!—very quickly, at every turn, and in a most concrete way. But to move from this general impression to an analytical explication—I thank heavens that I am not an archeologist and historian! But if you could name some books that are informative regarding four to five centuries of the Christian catacombs, I would be grateful. I also met up with Friedländer (from Freiburg)—he was very tired after gathering up about a thousand undifferentiated and unimportant pictures of churches for some commercial book.

And since I am already writing about *personalia*, here is one more addendum: last August in Freiburg, I once visited Fabricius at Brecht's house—these two are a virtually perfected model of philistine, intellectual snobbery—but, of course, brand new Dilthey, etc., [???] line the bookshelves in well-ordered rows. Compared to that, I think my friend Pastor Klein is more entertaining, as when he declaims in his sonorous preacher's voice while bathing in the sea: "perhaps Paul swam here, too"!! [I] recently got to see the book dealers' market register in the bookstore—a new book by Scheler is listed. Have you seen it? And if something new comes out by Jaspers or Dilthey, please write and tell me. There was also a book by Hans and Grete (Driesch), *Fern-Ost*—quite an oration in honor of a Buddha statue by Dr. Hans! What a perfectly European thing! A *Caesar* by the Gundolf factory. Good things by the Kaiser Verlag. I will write some other time about the actual, modern Italians here—here one can live more freely, unconventionally, naturally, and unselfconsciously than we do. And anyhow, from the very beginning I had brought with me a great affinity for all things Italian. The landscape of the *campagna*, the Sabina and Alban Hills, the sea coast, southern Etruria—it is all very beautiful, and on Sundays one can embark on many pretty day trips—always alone—but I am glad to be in Rome as an immigrant, to only have a few, nonbinding acquaintances and to finally get some peace and quiet; and if it's not all an illusion, to have entered into a state of real clarification, which also means a state of re-absorbing and continual work on most things. The table is once again full of little notes, and the primitiveness in which I am living here is only positive. Here and there lie dear letters from those people to whom my life has become connected through inclination, fate, and guilt—including his. It has been a long time since I have felt myself to be so uninhibited and free—my work is sanguine here.

I purposely did not take any of your lecture transcripts with me—just the notes from the "time" lecture; that which has crossed over into blood and bone will have to be effectual without the "black on white."

Up to now, I have physically tolerated the "adjustment" to the Roman climate and Roman food well—when it gets cold (stoves are nowhere to be found!) I will flee into the libraries. During the first month [I] had to work in the store eight hours a day; I learned all sorts of things, but it was too tiring for me to be able to also do my own work. The financial situation is pretty lamentable now, but by the skin of my teeth I should be able to stay here for the winter. You always stand before me as a silent and strict teacher and friend, and I don't need to keep telling you how much, and with what pleasure, I know myself to be your student. And now I would like to speak of still other things.

When I came to visit you at Christmas from Baden-Baden, you gave me Thomas à Kempis. Only now am I truly "reading" it, and the time has come for me to catch up with my history (similar to how so much that was crammed into us about "antiquity" in school begins to make sense retroactively while in Rome). It requires strange wrong turns, departures, and collisions. I have also dared to read a few of Luther's exegetical writings and am happy about it; what my pathetic religion teachers at school were unable to accomplish, life itself has ultimately brought about. It is depressing to consider the many years we spent on empty nonsense. And [it] is really not so easy to become "simple-minded."

This confession—which is intended in a sober way and does not wish to conceal any mysterious allusions!—would only be half of one, were I not about to tell you that another person's life is not without influence regarding my constitution: Charlotte Grosser. And no truth is more convincing than a truth that confronts one in the actual life of another. Anyone who looks at her fate from the outside would pity her—she became quite ill here and is now in Arosa, ready for anything, equally prepared to live as to die and always upbeat, gracious, and there for others. She does not pity herself, and does not wish for others to pity her; and I can't think of anyone else among my friends about whom I am less worried than her. For she went as far as the threshold and from there got underway. During the summer semester I often tasked myself with telling you about her—but ultimately I couldn't bring myself to do so. I now believe that I have no choice. Regarding what is essential, from the very beginning you have "understood" Charlotte Grosser, and Charlotte Grosser has "understood" you.

In closing, I would like to take one more liberty—not out of nepotism or a purported solicitude for Marseille, but rather based on my own experience. If you are able, and think it is right, don't make things harder than [is] necessary for a person who, in any case, is already cautious, grave, and almost paralyzingly thorough—perhaps sometimes a comment encouraging a faster pace moving forward with the work might be more helpful than a principled reticence and careful hesitation that does not wish to interfere?

In my own case, I am not deluding myself when I think that you and Jaspers considered it of utmost importance to point out my bad habits—but I am also not able to cough up enough benevolent self-deception in order to trick myself into believing after the fact that it would have been particularly dangerous if no one had said anything to me.

Of course, this remark was neither suggested by W. Marseille, nor does he know anything about it—I just know his way and manner of working, and because I know that you value him, I would like to contribute to a greater ease in your relationship. But, be honest—do you take offense at this?

Did you ever hear anything from Becker? And did Gadamer finish his thesis yet?

My heartfelt best for the beginning of the semester—your Karl Löwith.

You must have received my card from eight or so days ago?

**63.** *Martin Heidegger to Karl Löwith*
Marbg, Nov. 6. 24

Dear Herr Löwith,

First off, my heartfelt thanks for thinking of my birthday, and in such an appropriate way. The little text is instructive, and the author is also well-versed in patristics.

And thank you for the beautiful postcards from Rome; you even addressed one of them to *Schwanallee 21*, Freiburg. But thank you most of all for your splendid description of contemporary Rome, which sounds like a syncretism that borders on the unbelievable.

Moreover, I noticed in your letter that Rome is not failing to have an effect on you. Most valuable is the fact that you yourself have found the path toward simplicity—also in human relations. With that, the conditions for true work arise on their own. True work only flourishes when one has learned to be earnestly alone. Whoever doesn't understand that has never truly worked. The vibrating excitation surrounding Rotenberg is only justified if something comes of it. It seems today that "one" constantly buckles down and studies. If everyone were to find their proper work and become independent through it, then the goal of philosophical teaching would be achieved.

I think often of the Freiburg years. It was truly a strange "coincidence" that in the summer semester of 1919, a very specific circle of people came together. Now everything unfolds as "more objective" and more unhistorical {*unhistorischer*}. The nature of the "academic appointment" is to blame.

Even if one doesn't allow oneself to be bothered by it, it nevertheless exists for others and is perhaps best made to disappear again through the intensity of sober work. Here, everything is calibrated too much with an eye toward examinations—in Freiburg, the world was wide-open for us.

And we risked everything, feeling it as we did; here one wishes to hear "truths." Privately, I am still living completely in the tempo of my time in Freiburg, and I also hope to do so again openly, when I next begin to experiment again with "systematic" matters.

And if in doing so, the "students" become frightened by the fossils they have collected in their notebooks, then all the better. The Plato lecture is better attended than the Aristotle was over the summer—for the time being, at least. I now have the entire Academic Association in the department and most of them are in my seminar. The audience gives a curated impression in other ways, as well. An old Freiburger showed up from Munich—Schilling, a friend of Luschka, the one who previously gave up on his work and is now earning his doctorate with Vossler. One special acquisition should be mentioned: Herr Dr. Stern—also, some additional prospects from Berlin and Leipzig. Herr Martin is in a rural reform school.

I recently corresponded with Becker concerning "time." In addition, he sent me a review of the Frank book on Plato and the Pythagoreans. It all makes an excellent impression. I think it is premature to discuss the actual point of difference between us. You will get a copy when the essay comes out in January. Unfortunately, I had to leave out much that was important, above all the "hermeneutic indication," which is indispensable for an ultimate understanding—I worked on it extensively. For the coming summer I have announced a four-hour a week history {*Geschichte*} of the concept of time and tutorials on Descartes.

I remember Charlotte Grosser very well. If you could send me her address when you get the chance, I would like to write to her.

Friedländer recently told me that a secret gathering of classical philologists got together in Weimar in October, under the direction of Jaeger. They desire a new humanism, and to that end there are two new periodicals, one that is strictly scholarly (edited by Jaeger) and one "for the masses" (with pictures).

Apparently, on a personal level, Jaeger gives a very refined and superior impression, while at the same time wearing out his welcome in Berlin. Miki wrote from Paris and wants to go to Oxford in the spring. A big catalog of philosophical titles with great prices just came out with Fock—along with an awful lot of pulp fiction.

Please keep an eye out for when the following comes out in Quaracchi: Alexander Halensis, *Summa*. In addition, around 1903 quite a bit must have come out by Matthäus von Aquasparta.

Grabmann is supposed to have discovered Dante's "scholastic library."

Things are well with us. Drop a line about your work.
With warm regards,
  Your
    Martin Heidegger

**64.** *Martin Heidegger to Karl Löwith*
Marbg, 12.17.24

Dear Herr Löwith—I got your letter and the two notebooks. I am writing in bed—I am forced to do so by the flu and overexertion. I hope for recuperation up at the hut.

My piece on "time" was too long for Rothacker (five sheets); it will come out a few pages longer in the *Jahrbuch*. Publication begins at the end of January. I was together with Scheler for three days in Cologne and stayed with him. He is writing an anthropology and a metaphysics. This time we understood each other better. At this point he is no longer so dogmatic. He is particularly impressed by Ed. v. Hartmann. Hopefully, you will continue to keep up the good progress. I think Marseille's work will also turn out well. Bröcker gave me some very clever things on economy and economizing.

A heartfelt Christmas greeting, also from my wife—
  Your
    Martin Heidegger

**65.** *Martin Heidegger to Karl Löwith*
[Todtnauberg, 3.27.25]

Dear Herr Löwith,

Thank you for your letter. Whether I can even manage a correspondence right now seems questionable, given that I am unable to take care of even the most pressing things. For a few days now, our Jörg has been bedridden with a strain of the left leg. I am not able to work much, and my plans for the rest of the break are still indeterminate. Over the summer, I want to prepare myself for the winter lecture course, which is to be purely phenomenological. It is for this reason that I am offering only a beginner's seminar on Descartes and not allowing the older students to take part. I think you will have more students in the winter, and I also hope to get new people then, as well. I have your notebooks up here with me and I still hope that I will get the opportunity, and be able, to write to you more extensively. My piece on "time" will appear in the next edition of the *Jahrbuch*, and in the context out of which it arose—namely, as the foundation for the destructuring of Greek ontology and logic.

A second volume by Cassirer has now come out—Husserl is very impressed by it—presumably a lot of the material will have been worked through as smoothly as in Volume 1. I had a lot of fun lecturing last semester—but in the seminar I was let down by the presentations Klein, Gadamar, and others delivered—and the younger, more active people simply lack any phenomenological education—this is also the case with the aforementioned.

The theologians are convulsing over discussions about Barth-Gogarten and fail to get to the real issues and difficulties.

Landsberg was here for a few days—presumably he is working on Augustine in the same manner as he works on Plato and the Middle Ages—but he is no longer as arrogant, and is slowly noticing the literary character of his writings.

Among the students, there has never again arisen the liveliness and excitement that was present during the first semesters in Freiburg: perhaps the exclusively positive assessment of my work is at fault. I would like to suggest one more semester in Rome to you—there will be little for you in Marburg.

Three new periodicals on classical antiquity are to appear. One is academic—*Die Antike*, edited by Jaeger; one is critical—*Gnomon*, headed by a student of Jaeger's; and one is positively scientific. The third scholarly philological periodical published by Stroux is now in Munich—the one that just came out is called "Nietzsches Professur in Basel," page 104. For whom—and, above all, by whom—all of this is to be written is not clear to me. I was invited by the Kant society to a discussion on "metaphysics" for this year's Pentecost meeting, but I declined. As soon as I am free again, I will get to your notebooks. With warm regards,

    Your
       Martin Heidegger

[Handwritten note in pencil by Löwith:]

I wrote to Heidegger that I would need to know "by the end of March"—he wrote so that I got it on the 31st [sic].

**66.** *Martin Heidegger to Karl Löwith*
Marburg VI.30.25

Dear Herr Löwith,

Thank you kindly for your letters and cards. You are not the only one affected by my criminally negligent approach to letters. Surely no circle of correspondents—and not only in regard to "enactment"—is smaller than mine. The obstacle has been work, and indeed, good work ("good" from my perspective); and yet, still not sufficient for me to say in good conscience that I will be able to lecture on the "Logic" in the winter.

Unfortunately, the eye I kept out for the Japanese students was in vain. I still have two in the department, but they have become frugal regarding lessons since the financial conditions have changed. Karsch is already on his way to Japan; he got a position there as lecturer of German.

Otherwise, little has changed here. Hartmann will be going to Cologne next semester. What will follow, and when, is indeterminate. In any case, Jaensch is against more phenomenology. Tillich has been offered a professorship in ideology at the Technical University in Dresden.

The theologians here are very quiet—the students are discordant and mainly grouped around Bultmann, who is cautious and sober in all things and provides a positive contrast to Barthianism, and even more so to Kierkegaardianism. The commotion that I mentioned previously is slowly becoming terrifying; the most incompetent people showed up for this dialectic, and now use it so naturally that at the same time they say that they actually can't be speaking in such a way!

Again and again the theologians reveal themselves as vacuous and eager to compromise, and as long as Overbeck is not "refuted," all will remain artificial and escapist.

I wonder what will come into fashion in the next few years? Phenomenology has clearly fallen out of favor, and can thus return to its work all the more undisturbed.

Of course, it is also a question if the "metaphysics of insoluble problems" will remain attractive. One can be happy today if one stands apart from what attracts and what doesn't. Where things pass away so quickly, there must be something wrong with the soil. It gives one pause that something like that meeting of the Kant Society exists. Apparently, we have not exceeded the high point of an "interest in philosophy." Next, it will rain "ontologies" in the coming years; one "works" by following certain "scents." And since cleverness and writing skills have grown exponentially and are propagating themselves more and more, one will only be able to demonstrate the other differences "objectively" with great difficulty.

Jaspers wrote to me recently and said that he is also publishing a "collection": *Philosophische Forschungen* (!) Volume I—"Der Dandy"!—and he has his familiar, sociologically practical "excuse" for it: because dissertations are once again under pressure to be published, an "opportunity" to do so must be created for the students. But I will not write more to you about our intellectual business here, except for one more thing: Jaensch has discovered that his notion of the "eidetic" (i.e., Gestalt) stands in the closest of relations to what George is after—it is "in fact, the same."

The days in Kassel (at the end of April) were very nice. I stayed out in Wilhelmshöhe; the audience was very interested, and it was more important to me to give an "impression" of Dilthey's work and personality than to demonstrate insights.

It was very taxing—two lectures each night for five nights. Boehlau the elder was charming, the younger has remained the same—he is a little Berlin "big shot." At the end of the "conference," Boehlau (the younger), Bröcker (who was obligatorily present, of course), and I took a car to Fritzlar, where there was much to see that was beautiful. At the end of the semester, I will immediately go up to the hut and stay there until October. On the way back, I will stop off in Messkirch and Heidelberg. Unfortunately, I only got to speak with Bröcker briefly during the ski trip and the stay in Freiburg. But he appears to be working well, and it seems like the business of philosophy is once again doing better in Freiburg. This summer, Husserl will be lecturing on phenomenological psychology, aka, an orthodox, rectified hermeneutics of facticity. He is starting with Dilthey!

About Dr. König, [I] once heard from someone that he is writing a great "work" on "intuition" and plans to habilitate with Misch.

Soon, the first half-volume of the new philosophical journal *Philosophischer Anzeiger*, edited by Plessner, will come out. I am also featured on the cover, with the purpose of contributing to the critical task of the "endeavor." But for the moment, my wishes are being ignored, presumably because "one" does not wish to ruin relations with those in power. Should the whole thing take off, you will also have to work on it. Cassirer has published Volume II—*Das mythische Denken*—I will review it in the *Deutsche Literatur-Zeitung*. The same schema as Volume I, but presumably a bit better—I was only able to skim it. His positive analyses of primary phenomena fail every time, and he sees everything before him—and at the moment that is no small thing—from the lofty heights of Kantian concepts. Necessarily, Volume III, on art, will now follow. But the whole thing does have a certain substance. Have you finished the work on personalism? And what else do you have up your sleeve? I have read through your notebooks completely—all over I find continual reflections—they are strung like beads on a necklace but not worked through into a particular, self-imposed question. That is the next thing I expect from you. You will probably already be back in Germany before I get up to the hut. Otherwise you could visit us via Basel. Until next time.

With warm regards
   Your
      Martin Heidegger

My wife also sends her greetings.

**67.** *Karl Löwith to Martin Heidegger*
[Munich, Aug. 17. 25]

Dear Herr Heidegger,

For ten days now, I am once again transalpine, and I wonder why everyone here speaks German and everything is gray and the color of water. I have brought much with me from this year in Italy—but nothing that I can't or won't assimilate. Even "existence" does not remain untouched when one has lived in the south, in Rome, in Italy. In a certain sense, one must be visually oriented for this—but it all only remains "ocular" for someone who really knows how to use his eyes. It is a shame that I have no one among my friends who knows these experiences from out of their own perspective. Are things well with you and yours up at the hut? And have you already figured out the content for your lecture and seminar? In case certain books would [be] necessary or welcome for it, I ask that you please let me know. A long letter for you has not yet come to the tip of the quill.
  Warm regards,
    Your
      Karl Löwith

The photograph shows a mosaic from the end of the 2 century before Christ—I found it on the Via Appia.

**68.** *Martin Heidegger to Karl Löwith*
Todtnauberg, VIII. 24.25

Dear Herr Löwith,

Many thanks for your postcard. It arrived on my "desk" at the very moment in which I was bringing the chapter in my "time" lecture concerning death "to its end." In the winter I will lecture on logic. I am not far enough along to take it up and carry it out the way in which I imagine it. Given this, it will become an embarrassment. But for once I do wish to "lecture" from out of the context of these works. For often thereby a certain momentum unexpectedly comes about that would otherwise fail to materialize. In these matters, one must always give oneself over to "chance" at the right time. For only then is it revealed whether the originary, untouchable flow is there in work and existence.
  In the advanced seminar I will be working on Hegel's *Logic*, Book 1. But I would like to limit the discussions to a few particular concrete questions, and from the beginning not fall victim to the diffuseness of the text. At the same time, the participants should also have their say, if possible.

I gave tutorials on Descartes this summer; there were a few capable people among the participants, mostly theologians, but unfortunately they are leaving for Berlin and Tübingen. Life at the university is once again developing a satiated and "safe" habitus—that is, one no longer gets too excited about questions and challenges—rather, one "rehabilitates" and becalms and plants the wonderful awareness that it will all soon be as glorious as it was before the war.

What still shows some "life" is the Barth-Gogarten movement, which is being represented in Marburg—independently and cautiously—by Bultmann. And because I am constantly at risk of being counted as belonging to theology, I am allowed to travel along with this movement, although I made my skepticism clear enough in a recent disputation that "erupted" in the wake of a lecture given by Heitmüller (Tübingen) on understanding and interpretation of the New Testament. If something results from my work indirectly, I can't prevent that. But I do deny any intention and responsibility.

I am not suited to teach you anything about "what's new" in academic and printed things, and becoming ever less suited. Such things would be easiest for you in Munich. The *Anzeiger* has published the first half-volume according to the following principle: something must be published by August 1st, regardless of what it is. And that's exactly what has happened. An article on Yorck-Dilthey that I was flipping through—by one of Misch's students—is absolute kitsch.

Anything like a critical character in the true sense will hardly gain traction, and all will remain the same over the course of the year. In addition, there now also exists *Symposion*, and in addition to *Logos*, there is now also *Ethos* for sociology—and soon *Kairos* will also come out.

There is one advantage that comes from this feverish activity: in this way, phenomenology will quickly join the ranks of "retired" things, and one will no longer be importuned by the public and its dubious interest.

For a change, Scheler is "updating" Eduard von Hartmann. And what will next week's joke be? I think that a madhouse has a clearer and more reasonable inner aspect than this era.

During a small gathering of students to which I was invited at the end of the semester, I lectured to them from, and about, Jacob Burkhardt—they became very perplexed when faced with the inner calm and surety of a creative life.

You will probably only slowly begin to sense the expansions and overturnings that your stay in Italy must bring. I also wish a refreshment for myself—although for now I have to allow the continuing momentum to run out first.

Up here we live very quietly and happily. The boys are wild and healthy. Becker was here for a few days recently, but the time was too short to allow for real communication; additionally, he was severely handicapped by a jaw issue.

Shortly before the break, Fräulein Gerling suddenly showed up in Marburg and stayed a few days. Unfortunately, my wife and the boys had already left. I had a great time with her. But she doesn't seem to be totally satisfied with the whole school business.

By the way, Becker told me that you might come to Freiburg; if so, then you could also come up here. Although my time is in short supply, there would still be some opportunities for discussion.

What's more, Wiesemann has showed up in Marburg and is still as crazy as ever—if only he were at least resolute and would found a sect or something; but don't come to me, of all people, to earn a doctorate.

I will travel to Marburg via Messkirch and Heidelberg at the end of September, and I probably won't begin again before early November. For in that dreary little nest, one can do little else but work, and even that takes more energy than elsewhere.

Please write in more detail.

Warm greetings to you

Your

Martin Heidegger

**69.** *Karl Löwith to Martin Heidegger*
[Munich, August 22 or 29, 1925]

Dear Herr Heidegger,

It is already late, and everyone is asleep—I am now doing the opposite of what I was doing in Settignano; instead of rising early in the morning, I go to sleep early in the morning: for in the land of the Cimmerians—or, as Goethe sometimes also called them, the Zimmerians—it's just not worth it to look the new day in the eye at 5 a.m.—for that day will be of a bleak, watery color, and if it's clear for more than two hours at a stretch, one is once again obliged to pull out that standard piece of furnishing, the umbrella. Back there, the Italian nights shone more brightly than the day does here—*ohimè*! How knowingly I am now able to read Goethe's diaries chronicling his journey through Italy, or the last Winckelmann letters, or Gregorovius, Hehn, and all the rest. And I foresee that I will be in yet another analogous position in Marburg—without echo—somehow in solitary possession of an Italian year, which due to the force of its temporal meaningfulness is a year *sui generis*, during which I came more into myself than in all previous years, but also as a consequence of them—I don't wish to articulate it prematurely—but I sense that somehow a true epoch in my life has been reached whose most insistent initial characteristic is the feeling of a changed stance regarding my shared world, even with my closest friends. Much has simply fallen away, all on its own—a few prior relationships have engulfed each other and thereby became stronger—many others have lost efficacy and importance.

When I arrived here, I found two letters waiting for me—one from a baroness who wanted me as a private tutor (!), and one from Charlotte Grosser, sent from Göttingen—about Barth (!), with whom she studied last semester and whose departure for Münster is very depressing for her. She is preparing herself for the state university examination.

I had planned to travel to Marburg via Freiburg during the first days of September, but Becker wrote to say that he wouldn't be back until the middle of September, and I can't sit around here doing nothing for that long—for as an Italian traveler, I just can't get to work in this house with the dubious blessing of a telephone. At the moment, my father is at the Zeppelin commemoration on Lake Constance—he is representing art—and I am being pushed to take a look at the "transportation exhibit" and the "German (technical) museum" here—I don't know why—for I don't even go look at the antiquarian bookshops. And "new releases"? On my desk there lay, carefully preserved, several months' worth of book announcements and periodicals—I made the effort to fill the wastepaper basket with it all. It's great how much is being printed. Good old Gutenberg—if only he had known! The main success to be had is in the resolute renunciation, even if only in one's thoughts, of wanting to compete with this dizzying productiveness—the desire to come out on top in this sweeping current of periodicals and "works"—no, you are quite right in calmly allowing others to rush to print—this deluge is depressing, and the "scholarly airship" to which one is called should drop bombs on the printing presses rather than heading off on an expedition to the North Pole. On Becker's recommendation, I read one of the newest products—Scheler's *Formen des Wissens und der Bildung*—he still remains the same old clever and erudite guy, using and expanding his few, stereotypical ideas ever anew in the same old tracks: the outlining of systems, programs, and "metaphysical" vantages and the charging of open doors. His style suffices for one to see the implausibility of his educated "knowledge of salvation." Meanwhile, C. G. Carus—a true psychologist whom I "discovered" years ago—has been republished—but not his good *Psyche*, but rather his *Symbolik*. In the display [I] saw a book on philology by Vossler.

Yet, one could learn more from a certain modern Italian—Pirandello—than one could learn from all of that. My pastor there made me aware of him—he's a dramatist and an author of very studied and very philosophical novellas (but he is also the only one they have, and he appears extremely un-Italian, insofar as one thinks it un-Italian that an Italian writes works which breathe the air of Strindberg). Among other things he wrote a parable—*"Così è, se vi pare"*—in which, through utmost clarity, acuity, and vividity, the following problem is developed: "What does one actually know about another?" When, in response to this question, a lady says, "*chiedendo notizie ed informazioni*," Shakespearean laughter rings out. When I am in Marburg, I have to translate the main point for you in person—it is worth it, and I was childishly delighted to find my analyses of the shared world so well validated. This work is being performed here right now at the *Kammerspiele*—but at the end, to my right and left, I only heard the typical, moronic, annoying questions: "Who is the crazy one, after all—him or her?"—and this after Pirandello made an effort throughout the whole piece to push aside this initiating, "curious" question about the "reality" and "truth" of the object-like relatedness between people, in favor of calling attention to the being "in" of the relationships between the two—i.e., "we"—that is, calling attention to their reciprocal, jointly liable attunement.

I would rather not even get started on "Munich"—it is now even more idle than it was, as easily caricatured in the abstract as in the particular (the Walthers!). Most striking are two new, shameless, huge inscriptions—one on the *Feldherrnhalle* (a bad copy of a Florentine structure, by the way), and the other on the newest veterans' monument (i.e., a huge block of stone!). The first one says: "Lord, make us free"—the second: "they will rise again"— What do you say to such Christian politics?!

I reread the Rome travels chapter in Scheel's beautiful biography of Luther. In general, I was truly ravenous for German–Italian readings, and saw with astonishment with what fortuitousness one gets ahead of oneself—and if things work out, then catches up with oneself: for almost everything that I need in order to reinforce my time in Italy has been among my books already for years—provisional purchases, but as it turns out made with the right foresight. The congruity of life is often uncanny to me. I can't stand it here much longer, being so idle, especially given that already during the hottest month in Settignano I was not really able to work, and then I spent fourteen days traveling back. I passed through the fairytale-like Ravenna with its buildings and mosaics from the sixth century—what a grand and relaxed century in which these things emerged; Gregory the Great was ruling in Rome, and Benedict founded the monastery above Subiaco.

Here one speaks comfortably of the "royal-Bavarian Republic," and it is unbelievable to observe how quickly the world once again adapts itself, how strong the need for security is, and how bad the memory of a people is—1914 to 1918—no big deal, just a lost war; now, a "reconstruction," as orderly as possible—so it goes with the state as it does in philosophy. On the other hand, it is astonishing to see how far removed someone like Burkhardt—hungry for beauty but nevertheless a great man—was from any form of that optimistic, aesthetic, and humanistic view of history {*Geschichtsauffassung*}—most of all in his *Konstantin*, the Basel lectures, and some of his correspondences.

In Marburg work will begin again in earnest—there is little else there for us to do: for even human lassitude is ugly at these latitudes. I hope you will take pleasure in the photos that I will bring; and hopefully new blood has arrived in regard to students—I myself actually don't take myself to be "older," but the fact of twenty-eight chronological years does aggrieve the already bad conscience—for I have not yet achieved anything of consequence, even though I had the unforgettable "fortune" to begin my studies with you in Freiburg.

I wish you and your family good days
  Your
    Karl Löwith

About a month ago, I got a letter from von Rohden, posted from a Silesian seminary in Halle.

**70.** *Martin Heidegger to Karl Löwith*
Aug. 31. 25

Dear Herr Löwith,

The discontinuity of our correspondence is not a mystery, given the local postal conditions.

I brought my letter to you down to Schneider's the same day, as the weather was too poor to go into the village. The postman, when delivering the mail, was to have taken it with him from there. We did not get any mail on the 24th and 25th, presumably because the postman was not able to make it up to the hut on our account due to the bad weather. On the 26th, I found your letter to me down at Schneider's; mine to you was gone and it was stamped the next day. The mail only goes out once in the morning, at 9 o'clock. And because postman Brender also died during these days, yet another delay could have occurred.

When, before travelling here, I had to send a telegram from Marburg concerning a sudden hindrance, it arrived here the next day at 11 a.m. (although posted at 6 in the evening in Marburg).

When I had read your letter, I said to myself: you could have spared yourself the one you wrote, especially because in Italy you have come to understand that what is truly "new" must already be very old. I don't know of any other address for Fräulein Gerling; at the moment she is definitely at the school in Elmshorn.

After a few days of rain, the weather is once again beautiful and stable. It is a shame that you are in such a hurry to get to Marburg—although to me this seems more like a hurry to get *away from* than a hurry *to get to*.

With warm regards,
   Your
      Martin Heidegger

Please give my greetings to the Gadamers, the Krügers, and Marseille.

**71. Karl Löwith to Martin Heidegger**
III.16.26, Rotenberg 8 [Munich]

Dear Herr Heidegger,

I am sending you the Dilthey along with this letter. I had set a deadline for myself of III.15, and I actually succeeded—working day and night toward the end until 4 in the morning! Since the beginning of the break, I have almost gotten into the swing of things—for it isn't possible to keep the "semester" completely at bay, and one can only truly work on one thing, and work on it continually. It's nice and quiet in my garret—Marburg and the Hessian hills don't tempt me to go on excursions like the Sabina and the Volsci. You probably have snow up there and are, as always, "working."

Wiesemann came to visit me at the end of the semester; I had a long conversation with him, and if he has a clear head, he will take the appropriate steps, even though he does not at all live within the possibilities of "conceptuality"; everything that he said was much more philosophical than the usual rush of words. Also, the manner in which Marseille has penetrated into graphology has a lot more substance than the usual, empty discussions of what is "fundamental," which always lack any concrete background. By the way, he has been well underway the whole time already, but it will become a very dense matter, advancing critically into even the greatest details. We spoke often of these matters; he is the only one from whom I can learn something, since he knows how to make use of his factical "experiences," and knows what he wishes to accomplish with them. Gadamer always assures himself by way of a concept of "objectivity" that is not philosophical. [He] is recovering during th[is] break and hopes to be back at the beginning of the semester.

Will you see Becker and von Rohden at all? The latter once wrote from Davos—he heard a Shrovetide sermon by Brunner in Zurich and wrote quite fittingly about it: "A showpiece *à la* Kierkegaard—big on concepts, abysmal regarding exegesis—all energy deployed toward floundering about among misunderstandings and false assurances—and thereby no assurance at all and no existent relationship!" Charlotte Grosser stayed in Munich for the break, and, as before, has much of Barth. Despite the latter's methodological dogmatism, he appears to have capabilities of understanding similar to Jaspers, only transferred to the gravely theological. What bothers me concerning Barth's *Zwischen den Zeiten* essays is the *stereotype* of method therein—for while he owes to it a certain superior assurance, he gets perplexed wherever that methodical style consolidates and expands itself, when all the while the themes are so unsubstantial. The intellectual riches at the disposal of Hegel and Kierkegaard prevent the paltriness of their methodical possibilities from becoming immediately apparent. A certain lack of freedom always exists when a method becomes dogmatic. That is why the concept of "possibility"—of "encountering," etc.—is so important to me. The danger increases along with the higher level of "categorial" elaboration—with Hegel it is at an absolute denseness, so to speak, with every word a Hegelian category—he actually should have come up with his own language—it's fortunate that this isn't possible, and what remains is the embarrassing residue of "natural logic" and hazy "representation," etc. That is exactly why I find the study of Dilthey to be so fruitful, since he was *not yet* able to ground himself through conceptually-formal elaboration—expressions such as "will" or "resistance," etc., may be so primitive and he may still superficially pair them with "to feel" and "to understand"—but because such traditional terms are not simply invented, they still deliver a result that reveals three factical differences. Precisely because the formal *how* is here still expressed in a fixed *what*, the attempt becomes palpably visible in its insecurity—for one can clearly see the anticipation of "world view" and "life interpretation." And as it turns out, Dilthey actually does have very sophisticated views.

In this sense, things are going for me much like they are for Becker, and also for you—namely, I am very glad not to have begun my studies here, but rather in Freiburg in 1919 with you, and for my part I foresee that, in order truly to attain to the issues that concern me, I must first start at the beginning, that is, by renouncing an already existing, transparent conceptuality, and resist the temptation to formulate a purely reactive one—and to allow the appropriate categories to arise out of the intuitions over time. In the work I gave you, and also in the Dilthey, I could not prevent making use (as it were) of things I have learned from you, but things that go beyond my actual needs and means of engagement right now. Simply because I need to finish something.

The only fitting means of expression for me would be one structured by the temporality of ongoing investigations—lectures in the style of those you first gave in Freiburg—based on manuscripts that become ever more outdated with each semester and are not even typed up, for that only makes sense when one is as far along as you are.

By the way, the Dilthey is still missing an annotation at the beginning that would indicate the methodical "determination of provenance"—that is, your name—because I first wanted to ask you what form you would like it to take. Can I make reference to something that is forthcoming "soon," or to lectures that have been typed up, or perhaps simply say *en bloc* that I did not materialize the whole thing from inside my "I"? The practical glitch of the matter is the following: I had agreed with Plessner to keep it around one sheet—but now these 115 pages are awfully close to 80 printed pages! It is thus better for me—even just regarding the money—if I could get rid of it—but now that seems very doubtful to me. What's your opinion? (N.B.: If I hear anything back from the emergency assistance program, I will let you know immediately.) And publishing just Chapters I and II seems too cheap to me. Conversely, it would honestly be a shame to publish only Chapter III in such a periodical, apart from the fact that Chapter III alone is already much longer—and I can't simply begin with the interpretation of the title. If at all possible, I think it would be best if it all remains together and could thereby be an exemplum for Dilthey scholarship.

And there is one more thing I would like to know: Should I write an introduction to the other thing in the vein of what I wrote in my application? This week I will still be working through various notes that arose from the "Dilthey"—I would be very glad if I could hear from you toward the end of the month regarding the "shared world" so that I can make full use of the vacation.

N.B.: An advertisement full of Scheler-opuses arrived recently, along with a picture of Scheler—he looks great! It also contained parts of reviews: a big pile of trash by Nicolai Hartmann; witty platitudes by Troeltsch—"a Catholic Nietzsche"—that would be like a Catholic Protestant or a dogmatic skeptic—it was a lot of Nietzsche, but surely nothing Catholic!

Apart from the fact that right now I simply cannot take the hustle and bustle of the semester anymore, I have much to thank him for—namely, two things: (1) a serious introduction to Hegel, and (2) the same in regard to Kant; and when I see how you grasp things, and notice how I am finally past the stage of irritable receptivity and have gotten onto solid footing, I have hope for the "impending future" (in the sense of the "present"!)—a living-toward that I cannot prevent.

In case you still think it is a good idea to send the Dilthey to Plessner, please send it back to me about one week before the end of the month, as I have promised it to him by the end of March.

    Gratefully yours,
    Karl Löwith

Do you still want the Görres? The two volumes now cost 4 marks, instead of 8. In the meantime, second copy [???] of "Hegel" has come in, which I will put aside for you.

## 72. Martin Heidegger to Karl Löwith
Todtnaubg, March.17.27

Dear Herr Löwith,

Thank you for your letter; what you requested is enclosed. However, Marseille should have shown me the manuscript one more time before it went to print. Now I don't have any idea to what extent my demands and objections were fulfilled and considered. But there is nothing to be done now.

We have 1.5 meters of snow and the most wonderful sun. I am feeling great. I only saw Becker very briefly. It will be April before I can speak with him at length. One can only respond to Clauss' impertinence with silence. One shouldn't take such writings too seriously.

The fact that Kant's "metaphysics" of morals is ontology shows itself on every page. As does the generally inadequate foundation. What he wants and seeks in a positive, ontic way is clear, and in a sense our search is also nothing new. The crucial problems are all connected and always the "same old ones," and precisely thereby necessarily temporal. Nothing is accomplished by merely appealing to the fact that this or that person "also already wanted" this or that. Rather, through such observations we avoid what we are supposed to be doing—and what we are supposed to be doing precisely because those others also already wanted to do the same.

I wish you good progress with your work and send my greetings,
    Your
        Martin Heidegger

Because I don't know how Marseille ultimately formulated it, I would ask that you add the current title of the dissertation to the statement of print readiness (whose purpose I don't understand) next to the signature on the proof.

## 73. Karl Löwith to Martin Heidegger
Sunday, V.1.27

Dear Herr Heidegger,

I must revise my decision for the time being—until Pentecost—and drop the lecture and seminar. My initial decision to take part in both was already not that firm, for I was not sure whether it could be paired with the completion of my work. I am now noticing that it cannot, and I have to remain with my work as before—namely, undivided, for otherwise I will end up in disorder (especially now, while working on the final chapter, for which I need to have what came before present to me).

I hope that you will approve of this—for it is no longer the way it used to be, when I was able to juggle so much simultaneously, and I estimate the loss to the seminar by my absence to be minimal—perhaps it is rather an advantage if there are fewer "older folks" taking part! But the third systematic part of your work is so important, as is Hegel, that I would like to participate again after Pentecost, assuming that this is alright with you. You can, therefore, still count on the presentation I pledged to give, as long as a belated, additional admittance is not uncomfortable for you in regard to the other participants.

Thank you once again, very much, for leaving me a copy! I will have it solidly bound (in black) so that it can withstand some heavy use: for death is a theological principle of freedom. "Freedom"—to me this also seems to be the only true and specific idea of a philosophical existence, but I understand something different by it, because Nietzsche is my philosophical mother's milk, and my philosophical home is the south.

To the extent that I was able to do so without doing myself harm, I have tried to present in my own work my critical engagement with what I have understood of yours, and I have tried to do so in an objective and yet extremely "personal" manner. The actual reason why I am finalizing it two years later than I had initially intended is this: I needed that time in order to confront myself with it, for without such a critical engagement it would have had no meaning for me; I had already moved beyond the possibility of an entirely undemanding, high-school level phenomenological paper. I nevertheless remain a grateful student of my teacher—but I must ask that you think back to your former situation *vis-à-vis* Husserl in Freiburg in order to recognize the thankfulness within my unevenly matched assault.

I have also spoken with Afra about this; it is a blessing once again to see a person who by virtue of their nature *is* something, who *sees* and is internally free.

I hope you get new people for the department and the seminar.

 With best regards,
  Your
   Karl Löwith

PS: Should I keep an eye out in the catalogues for Feuerbach?

**74.** *Karl Löwith to Martin Heidegger*
[Munich] VIII.2.27

Dear Herr Heidegger,

I deeply regret that there was no opportunity to get together with you. There were so many points on my "agenda" that therefore had to remain unchecked, and the "ontic" difference between written and spoken speech is vast. For example (this is just such a case in point): my main concern with the all-too-rash application of a "principally" ontological analysis is that in such an analysis, the decisive, ontic-existentiell differences—the questions regarding emphasis—are lost in an "absolute indifference" (Hegel!) (pursuant to the demand of taking *Dasein* into consideration); however, as decisive ontic-existentiell differences, they are also decisive for ontological formalization—a formulation you would surely no longer accept! I believe that precisely your own insight into the difficulty of the ontic-ontological circle (I am thinking primarily of *Sein und Zeit,* pages 12–13, 166–167, and 199) must lead to this dialectical movement nevertheless being tied to an end—"foundationally"—but not to the ontological a priori—although that does appear to be the consequence of philosophizing (such as, in an extreme form, Husserl's way of delineating "essence" and "fact," where "essence" factically becomes inessential). But this is a danger that also exists when a "hermeneutics of facticity" develops itself into an ontological analytic of *Dasein.* (Concerning your work, I now feel myself to be in a position analogous to that of the "Munich circle" in regard to Husserl's going over to the phenomenology of constitution—although I hope to adopt this turn in a less pig-headed way then these "Munichians"!) This dialectical movement is, thus, not tied to the ontological a priori, but rather to the ontic-anthropological; or, said more psychologically, it is not scholarly philosophy that "substantiates" and makes "understandable" the original motives and tendencies of factical philosophizing—rather, it is the other way around. In what way, and from out of what something becomes "actually" understandable to someone—that is surely no longer able to be decided theoretically—yet, it nevertheless determines the concept of "understandability" as such. Although the methodological correctness of a possible objection to, say, Feuerbach, is clear to me in its "correctness," it nevertheless does not appear to me as sound and conforming to the true, but rather appears to me to be the sophism specific to philosophy as such. For example, some such responses as: "I don't think as a thinker, but rather as a thinking human," "philosophy must begin with the non-philosophical," "the birth certificate comes before the enrollment register," etc. Or: conscious understanding is to be understood from out of its unconscious drives.

However, I believe it to be indispensable that, from the beginning, the dialectical concurrence of being-present-to-hand and existing comes to the fore, a concurrence that can be better expressed with the following formulation: *Dasein* = "existing" (which, like all ontological determinations of "*Dasein,*" only appears to be so formal that it would not prejudice anything ontic-existentiell), and *Dasein* = "life" (as a result of which I referenced Kant: the human = "rational" "creature," "a being of nature conceived for freedom," which, according to Kant, cannot be "grasped" theoretically!). This is a "concurrence" that in the first place serves its purpose and prevents an unambiguous systemization and closing of the open question (the analytic of *Dasein*). I most certainly understand that through this "concurrence" the so-called substantial being-in-itself {*Ansichsein*} first comes into its own and its analytically explicit expression, and that the movement is first extreme in one direction, only then—in a countermovement—to come back to itself. But I do not believe that along this path the ("sensual") "nature" of the human comes to its positive manifestation in its naturalness; rather, this manifestation is an un-freedom, if all determinations lying therein (the nature of the human) are from the beginning mapped out by such an extremely "existentiell" concept as that of "thrownness." It is likewise concerning the determination of *Dasein* as being in each case "its own," in contradiction to which I have attempted to show—by way of an unavoidable "one-sidedness"—the "individual" as one who is able to be mediated, as a "persona," who from the beginning has its "roles" in the shared world. I thereby wished to lend support to Feuerbach's simple positing of the "I" as the I of an (older) you, the I designated as being the "first person" by the "second person." Phrased most generally, to thereby de-idealize "intentionality" even beyond "being-in-the-world" in such a way that I could make this "intentionality" clear to myself in its specifically real objectivity from out of the anthropological "world," as an "oppositional" intentionality of "relationships" (between humans). But this is something that cannot be written about briefly, so I will just be patient and wait until you are here once again.

Regarding the practical side of the matter, however, I do need to impose upon you via this letter and ask for your reply—for here it is also the same thing: ontically, "acting" is quite different from "knowledge," although ontologically it can be grasped "principally" and in total as concern. Regarding the present imposition, this time I cannot say whether I am only doing it in response to the pressure of my impatient and "success" oriented father, for what also matters to me is to do away with the uncomfortable state of oscillation between knowing and not knowing. In all honesty, the only reason I am mentioning this now, instead of waiting for the three months of break to pass, is to make you aware of this "state" (given that the question of my habilitation cannot be made relevant anyway until then). And this state is so discomfiting precisely because the uncertainty about the "success" of the matter up to now suppresses resumption of ongoing work, especially because the familiar shared-world of Marburg—a social "circle"—has become for me something that has run its course. (I feel the closest to Krüger, which is due, of course, to a "mutuality." And because he is a discreet person, I gave him a copy of my work to read some time ago. He studied it thoroughly and wrote a small booklet of comments for me; however, his theological grounding is a rather dark one, I think, and this is probably a sore point for him.) The possibility of engaging in philosophical work completely on my own account and on my own dime, continually finding the drive within myself to continue this work, is much more limited in my case than in yours. If I think about how intensely and uninterruptedly you have been working for ten years now, without significant communication, I am amazed; I would not be able to do the same, without the enlivening intermediaries of contacts, without opposition and "correspondence."

To be concise and direct: I am asking you to write me whether you would be willing to accept the whole thing as a habilitation thesis, and if I would then, in that case, have the chance to appear before the faculty at the beginning of the semester and—pass? Unfortunately, Jaensch is not really to be trusted. Has his doctoral student, Dr. Freiling, already habilitated? And how do things stand with the allocation of the second professorial chair? Or is this all academic arcana? Have you met Beck and Schmidt-Ott? Amongst the procession of the faculty I saw, to my great delight, the honorable and imposing figure of Goebel. But if one looks at Elwert and Ebel's photos, it does appear to be rather questionable whether the head is the organ of the spirit. Besides, we Germans really don't know how to celebrate—the torchlight procession was so boring and orderly it was as though it were heading toward a funeral. "*Festeggiare*"—that's something only the Italians understand. On Sunday night, we took in the castle festival, amazing operation—the most fun was to be had in the splendid cellar vault of the Bavarian beer hall—it was there that the Bavarians showed their best side.

My vacation plans are still undetermined due to a lack of funds; in that regard, Bröcker's parents are a laudable exception, for this time he even got to fly home—but it is questionable whether this is a good thing for Bröcker Junior. My godchild is growing up; now and again I coerce him into secret philosophical studies! In recent days, I read a collection of letters by Tolstoy—I simply must give it you—it is unparalleled in its radical, mutual understanding and its reciprocal critique. Once again one senses what it could mean to be a whole person, and to come to oneself through someone else.

For you I wish a partner (not to say an "opponent") of the same intellectual and scholarly level, but you will not easily encounter such a figure. Part of the fault for this circumstance lies in what Ebbinghaus wrote to you in the letter which you read to me—that is, the guarded way in which you approach him.

I need your advice concerning one other matter: How can I go about stepping on that damn Plessner's toes, that cowardly overachiever, so that he finally opens his mouth? He did not even respond to my ultimatum, but he also did not return the manuscript. I heard indirectly that my critique of Klages was recently belittled in the *Kölner Zeitung*, all in a few impertinent sentences—presumably, he is also the source of this! I will see about getting the edition.

From the Nietzsche archive, I received a rather curious acknowledgement in the name of Frau Förster-Nietzsche; in those quarters, there is rejoicing that Klages is getting his comeuppance! And in recognition of this, I am the recipient of Nietzsche's biography by Frau Förster-Nietzsche!! They even wish to make a copy of my dissertation for the archive—this all-too human "objectivity" is magnificent, isn't it? The best thing is that one doesn't publish anything, and sees it as a special privilege when one has the opportunity to present things to the people only in seminars and lectures, *le mieux est l'ennemi du bien*, particularly when it can't be taken home in print.

To you and yours, I wish pleasant days at the hut.
Warm regards
From your
Karl Löwith

**75.** *Karl Löwith to Martin Heidegger*
[Marburg] VIII.10.27

Dear Herr Heidegger,

As a follow-up to my letter from August 2nd, I am sending you the review from the almanac by a certain Herr "Teltaster"—could this be Plessner? Is he "Catholic"? (Cologne: Volkszeitung.) Incidentally—I grant everything that Teltaster says; it's just that he doesn't say anything substantial regarding the matters in question. Please save this article for me as a curiosity.

It is now very beautiful and calm here—everybody is away on holiday, including Gadamer and Krüger. Through Spitta I hear that Knittermeyer (in Bremen) will review your book in *Christliche Welt* (from the perspective of the theology of Barth-Gogarten, of course).

I am sure that you are now having wonderfully clear days and nights up there.

I send my warm greetings,
Your
Karl Löwith

**76.** *Karl Löwith to Martin Heidegger*
[Marburg] VIII.17.27

Dear Herr Heidegger,

Do not be alarmed that I am writing you again! The superficial reason is this: I have been looking backward after a long time—I sifted through a pile of correspondences, boxed up and sorted—I can now feel somehow the chronological fact of "30" "historical {*historisch*}" and existentiell years very clearly—both in relation to my philosophical work and in my personal relationships, no less the "private" ones with the "opposite sex," their development and dissolution. Among all of this, a pile of "Heidegger" correspondences came to be in my hands, and I recall how Thust once said to me the following: "Yes, Heidegger seems to me to be a kind of destiny for you—your relationship to him and his philosophy is remarkably intense"—but I am getting ahead of myself. What struck me suddenly was the name "Todtnauberg"—for as I read it, I worried that I had addressed my letter from August 2nd, and those following (a newspaper clipping and a photograph) to Todtnau. I will not analyze this possible slip of the pen "psychoanalytically"—I would only ask that you file a complaint in Todtnau if you haven't received anything from me!

But even without this discrepancy, I would have written to you again. It is no small thing to recapitulate the story of a personal and substantive relationship on the basis of letters and postcards—in other words, to "remember." Among these materials are letters that are four pages long! Letters from Munich, Freiburg, Mecklenburg, Baden-Baden, Rome, Settignano, and Marburg of course—containing statements that are for the most part in direct line with the position you hold today, but also some that are, at first sight, incompatible with it—you yourself can piece all of this together more easily than some "other" ever could. You were "30" (!) at the time when you wrote this: "In the course of this, I am increasingly losing any desire and aspiration to publish, and I think too highly of myself to be spoken about and discussed in places where philosophy is merely a pleasant opportunity to showcase one's talent. And at 30 years of age, one really is still too young; one has one's hands full making sure that one's own life doesn't get away from oneself in a way that can't be retrieved later—one then arrives at the system—and put in philosophical terms: that search is too expansive" (from 1921). Three years later you say: "The curse of my work, the work I must do, is that it has to move about in the region of the old philosophy and theology, and it must do so critically when it comes to certain irrelevances such as 'categories.' Thus an illusion arises, as though what has been negated should be confronted with what corresponds to it, with content. However, this work is uniquely limited—not for school, direction, continuance, supplementation—it can only be done by me—from out of the singularity of this constellation of conditions. This work is always antiquated, and grows out of a form of existence that perhaps remains completely untouched by 'today.'" At one point, you speak of the genuine difficulties of "being together," expressly reducing it to "existence." But the fact that we are no longer together in the same way as before, roaming around Freiburg, is not something I need to tell you—I didn't mean to infringe on you with my perhaps unrestrained, but at least always honest, letters—I, in particular, know how much the so-called responsibility in this relationship is "reciprocal" and "mutual"—insofar as it is possible to speak of "responsibility," and not only destiny, in a way that's not overly pathetic. Nothing can be done retroactively—to the contrary, such "stories" go ineluctably forward, and every attempt to cease or even reverse things only accelerates the progression against one's will. Thus: wisdom's last word is "do not resist evil."

I regard the development of the trajectory of your philosophical work in the same way—certainly, it had to continue in this way, and I respect the work that came about thereby with total and unconditional sincerity—I also do not believe that you need to wait on anything from me that will be decisive for you—but I do very much regret all of these inevitabilities and the corresponding lack of freedom, and therefore feel obligated to tell you at least this much: regarding the boundaries of our possible mutual understanding, I can communicate much better and more meaningfully with you—the "author"—than I can with any of your "students." Indeed, I understand nothing of Becker's work (for that to be possible, one has to be as unfortunate as Herr Seidemann! I once had dinner with him and his so-called wife at a tavern—it thoroughly ruined my appetite): I see that his opposition proceeds in an essentially different direction. Said more clearly: it comes from an entirely different region than mine—I believe that mine is more immanent insofar as I make no attempt to reestablish the lost "innocence" of "self-forgetful" and natural *Dasein*—because *Dasein* is principally a being-with-others that lies on the same plane of conflict as one's authentic existence, and through "nature" (sensibility) it does not become unproblematic but rather concretely and specifically problematic.

If the questions that were important to me that arose out of a critical engagement with your work were not exactly polite, and I did nothing to work around the all-too-human vulnerability that a "teacher" feels with respect to his "student," then I did so with the confident awareness that, whereas such caution may have been "appropriate" for Becker with respect to Husserl, in my case it would have indicated an unfounded and unforgivable cowardice and dishonesty. In fact, perhaps I even went too far in the other direction: for example, due to the simple fear of giving you the impression that I was kissing up to you, I did not take the opportunity to congratulate you on the publication of your book. My father is less burdened by such things—he is so accustomed to thinking of human affairs in transactional terms that he wanted to send me a box of cigars to give to you! Of course, when your opinion about my habilitation thesis is finalized, I will be freer regarding such things. I asked you about it in the letter to "Todtnau," since there was no more spoken conversation about it here, and three months of uncertainty over the holidays is a fairly embarrassing situation to be in.

Regarding the winter, I would definitely like to work only for myself—I cannot travel anywhere else, just in case the habilitation question becomes pressing—but at the very least I can isolate myself here. When I wanted to leave Mecklenburg and return to you in Marburg, you wrote to me and said that I should consider it carefully and decide for myself whether or not it would do me "more harm than good" to take part in your seminars and lectures—as it turned out, it was "thoroughly" useful that I participated. But now it is probably for the best that I deny myself the Schelling seminar and practice the laboriously acquired ability to walk on my own—I am not lacking "material"—if you have the desire, I can tell you what my plans are—"anthropology"—which is why it is very fortunate for me that I did not begin my studies in the first case with "ontology," but rather with the "hermeneutics of facticity."

I am—despite everything—
Your
Karl Löwith

**77.** *Martin Heidegger to Karl Löwith*
Todtnauberg, August 20, 27

Dear Herr Löwith,

I have received your three letters, and I thank you for them. I didn't respond earlier this August because I wanted first to read through your work to its end. It was packed in my box of books which, because it was treated as freight, took ten days to get here. In the meantime, Husserl asked me to come to Freiburg, and I was there for some time. I have been back now for several days and have read another portion of it.

I accept it as a habilitation thesis. It is fundamentally different from the draft, both in its level of questioning and also in its transparency of structure and linguistic expression.

Whether you substantively agree with me or not does not bear upon its acceptance or nonacceptance, nor does the question of whether or not you have understood my work in all of its fundamental aspects. The fact that you have been critical a bit too easily in places and have underestimated the difficulty of the problem and its foundations is something that I have only noted in the margins, and purely for your interest.

The veiled attacks and deliberate sideswipes are characteristic of the spirit in which one produces one's first real work. After a decade, such inclinations calm down, provided that one is able to channel all of one's ardor into the secure path of a vibrant life's work.

I will bring the matter before the faculty as soon as possible. The next steps depend upon whether the vacant position has been filled and whether Freiling's habilitation has concluded by then. Strong opposition has since arisen against the latter, and as a result Jaensch has not moved as quickly on the case as he had originally intended. He hoped that the work would be pushed through with the help of Mahnke as the "instructor"; since I do not understand the subject—that is, neither psychology nor pedagogy, but also with respect to your case—I have decided to remain neutral, which is not usually my style. Of course, I am also not going to engage in any bargaining regarding all of this. As far as I can fathom things, I do not believe that serious resistance can be expected. To be sure, Jaensch will become anxious when he realizes that you "also" do anthropology, and he will interpret the case in such a way as to think that I sent you against him. It is also possible that, when the habilitation gets underway, Hartmann will try to rally some opposition among his friends.

But these are things that you should not seriously worry about. Instead, you would do well to begin to consider some of the themes for your test lecture in front of the faculty and for your public inaugural lecture.

I do not know whether the nomination for the vacant spot has happened yet, since I left Saturday and have heard nothing more from Marburg since then. At the welcome dinner, the prominent gentlemen and their followers arrived rather late. There then unfolded a scene of such *ass-kissing* (*sit venia verbo* {"Pardon the expression"}) around the minister and Schmidt-Ott that I became sickened by the whole thing. I spent the next day stuck in a robe from 9 in the morning until 4 in the afternoon. The physical effort would have been bearable; but the spiritual toil was just too much. It's truly scandalous what banalities and barbarities are performed there. What transpired over the following two days was presumably still worse.

You should be clear in your mind about the step that you are venturing with your habilitation. One must be able to endure being ignored, and one must be prepared to wait. These days, the entire thing is a gamble. The fact that Natorp valued my Duns Scotus so highly; the fact that my days lecturing in Freiburg were so effective; the fact that people considered me to be an easy and harmless young man: all is happenstance. Today I would probably never be given an appointment. Whoever wants something will always be controversial; as a result, one is bound to fail from time to time. The fact that I may finish my days in Marburg is, however, not the greatest misfortune. For you, the bigger question is whether scholarship is so central to you that you advocate for the university, or whether you face the consequences of your work as Nietzsche did.

Regarding your work, it would be best to speak in person; I am not yet sufficiently proficient with it.

In Plessner's case, I have only one piece of advice: demand immediately that your manuscript be given back without any comments. Preferably, I would at the same time demand my removal from the editorial board, though for your sake I will refrain from doing so until after your habilitation. If I didn't, Hartmann—if I know him at all—would seek revenge by hobbling you in Marburg, if only through Jaensch. The Cologne review is obviously primarily a bashing of "the teacher," such things being most prevalent in Cologne. One has a trashcan for such things.

I would like to say only a few things in response to what you write regarding the problem of the ontic foundation of philosophy as ontology: first of all, I have always stressed, almost monotonously, the equiprimordiality of existence—thrownness and fallenness—and, correspondingly, the being of *Dasein* developed as care. The "approach" of fundamental ontology does not develop over the first ten pages, but rather through the entire treatise. Nonetheless, I say this: the analytic of *Dasein* is existential {*existenzial*}—it is thus guided by existence, because the "preparatory" analytic of *Dasein* (not ontological anthropology!) aims solely at the illumination of the understanding of being that belongs to *Dasein*. This understanding must also be made explicit by way of *Dasein*. The question is: Where and how do I obtain the horizon of the interpretation of this understanding? Yet, understanding characterizes existence—thus, the existential {*das Existenziale*} is both substantively and methodologically central, but in such a manner that, at the same time, the entirety of the fundamental structure of *Dasein* emerges. The "nature" of the human is not something appended to the "spirit." The question is: Is it possible to attain a foundation and a guideline regarding the conceptual interpretation of *Dasein* from out of nature or "spirit"—or from neither of the two, but rather originally from out of the entirety of the constitution of being, for which conceptual end the existential {*das Existenziale*} has a priority for the possibility of ontology? In that case, the anthropological interpretation can only be executed as an ontological one on the basis of a previously clarified ontological problematic. Thus, to my eyes, Becker's way of presenting the problem is perverse and philosophically impossible. Making mathematical "existence" a problem, while at the same time insisting that the difference between the ontic and the ontological is neither essential nor central: this simply demonstrates that he does not know what he wants or what he is doing.

What I expected was not so much an "application" of my investigations as an autonomous and foundational exposition of the mathematical problems of existence from out of what Becker takes to be the foundation of philosophy. But there is none of that—rather, my questioning has been forced onto a completely inappropriate plane.

Moreover, I am also convinced that ontology can only be grounded ontically, and believe that no one before me has grasped or articulated this. But ontic founding does not mean arbitrarily pointing to an ontic thing and then moving backward—rather, the ground for ontology can only be located when one knows what ontology is and then allows it, as ontology, to efface itself. The problems of facticity exist for me just as they did in the beginning in Freiburg, only much more radically and now seen from the perspectives that were also guiding me there. The fact that I constantly engaged with Duns Scotus and the Middle Ages, and then back to Aristotle, is no accident. And one cannot evaluate the work according to what one has said in lectures or tutorials. Previously, I had to go off into the extremes of the factical just in order to attain to facticity as a problem. Formal indication, criticism of common doctrines of a priori, formalism, etc., are all still present for me, even if I'm not writing to you about them now. Frankly, I am not interested in my development, but when it comes up for discussion, then one cannot just hastily patch it together out of the succession of lectures and what I am sharing with you now. Such a hasty consideration overlooks from all sides the central perspectives and underlying motivations.

"What one strives to understand as understandability cannot be decided theoretically." Indeed. But the question remains whether the psychoanalyzing of philosophizing, the ontic-psychological explanation of factical philosophizing, is itself already philosophy, or whether it is and must be something else in order for psychoanalytic questioning to have any meaning at all.

For a productive knowledge of the matter and a fruitful line of questioning, such analyses are not viable; they merely inhibit, prevent, and rigidify the complexes.

But, if you and Becker are already polemicizing against me in the sense of the battle against subjectivism, then I must insist that both you and Becker are much more characteriologically "subjective"—you are much more, and more intensively, occupied with the self than I am, and that the "with-others {*Miteinander*}" and the ["???"] grasped merely ontically by you both are determined in a highly subjective way. It is only a pretense if you believe you are thinking "more objectively."

Although ontically you appear to be bringing something more objective than "existence" to the table, at the same time you are unable—given what has come before—to gain and found ontologically the universal orientation that makes it possible to enter into that crucial communication with prior philosophy to which I aspire.

I have never been very interested in psychoanalysis, because both fundamentally and philosophically it does not seem relevant enough regarding the crucial issues. However, from the beginning, you and Becker have contorted my hermeneutics of facticity psychoanalytically, thereby forcing my work into perspectives in which it was never operative.

Thus, your relationship to me can only have changed on your end, and it apparently changed at that moment when you noticed that my work is not proceeding in the direction that you had anticipated, given your ontic interpretations.

On a personal level, I stand in the same relationship to you as before—excepting the differences brought to light in the development of our respective work. But for me this is yet one more reason to await—without pressuring or wooing—whether perhaps you will yet find a more confident path to a true friendship from out of a secured position regarding your own work and existence.

"Circles" are not friendships, a truth that reveals itself in the fact that at a certain point one tires of them.

With warm greetings,
   Your
      Martin Heidegger

The light in my little shack gave out, so I had to write almost completely in the dark.

**78.** *Martin Heidegger to Karl Löwith*
Todtbg, Oct.6.27

Dear Herr Löwith,

Many thanks for the birthday greeting and the "Aristotle." The picture is the best that I have ever seen. My holiday was ruined by a lengthy and arduous middle-ear infection. Indeed, I have only just recently recovered fully, and my work has not progressed as much as I had hoped. I will slowly make my way back to Marburg via Freiburg, Messkirch, and Heidelberg.

With warm greetings to you, and friendly regards to your parents,
   Your
      Martin Heidegger

**79.** *Karl Löwith to Martin Heidegger*
[Marburg] XII.29.27

Dear Herr Heidegger,

For the new year—Number 2 by Segantini. Since Christmas I have been reading Kaehler's "Humboldt" with the joy and excitement of those who encounter a book that they "understand" from A to Z and word for word. How different from the sterile mannequins of the Gundolf acolytes! This intellectual biography even surpasses Dilthey's *Schleiermacher* by a good amount—it's more "radical," because the actual story of Humboldt's spirit is revealed—the nature of his understanding of the undiminished reality of his personal life is grasped. Have you already looked at Kaehler's book?

Wishing you and yours a joyous ski-trip,
    Your
        Karl Löwith

**80.** *Karl Löwith to Martin Heidegger*
I.16.28

Dear Herr Heidegger,

Now that half a month has passed, I must request some money from my father—I had already written to him about the stipend failing to show up—he responded that he knows Schmidt-Ott personally from when he was still an advisor for art-related issues and recommended that I write to him—nothing like a little nepotism! I have responded that he should refrain from such suggestions and that I would rather he help me himself, in case my request, and an eventual inquiry on your part, should fail.

Now I would like to ask you whether I can count on receiving a salary for the position in the department beginning on May 1st, or whether I need to have habilitated first? (Also, what is the monthly amount?) Then I would need to rely on my father only for February, March, and April. Of course, I can change nothing regarding the psychological issues between fathers and sons regarding money.

I have now completed a first round of revisions on the draft, and have deleted everything that was askew in the introduction and the associated pages; in their place, I have prepended a short foreword in which the three concepts belonging to the title—"anthropology," "fundamental," and "ethical"—are clarified and delimited. Of course, I would like to rework the first part of the systematic chapter completely, but if I begin such revisions, there will be no end to them—the same is true with the Kant section, about which Krüger has given me some insightful comments. I will not be able to work on the two secondary topics for the inaugural and test lecture until month's end—revisions on the manuscript take a lot of time, often demanding the entire day. Hopefully Niemeyer gives a positive assessment soon. If my honorarium in any way complicates or hinders the progression of things, I will of course waive it.

I was at Klemperer's lecture last night—a very adroit speaker, but not much more than that—he blathered about terribly trivial things—afterward, the whole situation was very amusing. There was discussion amongst almost all of the professors who were present: Spitzer, Friedländer, Deutschbein, Hamann; the latter was the only one who made clever and considered comments and tried to "defend" the work of others, for example, Wechsler's book, etc. Friedländer threw himself into the arms of "classicism" with pathos—he began, somewhat unfortunately, with the point that it should have been the students and not the professors who were holding a discussion, for which point he received embarrassingly robust applause and became a bit flustered—he said that all of the terms Klemperer used ("culture," "patron," Volk, spirit of a Volk's culture, etc.) are "totally unclarified"—but luckily he also made no attempt to clarify them himself! Deutschbein, eager for popular approval, shouted (pro Klemperer) that in his field he would not allow for "working hypotheses" to be taken away, not "at any price"—why he said this, I don't know, because no one was trying to take such things away from him. Spitzer reconciled with Klemperer on the basis of a shared hostility toward Wechsler's book and concluded with a declaration of "love" for foreign literature—whereupon Hamann very sarcastically and deliberately brought reason back into the discussion and said that it is extremely important to be familiar with the foreign and exotic, the French, etc., and to learn how to regard one's own *Volk* as if it were foreign. Klemperer defended himself against Friedländer's "classical" indignation with the remark that classical philologists have it quite easy, owing to the fact that they are concerned with the dead—to which Friedländer replied, "I would never concern myself with the dead!!" In the end, Klemperer summarized all the objections very skillfully, and concluded with the nice statement that it all depends upon "intuition"!! Then they traded academic anecdotes over coffee in Café Markees. "Alma mater"—not even a circus could hold a candle to it! My well-behaved and disciplined Turazza, who is not accustomed to such "intellectual excitement" among Italian students, found it all very positive and said, *"che vita spirituale c'é in Germania* {what spiritual life there is in Germany}"—he is really my exact opposite; for example, he was impressed by the cafes here because the people are so well-bred and speak and sit so calmly and dispassionately that one can work or read as if one were "in a library"—the Italian cafes are dreadful to him, and what he finds unappealing about them is exactly what I find appealing. He feels as at home in Marburg as I do in Rome and regrets how ill-bred and cultureless Italians are. Incidentally, if you have the desire to get to know him sometime, please let me know—he is the polar opposite of Grassi!

With warm regards,
    Your
        Karl Löwith

**81.** *Martin Heidegger to Karl Löwith*
I.24.28

Dear Herr Löwith,

On the recommendation of Jaspers, a young Italian named Dr. Ernesto Grassi visited me from Milan; he has already been in Germany for some time and wishes to work on contemporary German philosophy. He would like to come here next winter for a year. Presently, he is here only until Monday.

Jaspers said to me that Grassi has an astonishing familiarity with my book; this was confirmed for me this morning. But even apart from this, he left a very pleasant and interesting impression—I think you would find a friend in him. Perhaps you could also help him along.

I invited him to a glass of wine this evening (at 8:30) and told him that I would ask you to join us.
    With warm greetings,
      Your
        Martin Heidegger

**82.** *Martin Heidegger to Karl Löwith*
II.7.28

Dear Herr Löwith,

On Saturday, I wrote to both Niemeyer and Husserl. However, it will take a few days for the response to reach us, since Niemeyer is incapable of making arrangements without all manner of ado. Also, Pfänder is keen to accommodate the work of his students that has already been lying around awhile. Under the present circumstances, I myself will be unable to publish in the fall, since I require an entire volume to do so. You will of course receive an honorarium, even though this will be your first time publishing in the *Jahrbuch*. In any case, I will make sure of it. With this you could then pay the interest.

The work is already back with me and has not progressed, since Jaensch also has a lot on his plate at the moment.

Come tomorrow at 11:30; I spent both Saturday and Sunday resting because of some boils, and have thus lost so much time.

There are some things that you can certainly still change—purely stylistic things and the "tone." Whether or not you will be able to get the commentary on my publication on the right track is another question entirely—but it is not important. I must only know approximately what you want to change, so that I can include a corresponding note with my report: for there of course must be no discrepancy between what the faculty sees and what you publish.

I have inquired with the curator regarding the premature awarding of the stipend. It appears also to have been a mistake on Gadamer's part. In any case, the submission can only be made if the curator himself has the habilitation in hand.

Whether it is advisable to make a request of the emergency assistance program at this point is a matter I must still consider.

Keep your head high; things are not so bad. When I was a student I faced every semester with nothing—I had to go into debt and go hungry.

    With kind regards,
      Your
        Martin Heidegger

**83.** *Martin Heidegger to Karl Löwith*
Mbg, II.21.[1928]

Dear Herr Löwith,

I have written to the emergency assistance program. I have received no reply from Husserl. Just in case, you could inquire in Munich about the publication of your book, so that if you decide to make use of it things can begin immediately.

By the way—wasn't Schmalenbach's Leibniz book published there?

As soon as the rest of it gets underway, we will make an application to the emergency assistance program.

    With kind regards,
      Your
        Martin Heidegger

**84.** *Martin Heidegger to Karl Löwith*
Todtnauberg, III.16.28

Dear Herr Löwith,

I will be here in the near future, and will be expecting your application. So far we have had marvelous weather and excellent snow. I stopped in Freiburg only for a very short while. I am still unsure when I will travel to Berlin.

Please send my best to Afra.

    With warm regards,
      Your
        Martin Heidegger

**85.** *Martin Heidegger to Karl Löwith*
Todtnaubg, III.20.28

Dear Herr Löwith,

I immediately forwarded your application and believe that it will be approved. My own matters are still undecided.
    One thing is certain: The goodwill of the Baden government is exceptional and grand, contrary to all expectation.
    It is still uncertain when I will go to Berlin.
    Before I do, I will indulge myself in a few weeks of work.
    With kind regards,
      Your
        Martin Heidegger

**86.** *Martin Heidegger to Karl Löwith*
IV.29.28

Dear Herr Löwith,

The committee's meeting was set for the evening of Tuesday, May 2nd, but had to be postponed for a few days. The committee stands in agreement; thus, your work can be disseminated to the faculty as quickly as possible.
    During this semester, which will be even more chaotic than the previous one, I will hardly have any time to study your book. To judge by the typeface, I think it will also be an attractive publication.
    When I have some free time in the near future, I will invite you for a stroll.
    With kind regards,
      Your
        Martin Heidegger

**87.** *Martin Heidegger to Karl Löwith*
[Summer 1928]

Dear Herr Löwith,

Since the final committee meeting regarding my successor took place the day before yesterday, and because there is a faculty meeting this evening, I am completely swamped with the drafting of the assessment, owing also to the fact that my other "colleagues" allow others to do their work for them.

It would only be possible Friday evening, but even then the time is just too short. But I also believe it is unnecessary. Regarding form, I would like to suggest this once again: to speak louder, more slowly, and, above all, stop "slurring" the last third of your sentences. After your practice lecture, a faculty member observed—and not incorrectly—that you have forgotten the "other": it was pure monologue.

Apart from that, I believe that your habilitation as a whole was much better than Fahrner's, which dragged on for much too long on account of the indefensible chatter of the gentlemen, as well as that of Fahrner himself. Yours was much shorter.

[Farewell and closing missing.]

**88.** *Martin Heidegger to Karl Löwith*
[End of summer, 1928]

Dear Herr Löwith,

I would like to extend my heartfelt gratitude for your kind and beautiful words of farewell. Unfortunately, there is now such a tumult that everything is happening with great commotion.

My application regarding your stipend was unanimously approved yesterday evening and will be sent to Berlin in the next few days.

I will be back during the first few days of September.

I wish you much joy and a wonderful time in Copenhagen.
    With kind regards,
      Your
        Martin Heidegger

**89.** *Martin Heidegger to Karl Löwith*
The hut, IX.28.28

Dear Herr Löwith,

Thank you so much for the birthday wishes. Memories leave quite an impression. I sent out the submission to the emergency assistance program along with my accompanying letter. I also sent out an official letter to the faculty, as well as one to Jacobsthal and your father. I am rooming very peacefully here with Jörg. Hermann is in Feldafing. On the last day I still had too much work; moreover, I was detained by Bultmann. I wish you a beautiful and productive semester.
    With warm regards,
      Your
        Martin Heidegger

**90.** *Martin Heidegger to Karl Löwith*
The hut, Oct.7.28

Dear Herr Löwith,

The robe is mine. However, the faculty will take it over, as in all such cases: all robes eventually become the property of the faculty. I need a different one here—different both in cut and in color.

You will not be able to do anything with mine, since non-Ordinarius professors have no lapels. I think that mine will be reserved for an Ordinarius Professor.

Regarding the lecture manuscript, it often comes about that one simply has too much, or, alternatively, that the revisions undertaken during the semester give the initial draft an entirely new form.

What to set as the maximum for the lecture is up to you; there is no general rule to follow. Depending on the material and the issue, both structure and execution can change. There is only one dictum that I would like to take the liberty of recommending to you: do not listen to the gossip of Deutschbein in these or in other matters, even if he is thought of as a bigshot amongst the students in Marburg.

Becker was up here recently for a few days. The waiting is slowly putting him on edge. Hopefully something happens before the semester begins.

Figure 5  Group of Six Philosophers; Martin Heidegger and Karl Löwith at Right (circa 1925).

We are moving back next week. I am very much looking forward to the winter, and hope for some quieter time to work.
With warm regards
Your
Martin Heidegger

The card is a Cézanne.

**91.** *Martin Heidegger to Karl Löwith*
Frbg, X.22.28

Dear Herr Löwith,

I heard from Gadamer just now, to whom I still owe an answer, that neither Jaensch nor Mahnke are still lecturing. Although I have nothing more to say in Marburg, I would strongly advise you—both for your sake and for the sake of the field—to hold at least a three-hour a week lecture concerning the history of modern philosophy since Descartes. You just have to immerse yourself and take from it what you can get. What you have planned for the other lecture won't go to waste.
Of course, it's best to wait until the appointment takes place. In any case, I would hold a bigger and more general lecture by means of which you could also introduce yourself to the students.
I make this suggestion in haste. Many thanks for the essay.
Your
Martin Heidegger

**92.** *Martin Heidegger to Karl Löwith*
[Freiburg] X.24.28

Dear Herr Löwith,

Frank already wrote me a few days ago; his letter was sent to me in a roundabout way. I had not expected this outcome. But Becker is taking the news very calmly. You will soon realize that Frank is different from the representatives there. And I believe that you will have his support.
It strikes me as unlikely that a representative will come after the appointment has been made. If so, then I can only wonder why it was not then also necessary when I held both professorships for two years. I *would* have to wonder such things, though I in fact won't do so, since I have tossed aside my time in Marburg in a gesture that is the opposite of a "repetition"—indeed, so much so that, since my time there, I have even physically felt to be in an entirely different condition.

Therefore, if representation does not come, you must absolutely lecture for three hour a week. This does not concern the faculty. Evidently, very good but hidden friends were all too worried about you, and who knows by what mysterious means. In the future, do not be too surprised if you come to experience more, and more powerfully, the demoralization of the university.

I hope that the collaboration here together will be pleasant.

Herr Grassi is already fervently annoying me.

Warm greetings, also from v. Rohden.

    Your

        Martin Heidegger

**93.** *Martin Heidegger to Karl Löwith*
[Freiburg] XII.23.28

Dear Herr Löwith,

Many thanks for your two letters. It especially pleases me that you are having such fine success with your teaching. And I also hope for you that you will find productive resistance. That one should have "followers" and the attending opponents are indeed only a side effect that cannot and should not become important for the first period of one's teaching experience. But what is essential is that the teacher harnesses the unfettered power to engage himself even more vehemently the less certain he is whether or not he is reaching his students.

The philosophizing Dozent has a completely different position in the university in relation to his "colleagues," though very few people understand this.

And it is nothing surprising that the students—even the clever and interested ones—do not even know what it takes for one to have to ascend to the lectern for months at a time and speak about essential things. With this I am not thinking about the requirements of formal preparation, which one can never take seriously enough, given that a lecture can only be good if the Dozent always understands quite a bit "more" (i.e., more originally) than what he says and how he says it. Of course, that does not mean that he must hold the pernicious opinion of having "settled" things once and for all.

I mean here the readiness of the commitment of one's entire person, which simply must *be* in place precisely where one should not feel obliged to speak about the personal.

But it is not good to reflect too much about such things.

On the other hand, your external situation requires much consideration. I hear from Schröer's daughter, who got married here and whom I only recently met (even though she and my brother were in the same class at the Gymnasium), that her father is coming here over the Christmas holiday. It would be best to deal with such a matter face-to-face. I will attempt to resolve both issues (i.e., the completion of the application and not endangering the Privatdozent scholarship). If Schröer does not come here or is inaccessible, I will have to write to him about the matter.

The obtaining of the retroactive increase of the Privatdozent scholarship is a simple duty of the dean and the faculty, and of certain individual members (Frank in particular). Certainly, it would be easier and more comfortable to avoid confrontation and to be viewed as an "affable colleague." In this way, one expends no energy and has the benefits of a reputation for being a polite person who takes care of others by doing absolutely nothing.

If you wish, I will write to Jacobsthal. However, I doubt that doing so will have any practical consequence, and it may even make the administration more stubborn. A similar thing happened to me two years ago; when I became Hartmann's successor, I was "granted" a meager increase in salary—not, however, on October 1st, the date of the official appointment, but rather two months later on December 1st. Such shabbiness, due to which I spent two years as the replacement for a representative and had to chase down the administration to get the pay owed to me as Ordinarius.

More important than all of this is the matter of the emergency assistance program.

The winter days here are glorious. I've already been up several times; after the holidays we will go to the hut. The boys are not currently up here, and they have such fun and comradery with the neighbor's children that they feel no desire to come.

I wish you a tranquil Christmas holiday, and send you my warm greetings.

    Your
        Martin Heidegger

**94**. *Martin Heidegger to Karl Löwith*
Frbg, IV.21.29

Dear Herr Löwith,

Thank you for your card. Unfortunately, Niemeyer is quite stingy with offprints, and I have so many obligations to official recipients that I must put an end to it at some point; otherwise, I would have been happy to send you one.

However, I have arranged with Niemeyer for the essay to appear separately in the bookstore, where (so Becker tells me) copies are already available.

Thus, Ebel is misinformed, or perhaps Niemeyer wants to hold back the offprints so that more people will purchase the entire volume.

Davos disrupted my holiday season; however, I did have the opportunity to go on a few wonderful ski trips.

I have had enough experiences with lecture reports that I no longer care about the echoes of my own lectures, and certainly not about the lectures of others—I simply "take note."

With kind regards, and the very best wishes for the second semester
    Your
        Martin Heidegger

**95.** *Karl Löwith to Martin Heidegger*
[Marburg] 5.9.29

Dear Herr Heidegger,

Thank you so much for the information. Meanwhile, the Hessian intelligentsia represented by a certain Ebel has delivered the offprint of your treatise.

The quantity of students—and, above all, of female students—is increasing to an alarming degree, and the quality is sinking proportionally—considered purely physiognomically, the impression one has of what's indiscriminately filling the lecture halls is devastating. Although Marburg, as a "summer university," should always be better in the winter, I nevertheless have the impression of a generalized, sociological shift—for now we have the mass arrival of all those children of small business owners and tradespeople, high-school diplomas in hand, who wish to become something "better," whereas the intelligentsia of the former middleclass, most likely due to economic reasons, is moving more into technical trades and technical universities, etc.—it is quite apparent, for example, that now many Marburg businesspeople allow their sons and daughters to study, when before they would have long since taken them into the family business. The consequence is that in most lectures, even those of the "philosophical" faculty, the "Deutschbein"-Jaensch-Mahnke type dominates—even Mommsen, whose first session I attended, made thousands of cheap concessions right off the bat to the educational background, ability to grasp concepts, and laziness of his students—elementary school stuff—and unfortunately, Frank lectures all too "mandatorily," as well—the first session of his course was essentially not that different from A. Messer's commentary on Kant—just a bit more verbally ecstatic. Although there are quite a number of people in my lecture series on Dilthey—about fifty to sixty—I have the impression that most of them find it terribly sophisticated and scholarly; and with some of them I have the impression that they must make quite an effort, for example, to figure out the difference between "to explain" and "to understand." Many from the prior semester are also among them. But because I myself would like to continue advancing my work, I don't even consider making concessions; instead, I just keep lecturing the way I have planned, and eventually one or another among them will notice that it pays off to engage one's intellect concerning objective questions, and that it does not pay off simply to listen to some generic, four-hour drivel.

In the seminar I'm running with Fahrner, the people are much better (but there is also, unfortunately, the abundantly confused senior Jacoby!), and I am really enjoying the collaboration with Fahrner. He has an admirable ability to subordinate himself to "language," despite differing opinions—he sees all things from out of the creative language of the "great poets"—and is always able to animate discussion in a fruitful way that does not simply pull us in another direction. Moreover, he is also very intelligent and logically rigorous.

In addition, along with some others from the A. V., I am reading Dostoevsky's *Notes from the Underground* and *The Dream of a Ridiculous Man*—the theological society arranged a lecture series on the Russian church for this semester: Nötzel, Stephun, Koch (Vienna), etc.

Gadamer will probably write to you himself.

I am now ordering many books for the department, since Frank received 2,000 marks for new acquisitions—and this place is wanting of the most important works. My personal antiquarian knowledge is actually of use here! That reminds me: While unpacking your library, did you find the Huizinga? If not, it's not a big deal.

It's only the third day of spring here, and everything is already blooming rapidly and outrageously.

If you see Becker, please give him my regards—I was sure he would write, but now I guess I will.

Do you have a little picture of your house, along with its inhabitants?

My warm greetings to you,

    Your

        Karl Löwith

**96.** *Martin Heidegger to Karl Löwith*
Todtnauberg, Sept. 3. 29

Dear Herr Löwith,

To you and your bride, whom I remember quite well, my wife and I send our most heartfelt congratulations for your betrothal.

I am especially happy for you. Not only because "appearances" will be easier and more relaxed for you, but also because it will be essentially enriching for you, which will also have a beneficial effect on your work.

The danger of becoming a member of the "bourgeoisie" is not very great—indeed, it would not exist at all if everyone knew how to initiate what is essential within themselves. Far more threatening for us living today is boredom with the tediousness of all things, from which one flees, together hand in hand, into "society" and artificial conviviality.

But none of this is really a problem if you two proceed along the chosen path decisively, and from out of your present reality.

Regarding your academic beginnings, you have the very best conditions and have accrued successes. Everyone must make their own ground here—that is the driving force in this profession, however manifold the shortcomings of our present-day universities may be. Human activity cannot flourish where there is no resistance. It is already enough if one maintains the security of one's own course, but in the adhering to and expanding of this course, one should not become the seemingly sole possessor of a single, paltry thought. In order to maintain this true center, one must be calm and tranquil and trust in the creative force that simply comes over one.

Only in this way is the individual strong enough to bear the burden for a truly free relationship to youth. For youth does not wish to know anything about sectarianism, and is thankful—not only theoretically, but authentically—if it is led out and away from all scholastic bickering and inflated, academic significances. As trying as the days in Davos were—due to an unremitting busyness and journalism—they were also valuable to me, for they confirmed my conviction that there must still be a new and good substantiality somewhere in the youth, and moreover, that this can be found and awakened—and this only through the resoluteness of actual, singular *Dasein*. It is only within this concretion that the spiritual and intellectual can uphold and renew itself—all of that Olympian and fluffed-up universal objectivity becomes shadowy and a mere fleeting pleasure for the aesthetes of the profession.

After a very work-intensive summer semester, I have spent some beautiful weeks at Lake Starnberg, and have also spent a long time with my brother back home. Because the mail was not forwarded to me there, I only received your announcement at the end of August.

The concluding remark of your postcard sounds as if you are seeing things. I have already written to you once before that I place no value on the telling of tales, and most especially that I don't interrogate people about others or, as has become common amongst my colleagues, request lecture transcripts. And if my own, inner contempt and easy transcendence regarding such activities should be insufficient to keep me away from them, then surely the many experiences I myself have had regarding the effect of the albeit necessary (but always half-understood and distorted) lecture reviews should do so.

The question of whether one goes along with *Being and Time* is of no concern to me. Never for a single moment have I expected that my work will bring about an effect directly or overnight. I wouldn't be understanding my own undertaking very well if I didn't know that everything must first, and for a long time, make its way through chatter. Of course, I never dreamed that it would become fashionable, nor that the apparently well-meaning explanatory palaver of the professors would become so boundlessly superficial (Misch, for example).

I thank Fate that I am truly made of the kind of stuff that cannot be harmed by all this whispering and whining. Despite the inner necessity of the creative process, I would rather choose to remain in utter silence than have my work be dependent on this profession.

You already know how I feel about psychoanalysis and an anthropologically/psychologically driven philosophy of reflection. You also know that I will not participate in this, and that I regret your inability to harden yourself in this regard. The inaugural lecture about Burckhardt that you presented to me and others differed from the published essay. The fact that you cannot get away from Dilthey, Nietzsche, and psychoanalysis was proven during your very first semester when you did not follow my advice to study a wider range of historical {*geschichtliche*} lectures, which would have forced you into other matters. But how could I blame you for such things! Then, I could have quite easily and effortlessly prevented your habilitation. You could search and search among the bigwigs in power for a single person who would habilitate a student with such contradictory work. I don't say this to make myself sound better—but I wonder more and more how little you really understand my position and my desires when you, as your remarks indicate, suspect an annoyance on my part. Becker is neither silent, nor does he have reason to be careful; rather, he has enough to do on his own, especially if you consider his two entirely unjust setbacks. He does not speak about it, but understandably finds it all very difficult. I have trust in you that your work, whichever way it may take, is bolstered by an earnest conviction with which you struggle and for which you take responsibility. Everything else is unimportant.

With warm greetings and sincere congratulations,
    Your
        Martin Heidegger

**97.** *Martin Heidegger to Karl Löwith*
[Freiburg] XI.17.29

Dear Herr Löwith,

Thank you so much for your letter, which I was very happy to receive. The way that you formulate the theme of your essays for the theological review very much piques my curiosity.

In the coming days, the last of Scheler's essays will appear under the title "Philosophische Weltschauung."

As a Christmas gift, here is my inaugural lecture, "What is Metaphysics," which demonstrates very clearly where I stand—and better still, where I am going. For I am now only in the decisive beginning and am able to direct destructuring against myself—without falling into nihilism.

It has been clear to me for some time that the contemporary world has not yet understood Nietzsche.

The other day I found Huizinga's *Herbst des Mittelalters*, to my great joy and relief. You should receive it within the coming days.

Will you and your wife be coming to our parts any time soon?

With kind regards from home to home
 Your
  Martin Heidegger

**98.** *Karl Löwith to Martin Heidegger*
Marburg a/L, Kirchhainerweg 22
XII.22.29

Dear Herr Heidegger,

Your letter from XI.17 has left me quite delighted. Thank you so much for it! I obtained your inaugural lecture given in Freiburg regarding the "nothing" from Ebel a few days ago and have just read it again word for word. The way you proceed in this essay is much clearer and more comprehensible to me than "The Essence of Ground"—the few sentences about "boredom" and the "boldness" of *Dasein* pleased me very much on a personal level, probably owing to the fact that I sense in such sentences the fact that you, even after having published a "system" about *Dasein*, have preserved an inner freedom and elasticity of thought that allows you always to be on the way toward new transformations and discoveries—to be sure, I never saw you as having "ossified" in any way, but the involuntary tyranny of one's own "work" seemed to me to be a danger for you from time to time. Thus, I can understand very well why you are only now confronting Nietzsche, and nothing would please me more than to have the opportunity to philosophize together with you and perhaps collaborate on some tutorials on Nietzsche's later writings—that is, nihilism and the doctrine of recurrence. I have once again become very attentive to the paramount importance and true radicalism of Nietzsche, just as when I worked for some weeks over the summer at the Nietzsche archive in Weimar; and I still hold the treasured thought of embarking on a systematic interpretation of Nietzsche, something I cannot imagine doing without recalling with gratitude the education in scholarly interpretation you imparted to me. According to the stated theme, it was about Augustine and Aristotle—but what was learned there can serve just as well in the study of Nietzsche.

It wasn't mere stubbornness or laziness on my part when I failed to take your advice about my first semester of teaching, namely, to cover Descartes through Kant, but then instead lectured for two hours about Nietzsche's later writings. In light of the question of nihilism, I am now (privately) reading Descartes' "view of certainty," etc.—Descartes, who was doubtlessly a daredevil and was in this respect anything but a "classicist"—do you know the portrait of Descartes by Franz Hals? I saw a brilliant sketch (of the great painting in the Louvre) in Copenhagen—what a fabulous face!

And it wasn't only the case that flashes of something fresh and new jumped out at me in your lecture—even seemingly definitive determinations from *Being and Time*, such as "anxiety," are now more comprehensible to me. Are you familiar with J. Conrad's wonderful story "The Shadow Line"? If you don't have it, I would like to send it to you—I know of nothing in world literature that has brought the "enthralled calm" of anxiety so vividly to light, and that has so clearly captured the existential decisiveness of this situation.

One more thing: whereas the final chapter of your Kant book did not make it clear to me why "*Dasein*" should be "more originary" than the human, and the claim that the character of *Dasein* "in" the human is more originary than just "the human," which should also not be a mere tautology according to the following elucidation: what the human "is," ontologically, according to its pure way of being can only be "understood" ontologically on the basis of a prior analysis of "*Dasein*"—for then it would indeed be tautological to say that the human only "is" the human on the basis of the *Dasein* within him—however, although this is the sense of this sentence, in reality it is neither tautological nor self-evident; and a justification for why this is so was lacking from *Being and Time*, a jettisoning of the "neutrality" of essential ontological claims, and I see the first signs of such an attempt on pages 17 and 18 of your lecture, where this "purity" of *Dasein* is proven on the basis of the "one" (and not "me" or "you") who experiences anxiety, and where you say that anxiety "transforms" the "human" into a pure "*Dasein*." In the article for the theological review, the corrected draft of which I received a month ago (though Bultmann has told me that it won't appear until the January issue), I have posed the question about the meaning of "neutrality." (The question serves as a transition to Part II, which will make significant reference to *Being and Time*.) However, because your lecture had not yet been published, I could not yet refer to it. I will make up for it in part two.

What I have seen in the reviews of *Being and Time* is almost completely impossible—P. Hofmann and H. Barth strike a balance with regard to the insubstantiality of their confused marginal notes—in my opinion, what Misch has written is still the best when compared with these so-called "critical engagements."

From what I heard, Bröcker is traveling today with Gadamer—but I decided not to go and fetch the latest news from "Freiburg," because as interested as I would be in hearing your lecture, I take Bröcker to be a very inadequate reporter—a perpetual schoolboy who has only changed his school colors and now gets bored in Berlin rather than in Freiburg—but not "authentically," though perhaps close to this dangerous boundary. Do you think you should simply give him something difficult to work on? For, he doesn't seem to have any initiative of his own, but through his negative savvy and his drawn-out and unfocused studies he has acquired a sterile air of superiority—it is probably high time that he makes some sort of decision—when he visited me on his way to Freiburg, I had the impression that he was slowly getting sick of himself. I myself do not know what to do with such northern Holsteiners and Hamann admirers—I saw within him once again the devastating effect that a pure study of philosophy can have. For example, this danger in no way exists here in Marburg under the protectorate of the triumvirate Jaensch-Mahnke-Frank. Since we three private Dozents are not eligible for exams and, as is commonly said, are so much more "difficult" in the lectures than the Ordinarius professors are, we don't serve as a counterweight in this regard. This difficulty consists simply in the fact that all three of us have learned from you not to be satisfied with mere words that come in one ear and go out the other.

In my lecture course "Freudian Psychoanalysis and its Anthropological Foundations," there were at first a lot of people, including doctors; however, about half of them dropped the course when they observed that I am not a psychoanalytic sexologist and that I was developing such "abstract" things as a philosophical interpretive approach grounded on the difference between "understanding" and "explanation," while also analyzing X concepts from the unconscious—now a reasonable number of thoughtful and diligent people remain, some of whom I have gotten to know a bit better through the course of the seminar.

Jaensch has sent a failed doctor of medicine to the seminar, one who knows nothing about either medicine or psychoanalysis, but who works as a physician in a "life education" sanatorium. I came across him in a tavern one time—he was good and drunk, and ever since then he has been very sheepish. The amazing thing is that Jaensch is working with him on "hysteria" in order to discover a C-type! Jaensch tells me that he has an article in press—it contains, among other things, a "critical engagement" with your Kant—he has discovered that eidetics also unifies the two types of cognition in an originary way, and wants, via eidetics, to "reach out a hand to you"! Isn't that precious? Mahnke is still brooding about "renaissance philosophers," and Frank is still cultivating his erudition.

Over the summer semester I will tackle the question of "concepts" under the title "Foundational Problems in the Philosophy of Language" (Hamann, Herder, Humboldt, perhaps also Leibniz). I will do this for one hour, and then also continue the "persona" analyses of the habilitation thesis for one hour, approaching it historically {*geschichtlich*}. I will do this second hour under the title "Introduction to Philosophical Sociology"—a seminar on the philosophy of language. Now, that title sounds very sprawling and unphilosophical—but it is unfortunately the case that with more specialized titles and topics the students would stay away, since our three Ordinarius professors are not the right ones to attract the students to specialized courses in philosophy. And despite a 15 percent deduction for purposes of tuition remission, the money from the college helps offset the meager stipend. Things are such with me presently that my stipend from the emergency assistance program of 150 runs out on December 31, 1929—the last extension was expressly approved as the "last" extension for the preceding one (and not as a new one befitting the extended topic that I had formulated), and there likely isn't even the slightest prospect of receiving another stipend from the emergency assistance program. Because I have received only 85 of state-supported money, apart from what I have from the emergency assistance program and the 50 from the seminar, I have requested by way of the curator an increase of the state-sponsored stipend starting on I.1.30—Frank is so cautious and fussy that it was better to approach the curator directly, who immediately forwarded and supported my application. This would be an increase to 150 starting on I.1—so that from now on I will receive 150 + 50 (from the seminar) totaling 200, rather than the 85 + 150 from the emergency assistance program + the 50 from the seminar (totaling 285)—for her work for the Liszt society my wife earns around 100—but since we are now entirely dependent upon ourselves, it is extremely tight with the 300, and Frank + the curator know of no other way to get beyond the state's stipend of 150. Occasionally, this is all regretted as an "undignified" state of affairs—but nobody does anything about it. I would be very thankful if you could give me any advice about how to improve my financial situation. The disastrous thing is that both the ministry and the emergency assistance program work against us, and to our disadvantage—reciprocally withdrawing their subsidies whenever the other entity steps in with a minimum. Moreover, under the general austerity of the minister along with the insufficient initiative of Frank, teaching positions don't appear to be possible.

Even so, the two of us live here on our pastoral and remote *Kirchhainerweg* in our cute miniature apartment cheerfully and with serenity, and with the confidence that even though it will be tight, we will make it through. Incidentally, the socialist student group recently asked me to give a free lecture—I told them that it is too contradictory to Marxist ideology to want to have a purely ideological lecture!

My wife, who heard you lecture while earning her degree in Frankfurt at the time, has asked me to send you her best. If our path should take us to your area, I will make certain to check with you about availability in a timely manner. For now, happy holidays!

Warmest greetings to you,
    Your
        Karl Löwith

**99.** *Karl Löwith to Martin Heidegger*
[Marburg] IV.2.30

Dear Herr Heidegger,

The press announces the news of your appointment and acclaim on all fronts, so much so that I received the news without even having read the newspaper. The news did not surprise me; it pleased me that the minister of culture chose you over little Spranger-like and Maier-like talking heads, and I am only curious about whether or not you will accept the position. In and of itself, "Berlin" is temptation personified, but you have successfully resisted the various temptations, and I can well imagine that even in the "midst" of this "way of being"—"The Berlin Chair"—you could remain who you are, namely, a steadfast individual whom the institution cannot harm. And the opportunities for political efficacy at the university level are naturally much greater in Berlin than they are in Freiburg. Thus, when I read the articles from the Munich papers that my parents sent me, and those from Berlin that my parents-in-law sent me, I was becalmed and satisfied: already in 1919/1920, when you didn't yet have any "press," let alone such glimmering praise, you possessed an adamantine instinct for the inner substance of what you presented to us at the time. Ever since then, an astonishing number of students have learned an unconditional respect for philosophy through you, and you have probably experienced more joy with some of them than you did with me. Indeed, the more distance I gain from the problem of the professor/student relationship—a problem for both sides of the equation, especially in philosophy—the more it appears to me like the relationship between "fathers and sons"—because at times both sides are the deciding factor: the proper and well-timed form of detaching, of becoming autonomous, and preserving what the young owe the old. This can never go smoothly—the unreflective imitations of schoolboys and "slave revolts" are the terrible extremes between which one must navigate.

My idea for "anthropological" philosophy has gained a fresh clarity, and thus, at the same time, a freer understanding of your own contribution to it. When Herr Driesch, in an article about both "unrestrained and cautious philosophy" (his, of course, being the "cautious" variant), speaks, without mentioning your name, of a "new value philosophy" that plays "acrobatically" with the "word" "nothing," it is easy to laugh—the praises are most of all easy to laugh at, because they, without knowing it, are the glistening testament of the "they." Everyone now shamelessly appropriates your fame, and nobody understands that it would be an honor to Troeltsch, and not to you, were you to be appointed as his successor—for nobody sees that Troeltsch failed to progress beyond Dilthey, but rather remained behind him.

Hopefully, you needn't lose the calm respite of your holiday as a consequence of the appointment.

I add the following as a subsequent question to my last letter regarding my financial situation: Would you strongly discourage me from possibly making myself available for the philosophical faculty at the pedagogical academies, just in case Frank cannot obtain a teaching appointment for me within the coming years? If I were still *solus ipse*, I probably never would have considered it; however, as a married man, I am compelled to contemplate such evils. I have learned by chance that the arranging of such things is conducted by a certain Herr von den Driesch from the Berlin ministry of culture.

Herr "Court-Photographer" Mauss has felt compelled to photograph me, on his own dime, in order to complete his pictures of the Dozents—*ecce* the results! He intended to capture something "beautiful," but it ended up turning out rather ordinary. Perhaps it will please you to have one of your first students in black and white in this way.

I send to you, and to your wife,
    My warm regards,
        Your
            Karl Löwith

**100**. *Karl Löwith to Martin Heidegger*
[Marburg] VII.17.30

Dear Herr Heidegger,

We were invited to the Jaceks yesterday evening—their very beautiful modern house is quite close to us—and so I was finally able to hear about you again, albeit indirectly: namely, about your river cruise from Aschaffenburg to Würzburg. Würzburg is well-known to me—as a young artist my father did many studies in the castle there, and for our wedding he gave us one of the paintings, because we got engaged in Würzburg one year ago. Have you ever seen the magnificent fresco by Tiepolo on the ceiling above the grand staircase? My wanderlust is as strong as ever; however, my salary does not reach as far for two as it did for one. But we did spend ten days in Paris and Chartres over Easter, owing to the fact that I have an uncle who was so kind as to have invited us. By now, you will also have heard about us through Afra Geiger—at least, she intended to travel back through Freiburg.

Your decision not to go to Berlin has made me very happy—it is not necessary that Berlin should swallow everything, and your intellectual efficacy would not be any lesser or less intensive in Freiburg than it would be in the formal center of things. Since your departure, Marburg is without a philosophical heart: it has even come about that neither theologians nor philologists here even study philosophy seriously, and one must be content if, among the many auditors, there are at least a few who remain devoted for multiple semesters.

The two lecture courses provide me with much pleasure, and my idea of an "anthropological" philosophy comes into clarity ever more concretely—in the philosophy of language, I exclusively interpreted Herder's treatise concerning the "origin of language" (and, additionally, Hamann's critique)—now I am carrying the matter up to J. Grimm's treatise in order to show the crisis in the philosophy of language and linguistics. The other course—philosophical sociology—allows me to extend somewhat the analyses of my habilitation thesis to the unique "societal" phenomena in which the I–You category is not captured. That provided me with the general opportunity to delve into sociology (I have also again been studying a lot of Max Weber), though most of it is not philosophically productive, and everywhere I am obliged to start from the ground up—that's how primitive this modern discipline of sociology is in all questions of principle. Most important to me was a foundational study of Hegel's *Philosophy of Right*—and the superb critique of it by Marx (published for the first time in its entirety in Volume 1 of the first half of the big collected works of Marx–Engels). I will lecture on these things for the first time next semester under the title "Marx and Hegel"—additionally, I will offer a follow-up course to the philosophy of language, from Humboldt to Leibniz.

I am less pleased with my seminar this go around. My intention was, on the basis of Klages' text "Ausdruckslehre und Charakterkunde," to offer the students a supplement to the philosophy of language—to clarify the difference between linguistic and unmediated "expression," but the very few who initially had interest in such things are so disparate and primitive in their training that each time it is a tedious labor just to get the cart moving, so to speak, and no real momentum can be reached in the tutorials. I did not want to take the usual Dozent path of lecturing, forcing them to cram, and testing them in the tutorials, but they were all too immature—and just lazy!—to have any real discussion. Freyer was here for a lecture—a good presentation as far as content goes, but very clever in a business-like manner, and rather cheap in a routine kind of way.

The second part of the phenomenology/theology essay was delivered to Bultmann some time ago, but unfortunately has not yet been published—most important for me in all of this was a critical discussion of the difference between the ontic and the ontological. I am curious what you will have to say about it, especially since I have not yet heard back about the first part.

I will be here through August—I will probably spend September with my parents in Munich. On the outside, our situation has not changed—so long as my wife is making money with her work on the Liszt edition, we will manage to make it through the winter, and I will continue to hope that Frank can secure me a lectureship in sociology. However, it all depends on the allocation from the state, and even if it were to be granted, it is highly questionable whether the payment will be as big as my current stipend of 160 marks. What wretched prospects. I don't really know what the prospects are for the possibility of philosophical work at a "pedagogical academy"—I've already written about this to you once before. So, one must live hand to mouth from semester to semester—in itself, this is not an unphilosophical way to live, but it is very unpleasant for one who is married. But at least I am all set for the winter semester, since Father Rochlow in Kassel has arranged a lecture series for me.

Will I ever again hear about you and your plans? I think of you very often and of all that I have received from you and will hold onto forever. The ascent to the lectern is sometimes a sour affair for me, but on the whole I believe that it was undoubtedly the right thing for me to pursue this task and none other, and it would make me very happy to hear that you also share this conviction about my habilitation. But the university is making great strides in its decline, and the popularity of people such as Deutschbein and Jaensch is increasing while that of more intellectually demanding lectures is diminishing—the purely professionalized and exam-oriented course of study dominates, and to that end there are countless "hoops" to jump through. "Academic freedom" is seen as purely negative, and is exactly as Nietzsche described it in his lectures on the future of German educational institutions.

Will you spend part of your holiday in Freiburg, or in the hut? If we travel your way, my wife and I would love to visit you.

With the warmest regards,
Your
Karl Löwith

**101.** *Martin Heidegger to Karl Löwith*
[Marburg] Dec. 4, 1930

Dear Herr Löwith,

Thank you so much for your card. I do not want to start having visitations here—it simply becomes too difficult to limit it without excluding someone. For that reason, I ask that you come early to Bultmann's on Saturday. We can arrange the precise time tomorrow after the lecture. Too bad that I will not meet your wife. I have brought the book along with me.
    With warm greetings—
    See you soon,
        Your
            Martin Heidegger

**102.** *Karl Löwith to Martin Heidegger*
[Marburg] 4.18.32

Dear Herr Heidegger,

Recently, I submitted an application to the director (a certain Prof. Gabetti) of the recently founded German–Italian Cultural Institute—*"casa di Goethe"*—in order to secure a study-visit, or even to collaborate with the aims of the institute. I alluded to the fact that I am your student. In the event that he should inquire with you, I would ask that you please provide him with information about me and support my application. Is Dr. Grassi now properly at Freiburg as a lecturer? If so, I would be grateful if you would mention this to him: I believe he knows Gentile, the head of the whole thing, and could thus perhaps recommend me as well. It would mean a lot to me if something were to come of it and I would be able to go to Rome again.
    There is nothing of consequence to report from here. Among the students who are evidently interested in philosophy, only a precious few work at it for its own sake and not just for their exams; the leveling down continues, but I see the matter a bit differently than Jaspers does.
    Although I know that your primary concern is not "philosophy of existence," but rather a repetition of the historical {*geschichtlichen*} origins of western philosophy in general, I am now teaching "Kierkegaard and the Philosophy of Existence" and offering, as an accompaniment, a tutorial on *Being and Time*—I have waited four years to do this, but can, I believe, risk it now. The significance that the problem of society (and not the "I–you" problem) has gained for me you will have already seen in *Weber and Marx*, even though my inquiries which appeared in the *Archiv für Sozialwissenschaft*

stopped just at the point at which the philosophical problem begins. The fact that the haphazard operations of modern bourgeois sociology are merely a headless Marxism is becoming clearer and clearer to me, but Marx at least knew why he looked into the question of society in the first place, and Kierkegaard's "individual" swings to the polar historical {*zeitgeschichtlich*} opposite, since Hegel's doctrine of objective and subjective spirit no longer had societal–historical {*gesellschaftlich-geschichtliche*} truth for him—and, therefore, could no longer be grasped.

After many years, I finally did some proper skiing—in Kitzbühel, from the middle to the end of March, with lustrous snow and much sun. I hope that you are also in good health. I will not complain to you about the economic situation. I will only say this: if you should have the opportunity to recommend me to any Kant societies that pay, please do so. I am currently very dependent on additional income. Without this I would have saved the *Weber–Marx* for a greater context.

 Best regards to you,
  Your
   Karl Löwith

P.S.: I would like to ask that you please send my greetings to Herr Dr. Brock, if possible.

**103**. *Martin Heidegger to Karl Löwith*
Frbg, IV.19.32

Dear Herr Löwith,

In the event of a request, I will respond in your spirit and will inform Herr Grassi. Thank you so much for your gifts. For a long time, I have been unable to respond to your correspondences; and this unfortunate state of affairs affects those closest to me as well. Since I am familiar with neither Marx nor Weber (apart from "Wissenschaft als Beruf" and a few methodological essays), I cannot take a position. However, just as you did with your habilitation thesis, I find that you have really immersed yourself into the matter here, and that you have the voice to do so. I find the "Theology" far-fetched. The havoc that my lecture "Phenomenology and Theology" wreaked on friend and foe alike seems still to be spreading. Even so, I have no desire and no need to intervene, particularly since I have reason to hope that everyone from Barth to Przywara (they are all the same) will pounce on Jaspers, who is ripe to be plundered and written about.

Of course now, even through Jaspers, the confusion about what I'm after becomes completely incalculable. This mishmash must also be given its due, and he will find those who will stir it all up and make "something" of it.

Every day I am thankful that I have retained my old standards and the joy of growing ever closer to the simple questions. They remain old-fashioned by their very nature, despite the ever-growing clamor about "ontology" and such.

Hopefully your Kierkegaard lectures will play a part in moving you forward in the task you have set yourself for years now.

With friendly regards,
Your
Martin Heidegger

**104.** *Martin Heidegger to Karl Löwith*
[Freiburg] XII.6.32

Dear Herr Löwith,

First, let me express my sincere condolences for the loss of your father, and also extend my deep sympathy to your mother. It must mean a lot to you that your previous conflicts finally resolved into a smooth and beautiful relationship. Memory holds a completely different revivifying power.

I am certainly willing to be a reference for your applications. Could you not also ask Jaspers? I believe also that Groethuysen has an important voice, especially regarding practical matters. Apart from this, I don't know any sociologists.

I would very much like to have you visit; however, it is very probable I will be at the hut at this time. Just in case, let me know the precise date of your lecture in Tübingen.

I am really looking forward to your review of Jaspers. To be sure, I haven't read the "great" work and will not have time to read it any time soon. Truth be told, I am not particularly interested in it. This pivoting toward a Christian worldview—because otherwise I cannot understand the threefoldness, a modification of the Kantian system—is repugnant to me. The productive way to the Greeks is once again entirely obscured. The actual thrust of my writings is nowhere understood or accepted and is rendered ineffectual through the label "philosophy of existence."

Nevertheless, I feel more comfortable in my own skin now than I have over the past few years, when such a fuss was being made out of my name. Now things have come so far that I am rejected, as one says, on all levels and in all registers. This is also a way in which the public, for its part, helps you to preserve your own inner law. To do this as well as one can is the only thing that remains—but it is enough.

With heartfelt greetings,
Your
Martin Heidegger

**105.** *Martin Heidegger to Karl Löwith*
Frbg, I.14.33

Dear Herr Löwith,

Thank you for your letter. I would be very happy were you to visit from Heidelberg. I would only ask that you let me know precisely when you would be coming. And if it proves necessary, you are of course welcome to stay the night with us.
    Warm greetings,
      Your
        Martin Heidegger

I never received the request from the administrative offices of the Rockefeller Foundation.

**106**. *Martin Heidegger to Karl Löwith*
[Freiburg, II.20.33]

advise unconditionally to accept
    Heidegger

**107**. *Martin Heidegger to Karl Löwith*
Freiburg, the 22nd of May, 1933

Dear Herr Löwith,

Thank you for your two letters. Regrettably, I currently have neither the time nor the quiet to address the important and difficult questions you raise. Perhaps there will be an opportunity in the near future for us to speak in person about these issues. My pairing with Jaensch in Frankfurt was made without my foreknowledge and against my will; I was thus compelled to withdraw my lecture entirely (as perhaps you have heard).
    If I am asked by Davis, I will step in.
    With kind regards,
      Your
        Martin Heidegger

**108**. *Martin Heidegger to Karl Löwith*
[Freiburg] June 12, 1933

Dear Herr Löwith,

I am just now returning from a long business trip. I politely ask that you refrain from dedicating the book to me; because so many people who at some point or another saw or heard me from afar are now seeking the support of my name, it would be embarrassing and damaging to me if this impression also arose with respect to the students. The way we consider and judge the behavior of "others" these days, such things are always a concern.

In reality, I know well how you feel about me, even when your work goes in other directions.

Also, with an eye toward possible situations in which I might be asked to render a judgment about you, I suggest that you omit the dedication.

It is quite doubtful that the semester will allow enough time for a discussion. I have not even been able to find time yet to dictate the completed rectorship address (which is taken from a greater context) into the recorder so that it can be set.

With kind regards,
Your
Martin Heidegger

**109**. *Martin Heidegger to Karl Löwith*
Freiburg, the 29th of July, 1933

Dear Herr Löwith,

Congratulations on the stipend, and I would advise you to take it this next spring. Unfortunately, it was not possible during my short stay in Marburg to drop in to see you.

With kind regards,
Your
Martin Heidegger

**110**. *Martin Heidegger to Karl Löwith*
[In Löwith's handwriting: June/July, 1936
(sent to Rome)]

Dear Herr Löwith,

I will try the various paths that I think are possible. I have already written to Berlin. To me, it does not seem immaterial that you are significantly younger that the competition—and that you represent an entirely different compliment to Reichenbach. It would really be nice if this time it worked out.

Regarding Jaspers' book—I am appalled. He is still basically where he began—with the "psychology of world-views." It is nothing more than the psychology of philosophy, and now in such a way that nothing remains but empty "transcendence."

Really, I find the idolization of the Nietzsche-Registry by Oehler fantastic—but Jaspers' book is merely a registry and a transcending index.

If he were to deal with other philosophers with this method, the results could be good.

If you have something urgent to communicate to me, it is best for you to write to the Freiburg address; I spend most of my time at the hut.

With kind regards
to your wife and Herr Dr. Antoni
Your
Martin Heidegger.

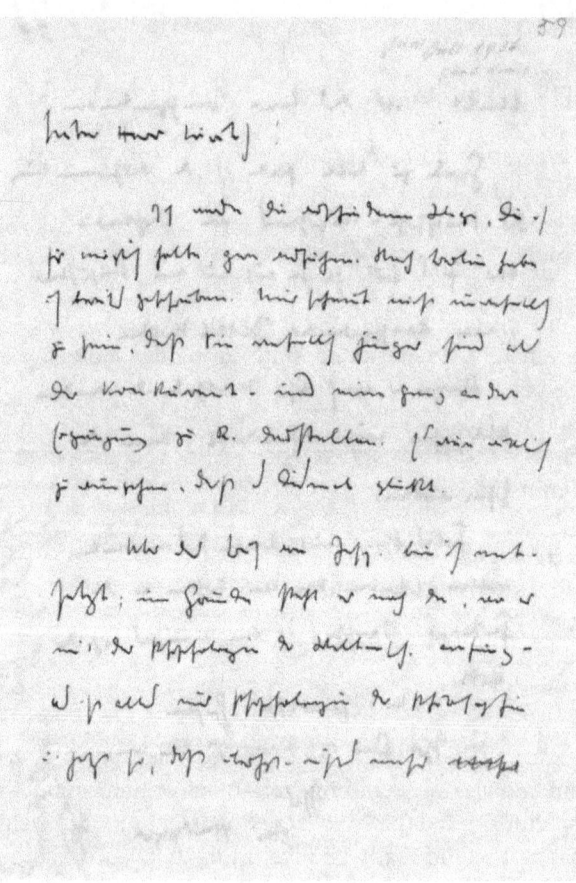

Figure 6    Facsimile of Heidegger's Letter (Document 110) from June/July 1936.

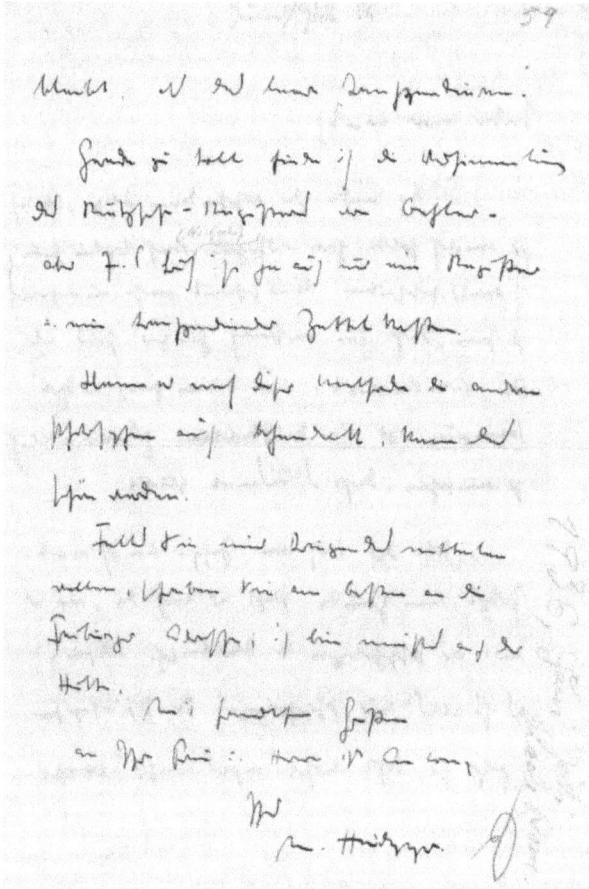

Figure 7  Facsimile of the back side of Heidegger's Letter (Document 110) from June/July 1936.

**111.** *Martin Heidegger to Karl Löwith*
Todtnauberg
July 18, 37

Dear Herr Löwith,

Thank you for your letter. I am all right with the idea of a Japanese translation, and the publisher is as well. Meanwhile, a French translation under the title *Qu'est ce que la métaphysique* has been published (by Gallimard) in a collection of translations of my work.

I have still not been able to see the published Italian translation.

I have not yet been able to read your books, owing to the fact that I have been very occupied with my own writing over the past month. But I hope to have a break soon, that I might write to you at length. The Hölderlin is already in its third, unchanged edition.

I am happy that you and your wife are settling in well, and that you have found a stable and worthwhile appointment.

**112**. *Karl Löwith to Martin Heidegger*
[New York]
Sept. 20, 1949

All the best wishes
  For your 60th!
    Your
      Karl Löwith

**113**. *Karl Löwith to Martin Heidegger*
July 26 [1958]
Philosophy Department
University of Heidelberg
Seminarienhaus Augustinergasse 15

Dear Herr Heidegger,

It pleased me to be able to hear your lecture; but academic conferences are not conducive to conversation, not even a short one. It would be nice if we could make up for this over the upcoming winter semester. Rumor has it that you will be speaking at the Bavarian Academy in November about "language." If that is correct, and it is not happening in early November, I would like to come to Munich, provided that the Academy can accommodate me. I myself will be flying to Japan in early August for a series of lectures, and will be returning at the beginning of November. I recently met a Herr Tsujimura here, who seems to me to be a serious man, in distinction to the Shintoist who equates the clearing of being {*die Lichtung des Seins*} with the sun goddess Amaterasu! I would like to hear your thoughts regarding Volume 3 of Schlecta's Nietzsche edition. I think that Schlechta has greatly overestimated his Nietzsche-philology and is thereby spreading a new Nietzsche legend. I have attempted to rectify the matter—it will be published in the *Merkur*.

  With kind regards,
    Your
      Karl Löwith

**114.** *Martin Heidegger to Karl Löwith*
Frbg, March 2, 1959

Dear Herr Löwith,

Thank you for your words. Unfortunately, I will be occupied for the entire week, and must leave on March 3rd.

Perhaps some other time you could stop here during one of your trips to the south.

My best wishes for your vacation, and greetings to both you and your wife.
    Your
        Martin Heidegger

**115.** *Karl Löwith to Martin Heidegger*
6.17.67

Dear Herr Heidegger,

I am here in Freiburg for two days for a colloquium being held by the Herder Foundation, and I have sought in vain for your telephone number—my hope was to see you, if possible. Also, I have a favor to ask: in the seminar by Marx, I saw an extraordinary photograph of you taken some four years ago. Would it be possible for me to get a copy? If so, please send it straightaway to the department in Heidelberg (although I myself will be in Carona until Autumn).

With best wishes for your well-being,
    Your
        Karl Löwith

I have since obtained your telephone number from Lili Szilasi—but, alas, it is now already too late to visit with you.

**116.** *Martin Heidegger to Karl Löwith*
Freiburg i. Br.
June 18, 1967

Dear Herr Löwith,

Thank you for the card and for your new book. I am looking forward to your visit on Friday at 10:30. Since I will be coming to your lecture tomorrow, we can discuss then whether or not that still works for you.

With best regards,
    Your
        Martin Heidegger

**117.** *Martin Heidegger to Karl Löwith*
[after 6.20.67]

For Karl Löwith
In commemoration
of our visit to Zähringen
on June 20, 1967.
Martin Heidegger

**118.** *Martin Heidegger to Karl Löwith*
Frbg, July 28, 1970

Dear Herr Löwith,

My heart-felt gratitude for your masterful presentation of the "Hegel-Renaissance," your insights, and the delineations of your thinking.
    Kind regards,
      Your
        Martin Heidegger

**119.** *Martin Heidegger to Karl Löwith*
[October 1971 or 1972]

Thank you for the remembrance;
Greetings and best wishes,
    Martin Heidegger

**120.** *Martin Heidegger to Karl Löwith*
Freiburg i. Br., II.25.72

Dear Herr Löwith,

Here is the only text of Nishitani that I possess. I ask that you please give Herr Nishitani my kind regards. Perhaps he will stay a while in Europe after the celebration. We will be away from Freiburg for the month of March at a spa.
    Thank you very much for providing me with Gadamer's precise address.
    There is so much to say about the subject of Mallarmé-Valéry.
      With kind regards,
        Your
          Martin Heidegger

My "Schelling" is being sent to you by the publisher (Niemeyer).

**121.** *Karl Löwith to Martin Heidegger*
March 10, 1972

Dear Herr Heidegger,

Many thanks for the Nishitani text (which I am herein returning), but especially for the copy of your Schelling lecture. I will tell Herr Nishitani that he should contact you, and that you will be away from Freiburg in March.
    With kind regards,
        Your
            (Prof. Dr. Karl Löwith)

Enclosed

**122.** *Martin Heidegger to Karl Löwith*
Freiburg, May 5, 1973

Dear Karl Löwith,

Gadamer wrote to me regarding your illness, and Herr Marx is sending me your address.
    During times of sickness, the world contracts and withdraws into the simple. In our old age, we think of the end—but also of the beginning—of our paths.
    The attached document, which originates from 1971, is not a poem; rather, it belongs to a series of "Thoughts."
    My wish is that this illness is without torment for you, and that it leaves your with the power of forward-thinking, which Rilke, in one of the "Sonnets of Orpheus," brought to the poetic word:
    "Be ahead of all departing…"
    My heartfelt wishes,
        Your
            Martin Heidegger

*Pathways*

    Pathways,
    pathways of thinking, on their way,
    escaping. Whence returning,
    bringing outlooks—onto what?
    Pathways, on their way,
    formerly open, suddenly closed,
    later ones; showing what came before:

refusing what has been attained,
fated to renunciation.
Pathways, footsteps loosening up,
echoing a humble fate.

And once again the distress of dusk,
hesitant,
in the waiting light.

**123**. *Martin Heidegger to Ada Löwith*
Freiburg i. Br., June 4, 1973

Dear Frau Löwith,

May the mercifulness of your husband's death diminish the pain of his departure, and with time transform it into thoughtful remembrance. Both at home and in foreign lands, the departed found a unique style for both his teaching and his written works, which he upheld successfully.

The circle of those awakened for thinking during the 1920s grows ever smaller. Soon, at the very most, they will only live on in the memory of a few individuals.

My wife and I send our sympathetic and sincere regards,
    Your
        Martin Heidegger

**124**. *Martin Heidegger to Ada Löwith*
Freiburg, XII.26.73

Dear Frau Löwith,

Thank you for the beautiful picture of your departed husband. It shows him in a state of calm and collected contemplation. I wish you a good new year of peaceful reflection.
    Yours,
        Martin Heidegger

# APPENDIX

*Supplement 1*

# Letter from Elisabeth Förster-Nietzsche to Karl Löwith

Dictated
Nietzsche Archive Foundation
Weimar

Weimar, August 13, 1927

Herr Doctor K. Löwith:
Marburg am Lahn

Honorable Herr Doctor:

I myself would like to say a few words in gratitude regarding the invaluable letter that you directed to Dr. Leonore Kulen.
    The compilation of a reference work to worthwhile books on Nietzsche would be of great interest to me; however, the archivist of the Nietzsche Archive is currently on holiday, and so it will be some time before he can compile the list. For the time being, I will identify some books that strike me as appropriate and some that strike me as exemplary. I would also like to stress how disappointed I am that Klages' books were not reviewed by an actual expert. Given how novel and groundbreaking his understanding of psychology in Nietzsche's philosophy is, it is truly incomprehensible to me how mistaken he is regarding the most fundamental points of Nietzsche's philosophy. If Klages' errors had been pointed out to him earlier on, he might not have persisted in being so misguided; however, I thought he would surely come to such discoveries on his own. Alas, such did not occur, and I am thus quite sympathetic to your little text.

Regarding your dissertation, I would like to say that we have in our possession a pretty good excerpt from it, but there is so much else to do at the moment that for now we will put off the rather cumbersome task of making a copy of it.

I am truly sorry that Dr. Prinzhorn has not understood your text; however, because he is a friend of Klages' and is very much under his spell, we must be a little patient with him while he attempts to understand Nietzsche's world of thought. I hold a very high opinion of Dr. Prinzhorn and also like him personally, and believe that it is possible that he, as well as others, will have a change of perspective. Perhaps it amazes you to hear that I believe in such transformation, but I do so entirely in the spirit of my brother: "I am akin {*verwandt*} only to those who transform themselves {*sich wandeln*}."

In the coming days you will receive the biography of my brother's life. Without taking recourse to any legends, I place great value on the actual facts and on the actual, wonderful life of my brother. Oswald Spengler even said to me once that my biography of my brother's life was the one text about Nietzsche from which a serious and scrupulous Nietzsche scholar could learn. Besides, this purportedly small biography is much better than the larger edition for providing actual knowledge about my brother. When I wrote the larger biography, it was still during a period of time when so much material from the estate remained unpublished, and I was obliged to make much use of the unpublished writings in order to make the course of his life comprehensible. As a result, the entire trajectory of his life story is often interrupted. By contrast, the little volume, which was rewritten after the works of the estate had been published, contains many more details from letters and personal reflections that I had since obtained. That is why the bookseller's title "little edition" is a bit erroneous; it is to be included without my instruction.

The final volume of the Musarion Edition will in fact be an autobiographical one, which will contain nothing entirely new, but will have a powerful and, as it were, fresh appearance. It will include my brother's first autobiography, written when he was 13, up to his last, *Ecce Homo*, which was written only weeks before he succumbed to illness.

Moreover, Musarion is releasing two volumes of additional autobiographical material which will make even more personal statements and letters of Nietzsche's available. Volume 1, entitled *Der werdende Nietzsche*, is already available; Volume 2, entitled *Friedrich Nietzsches Selbstbekenntnisse*, will likely be published in two years.

With kind regards,
    Your
Dr. h.c. Elisabeth Förster-Nietzsche

*Supplement 2*

# Martin Heidegger's Assessment of Karl Löwith's Habilitation Thesis (1928)

The study under consideration is a contribution to the foundation of ethical problems that sets itself the task of bringing to light the I–You relation as the foundational phenomenon from out of which, and in reference to which, all ethical problems in general are to be posed. Consequently, the question "what is the human being," upon which Kant had already based all further questions of philosophy (cf. Kant, *Logikvorlesung, Einleitung Abs. III*), finds a new exposition through the present work, which attempts to show that the grounding anthropological question *as a question*, quite apart from the nature of its answer, should not be posed either in the narrow orientation of an isolated subject, nor with the consideration of this isolated I in its bare relation to objects, but that, to the contrary, all personal relationships and all self-relations of the subject to the "world" are already constituted from out of the ground of the *originary being-with-others* of human beings.

Accordingly, the "Introduction" and Chapter 1 (1–19 [1–13]), in which Feuerbach's *Grundsätze der Philosophie der Zukunft* is developed, give a historical introduction to the problem of the function of the "shared world" for the general interpretation of human *Dasein*. Through the presentation of Feuerbach's doctrine, three questions arise: (1) How does a self encounter a "you" in the other? (Chapter 2, 20–196 [14–126]) (2) Are "you" really only the *you of an I?* (Chapter 3, 197–264 [127–168]) (3) Am "I" really only the *I of a you?* (Chapter 4, 265–285 [169–180]).

The answers to these questions are carried out through a concrete analysis of the essential structures of the fundamental relations of human beings to one another as particular lived-relations, which all "lived contexts" and "interrelated actions" bear and by which they are guided. The second chapter (20–70 [14–46]) provides an analysis of the concept of "world," and is in the first place oriented, at least in part, by W. Dilthey. It demonstrates the manner in which something like "world" is never a mere correlate to the solipsistic subject, but rather always already bears the equiprimordial relation to others like me. Accordingly, all experience and determination of the worldly environment is co-determined through the *Dasein* of individuals in a shared world with others. The central analysis of the structures of being with others {*Miteinanderseins*} (70–196 [46–126]) yields the following insight: the shared world is a collective relation of "personae" who play a "role" within and for each other's shared world, from out of which they determine themselves in their personhood. The shared world is thus no indifferent multiplicity of individuals who stand over against a subject. Human activity is therefore fundamentally determined through an originary obligation and responsibility to others, and not through a subsequent relation to them (see 173 ff. [112 ff.]). The I–You relation should thus not be grasped as a personified relation between a subject and an object. It is, therefore, valid to break with the traditional dominance of "thing-concepts" with regard to a clear interpretation of the relationship of one person to another. An excursus on Hegel's analysis of "something {*Etwas*}" (98 ff. [63 ff.]) elucidates this dominance of "anything at all {*Irgend Etwas*}" before "anyone at all {*Irgend Einer*}," that is, the world of things before that of people. This analysis of the structure of being-with-others now makes possible a fundamental clarification of the concepts of "egoism" and "altruism" (113 ff. [71 ff.]).

The considerations heretofore provide an important insight into the principal "ambiguity" of all relations of being-with-others (121 ff. [76 ff.]): namely, looking at the other contains a more-or-less inexpressible consideration of oneself and can thus be interpreted as "objective" only from this double-movement. Consequently, the examination leads to the accentuation of the genesis of the "absolute relation" of the individual to the other in his individualized "independence." The analyses of Chapter II are proven and extended by way of a thoroughgoing explication of an eminent form of being-with-others, namely, *speaking-with-others*. Here, then, we find a systematic employment of W. v. Humboldt's insights into the philosophy of language.

Chapter III addresses the following question: whether "you" are only really a "second-person," the "you" of an "I," and not rather a co-equal "first person," a "you yourself," even if there is no other "I." The critique of the relevant arguments of Scheler's (the other as "external-I"), Ebner's, and Gogarten's ("you" as "subject" of the I–You relation), and, moreover, the engagement with Dilthey's twofold concept of experience concerning the independence of the other person, lead back to the foundational systematic treatment of this question in Kant's practical philosophy. The interpretation of Kant is supplemented by an elucidation of Hegel's critique of Kantian moral philosophy (254 ff. [162 ff.]).

Finally, the third question regarding the "I-myself" is posed in Chapter IV. The irresponsible "individuality" in the face of others is, in the strict sense, constituted on the basis of a unique existential relationship to itself. Kierkegaard's concept of "the individual" and Stirner's concept of "the only person" clarify this specifically individual (and that means ineffable and therefore only indirectly communicable) situation, in which the "persona" determined through being-with-others finds its limit.

Both in its structure and realization, the work shows a scholarly independence that exceeds what is typical of habilitation theses in philosophy. Moreover, its relation to phenomenological research never comes off as sophomoric or superficial; indeed, it is at times even rather excessively independent, such that its critique of Scheler and of my own investigations does not always appear in a positive light. The primary focus of the work is less on systematic structure and more on the vivid implementation of concrete individual analyses and historical interpretations. The interpretation of Kant's practical philosophy does not penetrate to the ultimate fundamentals, as the author has imposed upon himself a prudent limitation in the consideration of the final systematic problems. I would also like to mention here two concrete concerns that the author simply must address in the published form. They relate to (1) the interpretation of Feuerbach (87–91 [56–58]), which is reinterpreted with the benefit of insights that Feuerbach himself never had; and (2) the analysis of speaking-with-others, which, while entirely worthwhile in its own right, places such emphasis on the relationship of those speaking to one another that the respective relationship of each speaker to *what is spoken about* is pushed aside.

On my recommendation, and in preparation for publication, the author has implemented the following changes to the manuscript:

1) The title will read: "Contributions to the Anthropological Foundation of Ethical Problems."
2) The Introduction (1–6 [1–4]) and Supplement I which refers to it (I–II), as well as sections 18 and 31, will be reworked with an eye toward a clearer distinction between the "ontological" and "anthropological" understanding of human *Dasein*.
3) A particular correction was made on page 260.
4) Supplement II (II–IV – to Comment 1, page 25 [17]) will be deleted.
5) Throughout the work, specific terminological and stylistic improvements will be made.

On the basis of the content of the work, the author has shown himself to be a diligent, experienced, and broad-minded individual with an extremely rich and rigorous education. Insofar as a habilitation thesis permits a prognosticating judgment, I am able to say that the author will doubtlessly make worthwhile and noteworthy contributions through his future scholarly works. His entire nature, which I have had the opportunity to observe over the past nine years, qualifies Dr. Löwith for a vibrant and distinctive teaching career. Moreover, the cultivation of his particular field of study will enrich the field of philosophy itself.

Therefore, I ask the faculty to accept the present study as a habilitation thesis and to approve the candidate's habilitation.

Marburg a./L., February 16, 1928         Martin Heidegger

*Supplement 3*

# Excerpt from Karl Löwith's Italian Diary (1934–1936)

Heidegger's Hölderlin lecture has now been published. As is the case with all of his works, it is masterfully constructed, artistic, focused, and not insignificant. However, it is not without its false notes. One hears them in the humility of the challenging inscription and at the end. Hölderlin as the "outcast" caught between the people and the gods! The idea that human beings are a conversation fits with his reticence like a square peg in a round hole. The inner uncertainty, which his increasingly dictatorial style and his "resoluteness" poorly conceal, evinces itself outwardly, but certainly not accidentally, in the way he desultorily floats from one publisher to the next: *Sein und Zeit* with Husserl's publisher (Niemeyer), the *Kant* book with Scheler's publisher (Cohen), the rectoral address with the Nazi publisher (Korn), and this Hölderlin text with the publisher of the "*inner*" Reich!

He brought his unappealing wife with him to Rome, along with his two full-grown sons, whom I used to watch in the evenings in Freiburg and Marburg when they were invited along.

We took a day-long excursion together to *Frascati* and Tusculum—with him wearing the party's insignia on his lapel! There was much discussion (though certainly not through *his* initiative) when I told him about the polemic in the newspaper regarding his Zurich lecture, and that in my opinion his philosophy ("Existence," "historicity {*Geschichtlichkeit*}") agrees *intrinsically* and *in principle* with National Socialism. He affirmed that it does. He has once again withdrawn entirely from university politics and thus has regained his former strength in aggressive isolation; but that does not prevent him from affirming "the whole" as such—without any concrete particulars! He did not speak with me about the Jewish question. Instead, he stressed his *critical* positions to me and said: never have things been as "irresponsibly" governed as they are now, through the elimination of all previously tried and true powers. He rejected Becker's reviews written from the racial perspective as laughable, as well as Jaspers' Nietzsche, which he called a "transcending index." Through his book, Heyse has compromised his (Heidegger's) work—Baeumler is nothing philosophical, and so forth—the remaining impression of all of this was *exclusively*: "Martin Heidegger," isolated and misunderstood, without true disciples or friends! He is currently on the scholarly committee of the Nietzsche Archives and also on the Academy for German Law—but the mediocre people, such as Krieck and the like, have been victorious everywhere. Regarding my question as to how he can sit together with *Streicher* (at the Academy for German Law) he was instinctively evasive: *der Stürmer* is nothing but pornography, and Hitler must indeed be afraid of him [i.e., Streicher]; otherwise, he could not explain how Hitler—"the Führer," even for Heidegger!—had failed to remove the wretch. But if everybody had felt themselves to be too "refined" to stand up for the "situation," then it would have been worse, though at the same time he could understand that many people were punched in the gut by the whole thing and failed to address the issue. It is always this way with Heidegger: by virtue of an enigmatic *reservatio mentalis*, this "radical" is ready to make practically any compromise, if only for the sake of a certain effectiveness. Despite all of his radicality and critical clarity, there is much uncertainty, opacity, and obscurity in his very being. His gaze is still the beautiful and self-assured sidelong glance, and his harmless friendliness is completely nonbinding. "É un bambino" was Antoni's impression. But one could see how far his intellectual tyranny reaches in the truly childish lecture of *Naumann*'s, who managed to dedicate his freshly baked book from 1933 to George and Hitler, the Fuhrer and the poet of the third Reich, and who, in his lecture on the "German worldview," in all seriousness construed Baldar and Odin along the lines of Heidegger's "They" and "being-a-self {*Selbstsein*}," with the customary additions of "heroism," "heroic pessimism," and longing for death. During dinner together, to which Gabetti had invited me, I brought up the speech of M. Weber and suggested that this man would probably have conducted himself differently with respect to the Jewish-question, to which he gave, as an answer, the truly decisive question: but was M. Weber not part Jewish?! Heyse was bland and entirely insignificant.

*Supplement 4*

# Letter from Ada Löwith to Elfride Heidegger-Petri (1976)

France, Île d'Oléron, 5.30.76

Dear and venerable Frau Heidegger,

Even at the risk of coming up short, I would nevertheless still like to express to you my deep anguish and heartfelt commiseration for your suffering. I hope that the end did not bring you and your esteemed husband much pain.

I see him before me even now, so hearty and friendly, with traces of freshly mowed lawn that he had just walked across still clinging to the soles of his shoes, all during a visit that was memorable and delightful for me. But above all I am mindful of the inescapable significance of this great teacher for the life of my beloved husband and the unbelievable luck of the renewed friendliness of their relationship over the last little while. It is almost exactly three years ago that my beloved husband departed from me, and I know well how much joy those last friendly letters from his great teacher brought him.

Dear Frau Heidegger, I am thinking of you from the bottom of my heart. You will likely have already heard that Frida Gadamer died recently. There are only a few of this generation still left, and already I have the impression that there can be no *proper* understanding where one no longer actually knows the people involved.

    Your
        Ada Löwith

P.S. I learned the news through the random purchase of the newspaper *Le Monde* from May 20, 1976 (N. 9748), in which there where three big articles.

# *Supplement 5*

# Entry from Karl Löwith in the Heidegger Family Guestbook at the Hut in Todtnauberg (1924)

III.1–III.11 at the hut of my destructor, burned brown by sun, wind, and light. Left behind half of a tooth and a ski-tip; the latter is being glued today. The "philosophy of language" came to expression in such a way that philosophy was not discussed. With heartfelt thanks to the hosts. Karl Löwith.

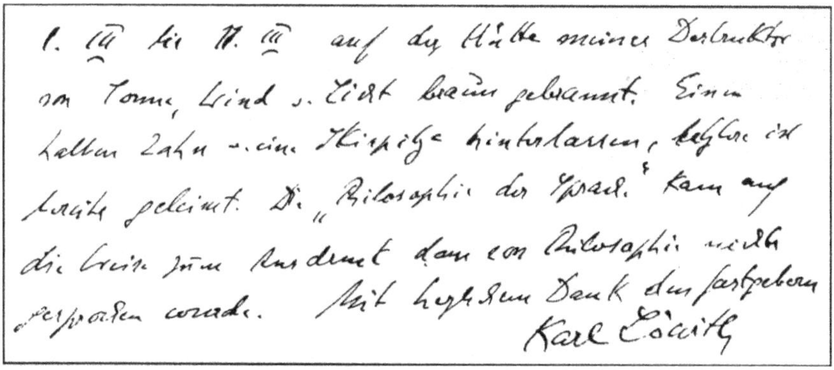
1. III bis 11. III auf der Hütte meines Destruktors von Sonne, Wind u. Licht braun gebrannt. Einen halben Zahn u. eine Skispitze hinterlassen, letztere ist heute geleimt. Die „Philosophie der Sprache" kam auf die Weise zum Ausdruck dass von Philosophie nicht gesprochen wurde. Mit herzlichstem Dank den Gastgebern
Karl Löwith

Figure 8 Löwith's Entry in the Guestbook.

## Supplement 6

# List of Martin Heidegger's Courses in which Karl Löwith Participated

**Summer Semester 1919**

On the enrollment list for "Phänomenologie und transzendentale Wertphilosophie" {Phenomenology and Transcendental Value-Philosophy}.

On the enrollment list for "Das Wesen der Universität und des akademischen Studiums" {The Essence of the University and of Academic Studies}.

**Winter Semester 1919/20**

On the enrollment list for "Grundprobleme der Phänomenologie" {Fundamental Problems of Phenomenology}.

On the enrollment list for the Colloquium.

**Summer Semester 1920**

On the enrollment list for "Phänomenologie der Anschauungen und des Ausdrucks" {Phenomenology of Intuition and Expression}.

In the seminar book for "Phänomenologische Übungen: Phänomenologie der Anschauung und des Ausdrucks" {Phenomenological Tutorials: Phenomenology of Intuition and Expression}.

**Summer Semester 1921**

On the enrollment list for "Augustinus und der Neuplatonismus" {Augustine and Neoplatonism}.

On the enrollment list for "Phänomenologische Übungen (für Anfänger)" {Phenomenological Tutorials (for Beginners)}.

In the seminar book for "Übungen über Aristoteles, De anima" {Tutorials On Aristotle's *de Anima*}.

In the seminar book for "Phänomenologische Übungen im Anschluß an Husserl, *Logischen Untersuchungen* II" {Phenomenological Tutorials in Connection with Husserl's *Logical Investigations II*}.

**Winter Semester 1921/22**
On the enrollment list for "Phänomenologische Interpretationen zu Aristoteles" {Phenomenological Interpretations of Aristotle}.

**Summer Semester 1922**
On the enrollment list for "Phänomenologische Interpretationen" {Phenomenological Interpretations}.

**Winter Semester 1922/23**
In the seminar book for "Phänomenologische Übungen zu Aristoteles" {Phenomenological Tutorials on Aristotle}.

**Winter Semester 1923/24**
In the seminar book for "Phänomenologische Übungen für Fortgeschrittene Aristoteles *Physik B*" {Advanced Phenomenological Tutorials on Aristotle's *Physics B*}.

**Winter Semester 1925/26**
In the seminar book for Phänomenologische Übungen für Fortgeschrittene Hegel, *Logik I. Buch*" {Advanced Phenomenological Tutorials on Hegel's *Logic*, Book I}.

**Summer-Semester 1926**
In the seminar book for "Übungen über Geschichte und historische Erkenntnis im Anschluß an J. G. Droysen" {Tutorials Concerning History and Historical Knowledge in Connection with J.G. Droysen}.

**Summer Semester 1927**
In the seminar book for "Die Ontologie des Aristoteles und Hegels *Logik*" {The Ontology of Aristotle and Hegel's *Logic*}.

# Annotations

**1.** M.H. to K.L., August 22, 1919, Postcard (copy)

*Many thanks for the postcard, and also the one from Munich*

The two postcards are not in the possession of the estate.

**2.** K.L. to M.H., September 8, 1919, Postcard

*a card sent by Prof. Pfänder*

Alexander Carl Heinrich Pfänder (1870–1941) became professor of philosophy at the University of Munich in 1908. He was an important advocate of Theodor Lipps' so-called "Munich phenomenology" and, beginning in 1913, served as co-editor of the *Jahrbuch für Philosophie und phänomenologische Forschung*. His most important works are *Zur Psychologie der Gesinnungen* (in *Jahrbuch für Philosophie und phänomenologische Forschung*, Volume I, 1913, 325–404, and Volume III, 1916, 1–125); *Logik* (Halle an der Saale: Max Niemeyer, 1920); and *Die Seele des Menschen: Versuch einer verstehenden Psychologie* (Halle an der Saale: Max Niemeyer, 1933).

*to Fräulein Walther*

Gerda Walther (1897–1977) studied economics, pedagogy, and psychology with Alexander Pfänder in Munich and with Edmund Husserl in Freiburg. The offprint of her dissertation, *Zur Ontologie sozialer Gemeinschaften*, appeared in 1921 and was included in Volume VI of *Jahrbuch für Philosophie und phänomenologische Forschung*, 1–158, in 1923. She also published *Zur Phänomenologie der Mystik* (Halle an der Saale: Max Niemeyer, 1923). See also Karl Löwith, *Mein Leben in Deutschland vor und nach 1933: Ein Bericht*, with a foreword by Reinhart Kosseleck and an afterword by Ada Löwith, republished by Frank-Rutger Hausmann (Stuttgart / Weimar: J.B. Metzler, 2007), 60 (*My Life in Germany Before and After 1933*, translated by Elizabeth King [London: Athlone Press, 1994]). The report was written in 1940.

*Spengler's Untergang des Abendlandes*

Oswald Spengler (1880–1936) was an independent scholar. His main work, *Der Untergang des Abendlandes*: Volume 1: *Gestalt und Wirklichkeit*, and Volume 2: *Christentum und Sozialismus* (Munich: C. H. Beck, 1918–1922), was one of the best-selling books of the Weimar Republic.

**4. M.H. to K.L., December 14, 1919, Postcard (copy)**

*I would prefer Gallery II, Row 4*

Presumably Löwith was supposed to buy a ticket for a concert.

*Fräulein Gerling*

Elisabeth Gerling took Heidegger's seminar *Phänomenologische Übungen über Descartes, Meditationes* ("Phenomenological Tutorials on Descartes' Meditations") in the summer semester of 1919. (The Natorp seminar was held privately—therefore, there is no record of enrollment.) Later, Gerling was a teacher in Schleswig-Holstein. No further information regarding her could be obtained.

*the Natorp seminar*

Heidegger held tutorials in connection with Natorp's *Allgemeine Psychologie* in the winter semester of 1919/20.

**5. M.H. to K.L., January 24, 1920, Postcard (copy)**

*that excellent presentation of yours*

Neither Löwith's nor Heidegger's estates are in possession of Löwith's presentation.

**6.** M.H. to K.L., February 15, 1920, Postcard (copy)

*Thank you so much for your card*

The postcard is not in the possession of the estate.

*I have nixed the entire summer lecture course*

In the summer semester of 1920, Heidegger lectured on the phenomenology of intuition and expression. See GA 59 (*Phenomenology of Intuition and Expression*, translated by Tracy Colony [London: Continuum, 2010]).

*a more inappropriate text than the Encyclopedia of Logic*

Heidegger is likely referencing a seminar given by Jonas Cohn in the summer semester of 1920 by the name of "Colloquium in Connection with the Lecture." The lecture itself was called "Philosophische Besprechungen (Hegel: Encyclopaedie)." Jonas Cohn (1869–1947) was a philosopher, psychologist, and pedagogue. From 1897 until his forced removal in 1933, he was a professor (and colleague of Heidegger) at the University of Freiburg. In 1919, he became Ordinarius Professor of philosophy, psychology, and pedagogy. He emigrated to Great Britain in 1939, where he died eight years later. He was an important representative of Neo-Kantianism. The following are among his most significant works: *Voraussetzungen und Ziele des Erkennens: Untersuchungen über die Grundfragen der Logik* (Leipzig: Engelmann, 1908); *Geist der Erziehung: Pädagogik auf philosophischer Grundlage* (Leipzig/Berlin: B. G. Teubner, 1919); and *Theorie der Dialektik: Formenlehre der Philosophie* (Leipzig: Felix Meiner, 1923).

*Dilthey's book Die Jugendgeschichte Hegels*

This work was published in 1905 in the papers of the Prussian Academy of Sciences in Berlin and was presented by Dilthey in a session of the philosophical-historical group on November 23rd, 1905. It is also available in Dilthey's *Die Jugendgeschichte Hegels und andere Abhandlungen zur Geschichte des deutschen Idealismus, Gesammelte Schriften* Volume IV (Stuttgart/Göttingen: Vandenhoeck & Ruprecht, 1974), 5–180. Wilhelm Christian Ludwig Dilthey (1833–1911) was a major proponent of the humanities, and was one of the most influential philosophers of the later years of the nineteenth century. His first major work was *Einleitung in die Geisteswissenschaften* (Berlin: Duncker & Humblot, 1883). His other works include *Der Aufbau der geschichtlichen Welt in den Geisteswissenschaften* (Berlin: Preußische Akademie der Wissenschaften, 1910) and *Das Erlebnis und die Dichtung: Lessing, Goethe, Novalis, Hölderlin* (Leipzig/Berlin: B. G. Teubner, 1906).

## 7. M.H. to K.L., March 23, 1920, Letter (copy)

*Besseler*

Heinrich Besseler (1900–1969) studied philosophy with Heidegger. In 1928, he became professor of musicology in Heidelberg. See also Karl Löwith, *Mein Leben in Deutschland*, 60 f. (*My Life in Germany*, 61 f.).

*Curjel*

Hans Curjel (1896–1974) studied art and music history. He was music director at the concert house in Düsseldorf in 1924/25. He worked as a playwright, producer, and assistant director from 1927 to 1931 at the Kroll Opera House in Berlin. Owing to persecution by the Nazis, he emigrated to Zürich in 1933, and was director of the Theater and Concert Collective in Zürich from 1942 to 1949. After 1948, he was active as a freelance writer and producer in Berlin, Paris, Venice, and Salzburg.

*I was very happy to receive your letter*

The letter is not in the possession of the estate.

*Lask*

Emil Lask (1875–1915) was a student of Henrich Rickert and a prominent representative of Baden's Neo-Kantians. His influence on Heidegger's philosophical development was significant. (See GA 1.)

*Hey.* [?]

This could refer to Gerardus Heymans, *Die Grenzen und Elemente des wissenschaftlichen Denkens* (Leipzig: Barth, 1905).

*Jaspers' Book*

Karl Jaspers, *Psychologie der Weltanschauungen* (Berlin: Springer, 1919). See Heidegger's criticism in GA 9, 1–44 ("Comments on Karl Jaspers' 'Psychology of Worldviews' *(1919/1921)*," translated by John van Buren, in *Pathmarks*, edited by William McNeill [Cambridge: Cambridge University Press, 1998], 1–38). Karl Theodor Jaspers (1883–1969) was a psychiatrist and philosopher. He became Extraordinarius Professor of psychology at Heidelberg University in 1916, and Ordinarius Professor in 1922. He became friends with Heidegger in 1920. His major works include *Allgemeine Psychopathologie* (Berlin: Springer, 1913); *Psychologie der Weltanschauungen* (Berlin: Springer, 1919); *Die geistige Situation der Zeit* (Berlin/Leipzig: Walter de Gruyter, 1931); and *Philosophie*, Volume 1: *Philosophische Weltorientierung*, Volume 2: *Existenzerhellung*, Volume 3: *Metaphysik* (Berlin: Springer, 1932). The correspondences between Heidegger and Karl Jaspers are also of interest—see Martin Heidegger and Karl Jaspers *Briefwechsel 1920–1963*, edited by Walter Biemel and Hans Saner (Frankfurt am Main: Vittorio Klostermann, and Munich/Zürich Piper, 1990) (*The Heidegger-Jaspers Correspondence (1920–1963)*, translated by Gary E. Aylesworth [New York: Humanity Books, 2003]).

*Bergson*

Henri-Louis Bergson (1859–1941) was a French philosopher. He received the Nobel prize for literature in 1927. His major works include *Essai sur les données immédiates de la conscience* (Paris: Presses Universitaires de France, 1889); *Matière et mémoire* (Paris: Presses Universitaires de France, 1896); *L'Évolution créatrice* (Paris: Presses Universitaires de France, 1907); and *Les Deux Sources de la morale et de la religion* (Paris: Presses Universitaires de France, 1932).

*by the "Society"*

In 1918/19, Edmund Husserl founded the Freiburg Phenomenological Society, to which both Heidegger and Löwith belonged. (See also Letter 8.) Edmund Husserl (1859–1938) was the founder of phenomenology and Heidegger's most important teacher. From 1901 to 1916, Husserl was professor of philosophy at Göttingen University, and in 1916 was appointed successor to Heinrich Rickert at Freiburg University. His major works include *Logische Untersuchungen* (2 Volumes) (Halle an der Saale: Max Niemeyer, 1900–1901); and *Ideen zu einer reinen Phänomenologie* (Max Niemeyer, Halle an der Saale, 1913). Regarding the relationship between Heidegger and Husserl, see *Heidegger-Jahrbuch* Volume 6, *Heidegger und Husserl* (2012).

*the new translator*

This likely refers to the new translation of Henri Bergson's *Matière et mémoire*, which appeared in Jena in 1919 under the title *Materie und Gedächtnis: Eine*

*Abhandlung über die Beziehung zwischen Körper und Geist* (translated into German by Julius Frankenberg and published by Diederich).

## *to speak for two hours about Spengler*

On April 14, 1920, Heidegger delivered a talk entitled "Oswald Spengler und sein Werk Der Untergang des Abendlandes" ("Oswald Spengler and his Work on the Decline of the West"). "Science week" was organized by the Federation of University Courses.

## *Born (Frankfurt)*

Max Born (1882–1970) was professor of theoretical physics in Frankfurt beginning in 1919, and was friends with Albert Einstein. In 1920, he published *Die Relativitätstheorie Einsteins und ihre physikalischen Grundlage* (Berlin: Springer).

## *Oncken (Heidelberg)*

Hermann Gerhard Karl Oncken (1869–1945) was professor of modern history at Heidelberg University at the time, and later in Munich and Berlin.

## *Wolzendorff (Halle)*

Kurt Wolzendorff (1882–1921) was professor of public law at the University of Halle at the time. He published *Vom deutschen Staat und seinem Recht: Streiflichter zur allgemeinen Staatslehre* (Leipzig: Veith, 1917), and *Geist des Staatrechts: Eine Studie zur Biologie des Rechts und zur Psychologie des Volksstaats* (Leipzig: Der Neue Geist-Verlag, 1920).

## *Stern*

This probably refers to Erich Stern, who participated in Heidegger's seminars from the summer semester of 1919 through the winter semester of 1920/21. He graduated on the basis of his thesis, *Über bewahrendes und verarbeitendes Gedächtnisverhalten* (Freiburg: J. A. Barth, 1922). Husserl authored the co-advisor report for his dissertation. See Edmund Husserl, *Briefwechsel*, in connection with Elisabeth Schuhmann, edited by Karl Schuhmann, Volume 8: *Institutionelle Schreiben* (Dordrecht: Kluwer, 1994, 176).

## *Scheler*

Max Ferdinand Scheler (1874–1928) was the most important representative of phenomenology after Husserl. He became professor of philosophy and sociology in Cologne in 1921, and in 1928 transferred to the University of Frankfurt am Main. His writings are collected in the sixteen volumes of the Scheler *Gesammelte Werke*, edited by Maria Scheler and Manfred S. Frings.

*Scheler's* Idole

Max Scheler, "Die Idole der Selbsterkenntnis," in *Abhandlungen und Aufsätze*, 2 Volumes (Leipzig: Weissen Bücher, 1915, Volume 2, 3–168); now also in *Gesammelte Werke* Volume 3, edited by Maria Scheler and Manfred S. Frings (Bonn: Bouvier, 1972, 213–292).

**8.** M.H. to K.L., September 1, 1920, Postcard (copy)

*The second lad*

Heidegger's second son, Hermann—who is not his biological son—was born in Freiburg on August 20, 1920. See the afterword by Hermann Heidegger in *Mein liebes Seelchen!: Briefe Martin Heideggers an seine Frau Elfride 1915–1970*, edited and annotated by Gertrud Heidegger (Munich: Deutsche Verlags-Anstalt, 2005, 382) (Martin Heidegger, *Letters to His Wife: 1915–1970*, translated by Rupert Glasgow [Cambridge: Polity, 2008], 317).

**9.** M.H. to K.L., September 13, 1920, Postcard (copy)

*one is sure to get enough "Simmel"*

Georg Simmel (1858–1918) was a philosopher and sociologist. Only in 1914 did he receive an appointment to the University of Strasbourg. He is often considered to be a proponent of *Lebensphilosophie* ["life-philosophy"]. Along with Max Weber and Ferdinand Tönnies, Simmel co-founded the *German Sociological Society*. Heidegger studied Simmel in his early years. The collected writings of Simmel, edited by Otthein Rammstadt and published by Suhrkamp (Frankfurt am Main), appeared in 1989.

*Szilasi*

Wilhelm Szilasi (1889–1966) studied with Heidegger during the summer semester of 1920 and later followed him to Marburg. The two developed a life-long friendship. After World War II, Szilasi became a professor in Freiburg, where he occupied Heidegger's chair from 1947 until 1964. His major works include *Macht und Ohnmacht des Geistes: Interpretationen von Werken von Platon und Aristoteles* (Bern: Francke, 1946), and *Philosophie und Naturwissenschaft* (Bern: Francke, 1961).

*In regard to the "cogito"*

The allusion to the "cogito" evidently refers to the seminar "Phänomenologische Übungen für Anfänger im Anschluß an Descartes, *Meditationes*" ("Phenomenological Tutorials for Beginners in Connection with Descartes' *Meditations*"), held in the winter semester of 1920/21.

*the other two metaphysical treatises*

This presumably refers to René Descartes, *Discours de la méthode*, in *Oeuvres*, published by Charles Adam and Paul Tannery, Volume VI (Paris: Leopold Cerf, 1902), 1–78, and the *Principia Philosophiae*, in *Oeuvres*, Volume VIII (Paris, 1905), 1–353.

*and the* Regulae

René Descartes, *Regulae ad directionem ingenii*, *Oeuvres* Volume X (Paris, 1908), 349–488.

*Perhaps we can dare to do it next summer*

Heidegger did not end up offering a philosophy of religion seminar in Freiburg over the following semesters.

*I then considered Plotinus*

In the summer semester of 1921, Heidegger gave a lecture entitled "Augustinus und der Neuplatonismus" ("Augustine and Neoplatonism"), now available in GA 60, 158–299 (*The Phenomenology of Religious Life*, translated by Matthias Fritsch and Jennifer Anna Gosetti-Ferencei [Bloomington: Indiana University Press, 2004], 113–184).

*The Luther edition is by Otto Clemen*

*Luthers Werke in Auswahl*, edited by Otto Clemen in collaboration with Albert Lietzmann, Volumes 1–4 (Bonn: Marcus and Weber, 1912–1913).

*Could you please send me the Kahler*

Erich von Kahler, *Der Beruf der Wissenschaft* (Berlin: Georg Bondi, 1920).

## Greetings to Dr. Becker

Oskar Joachim Becker (1889–1964) was a student of Husserl, and was friends with both Heidegger and Löwith. He became *außerplanmäßiger* professor in Freiburg in 1927, and went on to teach from 1931 to 1945 as a professor of history and mathematics at the University of Bonn. His major work *Mathematische Existenz: Untersuchungen zur Logik und Ontologie mathematischer Phänomene* appeared along with Heidegger's *Sein und Zeit* in Volume VIII of the *Jahrbuch für Philosophie und phänomenologische Forschung*. See also Löwith, *Mein Leben in Deutschland*, 45–57 (*My Life in Germany*, 45–58).

## 10. M.H. to K.L., September 19, 1920, Postcard (copy)

### Frbg

This must be an error on Heidegger's part, as he was in Messkirch at the time.

### his little, informal speech

This refers to a speech by Max Scheler held in Cologne at the beginning of 1919, entitled "Die Krisis der deutschen Universität—und die Notwendigkeit ihrer Reform im Zusammenhang mit der Reform des gesamten deutschen Bildungswesens." A later, extended version, under the title "Universität und Volkshochschule," was published as a chapter in the anthology *Zur Soziologie des Volksbildungswesen*, edited by Leopold von Wiese (Volume 1 of *Schriften des Forschungsinstitutes für Sozialwissenschaften in Köln* [Berlin: Duncker & Humblot, 1921]). It is currently available in Max Scheler, *Die Wissensformen und die Gesellschaft* (*Gesammelte Werke*, Volume 8), edited by Maria Scheler (Bern/Munich: Francke Verlag, 1960, 383–420).

### Ebbinghaus

Julius Karl Ludwig Ebbinghaus (1885–1981) habilitated from the University of Freiburg in 1921 with his work *Die Grundlagen der Philosophie Hegels*. In 1926, he became Extraordinarius Professor of philosophy there. In 1930, he accepted a position at the University of Rostock. He began teaching at the University of Marburg in 1940. His most important work is *Über die Fortschritte der Metaphysik* (Tübingen: J. C. B. Mohr, 1931).

## Kroner

Richard Kroner (1884–1974), along with Wilhelm Windelband and Heinrich Rickert, was affiliated with the Southwest German School of Neo-Kantianism. He studied with Georg Simmel, Wilhelm Windelband, Heinrich Richert, and Edmund Husserl (among others). He wrote the first German article on the philosophy of Henri Bergson. In 1919, he was appointed contingent Extraordinarius Professor at the University of Freiburg. In 1920, he received a triennial special lectureship in the philosophy of German Idealism. During this time he produced the two-volume work *Von Kant bis Hegel* (Tübingen: J. C. B. Mohr, 1921 and 1924). In 1928, he became professor of philosophy at the University of Kiel. He voluntarily went emeritus in 1935, owing to the fact that he was a Jew with frontline privileges, and moved to Berlin where he lived for three years. In 1938, he emigrated to England, where he taught for three years at the University of Oxford. In 1940, he moved to the United States, where he taught at the Union Theological Seminary (in New York City) from 1941 until he went emeritus in 1952.

## Dr. Metzger

Arnold Metzger (1892–1974) was Husserl's assistant from 1920 to 1924. He published his habilitation thesis *Phänomenologie und Metaphysik* (Halle der an Saale: Max Niemeyer) in 1933. In 1938, he emigrated to Paris, and then on to England in 1940, and finally to the United States in 1941. He taught at Harvard University in Cambridge, MA (among other institutions). From 1952 until 1974, he was an honorary professor at the University of Munich.

## I am an "Ostelbien aristocrat"

"Ostelbier" or "Junker" is the colloquial name for large land owners in Ostelbien, the regions of Prussia and Mecklenburg that lies to the east of Elbe. Heidegger makes use here of the opposition between the understandings of the "the Prussian nobility" as either "friends of the proletariat" or an ancient elite.

## to speak with your parents

Löwith's father Wilhelm (1861–1932) was a renowned artist. He was a student at the Wiener Academy with Christian Griepenkerl and August Eisenmenger, and at the Munich Academy with Wilhelm von Lindenschmidt. Löwith's mother's maiden name was Margerete Hauser. Both of his parents were Jewish.

*whoever else is there*

Heidegger did not sign the postcard.

## 11. M.H. to K.L., October 9, 1920, Postcard (copy)

*my lecture*

Martin Heidegger, "Einleitung in die Phänomenologie der Religion," in GA 60, 3–159 (*The Phenomenology of Religious Life*, 3–111).

*perhaps Thust will then also show up with something*

Martin Thust later published *Sören Kierkegaard, der Dichter des Religiösen: Grundlagen eines Systems der Subjektivität* (Munich: C. H. Beck, 1931). See also Karl Löwith, *Mein Leben in Deutschland*, 60 (*My Life in Germany*, 62).

*the Gurlitt seminar*

Wilibald Gurlitt (1889–1963) was professor of musicology at the University of Freiburg, and was friends with Heidegger. In the summer of 1920, they wanted to conduct a seminar together: "Dear Herr Doctor! I would like to propose something to you: to situate our planned colloquium for next semester in the course catalogue in the form of tutorials in the phenomenological foundation of musicology; *privatissime*, format still to be determined. Dr. Gurlitt along with H. If you are in agreement, I would advertise it among the 'philosophical seminars.' I think that we would satisfy an acute desire of the students' while also giving an example of concrete collaboration; and we would also very likely learn a great deal ourselves" (Letter from Heidegger to Gurlitt from July 1, 1920 [DLA: A: Heidegger. 90.90.2/1]. The seminar never took place.

*Dear Herr Löwith*

This is a later addition on the address side of the postcard. Heidegger had accidentally provided his own address (*Lerchenstrasse* 8). After noticing the mistake, he evidently sent the postcard in an envelope with the correct address on it.

*Afra Geiger*

Afra Geiger was a Jewish friend of Gertrud Jaspers who studied with both Karl Jaspers and Heidegger. She died at the Ravensbrück concentration camp.

Her future as a philosopher had been blocked by Husserl solely on the grounds that she was a woman. See also Karl Löwith, *Mein Leben in Deutschland*, 60 (*My Life in Germany*, 62). See also *Heidegger-Jaspers Briefwechsel*, 18, 22, and 223 (note 6 to letter 3) (*The Heidegger-Jaspers Correspondence*, 26, 30, and 215).

**12.** M.H. to K.L., October 20, 1920, Postcard (copy)

*Frau Szilasi*

Lili Szilasi was the wife of Wilhelm Szilasi. She later gave Heidegger's son Hermann piano lessons.

*your little club*

It cannot be determined who precisely belonged to this "little club."

*he is not to ruin the whole matter*

The "matter" referred to is Becker's planned habilitation.

*but he is "unfortunately a Jew"*

Heidegger's source in the matter of Becker's habilitation was probably Husserl.

*Please tell Wilke*

In the summer semester of 1920, Rudolf Wilke participated in Heidegger's seminar "Phänomenologische Übungen" ("Phenomenological Tutorials"). He earned his doctorate at the University of Cologne in 1923 with his work *Logischen Studien zum Problem teleologischen Geschehens*.

**13.** K.L. to M.H., 1920, Postcard

*[1920]*

The postcard must have been written before the letter from November 29, 1920, and likely after Heidegger's letter from October 20, since he had to have been in Freiburg at that time.

*The decision on Baden-Baden ended positively*

Löwith worked as a private tutor in Baden-Baden.

*Leyendecker*

Herbert Leyendecker (1885–1958) belonged to the Munich school of phenomenology. He published *Zur Phänomenologie der Täuschungen* (Halle an der Saale: Max Niemeyer, 1915). He later worked as an art dealer.

**14. K.L. to M.H., November 29, 1920, Letter**

*Rickert's tearjerker*

Löwith is probably referring to the following text: Heinrich Rickert, *Die Philosophie des Lebens: Darstellung und Kritik der philosophischen Modeströmungen unserer Zeit* (Tübingen: J. C. B. Mohr, 1920).

*the superb Nietzsche–Rohde correspondence*

Elisabeth Förster-Nietzsche and Fritz Scholl (editors), *Friedrich Nietzsches Briefwechsel mit Erwin Rohde* (Leipzig: Insel Verlag, 1902).

*the Hölderlin letters in Dilthey's Teubner edition*

This likely refers to the following text: Wilhelm Dilthey, *Das Erlebnis und die Dichtung: Lessing, Goethe, Novalis, Hölderlin* (Leipzig/Berlin: B. G. Teubner, 1919).

Passiones animae *by Descartes*

It cannot be determined to which edition of Descartes' book he is referring.

*Kierkegaard's* Furcht und Zittern *and* Wiederholung

Sören Kierkegaard, *Furcht und Zittern/Wiederholung*, translated into German by H. Gottsched. *Gesammelte Werke*, Volume 3 (Jena: Diederich, second improved edition, 1909).

*G. Keller's* Sinngedicht

Gottfried Keller, *Das Sinngedicht: Novellen* (Berlin: Wilhelm Hertz, 1882).

*all else I heard from F.*

This probably refers to Fritz Leopold Kaufmann (1891–1958). He habilitated with Husserl in 1926 with his work *Die Philosophie des Grafen Paul Yorck von Wartenburg*, which was published in 1928 in Volume IX of *Jahrbuch für Philosophie und phänomenologische Forschung* (1–235). He was an independent scholar in Freiburg until 1933, and emigrated to the United States in 1938. See Karl Löwith, *Mein Leben in Deutschland*, 61 (*My Life in Germany*, 62).

### Cleverness in the style of Neumann

Friedrich ("Fritz") Neumann. Regarding Neumann, see GA 60, 340 (*The Phenomenology of Religious Life*, 256). See also Theodore Kisiel, *The Genesis of Heidegger's Being and Time* (Berkeley: University of California Press, 1994), 167, and *Heidegger-Jaspers Briefwechsel*, 15–19 (*The Heidegger-Jaspers Correspondence*, 24–27).

### have you heard anything about Husserl getting an offer from Leipzig?

As Löwith himself suspected, the information was incorrect.

### How is it going, anyway, with the Husserl seminars?

In the winter semester, Husserl gave the following two seminars: "Phänomenologie der Abstraktion" and "Phänomenologie des Zeitbewußtseins." As his assistant, Heidegger also took part in the seminars.

### in the second investigation

The second logical investigation has the title: "Die ideale Einheit der Spezies und die neueren Abstraktionstheorien," in Edmund Husserl, *Logische Untersuchungen*, Volume II/1, Volume II/2, *Elemente einer phänomenologischen Aufklärung der Erkenntnis* (Halle an der Saale: Max Niemeyer, second revised edition, 1913). The sixth logical investigation first appeared in 1921 under the title *Logische Untersuchungen*, Volume II/2, *Elemente einer phänomenologischen Aufklärung der Erkenntnis*, in the second revised edition.

### how is the time-seminar going for the 'initiates'?

In the winter semester of 1920/21, Husserl gave a seminar entitled "Phänomenologie des Zeitbewußtseins." As Husserl's assistant, Heidegger also participated in this seminar.

*such as M. Weber*

Karl Emil Maximilian ("Max") Weber (1864–1920) was a political scientist, economist, and sociologist. He was given a chair of political economics at the University of Freiburg in 1894, and in 1897 he transferred to Heidelberg. His major works include *Die soziale Gründe des Untergangs der antiken Kultur*, in *Die Wahrheit*: Volume 3, Issue 63 (Stuttgart: Friedrich Frommanns Verlag, 1896), 57–77; *Die protestantische Ethik und der Geist des Kapitalismus* (Tübingen: J. C. B. Mohr, 1905); and *Wirtschaft und Gesellschaft: 1. Die Wirtschaft und die gesellschaftlichen Ordnungen und Mächte* (Tübingen: J. C. B. Mohr, 1921). In 1919, he gave the following two famous lectures in Munich: "Politik als Beruf" and "Wissenschaft als Beruf," the latter of which had a big impact on Löwith. See Max Weber, *Max Weber Gesamtausgabe*, Volume I/17: *Wissenschaft als Beruf 1917/1919 / Politik als Beruf 1919*, edited by Wolfgang J. Mommsen and Wolfgang Schluchter, along with Birgit Morgenbrod (Tübingen: J. C. B. Mohr, 1992).

*the Rickert text*

Heinrich Rickert, *Die Philosophie des Lebens*.

*your handwriting*

This probably refers to a manuscript of Heidegger's that Löwith had presumably given to Marseille. Walter William Marseille (1901–1983) was friends with Löwith and studied with Heidegger in Marburg. He graduated in 1926 with his work *Beiträge zur Untersuchung der den graphologischen Systemen von J. H. Michon und L. Klages zugrundeliegende Begrifflichkeit*. He moved to Vienna in 1933, and then emigrated to the United States in 1940. After World War II, he sent his essay "A Method to Enforce World Peace" to Albert Einstein and Bertrand Russell, both of whom welcomed it with interest. (This led to a series of correspondences between them.) In 1954, he became a psychoanalyst in Berkeley, California.

**15.** M.H. to K.L., December 17, 1920, Postcard (copy)

*Many thanks for your card*

The postcard is not in the possession of the estate.

*The graphological analysis*

The "graphological matter" likely refers to an early draft of the dissertation of Löwith's friend Marseille.

*Driesch*

Hans Adolf Eduard Driesch (1867–1941) became Extraordinarius Professor at the University of Heidelberg in 1911. In 1917, following the departure of Emil Lask, his position was converted to an Ordinarius honorary professorship. In 1920, Driesch accepted a position at the University of Cologne, and in 1921 he moved to Leipzig. He was prematurely retired in 1933, owing to the fact that he was considered to be a pacifist and a Jewish sympathizer. His major work is *Philosophie des Organischen* (Leipzig: Wilhelm Engelmann Verlag, 1921).

*system of religious philosophy*

Heinrich Scholz, *Religionsphilosophie* (Berlin: Reuther & Reichard, 1921).

*a discourse on Hegel*

Heinrich Scholz, *Die Bedeutung der Hegelschen Philosophie für das philosophische Denken der Gegenwart* (Berlin: Reuther & Reichard, 1921).

*the second edition of Spengler*

Oswald Spengler, *Preußentum und Sozialismus* (Munich: C. H. Beck, 1921).

*Vol. I of the* Logical Investigations

Edmund Husserl, *Logische Untersuchungen*, two volumes.

*Scheler is to speak here around this time*

This could refer to Scheler's 1920 lecture "Der Friede unter den Konfessionen." In Max Scheler, *Gesammelte Werke*, Volume 6: *Schriften zur Soziologie und Weltanschauungslehre*, second revised edition with supplements and lesser-known writings from the time of *Schriften*, edited with an appendix by Maria Scheler (Bern: Francke, 1963), 227–258.

**16. K.L. to M.H., January 22, 1921, Letter**

*Schapiro*

Karl Schapiro was a musician, and was friends with Löwith.

*a seminar on the history of medieval history and Aristotle?!*

In the summer semester of 1921, Heidegger gave a lecture on Augustine and Neoplatonism (in GA 60, 158–246 and 270–299) (*The Phenomenology of Religious Life*, 113–184). At the same time, Heidegger conducted tutorials on Aristotle's *De anima*. These are published in *Heidegger-Jahrbuch 3, Heidegger und Aristoteles* (2007), 9–22, with a postscript by Oskar Becker. A postscript for this seminar is also in the possession of Löwith's estate.

*Spemann*

Hans Spemann (1869–1941) was a professor of zoology at the University of Freiburg from 1919 until his retirement in 1937. He received the Nobel Prize for physiology and medicine in 1935.

*the problem of expression in Croce*

Probably prompted by Heidegger's lecture course "Phänomenologie der Anschauung und des Ausdrucks: Theorie der philosophischen Begriffsbildung" (GA 59), given in the summer semester of 1920, but in connection to Benedetto Croce and seeking out new directions (*Phenomenology of Intuition and Expression*, translated by Tracy Colony [London: Continuum, 2010]).

*the big edition of van Gogh's letters*

Vincent van Gogh, *Breife an seinen Bruder.*

*and also to your wife*

Elfride Heidegger (whose maiden name was Petri) (1893–1992).

## 17. M.H. to K.L., January 25, 1921, Postcard

*Ebbinghaus will address Hegel's essay on natural law in the seminar*

Since the course catalogue from the University of Freiburg does not advertise an Ebbinghaus seminar, Ebbinghaus probably discussed Hegel's essay on natural law in Heidegger's seminar, as Löwith had similarly done with a paper on Croce.

*the Stern-Neumann clique*

This refers to Erich Stern and Friedrich Neumann. Hans Jonas and Günther Stern also participated in this seminar. Hans Jonas (1903–1993) studied in Freiburg with Husserl and Heidegger and later in Marburg with Heidegger and Bultmann. He graduated in 1928 on the basis of his work on the concept of *gnosis*. While in Marburg, he made the acquaintance of Hannah Arendt, with whom he remained a lifelong friend. In 1933, Jonas was forced to emigrate from Germany, first to Great Britain and then later (in 1935) to Palestine. He later became a professor at Hebrew University in Jerusalem; then (in 1949) at McGill University in Montreal; and later (in 1955) at the New School for Social Research in New York. His works include *Gnosis und spätantiker Geist, Teil 1: Die mythologische Gnosis* (Göttingen: Vandenhoeck & Ruprecht, 1934), and *Das Prinzip Verantwortung: Versuch einer Ethik für die technologische Zivilisation* (Frankfurt am Main: Insel Verlag, 1979). Günther Siegmund Stern (1902–1992) commenced studying with Heidegger and Husserl in the winter semester of 1920/1921, and then followed Heidegger to Marburg. He graduated under Husserl in 1924 with his work *Die Rolle der Situationskategorie bei den "Logischen Sätzen": Erster Teil einer Untersuchung über die Rolle der Situationskategorie*. While in Marburg in 1925 he met Hannah Arendt, to whom he was later married (from 1929 to 1937). In Berlin in 1930, his attempt to habilitate (under Paul Tillich) failed. Thereafter, he became a freelance writer under the pseudonym Anders. In 1928, he published *Über das Haben: Sieben Kapitel zur Ontologie der Erkenntnis* (Bonn: Friedrich Cohen). His major work is *Die Antiquiertheit des Menschen. Volume I: Über die Seele im Zeitalter der zweiten industriellen Revolution* (Munich: C. H. Beck, 1956), and *Volume II: Über die Zerstörung des Lebens im Zeitalter der dritten industriellen Revolution* (Munich: C. H. Beck, 1980).

*In my lectures*

In the winter semester of 1920/21, Heidegger presented his "Einleitung in die Phänomenologie der Religion" ("Introduction to the Phenomenology of

Religion"), now in GA 60, 3–156 (*The Phenomenology of Religious Life*, 1–111).

*the annual edition containing Pfänder's logic*

Alexander Pfänder, *Logik*, in *Jahrbuch für Philosophie und phänomenologische Forschung IV* (1921), 139–499.

*the paper by Ingarden*

Roman Ingarden, "Über die Gefahr einer Petitio principii in der Erkenntnistheorie," in *Jahrbuch für Philosophie und phänomenologische Forschung* IV (1921), 545–568.

*Fräulein Stein has a new book*

Edith Stein, *Eine Untersuchung über den Staat*, in *Jahrbuch für Philosophie und phänomenologische Forschung VII* (1925), 1–123.

*the seminar on time*

Husserl held a seminar entitled "Phänomenologie des Zeitbewußtseins" during the winter semester of 1920/21. No additional information could be obtained regarding Dr. Erich Schwarz.

*I would like to come to your presentation*

Apparently, Löwith gave a presentation in the Husserl seminar.

**18. K.L. to M.H., February 18, 1921, Postcard**

*the historical*

This likely refers to the third and fourth chapters of Heidegger's lecture course "Einleitung in die Phänomenologie der Religion" ("Introduction to the Phenomenology of Religion") from the winter semester of 1920/21 (GA 60, 31–65) (*The Phenomenology of Religious Life*, 61–82). Heidegger canceled the meeting of the 30th of November, 1920. In the sessions following this cancellation, Heidegger interpreted concrete religious phenomena in connection with the letters of Paul.

*Will Afra Geiger be assigned the Romantics?*

Afra Geiger was supposed to edit a new edition of Hamann's letters. See Heidegger's postcard from April 2, 1921 (Document 21).

*Aus Schellings Leben in Briefen*

Gustav Leopold Plitt (editor), *Aus Schellings Leben in Briefen*, 3 Volumes (Leipzig: Hirzel, 1869–1870).

**19.** M.H. to K.L., Winter 1921, Postcard (copy)

*Rothacker gave a talk here yesterday*

No additional information regarding Erich Rothacker's speech could be found.

*Finke*

Heinrich Finke (1855–1938) was professor of history at the University of Freiburg starting in 1899. He was a father-like friend of Heidegger who advocated for him up through his habilitation. See also Finke's letters to Heidegger in *Heidegger-Jahrbuch 1* (2004), 71 ff.

*Schmitz-Kallenberg*

Ludwig Schmitz-Kallenberg (1867–1937) was professor of history at the University of Münster.

**20.** K.L. to M.H., February 26, 1921, Letter

*Keyserling*

Count Hermann Keyserling (1880–1946) was an ingenious thinker. After failing his habilitation at the University of Berlin, Keyserling traveled extensively. After a one-year trip around the world, he published *Reisetagebuch eines Philosophen* (two volumes, Darmstadt: Reichl, 1919). In 1920, he founded the "Schule der Weisheit" ("School of Wisdom") in order to disseminate his metaphysical philosophy of sense. His works include *Philosophie als Kunst* (Darmstadt: Reichl, 1920) and *Schöpferische Erkenntnis* (Darmstadt: Reichl, 1922).

## Kahler

Erich Gabriel von Kahler (1885–1970) was in the same circles as Stefan George and Max Weber. He fled to Zurich in 1933 and there developed a close friendship with Thomas Mann. He emigrated to the United States in 1938 and became professor of history and philosophy of history at the New School for Social Research in New York, and at Black Mountain College in North Carolina. He became professor of German literature at Cornell University in Ithaca in 1947. His works include *Der Beruf der Wissenschaft: Der deutsche Charakter in der Geschichte Europas* (Zurich: Europa-Verlag, 1937); *Die Verantwortung des Geistes* (Frankfurt am Main: S. Fischer, 1952); *Dichter wider Willen* (Zurich: Rhein-Verlag, 1958); and *The Disintegration of Form in the Arts* (New York: Braziller, 1968).

## Vaihinger

Hans Vaihinger, *Nietzsche als Philosoph*, fourth revised edition (Berlin: Reuther & Reichard, 1916).

## Kerler's pamphlet

Dietrich Henrich Kerler, *Nietzsche und die Vergeltungsidee: Zur Strafrechtsreform* (Ulm: Kerler, 1910).

## epicure of "that which is necessary!"

See Democritus, Fragment B85: ὁ ἀντιλογεόμενος καὶ πολλὰ λεσχηνευόμενος ἀφυὴς ἐς μάθησιν ὧν κρή. Hermann Diels translates as follows: "Wer widerspricht und viel schwätzt, ist unfähig zum Lernen dessen, was not tut." ("Whosoever contradicts and blathers on endlessly is incapable of learning what is necessary.") See also Martin Heidegger, "Anmerkungen zu Karl Jaspers Psychologie der Weltanschauungen," in GA 9, 4 ("Remarks on Karl Jaspers' 'Psychology of Worldviews,'" in *Pathmarks*, 3).

## Herr Bury

Curiously, the name Bury occurs neither in the enrollment list of Heidegger's lectures nor in his seminar books.

## 21. K.L. to M.H., March 19, 1921, Postcard

*Vaihinger*

This presumably refers to Hans Vaihinger, *Die Philosophie des Als-Ob: System der theoretischen, praktischen und religiösen Fiktionen der Menschheit auf Grund eines idealistischen Positivismus, mit einem Anhang über Kant und Nietzsche* (Berlin: Reuther & Reichert, 1911).

*Monrad*

This presumably refers to Olaf Peter Monrad, *Søren Kierkegaard: Sein Leben und seine Werke* (Jena: Diederichs, 1919).

*Balzac*

It could not be determined to which work of Honoré de Balzac's this refers.

*Gundolf (the Archipelagus essay)*

Friedrich Gundolf, *Hölderlins Archipelagus*, a public test lecture held on the 26th of April, 1911 (Heidelberg: Weiss'sche Universitäts-Buchhandlung, 1916).

## 22. M.H. to K.L., April 2, 1921, Postcard (copy)

*my lecture*

Heidegger lectured concerning Augustine and Neoplatonism in the summer semester of 1921. Now in GA 60, 158–299 (*The Phenomenology of Religious Life*, 113–184).

## 23. K.L. to M.H., August 15, 1921, Postcard

*the Walthers*

This refers to Gerda Walther and her friend.

*Augustine's Sermones 1521*

St. Augustine of Hippo, *Sermones* (Haganoae, 1521).

*Die psychische Dingwelt*

Wilhelm Haas, *Die psychische Dingwelt* (Bonn: Friedrich Cohen, 1921).

*young Bauer*

Walter Bauer (1901–1968) was a student of economics who attended Heidegger's courses in the early 1920s. He was a friend of Heidegger and his family. See Martin Heidegger and Elisabeth Blochmann, *Briefwechsel 1918–1969*, edited by Joachim W. Storck (Marbach am Neckar: Deutsche Schillergesellschaft, second revised edition, 1990), 140 f.

**24.** K.L. to M.H., August 17, 1921, Letter

*Blüher*

Hans Blüher (1888–1955) worked as an independent scholar in Berlin. Philosophically, he was oriented toward Nietzsche, and had a decisive influence on the *Wandervogelbewegung* ("Rambling Movement"). His works include *Wandervogel: Geschichte einer Jugendbewegung*, two volumes (Berlin-Tempelhof: Bernhard Weise, 1912); *Die deutsche Wandervogelbewegung als erotisches Phänomen: Ein Beitrag zur sexuellen Inversion* (Lichtenrade-Berlin: Friedrich Ruhland, 1912); and *Die Rolle der Erotik der männlichen Gesellschaft: Eine Theorie der Staatsbildung nach Wesen und Wert*, two Volumes (Jena: Diederichs, 1917–1919).

*akin to the "temptations"*

In German: "Versuchung" ("Temptation"). This is probably an allusion to Augustine. Heidegger had lectured on Augustine and Neoplatonism in the summer semester of 1921.

*"stages of despair"*

Kierkegaard describes three stages of despair in his book *The Sickness Unto Death*.

*Notes from the Underground*

Fyodor Dostoevsky, *Aus dem Dunkel der Großstadt: Acht Novellen*, translated by E. K. Rashin, in *Sämtliche Werke* (with the assistance of Dmitri

Mereschkoski), edited by Moeller von den Bruck, Volume 20 (Munich: R. Piper & Co., 1916).

## Gustav Landauer

Gustav Landauer (1870–1919) was one of the most important theorists of anarchism and pacifism. In April 1919, he became a member of the so-called "Munich Soviet Republic." He was killed by soldiers of the volunteer corps.

## Percy Gothein

Percy Paul Heinrich Gothein (1896–1944) was a university friend of Löwith. He later became known as an author and renaissance scholar. He also belonged to the George Circle. After failing to complete his dissertation, he pursued his own path outside of academia. His publications include "Die antiken Reminiszenzen in den Chansons de Geste," in *Zeitschrift für französische Sprache und Literatur* 50 (1927), 39–84; *Francesco Barbaro: Früh-Humanismus und Staatskunst in Venedig* (Berlin: Die Runde, 1932); and *Zacharias Trevisan-Leben und Umkreis* (Amsterdam: Pantheon, 1944). He also translated Francesco Barbaro's *Das Buch von der Ehe (De re uxoria)* (Berlin: Die Runde, 1933).

## Knut Hamsun

Knut Hamsun, *Mysterien*, translated by J. Sandmeier (Munich: Albert Lang Verlag, 1894).

## "Ein Gespräch mit dem jungen Bauer"

It is not clear to what Löwith is referring.

## Reinach's collected works

Adolf Reinach (1883–1917) habilitated with Husserl in 1908 with his *Entwurf zur Urteilstheorie*. See Adolf Reinach, *Gesammelte Schriften*, edited by his students (Halle an der Saale: Max Niemeyer, 1921).

## the complete writings of Rickert

Heinrich Rickert (1863–1936) was Heidegger's habilitation director and was (along with Wilehelm Windelband) the most important representative of the

Baden school of Neo-Kantianism. He was Ordinarius Professor of philosophy at the University of Freiburg from 1896 until 1916, after which time he transferred to Heidelberg. For more about Rickert and Heidegger, see Martin Heidegger/ Heinrich Rickert, *Briefe 1912 bis 1933 und andere Dokumente*, edited by Alfred Denker (Frankfurt am Main: Vittorio Klostermann, 2002).

*your lectures on the transcendental*

Löwith is referring to Heidegger's lecture "Phänomenologie und transzendentale Wertphilosophie" ("Phenomenology and Transcendental Philosophy of Value") from summer semester 1919. The critique of Rickert forms the conclusion of the lecture, which is available in GA 56/57, 177–203 (*Towards the Definition of Philosophy*, translated by Ted Sadler [London: Continuum, 2000], 135–152).

*(second level!)*

This is an allusion to Emil Lask. In his book *Die Logik der Philosophie and die Kategorienlehre*, Lask differentiates between what he refers to as the first, second, and third levels. The first level includes all essential points that can be grasped about a logical form. Logical form is validity-content and takes, at the third level, the form of validity. See Emil Lask, *Die Logik der Philosophie und die Kategorienlehre* (Tübingen: J. B. C. Mohr, 1911), 112.

*"what is decisive in Kierkegaard is the methodological consciousness"*

Löwith here cites freely from a sentence in Heidegger's "Anmerkungen zu Karl Jaspers 'Psychologie der Weltanschauungen'" (GA 9), 41 ("Remarks on Karl Jaspers' 'Psychology of Worldviews,'" in *Pathmarks*, 36): "Concerning Kierkegaard, we should point out that such a heightened consciousness of methodological rigor as his has rarely been achieved in philosophy or theology (the question of where he achieved this rigor is not important here). One loses sight of nothing less than the most important aspect of Kierkegaard's thought when one overlooks this consciousness of method, or when one's treatment of it takes it to be of secondary importance."

*Christian Discourses*

Søren Kierkegaard, *Ausgewählte Christliche Reden*. Translated from the Danish by Julie von Reincke. The volume includes an appendix regarding Kierkegaard's familial and private life as told by his niece K. Lund; it also includes a drawing of Kierkegaard and his father (Giessen: Alfred Töpelmann, 1909).

*You speak of the historically enacting life*

Martin Heidegger, "Anmerkungen zu Jaspers 'Psychologie der Weltanschauungen'" (GA 9), 35 ("Remarks on Jaspers' 'Psychology of Worldviews,'" in *Pathmarks*, 30–31): "That our factical, historically enacted life is at work right within 'how' we factically approach the problem of 'how' the self, in being anxiously concerned about itself, appropriates itself—this is something that belongs originally to the very sense of the factical 'I am.'"

*(quaestio mihi factus sum)*

St. Augustine of Hippo, *Confessions* X, 50.

*defluxus in multa*

See GA 60, 206 ff. (*The Phenomenology of Religious Life*, 152 ff.).

*robustus in existentia sua*

"The hidden motto of his existential ontology—'*Unus quisque robustus sit in existentia sua*' [Johannes Ficker, *Luthers Vorlesung über den Römerbrief*, Volume 1, with commentary (Leipzig: Diederichs, 1908), 122]—also comes from Luther. Heidegger [. . .] translates it into German by ceaselessly insisting on that which alone is important to him: that 'each individual do what his capacities permit'—that is to say, 'the authentic capacity-for-Being always specific to an individual,' or the 'existential limit of our ownmost particular historical facticity'" (Löwith, *Mein Leben in Deutschland*, 32) (*My Life in Germany*, 31).

*Geiger's* Unbewußte

Moritz Geiger (1880–1937) was Extraordinarius Professor of philosophy in Munich. From 1923 until 1933, he was Ordinarius Professor of philosophy in Göttingen. In 1933, he emigrated to the United States, and later taught at Stanford University. He belonged to the Munich school of phenomenology. His publications include *Beiträge zur Phänomenologie des ästhetischen Genusses*, in *Jahrbuch für Philosophie und phänomenologische Forschung* I (1913), 567–684; and *Das Unbewusste und die psychische Realität*, in *Jahrbuch für Philosophie und phänomenologische Forschung* IV (1921), 1–138.

*you speak of a different anteriority in "reflection"*

Martin Heidegger, "Anmerkungen zu Karl Jaspers 'Psychologie der Weltanschauungen'," in GA 9, 42–44 ("Comments on Karl Jaspers' 'Psychology of Worldviews,'" in *Pathmarks*, 36–38).

*Rieniets*

Karl Rieniets was a physician and a university friend of Löwith. He was a member of the Munich Fraternity of Free Students. No additional information regarding Rieniets could be obtained.

*those lectures on the future of German educational institutions*

Friedrich Nietzsche, "*Über die Zukunft unserer Bildungsanstalten*," in Friedrich Nietzsche, *Nietzsches Werke* 9, Part 2, Volume 1, *Nachgelassene Werke aus den Jahren 1869–1872* (Leipzig: Naumann; completely revised edition, 1903), 295–382.

*"in German one lies when being polite"*

Johann Wolfgang Goethe, *Faust 2*, chapter 20.

**26.** K.L. to M.H., October 1, 1921, Postcard

*the new Augustine book by W. Achelis*

Wilhelm Achelis, *Augustinus, Bischofs von Hippo: Analyse seines geistigen Schaffens auf Grund seiner erotischen Struktur* (Prien am Chiemsee: Kampmann & Schanel, 1921).

**27.** M.H. to K.L., October 3, 1921, Postcard (copy)

*your postcards from Heilbronn and Munich*

The postcard from Heilbronn is not in the possession of the estate.

*a 2-hour tutorial for wider circles*

Husserl held his "Phänomenologische Übungen" ["Phenomenological Tutorials"] in the winter semester of 1921/1922.

*I could easily give a 4-hour a week lecture and still not be finished*

> GA 61 (*Phenomenological Interpretations of Aristotle: Initiation into Phenomenological Research*, translated by Richard Rojcewicz [Bloomington: Indiana University Press, 2008]).

*tenacious go-getters like Bauer*

> According to the list of students for the summer semester of 1921, this was Walter Bauer.

*preliminary discussion for the tutorials*

> "Phänomenologische Übungen für Anfänger im Anschluß an Husserl, *Logische Untersuchungen* II" ("Phenomenological Tutorials for Beginners in Connection with Husserl's *Logical Investigations* II").

*the Augustine book*

> Wilhelm Achelis, *Augustinus*.

**28.** K.L. to M.H., October 17, 1921, Letter

*a wonderful evening of Beethoven (featuring Lamond)*

> On the 16th of October, 1921, the Scottish pianist Frederic Lamond performed an evening of Beethoven in the concert hall at the hotel *Vier Jahreszeiten*. Thomas Mann (among others) was in attendance. See Gert Heine & Paul Schommer, *Thomas Mann Chronik* (Frankfurt am Main: Vittorio Klostermann, 2004), 122.

*Johannes Müller*

> Johannes Müller (1864–1949) was a Lutheran theologian. Beginning in 1916, he led a "Sanctuary for Private Life" at the Elmau castle, which was specially built for the purpose. His publications include *Die Reden Jesu*, 3 volumes (Munich: C. H. Beck, 1908–1918).

*"Wesen und Beziehung"*

> Friedrich Gundolf, "Wesen und Beziehung," in *Jahrbuch für die geistige Bewegung* 2 (1911), 10–55.

*"Der Teppich des Lebens"*

> Stefan George, *Der Teppich des Lebens und die Lieder von Traum und Tod mit einem Vorspiel* (Berlin: Georg Bondi, 1921).

*Blüher's Christology*

> Hans Blüher, *Die Aristide des Jesus von Nazareth: Philosophische Grundlegung der Lehre und Erscheinung Christi* (Prien am Chiemsee: Kampmann & Schnabel, 1921).

*Wyneken*

> Gustav Wyneken (1875–1964) was an education reformer and founder of *Der Freien Schulgemeinde Wickersdorf* ("The Free Community School of Wickersdorf"). He temporarily played a leading role in the German youth-movement; however, in 1920 he was convicted of engaging in sexual misconduct with his students. His writings include: *Die neue Jugend: Ihr Kampf um Freiheit und Wahrheit in Schule und Elternhaus in Religion und Erotik* (Munich: Steinicke, 1914), and *Der Kampf um die Jugend – Gesammelte Aufsätze* (Jena: Diederichs, 1919).

*Franz Marc*

> Franz Marc, *Briefe aus dem Feld* (Munich: Piper, 1920).

*a big Lehmbruck exhibit*

> August Wilhelm Lehmbruck (1881–1919) was a sculptor. In 1919, he was elected to the Prussian Academy of Arts; on the 25th of March of that same year, he committed suicide. A memorial exhibition of his work was held in Munich in July/August of 1921.

## 29. K.L. to M.H., August 17, 1922, Letter

*von Rohden*

> Wilhelm von Rohden (1901–1990) was an evangelical theologian and student of Heidegger and Bultmann.

*the Logos article*

> Edmund Husserl, "Philosophie als strenge Wissenschaft," in *Logos* I (1910–1911), 289–340.

*this summer regarding Göttingen*

Moritz Geiger and Heidegger were both candidates for a position at the University of Göttingen. In 1923, Geiger was appointed there as Ordinarius Professor of philosophy. Löwith had considered following Heidegger to Göttingen in the event of his transfer.

*the Nietzsche volume with his (hitherto unpublished) early writings*

Friedrich Nietzsche, *Nietzsches Werke* 9, Part 2, Volume 1, *Nachgelassene Werke aus den Jahren 1869–1872.*

*Overbeck*

Franz Overbeck (1837–1905) was a Swiss theologian and a friend of Friedrich Nietzsche. In 1870, he became professor of New Testament exegesis and ancient church history at the University of Basel.

*Lucus a non lucendo*

"'Grove' is derived from 'not shining'" (a proverbial, false etymology).

*Are you sure that you will come to Feldafing in September?*

The Szilasis lived in Feldafing.

**30.** M.H. to K.L., before September 1922, Postcard (copy)

*The old man*

Edmund Husserl.

*Regarding the other things by Ritschl, Sulpicius Severus, and Sedulius*

This probably refers to the following books: P. Bihlmeyer, *Die Schriften des Sulpicius Severus über den Heiligen Martin, Bischof von Tours*, Bibliothek der Kirchenväter, Volume 20 (Kempten/ Munich: Kösel Verlag, 1914), and an edition of Sedulius' *Paschale Carmen*. Albrecht Benjamin Ritschl (1822–1889) was a theologian; it is not known which of his works Heidegger wanted to buy.

**31.** M.H. to K.L., September 20, 1922, Letter (copy)

*a registered letter including travel money arrived from Jaspers*

> See *Heidegger-Jaspers Briefwechsel*, 32–35 (*The Heidegger-Jaspers Correspondence*, 39–41).

*I will now write an "introduction" after all (though a very condensed and propaedeutic one)*

> Martin Heidegger, "*Phänomenologische Interpretationen zu Aristoteles: Anzeige der hermeneutischen Situation*" (known as "*Bericht an Natorp*," "*Aristoteles-Einleitung*," or just "*Einleitung*"). First published in *Dilthey-Jahrbuch* (6) 1989, 236–274, with an introductory essay by Hans-Georg Gadamer, 228–234, and an afterword by the editor Hans-Ulrich Lessing, 270–274. Now available as "Phänomenologische Interpretationen zu Aristoteles: Ausarbeitung für die Marburger und die Göttinger Philosophische Fakultät," 575, edited by Günther Neumann, with Gadamer's essay "Heideggers 'theologische' Jugendschrift," 76–86, an afterword by the editor, 87–100, and notes, 101–106 (Stuttgart: Reclam, 2003). Now also in GA 62, 345–419 ("Phenomenological Interpretations in Connection with Aristotle: An Indication of the Hermeneutical Situation," in *Supplements: From the Earliest Essays to "Being and Time" and Beyond*, ed. John Van Buren [Albany: State University of New York Press, 2002], 111–145).

*the critique*

> Martin Heidegger, "Anmerkungen zu Karl Jaspers 'Psychologie der Weltanschauungen'," in GA 9, 144 ("Comments on Karl Jasper's 'Psychology of Worldviews,'" in *Pathmarks*, 1–38).

*Marianne Weber*

> Marianne Weber (1870–1954) was Max Weber's widow and was very active in the women's movement. She published *Fichtes Sozialismus und sein Verhältnis zur Marxschen Doktrin* (Tübingen: J. C. B. Mohr, 1900), and her major work *Ehefrau und Mutter in der Rechtsentwicklung: Eine Einführung* (Tübingen: J. C. B. Mohr, 1907). After Max Weber's death in 1920, Marianne focused her efforts on publishing his manuscripts. Max Weber's major work *Wirtschaft und Gesellschaft*, and the seven volumes of his *Gesammelte Aufsätze*, were

published by her between 1921 and 1924. Her influential biography *Max Weber: Ein Lebensbild* (Tübingen: J.C.B. Mohr) appeared in 1926. She was friends with Gertrud Bäumer, who was also a friendly acquaintance of Elfride Heidegger.

## The second edition

The two revised editions of Jaspers' *Psychologie der Weltanschauungen* (Berlin: Springer) appeared in 1922.

### 32. K.L. to M.H., September 22, 1922, Letter

*"phenomenology of race"*

Ludwig Ferdinand Clauss (1892–1974) was a psychologist. From 1917 until 1921, he studied with both Husserl and Heidegger in Freiburg, where he also came to know Löwith. He attempted to habilitate in 1923 with his publication *Die nordische Seele: Artung, Prägung, Ausdruck* (Halle an der Saale: Max Niemeyer, 1923), which Husserl firmly rejected on the grounds of its personal attacks on Jewish "degeneracy." Löwith later reviewed his book *Rasse und Seele: Eine Einführung in die Gegenwart* (Munich: J. F. Lehmann, 1926), available in *Mensch und Menschenwelt,* LSS 1, edited by Klaus Stichweh (Stuttgart: J. B. Metzler, 1981, 198–208), first published in *Zeitschrift für Menschenkunde* 2 (1926/1927), 18–26). Clauss later became a leading race theorist.

*("Erkenntnis Gottes")*

Auguste Joseph Alphonse Gratry, *Über die Erkenntnis Gottes,* 3 Volumes; Volume 1: *Über die Erkenntnis Gottes;* Volume 2: *Über die Erkenntnis des Menschen in seiner Denkthätigkeit;* Volume 3: *Über die Erkenntnis der Seele* (Regensburg: Verlag von Georg Joseph Manz, 1858).

*"Der Monat Mariä: 31 Betrachtungen"*

Auguste Joseph Alphonse Gratry, *Der Monat Mariä von der unbefleckten Empfängnis.* Translated into German by K. J. Pfahler (Regensburg: printing and publication by Georg Joseph Manz, 1859).

*"Les sources conseils pour la conduite de l'esprit"*

Auguste Joseph Alphonse Gratry, *Les sources, conseils pour conduire l'esprit* (Paris: Téqui, 1862).

*"a certain Herr Dr. Scheler and a certain Dr. Hildebrandt"*

Dietrich von Hildebrandt (1889–1977) was a Privatdozent at the University of Munich from 1918 to 1924, and Extraordinarius Professor from 1924 to 1933. He emigrated to Austria in 1933, then to France in 1939, and finally to the United States in 1940. From 1941 to 1960, he was a professor at Fordham University, New York. His major works are *Metaphysik der Gemeinschaft* (Augsburg: Haas & Grabherr, 1930) and *Christian Ethics* (Chicago: Franciscan Herald Press, 1953).

*Vorgeschichte und Jugend der mittelalterlichen Scholastik*

Franz Overbeck, *Vorgeschichte und Jugend der mittelalterlichen Scholastik: Eine kirchengeschichtliche Vorlesung*, edited by Carl Albrecht Bernouilli (Basel: Schwabe & Co., 1917).

*the first edition of Luther's twelve volumes in parchment by H. Lufft Wittenberg*

The *Wittenberger Luther Ausgabe* was edited by Luther and appeared in both a twelve-volume German set and a seven-volume Latin set.

*Will you skip Sextus Empiricus?*

It cannot be determined to which publication he is referring.

*The old Pappenheim translation*

Sextus Empiricus, *Pyrrhonische Grundzüge*, translated from the Greek with an introduction and annotations by Eugen Pappenheim (Leipzig: Dürr, 1877).

Overbeck's *Über die Christlichkeit der heutigen Theologie*, second edition

Franz Overbeck, *Über die Christlichkeit der heutigen Theologie*, second edition, revised with an introduction and an afterword (Leipzig: C. G. Naumann, 1903).

*Études sur Pascal*

Alexandre Rodolphe Vinet, *Études sur Pascal* (Paris: Les Éditeurs, 1848) and Victor Cousin, *Études sur Pascal*, 5, edited, revised, and augmented (Paris: Didier, 1857).

## Schleiermacher's Einleitung in das Neue Testament

This perhaps refers to Friedrich Schleiermacher, *Sämtliche Werke*, Volume 8: *Friedrich Schleiermachers literarischer Nachlaß zur Theologie*, Volume. 3: *Einleitung in das Neue Testament* (Berlin: Reimer, 1845).

## F. Schlegel's Briefe

This perhaps refers to *Friedrich Schlegels Briefe an seinen Bruder August Wilhelm*, edited by Oskar F. Walzel (Berlin: Speyer & Peters, 1890).

## Winckelmann's Schriften

Johann Joachim Winckelmann, *Winckelmanns Kleine Schriften zur Geschichte der Kunst des Altertums: mit Goethes Schilderung Winckelmanns*, edited by Hermann Uhde-Bernays (Leipzig: Insel Verlag, 1913).

## F. von Baader's Religionsphilosophie

It could not be determined which edition of Baader's work is being referenced. In his sixteen-volume *Sämtliche Werke*, edited by Franz Hoffmann (Leipzig: Bethmann, 1951–1960), there are four volumes that contain writings regarding the philosophy of religion.

## the complete Seneca (Teubner)

Lucius Annaeus Seneca, *Opera* (quae supersunt recognovit et rerum indicem locuplettissimum adiecit Fredericus Haase), three volumes (Leipzig/Berlin: B. G. Teubner, 1852/1853).

## the complete letters of Cicero

This perhaps refers to Marcus Tullius Cicero, *Sämtliche Briefe*, three volumes, translated by K. L. F. Mezger (Berlin-Schöneberg: Langenscheidt, 1914).

## the Manutius Commentary

This perhaps refers to Paulus Manutius, *Commentarius in M. Tulii Ciceronis epistolas ad diversos* (Leipzig: Cur. C. G. Richter, 1780).

*I am still working on a concluding chapter, in which I will retract the moments of "over-focus"*

Löwith's still-unpublished dissertation (*Auslegung von Nietzsches Selbstinterpretation und von Nietzsche-Interpretationen*) [*Exegesis of Nietzsche's Self-Interpretation and of Interpretations of Nietzsche*] was accepted on March 31, 1923, by Prof. Dr. Erich Becher, dean of the philosophy faculty. The dissertation is divided into the following sections: Review of Literature (IV); Exegesis of Nietzsche's Self-Interpretation and Interpretations of Nietzsche (1–2); Introduction (3–24); I. Elucidation of Nietzsche's Self-Interpretation (25–67); II. Self-Reflection and Self-Awareness (68–105); III. Nietzsche Interpretations (106–153); IV. Interpretation of the Doctrine of Eternal Recurrence (154–181); Review and Prognosis (182–198); Notes and Supplements (199–254).

## 35. K.L. to M.H., November 20, 1922, Letter

*Baeumker*

Clemens Baeumker (1853–1924) became a professor of philosophy in Breslau in 1883, in Bonn in 1900, and succeeded Wilhelm Windelband in Strasbourg in 1903. He transferred to the University of Munich in 1912. His areas of focus were ancient and medieval philosophy. His major work was *Witelo: Ein Philosoph und Naturforscher des 13. Jahrhunderts* (Münster: Aschendorff, 1908). See also Karl Löwith, *Mein Leben in Deutschland*, 18 (*My Life in Germany*, 16).

*Becher*

Erich Becher (1882–1929) succeeded Oswald Külpe at the University of Munich in 1916. His work was concerned with problems of psychology, natural philosophy, epistemology, and ethics.

*Wölfflin*

Heinrich Wölfflin (1864–1945) was an art historian who was friends with Jacob Burkhardt. He was appointed to the Burckhardt Chair in Basel in 1893. In 1901, he moved to Berlin, and then on to Munich in 1912. His major work is *Kunstgeschichtliche Grundbegriffe: Das Problem der Stilentwicklung in der neueren Kunst* (Munich: Bruckmann, 1915).

## E. Schwartz

Eduard Schwartz (1858–1940) was a classical philologist, and became professor and chair of classical philology at Ludwig-Maximilians University in Munich in 1919.

## Geyser

Joseph Geyser (1869–1948) was professor of philosophy in Münster from 1904 until 1917, and worked within the Aristotelian/Scholastic tradition. He transferred to the University of Freiburg in 1917, thereby putting an end to any hope Heidegger had for the Catholic Chair of philosophy there. His major works include *Lehrbuch der Psychologie* (Münster: Schöningh, 1908), *Grundlage der Logik und Erkenntnislehre: Eine Untersuchung der Formen und Prinzipien objektiv wahrer Erkenntnis* (Münster: Schöningh, 1912), and *Allgemeine Philosophie des Seins und der Natur* (Münster: Schöningh, 1915). Regarding Geyser, see also Martin Heidegger/Heinrich Rickert, *Briefe 1912 bis 1933 und andere Dokumente*, 38 f.

## Hagemann

Georg Hagemann (1832–1903) was professor of philosophy in Münster. He worked within the tradition of Aristotelian/Scholastic philosophy.

## Mercier

This likely refers to Désiré-Joseph Mercier (1851–1926), professor of philosophy at the Catholic University of Leuven from 1882 to 1905. In 1906, he became Archbishop and Cardinal of Mechelen, Belgium. Like Baeumker, he was a representative of Neo-Scholasticism.

## *"You can also read this in print in my essay in Deutschen Philosophie der Gegenwart."*

Clemens Baeumker, "Selbstdarstellung," in Raymund Schmidt (ed.), *Deutsche Philosophie der Gegenwart in Selbstdarstellungen* (Leipzig: Felix Meiner, 1921), 31–60.

## Bösemann

No information regarding Bösemann could be found. His name appears in neither the enrollment list nor in Heidegger's seminar book.

## *L. Klages once spoke during a lecture*

Presumably Klages had spoken about the cosmogonic *eros*. See Ludwig Klages, *Vom kosmogonischen Eros* (Munich: Müller, 1922).

## *Tirpitz*

Alfred von Tirpitz (1849–1930) was an admiral. In 1907, as the Secretary of State for the Reich's Naval Division, he developed the so-called "Tirpitz Plan" for expanding the German naval fleet. He later became a politician for the German National People's Party. He was friends with von Hindenburg and Ludendorff.

## *Ludendorff*

Erich Ludendorff (1865–1937) became a brigade commander in Strasbourg in 1914. During World War I, he was the leading general along with Paul von Hindenburg. After the end of the war, he went into politics along with Adolf Hitler and was involved in his coup attempt in Munich on the 9th of November, 1923. See Löwith, *Mein Leben in Deutschland*, 17 f. (*My Life in Germany*, 15 f.).

## *Walther*

Walther W. Marseille

## *Reflexionen und Maximen* by Augustine

Augustine, *Reflexionen und Maximen*, complied and translated by Adolf von Harnack (Tübingen: J. C. B. Mohr, 1922).

## *supplement to Overbeck's Harnack encyclopedia*

Overbeck's *Church Lexicon* was first made available in 1995, published by the estate.

## *those philosophies of religion (of course: a monologue) by Herr O. Gründler*

Otto Gründler, *Elemente zu einer Religionsphilosophie auf phänomenologischer Grundlage* (Munich: Kösel & Pustet, 1922).

## *Some weak stuff by Haas*

Wilhelm Haas, *Kraft und Erscheinung: Grundriss einer Dynamik des Psychischen* (Bonn: Friedrich Cohen, 1922).

*a botched book by Troeltsch*

Ernst Troeltsch, *Gesammelte Schriften*, Volume 2: *Zur religiösen Lage, Religionsphilosophie und Ethik* (Tübingen: J. C. G. Mohr, 1922).

*Utitz talked about F. Brentano*

Emil Utitz (1883–1956) lived in Prague and associated with Franz Kafka and Hugo Bergmann. He became professor of philosophy in Halle in 1924 and taught at the University of Prague from 1933 until 1939. He was strongly influenced by Franz Brentano.

*The Englishman to whom I gave lessons*

The Englishman was a certain Mr. Cuckow. The Russell text in question is: Bertrand Russell, *The Principles of Mathematics* (Cambridge: Cambridge University Press, 1903).

**36. M.H. to K.L., November 22, 1922, Letter (copy)**

*in my introductory tutorials*

Heidegger's seminar "Phänomenologische Übungen für Anfänger im Anschluß an Husserl, *Ideen I*" ("Phenomenological Tutorials for Beginners in Connection with Husserl's *Ideas I*").

*the likes of Alpheus, Mertens, Wiesemann, and Elken*

The seminar records list the participation of Hans Elken, Hans Mertens, Gustav Wiesemann, Paul Mertens, and Karl Alpheus.

*Regarding the Aristotle tutorial*

Heidegger's Seminar "Phänomenologische Interpretationen zu Aristoteles" ("Phenomenological Interpretations of Aristotle"). GA 61 (*Phenomenological Interpretations of Aristotle: Initiation into Phenomenological Research*).

*Fräulein Bondi*

Elisabeth Bondi was a philosophy student in her fifth semester at the time. She participated in Heidegger's seminars from the winter semester of 1921/1922 to the winter semester of 1922/1923.

*a new habilitation candidate from Amsterdam (classical philology)*

During the early 1920s, Hendrik Josephus Pos (1898–1955), a Dutch philosopher and classical philologist, studied with Rickert in Heidelberg and Husserl in Freiburg (where he came to know Heidegger). He graduated from Heidelberg in 1922. He was present for the Heidegger/Cassirer debate in Davos in 1929. In 1931, Heidegger wrote an assessment of Pos, which was first published in 1991 (Jan Aller, ed.) in *Martin Heidegger 1889–1976: Filosofische Weerklank in de Lage Landen* (Amsterdam/Atlanta: Rodopi, 1991), 173.

*a Jesuit*

This perhaps refers to Karl Klinkenberg, who was the only theology student who participated in Heidegger's seminar.

*and also a "Marburger"*

Hans-Georg Gadamer (1900–2002) came to the University of Freiburg in the winter semester of 1922/23 to study with Heidegger. He was in the thirteenth semester of his studies at the time. He habilitated in 1929 with Heidegger and Friedländer with his work *Platos dialektische Ethik: Interpretationen zum 'Philebos'* (Leipzig Felix: Meiner, 1931). In 1939, he was made Ordinarius Professor at the University of Leipzig. In 1949, he succeeded Karl Jaspers at the University of Heidelberg. Gadamer and Heidegger were life-long friends. His major work *Wahrheit und Methode: Grundzüge einer hermeneutischen Philosophie* was published in 1960 (Tübingen: J. C. B. Mohr). See Jean Grondin's *Hans-Georg Gadamer: Eine Biographie* (Tübingen: J. C. B. Mohr, 1999).

*The lecture course*

I.e., Oskar Becker's.

*In the summer I would like to give my "logic" lecture*

The lecture was given under the title "Ontologie." Available as GA 63 (*Ontology—The Hermeneutics of Facticity,* translated by John Van Buren [Bloomington: Indiana University Press, 1999]). Regarding the title, see German page 113.

## As you well know, Göttingen is finished for me

Heidegger hoped to be appointed chair of philosophy at Göttingen. Georg Misch had informed Husserl about Heidegger. Husserl sent him a copy of Heidegger's "Phänomenologische Interpretationen zu Aristoteles" ("Phenomenological Interpretations of Aristotle"). Instead of Heidegger, Moritz Geiger was appointed.

## Natorp

Paul Natorp (1854–1924) was the most important student of Hermann Cohen. In 1893, he became chair of philosophy and pedagogy at the University of Marburg. In 1912, he published *Die logischen Grundlagen der exakten Wissenschaften* (Leipzig/Berlin: B. G. Teubner) and *Allgemeine Psychologie nach kritischer Methode* (Tübingen: J. C. B. Mohr). His interests lay primarily in Husserl's phenomenology, and he was the leading power behind Heidegger's appointment to the University of Marburg in 1923, where he and Heidegger had lively exchanges. See also "Nachruf auf Paul Natorp" ("Obituary for Paul Natorp") in GA 19, 1–5 (*Plato's Sophist*, translated by Richard Rojcewicz and André Schuwer [Bloomington: Indiana University Press, 1997], 1–4).

## Hartmann

Nicolai Hartmann (1882–1950) succeeded Paul Natorp at the University of Marburg in 1922. In 1925, he accepted an appointment at the University of Cologne; in 1931, he was appointed to the University of Berlin; finally, in 1945, he was appointed to the University of Göttingen. He was a student of Hermann Cohen. He later implemented a reversal of Kant's "Copernican revolution" and construed the epistemological subject/object distinction as a relation between two beings, and thus as a relation of being. His most important works include *Platos Logik des Seins* (Giessen: Töpelmann, 1909); *Grundzüge einer Metaphysik der Erkenntnis* (Berlin/Leipzig: de Gruyter, 1921); *Die Philosophie des deutschen Idealismus*, Volume 1: *Fichte, Schelling und die Romantik*; Volume 2: *Hegel* (Berlin/Leipzig: de Gruyter, 1923–1929); *Ethik* (Berlin/Leipzig: de Gruyter, 1926); and *Zur Grundlegung der Ontologie* (Berlin/Leipzig: de Gruyter, 1935). On the relation between Hartmann, Natorp, and Heidegger, see Hans-Georg Gadamer, *Philosophische Lehrjahre: Eine Rückschau* (Frankfurt am Main: Vittorio Klostermann, 1977), 21–43.

## if Geiger is only there until February

See also Heidegger's letter to Jaspers from November 19, 1922: "Löwith has evidently made things easier for himself. The work is supposed to be turned in via Geiger. Since I was given nothing to see of the revision that was demanded, I have renounced all responsibility" (*Heidegger-Jaspers Briefwechsel*, 34) (*The Heidegger-Jaspers Correspondence*, 41).

*The French Academy edition of Descartes*

René Descartes, *Oeuvres* I-XI (Paris, 1897–1913).

*Throw in a Hume, for all I care!*

*The Philosophical Works of David Hume*, Volumes 1–4, ed. by Thomas H. Green (London: Longmans, Green and Co., 1882–1886).

*All three new volumes of Dilthey's collected works are gone*

This likely refers to Wilhelm Dilthey, *Einleitung in die Geisteswissenschaften: Versuch einer Grundlegung für das Studium der Gesellschaft und der Geschichte* (*Gesammelte Schriften*, Volume I, Leipzig/Berlin: B. G. Teubner, 1922); *Weltanschauung und Analyse des Menschen seit Renaissance und Reformation* (*Gesammelte Schriften* Volume II, Leipzig/Berlin: B. G. Teubner, 1921); and *Die Jugendgeschichte Hegels und andere Abhandlungen zur Geschichte des deutschen Idealismus* (*Gesammelte Schriften* Volume IV, Leipzig/Berlin: B. G. Teubner, 1921).

*Schleiermachers Leben*

Wilhelm Dilthey, *Leben Schleiermachers*, Volume 1 (Berlin: G. Reimer, 1870).

*The old man is writing contributions to a Japanese newspaper*

In 1923/24, and subsequent to Russell and Rickert, Husserl published three articles in *The Kaizo: A Monthly Review of Politics, Literature, Social Affairs, Etc.* Edmund Husserl, "Erneuerung: Ihr Problem und ihre Methode," in *The Kaizo* 5 (1923, Issue 3, 84–92); "Die Methode der Wesenforschung," in *The Kaizo* 6 (1923, Issue 2, 107–116), and "Erneuerung als individualethisches Problem," in *The Kaizo* 6 (1924, Issue 3, 2–31). The second and third articles were reversed. Two additional articles, "Erneuerung und Wissenschaft" und "Formale Typen der Kultur in der Menschheitsbildung," remained unpublished on account of the earthquake of 1923.

## Some guy named Wasmund

Joseph Wasmund participated in Heidegger's seminar, "Phänomenologische Übungen für Anfänger: Husserl, *Ideen I*" ("Phenomenological Tutorials for Beginners: Husserl, *Ideas I*"), held in the winter semester of 1922/23.

## one of Ephraim's friends

Richard Ephraim studied with Heidegger from the winter semester of 1921/22 until the summer semester of 1923. He graduated in 1924 from the University of Freiburg with his work *Zum Problem der Objektivität bei Gottfried Keller*.

## Hans Freyer

Hans Freyer (1887–1969) was professor of philosophy at the University of Kiel from 1922 until 1925. In 1925, he accepted the first ever chair for sociology offered in Germany (at the University of Leipzig). He was also a member of the conservative revolution.

## 37. K.L. to M.H., December 7, 1922, Letter

## two essays by E. Gundolf and K. Hildebrandt

Ernst Gundolf and Kurt Hildebrandt, *Nietzsche als Richter unsrer Zeit* (Breslau: Hirt, 1923). (The book had already appeared in 1922.)

## "priestly knowledge of path and destination"

This is probably an allusion to Nietzsche. See, for example, Friedrich Nietzsche, *Nietzsches Werke*, Division II, Volume XV, *Ecce homo: Der Wille zur Macht, Erstes und Zweites Buch* (Leipzig: Alfred Kröner, 1912), 247 ff. (i.e., numbers 140 and 141).

## George

Stefan George (1868–1933) was one of the most important poets during the first half of the twentieth century. Along with C.A. Klein, he founded a journal for poetry entitled *Blätter für die Kunst*. His first collection of poetry appeared in 1903. He also took an active part in compiling the first critical edition of Hölderlin's poetry, organized by Norbert von Hellingrath. He formed a select group of young people and students into an "intellectual society," the so-called "George Circle." Wolfskehl and the Gundolf brothers belonged to this circle of poets, as did Friedrich Wolters, Berthold Vallentin, Kurt Hildebrandt, Robert Boehringer, Ernst Morwitz, Ludwig Thormaehlen, Erich Boehringer, Max Kommerell, Ernst Kantorowicz, Bernhard and Woldemar Graf von Uxkull-Gyllenband, and the brothers Alexander, Berthold, and Claus Schenk Graf von Stauffenberg.

Gundolf-*Goethe*

> Friedrich Gundolf, *Goethe* (Berlin: Georg Bondi, 1916).

*I kept only the Shakespeare*

> Friedrich Gundolf, *Shakespeare und der Deutsche Geist* (Berlin: Georg Bondi, 1911).

*his Kleist*

> Friedrich Gundolf, *Heinrich von Kleist* (Berlin: Georg Bondi, 1922).

*with Steiner*

> Rudolf Steiner (1861–1925) was the founder of "Anthroposophy." In 1895, he published *Friedrich Nietzsche: Ein Kämpfer gegen seine Zeit* (Weimar: Felber).

*bound in three volumes*

> Bruno Bauer, *Kritik der evangelischen Geschichte der Synoptiker* (Leipzig: Wigand, 1841).

*three volumes; also around 600–700 marks*

> Bruno Bauer, *Kritik der Evangelien und Geschichte ihrer Ursprünge*, three volumes (Berlin: Hempel, 1850–1851).

**38.** M.H. to K.L., December 9, 1922, Postcard (copy)

*Overbeck's Christentum und Kultur*

> Franz Overbeck, *Christentum und Kultur: Gedanken und Anmerkungen zur modernen Theologie*, edited by Carl Albrecht Bernoulli (Basel: Schwabe & Co., 1919).

*I will show it to you when you come*

Letter from Jaspers to Heidegger, dated November 24, 1922; in *Heidegger-Jaspers Briefwechsel*, 37 (*The Heidegger-Jaspers Correspondence*, 43): "Thanks as well for the *Overbeck* volume. You bought it for me. How much do I owe you? I read it immediately—with much sympathy but, at the end, with the same mistrust with which I read him before. A thin, bloodless sort, with much discretion but only as a shield—without any impulse for me—nevertheless, an honest man, of proven faithfulness in his friendship with Nietzsche and an unimpeachable scholar. [. . .] He is altogether striking in his critique, to be sure. We, or at least I, see the positive that comes out of the critique so thinly that, for me, it disappears. It is itself simply too negative to describe—but he comes from the world of Nietzsche and Burckhardt and, just because of this, I read him with reverence and with the consciousness of being in one of the few oases of the modern European desert."

*"No news from the Paris front."*

There was no news on the matter of his appointment, and Heidegger had given up hope regarding the Ordinarius professorship in Göttingen. The phrase "no news from the Paris front" refers to the dispatches of General von Podbielski during the siege of Paris in 1870/71. *Geflügelte Worte: Der Zitatenschatz des deutschen Volkes*, edited and annotated by Georg Büchmann, 31st edition. Updated to the present era by Werner Rust, revised by Alfred Grunow (Berlin: Haude & Spenser, 1964), 717 f.

*publishing business*

Heidegger planned to publish his "Aristoteles-Einleitung" ("Introduction to Aristotle") in Husserl's *Jahrbuch für Philosophie und phänomenologische Forschung*; however, by the end of 1924, he had abandoned this plan.

*Rudolf Unger*

Rudolf Unger (1876–1942) was a Germanist and literary historian who taught at the University of Königsberg from 1921 to 1924. In 1922, he published his book *Herder, Novalis und Kleist: Studien über die Entwicklung des Todesproblems in Denken und Dichten vom Sturm und Drang zur Romantik; mit einem ungedruckten Briefe Herders* (Frankfurt am Main: Diesterweg).

**40.** K.L. to M.H., February 15, 1923, Letter

*Is it still headed by Spemann?*

Hans Spemann was chairman of the Peoples University of Freiburg from 1920 to 1923.

*Külpe's "critical realism"*

Oswald Külpe (1862–1915) was an assistant to Wilhelm Wundt at the Institute of Experimental Psychology in Leipzig from 1887 to 1894. In 1894, he became professor of philosophy and aesthetics in Würzburg; and in 1896, he founded an Institute for Experimental Psychology, whose studies on the psychology of thinking found worldwide recognition. He became a professor in Bonn in 1909, and then in Munich in 1914; at both universities, he founded institutes modeled on the institute in Würzburg. After 1898, he turned away from positivism and developed a critical realism. He studied the intentionality of consciousness through the description of thought-processes and the experience of thought. His major works include *Grundriss der Psychologie: Auf experimenteller Grundlage* (Leipzig: Engelmann, 1893); *Einleitung in die Philosophie* (Leipzig: Hirzel, 1895); and *Die Realisierung: Ein Beitrag zur Grundlegung der Realwissenschaften*, 3 Volumes (Leipzig: Hirzel, 1912–1923).

*A forbidden little book on Nietzsche by Schrempf*

Chrisoph Schrempf, *Friedrich Nietzsche* (Göttingen: Vandenhoeck & Ruprecht, 1922).

*Rittelmeyer recently spoke here*

Friedrich Rittelmeyer (1872–1938) was a pastor and theologian. He was cofounder and coordinator for the Movement for Christian Reformation, founded in 1922. Presumably he spoke on such a theme in Munich at this time.

*Schweitzer*

Albert Schweitzer (1875–1965) was a Franco-German doctor, an evangelical theologian, and a philosopher. His *Gesammelte Werke in fünf Bänden*, edited by Rudolf Grabs (Munich: C. H. Beck), was published in 1974.

*the paragraph regarding "death" as "the how of life"*

Martin Heidegger, "Phänomenologische Interpretationen zu Aristoteles (Anzeige der hermeneutischen Situation)," in GA 62, 358 ff. ("Phenomenological Interpretations in Connection with Aristotle: An Indication of the Hermeneutical Situation," in *Supplements*, 111–145).

**41. M.H. to K.L., February 20, 1923, Letter (copy)**

*the Gsellius catalogue*

An antiquarian bookstore in Berlin.

*the Calvin commentary*

This probably refers to Johannes Calvin, *Ioannis Calvini in Novum Testamentum commentarii, ad editionem Amstelodamensen, accuratissime exscribi curavit et praefatus est August Tholuck*, Guilelmum Thome (Berolini, 1833–1838).

*De Wette, the Apostle story (the edition that Overbeck published)*

Wilhelm Martin Leberecht De Wette, *Kurze Erklärung der Apostelgeschichte*, ed. Franz Overbeck (Leipzig: Hirzel, 1870).

*Did you ultimately snatch up the Overbeck?*

This probably refers to Franz Overbeck, *Über die Christlichkeit unserer heutigen Theologie*, second revised edition (with an introduction and afterword) (Leipzig: C. G. Naumann, 1903).

*the preliminary interpretations*

Heidegger's Seminar: "Übungen über Phänomenologische Interpretationen zu Aristoteles (*Nikomachische Ethik VI*; *De anima*; *Metaphysik VII*)" ("Tutorials Concerning Phenomenological Interpretations of Aristotle: *Nicomachean Ethics VI*; *De anima*; *Metaphysics VII*").

*Fräulein Victorius*

Beginning in the summer semester of 1922, Käte Victorius participated in all of Heidegger's seminars at the University of Freiburg; she later became a psychoanalyst. She and Heidegger became lifelong friends; the correspondence between the two remains unpublished. See *Heidegger-Jaspers Briefwechsel*, 283 f. (*The Heidegger-Jaspers Correspondence*, 270–271.) She published "'Der Moses des Michelangelo' von Sigmund Freud: Eine Studie," in Alexander Mitscherlich (ed.), *Entfaltung der Psychoanalyse: Das Wirken Sigmund Freuds* (Stuttgart: Klett, 1956), 1–10.

## Aquinas' Aristotle commentaries

Thomas Aquinas wrote commentaries on the following Aristotelian texts: *Metaphysics, Logic, Ethics, Politics, Physics, On the Heavens, On Generation and Corruption, Meteorology, On the Soul,* and *Sense and Sensibilia*.

## Rothacker

Erich Rothacker (1888–1965) was a professor of philosophy at the University of Heidelberg from 1924 to 1928. From 1928 until 1954, he was professor of philosophy at the University of Bonn. In 1923, he became editor for the then new journal *Deutsche Vierteljahresschrift für Literaturwissenschaft und Geistesgeschichte*. Heidegger was to publish his essay "*Der Begriff der Zeit*" in this journal in 1925. (Available as GA 64, 1–103) (*The Concept of Time*, translated by William McNeill [Oxford: Blackwell, 1992]. Also translated in *Becoming Heidegger: On the Trail of His Early Occasional Writings, 1910–1927*, edited by Theodore Kisiel and Thomas Sheehan [Evanston: Northwestern University Press, 2007], 192–210.) See also "Martin Heidegger und die Anfänge der 'Deutschen Vierteljahresschrift für Literaturwissenschaft und Geistesgeschichte': Eine Dokumentation," edited by Joachim W. Storck and Theodore Kisiel, in *Dilthey-Jahrbuch* 8 (1992–1993), 181–225. The correspondence between Heidegger and Rothacker is also published in this chronicle.

## Husserl's Ideas

Edmund Husserl, *Ideen zu einer reinen Phänomenologie und einer phänomenologischen Philosophie*.

## What you say about "death"

This refers to the analysis of death from Heidegger's *Phenomenological Interpretation of Aristotle*, available in GA 62, 358–360. [Only the appendix has been published into English.]

*Jörg*

> Heidegger's oldest son, Jörg, born on January 21, 1919.

**42. M.H. to K.L., April 21, 1923, Letter (copy)**

*Thank you for the letter and cards*

> Neither the letter nor the postcards are in the possession of the estate.

*'Ontology'*

> GA 63 (*Ontology: The Hermeneutics of Facticity*).

*in order to complete the required workload for the winter*

> Continuation of the *Phenomenological Interpretations of Aristotle*.

*The tutorial with Ebbinghaus*

> A colloquium concerning the theological foundations of Kant, entitled "Religion innerhalb der Grenzen der bloßen Vernunft" ("Religion within the Limits of Pure Reason").

*the tutorials for beginners on Aristotle's Nicomachean Ethics*

> "Phänomenologische Übungen für Anfänger, Aristoteles, *Nicomachische Ethik*" ("Phenomenological Tutorials for Beginners: Aristotle's *Nicomachean Ethics*").

*Schlatter*

> Adolf Schlatter, *Erläuterungen zum Neuen Testament*, ten volumes (Stuttgart: Calwer Vereinsbuchhandlung, 1910).

*Finke*

> Heinrich Finke had strong connections with Spain and Italy. He held honorary doctorates from universities in Barcelona, Valladolid, Milan, and Salamanca, and was an honorary member of Madrid's Academy of History.

*Göller*

> Emil Göller (1874–1933) was professor of church history at the university of Freiburg beginning in 1909. Heidegger heard Göller's four-hour lecture on

Catholic cannon law (Part 1: Introduction, Sources, and Constitution) during the winter semester of 1910/1911.

*Kiba*

Ryôhon Kiba participated in Heidegger's seminar "Phänomenologische Übungen im Anschluß an *Logischen Untersuchungen* II" ("Phenomenological Tutorials in Connection with *Logical Investigations* II") in the winter semester of 1921/1922.

*Tanabe*

Hajime Tanabe (1885–1962) traveled to Freiburg in 1922 in order to study with Husserl and Heidegger. He later became successor to Kitarô Nishida at the Imperial University in Kyoto.

*"Zur Geschichte der Fuge"*

Joseph Müller-Blattau presented a musicology seminar in Königsberg in 1923 under the title *Grundzüge einer Geschichte der Fuge*.

*Young Baumgarten*

Eduard Baumgarten (1898–1982) got his Ph.D. with his uncle Max Weber in Heidelberg. From 1927 through 1931, he was a professor of philosophy at the University of Wisconsin. In 1929, he became the Abraham Lincoln Fellow at theUniversity of Freiburg. In 1940, he became professor of philosophy at the University of Königsberg. After World War II, he received an appointment to the University of Mannheim. See the *Heidegger-Jaspers Briefwechsel*, 270–274 (*The Heidegger-Jaspers Correspondence*, 208–212). See also Heidegger's negative assessment of Baumgarten from December 17, 1933 (in GA 16, 774 f.). The assessment also played a role in Heidegger's denazification process. See Lutz Hachmeister, *Heideggers Testament: Der Philosoph, der Spiegel und die SS* (Berlin: Propyläen, 2014), 76.

*he is helplessly "Georgine"*

"Georgine" refers to Baumgarten's adoration of Stefan George.

*Friendly regards to your parents*

Martin Heidegger visited Löwith in Munich in March 1923. In a letter to his wife from March 27th, Heidegger spoke of the visit: "I've been very kindly received at Löwith's—the young man has a splendid library—much bigger and better than mine—though at bottom it doesn't have any use—something for sophisticates. The old man is a petty bourgeois 'schoolmaster' (painter)—he received me in his studio—as the enclosed didn't turn out well—twice again today [....] Löwith has shown me the most beautiful parts of Munich—in particular the collection of Greek vases—this is one of the things that has left the deepest impression on me so far. For the rest I've had more than enough of the city and will be glad to be out of it again" (*Mein liebes Seelchen*, 127) (*Letters to His Wife*, 90).

**43.** M.H. to K.L., May 8, 1923, Letter (copy)

*Many thanks for your letter*

The letter is not in the possession of the estate.

*the little book*

It could not be determined which volumes are being referenced.

*There are six here from Marburg*

One of the six was Hans-Georg Gadamer, of whom Heidegger was initially very critical.

*A female licentiate from Berlin*

It could not be determined to whom this is referring.

*Troeltsch*

Ernst Troeltsch (1865–1923) was a theologian, philosopher, and politician. He became professor of philosophy at the University of Berlin in 1915. One of his major works was *Die Soziallehren der christlichen Kirchen und Gruppen* (Tübingen: J. C. B. Mohr, 1912). The letters from Troeltsch to Heidegger were published in *Heidegger-Jahrbuch* 1 (2004).

*Fräulein Stein has already reserved a place for herself in the next volume*

Edith Stein, *Eine Untersuchung über den Staat*, in *Jahrbuch für Philosophie und phänomenologische Forschung* VII (1925), 1–123; now also in Edith Stein, *Gesamtausgabe*, Volume 7 (Freiburg/Basel/Vienna: Herder, 2006).

*a statement Van Gogh made to his brother*

Vincent van Gogh, *Briefe an seinen Bruder*. Compiled by his sister-in-law J. van Gogh-Bonger. Translated into German by Leo Klein-Diepold, two volumes (Berlin: Paul Cassirer, 1914), number 592.

**44.** K.L. to M.H., May 10, 1923, Letter

*Söderblom's guest lecture*

Nathan Söderblom (1866–1931) was a Swedish Lutheran theologian and was the Archbishop of Uppsala. He advocated ecumenicalism and world peace, for which efforts he received the Nobel Peace Prize in 1930.

*that Bavarian Pfeilschifter, brutal and falsely solemn*

Georg Pfeilschifter (1870–1936) was a theologian and religious scholar. From 1903 until 1917, he was professor of church history at the University of Freiburg. Heidegger heard Pfeilschifter's lectures concerning church history while he was a theology student (from the winter semester of 1910/1911 to the winter semester of 1911/1912). In 1917, Pfeilschifter transferred to the Ludwig Maximilian University in Munich, where he served as rector in 1922/1923.

*prelate Mausbach*

Joseph Mausbach (1861–1931) was a theologian and politician. He became a professor of moral theology and apologetics in Münster in 1892. One of his major works was the three-volume work *Religion, Christentum, Kirche*, co-authored with Gerhard Esser (Kempten: Kösel, 1911–1913), which Heidegger studied intensely.

*"Döllinger, the crown of Munich's theology faculty"*

Johann Joseph Ignaz von Döllinger (1799–1890) was appointed to the University of Munich in 1826. He had a decisive influence on the Catholic theological discourse of the time, and was also engaged in politics during the 1840s. He was excommunicated in 1871 owing to his rejection of the papal dogma of infallibility. Not long after, he became rector at the University of Munich and the president of the Bavarian Academy of Science. He was a supporter of the "Old Catholic" movement.

*(Heiler!)*

Friedrich Heiler (1892–1967) was a religious scholar. He was influenced by Söderblom and moved between Catholicism and Protestantism. He neither resigned from the Catholic Church nor joined the Protestants, though he was very sympathetic to Söderblom's desire for ecumenism.

*the Barth-Gogarten movement*

The Barth–Gogarten Movement (also referred to as "dialectical theology") was a new direction in Protestant theology that emphasized the absolute antithesis of god and human beings. Karl Barth (1886–1968) was an Evangelical theologian and co-founder of dialectical theology. (The founders were principally Barth, Gogarten, and Schule, but also included Rudolf Bultmann and Eduard Thurneysen.) Barth's most famous work, *Der Römerbrief* (Bern: Bäschlin, 1919), appeared in 1918. (The second, revised edition, published by Christian Kaiser in Munich, was released in 1922.) He was made an honorary professor for reformation theology at the University of Göttingen in 1921, though he had neither a doctorate nor had he habilitated. In 1925, he was appointed professor of dogmatic and new-testament exegesis at the University of Munster. In 1930, he became professor of systematic theology in Bonn, where (in 1931) he began his monumental work *Kirchliche Dogmatik*, the final edition of which appeared in 1967. Because Barth refused to take Hitler's oath of office, he was forced into retirement in 1935. He then received an appointment at the University of Basel, where he continued to teach. Friedrich Gogarten (1887–1967) was a Lutheran theologian and co-founder of dialectical theology. He was a professor in Breslau, Bonn, and Göttingen. His works include *Illusionen: Eine Auseinandersetzung mit dem Kulturidealismus* (Jena: Diederichs, 1926); *Glaube und Wirklichkeit* (Jena: Diederichs, 1928); *Politische Ethik: Versuch einer Grundlegung* (Jena: Diederichs, 1932); and *Das Bekenntnis der Kirche* (Jena: Diederichs, 1934).

*Bishop Martensen*

Hans Lassen Martensen (1808–1884) was a Danish theologian and bishop. According to Kierkegaard, he represented everything that was wrong with the church.

*A quote from Luther's text*

Martin Luther, *Von den Juden und ihren Lügen*, in *Weimarer Ausgabe*, Volume 53, Writings from 1542/1543, edited by Ferdinand Cohrs and Oscar Brenner (Weimar: Böhlaus, 1920), 417–552.

*Bruckner*

    Joseph Anton Bruckner (1824–1896) was an Austrian composer of the romantic era.

*In Bischofstein*

    The Bischofstein castle sits under the boulders in Lengenfeld. It was a country reform school from 1908 until 1945.

*the Ruhr occupation*

    The occupation of the area from the Ruhr region to Dortmund in January of 1923—a strategy of reparations—was construed by the right-wing conservative circle as a humiliation for Germany forced upon them by the Allies. For purposes of propaganda, it was referred to as "the shame of Versailles."

*Some famous actor is "playing Luther"*

    This refers to the 1923 film *Martin Luther* by Karl Wüstenhagen. The lead actor was Wilhelm Diegelmann.

*I will have to take a position as private tutor in Mecklenburg*

    See Löwith, *Mein Leben in Deutschland*, 62 f. (*My Life in Germany*, 64 f.).

**45. K.L. to M.H., June 1923, Postcard**

*your letter*

    The letter is not in the possession of the estate.

*Ch. Grosser*

    Regarding Charlotte Grosser, see also Löwith, *Mein Leben in Deutschland*, 61 (*My Life in Germany*, 62).

*"Mystische Phänomenologie"*

    Gerda Walther, *Zur Phänomenologie der Mystik*.

*Nohl*

Hermann Nohl (1879–1960) was a professor of philosophy in Göttingen beginning in 1920 who worked within the tradition of Dilthey. He was among the promoters of the pedagogy reformation movement of the 1920s, and was founder of the Göttingen School of Humanistic Pedagogy. Along with his colleague Georg Misch, Nohl considered offering Heidegger an appointment at the University of Göttingen in 1922.

*W. Stern, Person und Seele*

Löwith is perhaps referring to the new edition of William Stern's *Person und Sache: System des kritischen Personalismus*, Volume 1: *Ableitung und Grundlehre des kritischen Personalismus* (Leipzig: Barth, 1923), and Volume 2: *Die menschliche Persönlichkeit* (Leipzig: Barth, 1923).

*Litt, Leben und Erkennen*

Theodor Litt, *Erkenntnis und Leben* (Leipzig/Berlin: B. G. Teubner, 1923).

**46.** M.H. to K.L., June 18, 1923, Postcard (copy)

*a Japanese student who is in Heidelberg at the moment*

This refers to Kiyoshi Miki (1897–1945), who attended Heidegger's lectures and seminars in the winter semester of 1923/1924. He later became a Marxist, which brought his academic career to an end. This likely also refers to Shûzô Kuki (1888–1941) who, between the years of 1921 and 1929, studied in Germany with Rickert, Husserl, and Heidegger, and in Paris with Bergson. Jean-Paul Sartre was his tutor, and he also took private lessons with Heidegger. He taught at the Imperial University in Kyoto beginning in 1935.

*Jaeger's book on Aristotle*

Werner Wilhelm Jaeger, *Aristoteles: Grundlegung einer Geschichte seiner Entwicklung* (Berlin: Weidmann, 1923).

*the earlier one*

Werner Wilhelm Jaeger, *Studien zur Entstehungsgeschichte der Metaphysik des Aristoteles* (Berlin: Weidmann, 1912).

*Reinhardt's Poseidonius*

Karl Reinhardt, *Poseidonius* (Munich: C. H. Beck, 1921).

*Fräulein Walther's opus*

Gerda Walther, *Zur Phänomenologie der Mystik*.

*Ricarda Huch*

Ricarda Huch (1864–1947) was an author and historian.

*Hedwig Conrad-Martius*

Hedwig Conrad-Martius (1888–1966) studied with Theodor Litt, Edmund Husserl, and Alexander Pfänder. She received an honorary professorship at the University of Munich in 1955. Her work is extensive. In 1916, she published "Zur Ontologie und Erscheinungslehre der realen Außenwelt: Verbunden mit einer Kritik positivistischer Theorien" in Volume III of *Jahrbuch für Philosophie und phänomenologische Forschung* (345–542), and in 1925 her "Realontologie" appeared in Volume VI of the same (159–333). She contributed "Farben: Ein Kapitel aus der Realontologie" to the Husserl Festschrift (*Festschrift für Edmund Husserl zum 70 Geburtstag*, published as a supplementary volume of *Jahrbuch für Philosophie und phänomenologische Forschung*, 1929, 339–370).

*the third edition of the Psychopathologie*

Karl Jaspers, *Allgemeine Psychopathologie: Für Studierende, Ärzte und Psychologen*, third augmented and revised edition (Berlin: Springer, 1923).

*Stern*

Günther Stern.

*I will respond to your letter*

The letter is not in the possession of the estate.

**47.** K.L. to M.H., June 21, 1923, Postcard

*you will always remain, in principle and in the end, "Extra-Ordinarius"*

Heidegger's appointment in Marburg was to an Extraordinarius chair, but as Ordinarius.

*Fräulein Walther sent me her book*

Gerda Walther, *Zur Phänomenologie der Mystik*.

*"the Japanese student"*

This refers to Japanese students of Heidegger to whom Löwith was giving private language instruction.

**48.** K.L to M.H., July 9, 1923, Postcard

*a short paper on Romans 5–8*

No additional information could be found regarding this work.

**49.** K.L. to M.H., July 27, 1923, Postcard

*The George enthusiast Wolters*

Friedrich Wilhelm Wolters (1876–1930) was a historian, a poet, and a translator. In 1904, he began associating with the George Circle. He edited the *Jahrbuch für die geistige Bewegung* along with Ernst Gundolf. In 1913, he began working on his magnum opus, *Stefan George und die Blätter für die Kunst: Deutsche Geistesgeschichte seit 1890* (Berlin: Georg Bondi, 1929).

*The appointment Husserl got at the O3 [?]*

On July 4, 1923, Husserl was offered the chair at the University of Berlin, which had been vacated by the death of Ernst Troeltsch. He refused the offer on July 31st.

*Mystik*

Gerda Walther, *Zur Phänomenologie der Mystik*.

*a little work on "Augustine's inner development" by K. Holl*

> Karl Holl, *Augustins innere Entwicklung* (Berlin: Verlag der Akademie der Wissenschaften, 1923).

**50. M.H. to K.L., July 30, 1923, Postcard (copy)**

*Jaensch*

> Erich Jaensch (1883–1940) was a philosopher and psychologist. He was a professor of psychology, head of the psychology department, and director of philosophical seminars at the University of Marburg from 1913 until 1940. His publications include *Wirklichkeit und Wert in der Philosophie und Kultur der Neuzeit: Prolegomena zur philosophischen Forschung auf der Grundlage philosophischer Anthropologie nach empirischer Methode* (Berlin: Elsner, 1929).

*Karsch*

> Fritz Karsch (1893–1971) graduated in 1923 under the direction of Nicolai Hartmann. He taught German language and German literature at the Senior *Gymnasium* in Matsue, Japan, from 1925 until 1939.

*Die Idee der Universität (Springer)*

> Karl Jaspers, *Die Idee der Universität* (Berlin: Springer, 1923).

*Fabricius*

> Ernst Fabricius (1857–1942) was professor of ancient history at the university of Freiburg, and was Heidegger's friend.

**51. K.L. to M.H., August 6, 1923, Letter**

*transcript of your lecture*

> This refers to Heidegger's lecture course *Ontologie: Hermeneutik der Faktizität* (GA 63) (*Ontology—The Hermeneutics of Facticity*), offered in the summer semester of 1923.

*Bröcker*

> Walter Bröcker (1902–1992) was a philosopher, a student of Heidegger, and also one of Heidegger's assistants. He graduated under Heidegger's direction

in 1928 with his work *Kants 'Kritik der ästhetischen Urteilskraft': Versuch einer phänomenologischen Interpretation und Kritik des I.T. der 'Kritik der Urteilskraft,'* and went on to habilitate under Heidegger in 1934. His habilitation thesis, *Aristoteles*, was published in 1935 (Frankfurt am Main: Vittorio Klostermann). He worked as a private tutor from 1937 until 1940 in Freiburg, and was professor of philosophy at the University of Rostock from 1940 to 1948, after which time he was at the University of Kiel until he went emeritus in 1967.

## *Friedländer*

Paul Friedländer (1882–1968) was a classical philologist. He was a professor at the University of Marburg from 1920 until 1932, after which time he taught at the University of Halle. He was dismissed in 1935, and was arrested in 1938 and sent to the Sachsenhausen concentration camp. In 1939, he emigrated to the United States, where he taught at Johns Hopkins University and later at UCLA. His publications include *Platon*; Volume 1: *Eidos, Paideia, Dialogos*; Volume 2: *Die platonischen Schriften;* and Volume 3: *Die platonischen Schriften: Zweite und dritte Periode* (Berlin: de Gruyter, 1928).

## *his student, Dr. Klingner*

Friedrich Klingner (1894–1968) was a classical philologist and student of Paul Friedländer; he followed Friedländer to Marburg in 1920. He graduated from Marburg in 1921 with a dissertation on Boethius' *Consolation of Philosophy*. In 1925, he became a professor at the University of Hamburg; from 1930 until 1947 he was a professor at the University of Leipzig; and in 1947, he transferred to the University of Munich.

## *the four-hour Augustine lecture over the summer*

In the summer semester of 1924, Heidegger lectured on Aristotle rather than on St. Augustine. See GA 18 (*Basic Concepts of Aristotelian Philosophy*, translated by Robert D. Metcalf and Mark Basil Tanzer [Bloomington: Indiana University Press], 2009).

## *Holl's little work*

Karl Holl, *Augustins innere Entwicklung* (Berlin: Verlag der Akademie der Wissenschaften, 1923).

## the pastor from Gatow

No additional information could be determined regarding the pastor from Gatow.

## Pastor Slotty

Martin Slotty (1884–1945) graduated from the University of Erlangen with the following dissertation on Kierkegaard: *Die Erkenntnislehre S. A. Kierkegaards: Eine Würdigung seiner Verfasserwirksamkeit vom zentralen Gesichtspunkte aus* (Cassel: Pillardy & Augustin, 1915).

## a talk on Schleich

Carl Ludwig Schleich (1859–1922) was a surgeon and writer. His works include *Erinnerungen an Strindberg: Nebst Nachrufen für Ehrlich und von Bergmann* (Munich: Georg Müller Verlag, 1917); *Das Problem des Todes* (Berlin: Rowohlt, 1920); *Das Ich und die Dämonien* (Berlin: S. Fischer, 1920); and *Bewußtsein und Unsterblichkeit* (Stuttgart/Berlin: Deutsche Verlags-Anstalt, 1920). No further information could be obtained regarding the lecture in question.

## Falckenberg

Richard Friedrich Otto Falckenberg (1851–1920) was professor of philosophy at the University of Erlangen from 1889 to 1920. His emphasis was on the history of modern philosophy. Falckenberg was the first professor in Germany to support a number of doctoral projects on Kierkegaard. Between 1909 and 1915, four dissertations on Kierkegaard were submitted in Erlangen.

## Leben und Walten der Liebe

Søren Kierkegaard, *Leben und Walten der Liebe*, translated by Albert Donner (Leipzig: Friedrich Richter, 1890).

## Has Metzger habilitated?

At the time, Arnold Metzger was working on his habilitation thesis "Der Gegenstand der Erkenntnis: Studien zur Phänomenologie des Gegenstandes, 1. Teil" (later published in *Jahrbuch für Philosophie und phänomenologische Forschung* VII [1925], 613–769). However, he was unable to submit it owing to unforeseeable circumstances. He habilitated in 1933 with his work *Phänomenologie und Metaphysik* (Halle an der Saale: Max Niemeyer).

## 52. M.H. to K.L., August 23, 1923, Letter (copy)

*Hönigswald*

Richard Hönigswald (1875–1947), a Neo-Kantian, was a professor of philosophy at the University of Breslau from 1911 to 1930. In 1930, he accepted an appointment at the University of Munich; however, he was dismissed in 1933 owing to his Jewish descent, and in 1938 he was imprisoned at Dachau. In 1939, he emigrated to New York (USA), where he worked as an independent scholar. See Heidegger's negative assessment of Hönigswald from June 25, 1933, in GA 16, 132 ff.

*his father*

Johannes Georg Gadamer (1867–1928) was a chemist. He was a professor of pharmaceutical chemistry at the University of Breslau from 1902 until 1919. He transferred to the University of Marburg in 1919.

*a critique of Hartmann's Metaphysik*

Hans-Georg Gadamer, "Metaphysik der Erkenntnis." On the book by Nicolai Hartmann with the same name, see *Logos* 12 (1923/1924), 340–359.

*Do you have your current position*

The tutoring position was in Kogel (Mecklenburg). His employer was the chamberlain August Freiherr von Flotow.

## 53. M.H. to K.L., September 27, 1923, Postcard (copy)

*I will be lecturing two hours on an introduction to phenomenology*

GA 17 (*Introduction to Phenomenological Research*, translated by Daniel O. Dahlstrom [Bloomington: Indiana University Press, 2005]).

*two hours on Aristotle*

Heidegger held this seminar a semester later. Available as GA 18 (*Basic Concepts of Aristotelian Philosophy*).

*the coming course of lectures on Augustine*

The lecture was never held.

*Niemeyer has shelved all publications*

This was owing to the inflation crisis in Germany.

*Logical Investigations for beginners*

Martin Heidegger "Phänomenologische Übung für Anfänger: Husserl, *Logische Untersuchungen* II,1" ("Phenomenological Tutorials for Beginners: Husserl, *Logical Investigations* II.1").

*Aristotle and the middle ages*

This then became "Phänomenologische Übung für Fortgeschrittene: Aristoteles, *Physik* B" ("Advanced Phenomenological Tutorials: Aristotle, *Physics* B").

**54.** M.H. to K.L., October 1, 1923, Postcard (copy)

*(my father is in very bad shape)*

Friedrich Heidegger (1851–1924) was a sexton and a master cooper. He died on May 1, 1924, following a stroke.

**55.** M.H. to K.L., March 19, 1924, Postcard (copy)

*The Überweg book*

Friedrich Überweg, *Grundriss der Geschichte der Philosophie* (four volumes; tenth edited and enhanced edition) (Berlin: Mittler & Sohn, 1915).

*the Seidmann edition*

This perhaps refers to Martin Luther's *Erste und Älteste Vorlesungen über die Psalmen aus den Jahren 1513–1516* (two volumes in one), based on the handwritten (Latin) manuscript of Luther and housed in the royal public library in Dresden. Edited by Johann Karl Seidemann, with assistance by the High Royal Ministry of Culture and Public Education, and under the general direction of the Royal Library of Art and Science. Contains facsimiles and lithographs (Dresden: R von Zahns Verlag, 1876).

*the Weimar edition*

Martin Luther, *Werke, Kritische Gesamtausgabe*, Group 1: *Schriften*, Volume 3, *Psalmenvorlesungen* 1513/1515 (Psalms 1–84) and Volume 4, *Psalmenvorlesungen* 1513/1515 (Psalms 85–150); *Randbemerkungen zu Faber Stapulesis*; *Richtervorlesungen* 1516/1517; *Sermone* 1514/1520 (Weimar: H. Böhlau, 1885 and 1886; reprinted 1923).

*the one medieval seminar*

"Die Hochscholastik und Aristoteles: Thomas, *De ente et essentia*; Cajetan, *De nominum analogia*" ("The Scholastics and Aristotle: Thomas, *De ente et essentia*; Cajetan, *De nominum analogia*").

*the Christiania turn*

The "Christiania turn" is the name of a manner of changing direction while skiing.

**56.** M.H. to K.L., March 26, 1924, Letter (copy)

*Many thanks for your letter*

The letter is not in the possession of the estate.

**57.** K.L. to M.H., August 17$^{th}$, 1924, Letter (privately held)

*You will already have understood everything essential in my postcard*

The postcard is not in the possession of the estate.

*"the way in which people can be together"—and are allowed to be together— "in existence"*

See Heidegger's letter from August 19, 1921 (i.e., document 25).

*3-Masken Verlag*

This refers to the Munich publisher *Drei Masken*, with whom Löwith published his habilitation thesis *Das Individuum in der Rolle des Mitmenschen* (*The Individual in the Roll of Fellow Human Being*) in 1928.

**58.** M.H. to K.L., August 21, 1924, Letter (copy)

*The Rome opportunity is right on cue*

> Löwith traveled to Italy in 1924 and spent the year there. See Löwith, *Mein Leben in Deutschland*, 63–65 (*My Life in Germany*, 65–66).

*presumably Hartmann will no longer be here by then*

> Nicolai Hartmann accepted an appointment at the University of Cologne in 1925. Heidegger was his successor in Marburg.

*Natorp has died*

> Paul Natorp died on August 17, 1924. See Heidegger's "Nachruf auf Paul Natorp" ("Obituary for Paul Natorp") in GA 19, 1–5 (*Plato's Sophist*, 1–4).

*Dott. P. Bruno Katterbach O. F. M.*

> Bruno Katterback O. F. M. (1883–1931) was an archivist and paleographicist. He obtained his doctorate in Freiburg in 1908 under Heinrich Finke and later relocated to Rome. Heidegger knew him from his time as a student.

*Festschrift for P. Franz Ehrle S.C. in 5 volumes*

> *Miscellanea Francesco Ehrle. Scritti di storia paleografia, pubblicati sotto gli auspici di S. S. Pio XI in occasione dell'ottantesimo natalizio dell'Emo Cardinale Francesco Ehrle*, five volumes (Rome: Biblioteca Apostolica Vaticana, 1924).

**60.** K.L. to M.H., September 22, 1924, Postcard (privately held)

*By the 26th*

> September 26th was Heidegger's birthday.

*in the Calixtus catacombs*

> The Calixtus catacombs between *Via Appia Antica*, *Via Ardeatina*, and *Vicolo della Sette Chiese* is an ancient network of underground grave sites in Rome.

*I hope that you are enjoying Aristotle/Luther*

> This likely refers to Karl Immanuel Nitzsch, *Luther und Aristoteles: Festschrift zum vierhundertjährigen Geburtstage Luthers* (Kiel: Universitäts-Buchhandlung, 1883).

**61. K.L. to M.H., October 18, 1924, Postcard (privately held)**

*Lietzmann*

> Hans Lietzmann (1875–1942) was a theologian and church historian. In 1923, he succeeded Adolf von Harnack at the University of Berlin.

*Tillich*

> Paul Johannes Tillich (1886–1965) became professor of theology in Dresden in 1925. From 1929 to 1933, he was professor of philosophy and sociology in Frankfurt am Main, and from 1940 until 1955 he taught at the Union Theological Seminary in New York, after which time he taught both at Harvard Divinity School and at the University of Chicago.

*opera varia A. Maii: nova patrum bibliothecae Volumes I–VII*

> *Nova patrum bibliotheca*, edited by Angelus Maius (Rome: Sacri Consilii propagando Christiano nomini, 1844–1855).

*Augustinus Sermones CCI ex codice vaticanis mit 5 paläographischen Tafeln, etc.*

> *Sancti Augustini Novi ex cod. Vaticanis sermones* (Rome: Sacri Consilium propoganda Christiano nomini, 1852).

*(S. Cyrilli alexandrine adlocutio et fragmenta commentarium in Matheam et Lucam)*

> The edition in question could not be determined.

*complete Summa with the Gaietan Commentary*

> *Summa Sancti Thomae Aquinatis universam sacram theologiam complectens cum commentariis Thomae de Vio Caietani* (Bergamo, 1590).

*Amelung*

Löwith is likely referring to the evangelical theologian Karl Amelung (1858–1939).

**62. K.L. to M.H., October 28, 1924, Letter (privately held)**

*the actor Jacki Coogan*

Jacki Coogan, born John Leslie Cooper (1914–1984), was an American actor and child star. He was discovered by Charlie Chaplin and had his first rolls in his films.

*Herr Dr. Gründler*

Otto Gründler was editor of the Catholic newspaper *Hochland* from 1921 to 1926.

*Dürer's "Hare"*

Regarding Dürer's hare, see the presentation by Werner Körte in Martin Heidegger "Übungen für Anfänger: Schillers Briefe über die ästhetische Erziehung des Menschen" ["Tutorials for Beginners: Schiller's 'Letters on the Aesthetic Instruction of Humankind'"] from the winter semester of 1936/1937. Edited by Ulrich von Bülow, with an essay by Odo Marquard (Marbach: Marbacher Bibliothek 8, Deutsche Schillergesellschaft, 2005), 149–68.

*Botticelli*

Sandro Botticelli (1445–1510) was an Italian painter and draftsman from the early Renaissance.

*"Lippert"*

Peter Lippert (1879–1936) was a Catholic priest and theologian. His publications include *Gott* (Freiburg im Breisgau: Herder, 1913); *Gott und die Welt* (Freiburg im Breisgau: Herder, 1917); *Die Sakramente Christi* (Freiburg im Breisgau: Herder, 1923); and *Das Wesen des katholischen Menschen* (Munich: Theatiner Verlag, 1923).

*Friedländer (from Freiburg)*

Walter Friedländer (1873–1966) was an art historian. In 1914, he became a Privatdozent at the Wilhelm Vöge institute at the University of Freiburg. He was named Extraordinarius Professor in 1921, and continued to teach in Freiburg until 1933. Following his dismissal (on the basis of the Law for the Restoration of Professional Service), Friedländer emigrated to the United States. He found a position at the Institute of Fine Arts at New York University in 1935.

*at Brecht's house*

Franz Josef Brecht (1899–1982) studied with Heidegger in the 1920s. He became a Privatdozent at Heidelberg University in 1932, and then an *Außerplanmäßig* professor of philosophy in 1941. From 1952 until 1967 he was a professor at the University of Mannheim. His publications include *Platon und der George-Kreis* (Leipzig: Dieterich, 1929); *Heraklit: Ein Versuch über den Ursprung der Philosophie* (Heidelberg: Carl Winter Verlag, 1948); *Einführung in die Philosophie der Existenz* (Heidelberg: Schmidt-Carstens, 1948); and *Heidegger und Jaspers: Die beiden Grundformen der Existenzphilosophie* (Wuppertal: Marées-Verlag, 1948).

*the book dealers' market register*

*Gesamtkatalog der deutschen philosophischen Literatur*: From the International Philosophical Congress in Naples (May 5–9, 1924), handed over by the German publishers as contracted by the Trade Association of German Booksellers, edited by August von Löwis of Menar and Friedrich Michael (Leipzig, 1924).

*a new book by Scheler*

Max Scheler, *Schriften zur Soziologie und Weltanschauungslehre*: Volume 3, *Christentum und Gesellschaft*; Volume 1, *Konfessionen*; and Volume 2, *Arbeits- und Bevölkerungsprobleme* (Leipzig: Neue Geist-Verlag, 1924).

*There was also a book by Hans and Grete (Driesch)*

Hans and Margarete Driesch, *Fern-Ost: Als Gäste Jungchinas* (Leipzig: F. A. Brockhaus, 1924).

*A Caesar by the Gundolf factory*

Friedrich Gundolf, *Caesar* (Berlin: Georg Bondi, 1924).

*the notes from the "time" lecture*

> On July 25, 1924, Martin Heidegger delivered his talk "Der Begriff der Zeit" ["The Concept of Time"] to the Marburg Theological Society. This was later published as Martin Heidegger, *Der Begriff der Zeit*, edited (with an afterword) by Hartmut Tietjen (Tübingen: Max Niemeyer, 1989). The lecture also appears as GA 64, edited by Friedrich-Wilhelm von Herrmann (Frankfurt: Vittorio Klostermann, 2004), 105–125 (*The Concept of Time*, translated by William McNeill [Oxford: Blackwell, 1992]; a different translation also appears in *Becoming Heidegger: On the Trail of His Early Occasional Writings, 1910–1927*, 192–210).

*you gave me Thomas à Kempis*

> Thomas à Kempis, *De imitatione Christi* (Toulouse, 1488). It could not be determined which edition Heidegger gave to Löwith.

*You must have received my card from eight or so days ago?*

> The postcard in question is from October 18, 1924 (i.e., document 60 above).

**63.** M.H. to K.L., November 6, 1924, Letter (copy)

*the beautiful postcards from Rome; you even addressed one of them to Schwanallee 21, Freiburg*

> The postcard in question is from October 18th, 1924 (i.e., document 60 above). Heidegger's address in Marburg was 21 *Schwanallee*.

*The vibrating excitation surrounding Rotenberg*

> This perhaps refers to Heidegger's remark regarding the German burse. At the time, Löwith's address was *Rotenberg* 8; that of the German burse was *Rotenberg* 21. It was founded in 1918 as the *Institut für Grenz- und Auslanddeutschtum* by the sociologist Johann Heinrich Mannhardt (1883–1969). Mannhardt habilitated in 1925 and was Extraordinarius Professor at the University of Marburg from 1927 until 1929, at which point he become Ordinarius Professor. He joined the Nazi Party in 1933. From their inception, the two institutes had a German nationalist orientation. The first summer school took place in August of 1922, under the motto "German culture in the life of the present." The aim of the course was to support those who had been forcibly ejected from the Reich by the Treaty of Versailles. The "existential struggle [*Dasinskampf*]" of the Germans following World War I was thematized in several summer courses, which also

included reactionary activities on "race theory" and "racial hygiene," as well as lectures on then modern topics such as "expressionism" and "the constitutional foundations of the Weimar Republic." Mannhardt's efforts were quite successful, and he obtained accomplished and renowned humanist scholars for his courses, such as, for example, the cream of the crop of academic Germanists in Marburg (Oskar Walzel, Leo Weisgerber, and Andreas Heusler), as well as the author Rudolf G. Binding and the philosopher-pedagogues Theodor Litt and Eduard Spranger.

*An old Freiburger showed up from Munich—Schilling*

Kurt Schilling (1899–1977) studied philosophy, history, and German in Munich, Freiburg, Marburg, and Göttingen. Following his habilitation, he joined the Nazi Party and became chair of the philosophy department. He later became professor of philosophy in Prague and Munich.

*a friend of Luschka*

Werner Herbert Luschka (born in 1900) was a student of Heidegger and Karl Vossler. He graduated in 1925 from the University of Munich with his doctoral thesis *Die Rolle des Fortschrittsgedankens in der Poetik und literarischen Kritik der Franzosen im Zeitalter der Aufklärung*.

*Vossler*

Karl Vossler (1872–1949), a professor at the University of Munich, was a German literary-historian, Dante scholar, and one of the most important Romance scholars of the first-half of the twentieth century.

*Herr Martin*

Gottfried Martin (1901–1972) studied philosophy with Natorp and Heidegger. He later became a philosophy professor in Cologne, Mainz, and Bonn.

*the Frank book on Plato and the Pythagoreans*

Erich Frank (1883–1949) became Heidegger's successor in Marburg in 1928. The book in question is *Plato und die sogenannten Pythagoreer* (Halle an der Saale: Max Niemeyer, 1923). He emigrated to the United States in 1939. Becker's review appeared in *Logos* XIII (1924/1925), 133–137.

*a four-hour a week history of the concept of time*

> GA 20 (*History of the Concept of Time: Prolegomena*, translated by Theodore Kisiel [Bloomington: Indiana University Press, 1992]).

*tutorials on Descartes*

> Martin Heidegger, "Anfängerübungen im Anschluß an Descartes, Meditationes" ["Beginner Tutorials in Connection with Descartes' *Meditations*"].

*They desire a new humanism*

> In 1924, Jaeger co-founded *Die Gesellschaft für antike Kultur* ("The Society for Ancient Culture"). He was also a great supporter of humanistic education in high schools. Along with his friend Eduard Spranger, Jaeger advocated for ancient language and a philosophy of education. He viewed human beings as the greatest work of art that could be created: "Our German word *Bildung* signifies the essence of upbringing in the most vivid Greek, Platonic sense. It contains within itself the connection to that which gives form artistically, the sculptural, as well as to the creator having in his mind's eye the normative image, the 'idea' or the 'type.' Wherever this thought again appears in subsequent history, it is an heir to the Greeks..." (Werner Jaeger, *Paideia*: *Die Formung des griechischen Menschen*, three volumes [Leipzig/Berlin: Walter de Gruyter, 1934–1947], Volume 1, 12 f.).

*"for the masses"*

> Jaeger edited the journal *Die Antike: Zeitschrift für Kunst und Kultur des klassischen Altertums* from 1925 to 1944, and this is what is referred to with the phrase "for the 'masses.'" In 1925, he co-founded the critical journal *Gnomon*, whose editorship his pupil Richard Harder took over. See also Heidegger's letter from March 27, 1925 (i.e., document 65).

*with Fock*

> Gustav Fock Antiquariat, in Leipzig.

*Alexander Halensis, Summa*

Alexander of Hales OFM, *Summa Theologiae*, five volumes, edited by Bernardinus Klumper OFM (Quaracchi, 1924).

*Matthäus von Aquasparta*

Matthew of Aquasparta (1237–1302) was an Italian Franciscan, scholastic theologian, and philosopher of the Parisian school. He studied with Bonaventure in Paris. It could not be determined which texts are being referenced.

*Grabmann*

Martin Grabmann (1875–1947) was an expert in Medieval philosophy and scholasticism. He was a professor at the University of Vienna, University of Munich, and University of Eichstätt. See also Hermann Köstler, "Heidegger schreibt an Grabmann," in *Philosophisches Jahrbuch* 87 (1980), 96–109.

**64.** M.H. to K.L., December 17, 1924, Postcard (copy)

*I got your letter and the two notebooks*

The letter is not in the possession of the estate, and it could not be determined which notebooks are being referenced.

*it will come out a few pages longer in the Jahrbuch*

In 1925, Heidegger was to publish his review of the recently published correspondence between Wilhelm Dilthey and Count Yorck von Wartenburg under the title "Der Begriff der Zeit" in the *Deutsche Vierteljahresschrift für Literaturwissenschaft und Geistesgeschichte*. (Available as GA 64, 1–103.) However, because it was too long, Rothacker decided against including the review.

*He is writing an anthropology and a metaphysics*

This perhaps refers to Max Scheler's late publications *Die Stellung des Menschen im Kosmos* (Darmstadt: Reichl, 1928) and *Idealismus-Realismus*, which appears in Volume 9 of his collected works (Bonn: Bouvier, 1976).

*Ed. v. Hartmann*

> Eduard Karl Robert von Hartmann (1842–1906) was a philosopher and independent scholar in Berlin. His major two-volume work, *Philosophie des Unbewußten* (Berlin: Duncker, 1869), was highly regarded by Scheler.

**65. M.H. to K.L., March 27, 1925, Postcard (copy)**

*Thank you for your letter*

> The letter is not in the possession of the estate.

*the winter lecture course*

> GA 21 (*Logic: The Question of Truth*, translated by Thomas Sheehan [Bloomington: Indiana University Press, 2016]).

*a beginner's seminar on Descartes*

> In place of a seminar on Descartes, Heidegger held two other seminars: "Übungen für Anfänger: Kant, *Kritik der reinen Vernunft*" ("Tutorials for Beginners: Kant's *Critique of Pure Reason*") and "Phänomenologische Übungen für Fortgeschrittene (Hegel, *Logik I*)" ("Advanced Phenomenological Tutorials: Hegel's *Logic I*").

*A second volume by Cassirer has now come out*

> Ernst Cassirer, *Philosophie der symbolischen Formen*, Volume 2: *Das mythische Denken* (Berlin: Bruno Cassirer, 1923). (The foreword is dated December 1924.)

*the presentations by Klein*

> Jacob Klein (1899–1978) studied with Husserl, Hartmann, and Heidegger. He emigrated to the United States in 1937 and taught at St. John's college in Annapolis, Maryland. He was a distinguished expert on Plato and Platonism.

*Landsberg*

> Paul Ludwig Landsberg (1901–1944) habilitated in 1928 from the University of Bonn with his *Augustinus: Studien zur Geschichte seiner Philosophie*. He emigrated to France in 1933, and in 1934 moved to Spain. He returned to France

in 1937 and taught at the Sorbonne in Paris, and in 1939 worked for Radio Paris. In 1940, he fled to Lyon, and later lived in Pau. He was arrested by the Gestapo in 1943, and on April 2nd of that year he died from tuberculosis at the Oranienburg concentration camp. Heidegger is referring to Landsberg's early publications *Die Welt des Mittelalters und wir: Ein geschichtsphilosophischer Versuch über den Sinn eines Zeitalters* (Bonn: Friedrich Cohen, 1922) and *Wesen und Bedeutung der Platonischen Akademie: Eine erkenntnissoziologische Untersuchung* (Bonn: Friedrich Cohen, 1923).

*"Nietzsches Professur in Basel"*

Johannes Stroux, *Nietzsches Professur in Basel* (Jena: Frommannsche Buchhandlung, 1925).

**66.** M.H. to K.L., June 30, 1925, Letter (copy)

*Thank you kindly for your letters and cards*

Neither the letters nor the postcards are in the possession of the estate.

*as long as Overbeck is not "refuted"*

In his major work *Über die Christlichkeit unserer heutigen Theologie*, Overbeck attempted to prove that original Christianity is in stark opposition to every mode of knowing. The theological attempt to bring faith and knowledge into harmony was thus in vain; therefore, any Christian theology was in principle impossible. The refutation of Overbeck's thesis on the impossibility of Christian theology became an urgent task for theology at the time.

*the "metaphysics of insoluble problems"*

This is probably an allusion to Nicolai Hartmann.

*Philosophische Forschungen (!) Volume I—"Der Dandy"!—*

Otto Mann, *Der moderne Dandy: Ein Kulturproblem des 19. Jahrhunderts* (*Philosophische Forschungen*, Volume 1) (Berlin: Springer, 1925).

*The days in Kassel (at the end of April)*

From April 16 to 21, 1925, Heidegger (on invitation) held ten lectures for The Kurhessen Society for Art and Science under the title "Wilhelm

Diltheys Forschungsarbeit und der gegenwärtige Kampf um eine historische Weltanschauung." Now in: Martin Heidegger, *Vorträge*, Part 1: 1915–1932, edited by Günther Neumann (GA 80.1) (Frankfurt am Main: Vittoria Klostermann, 2016), 103–157 ("Wilhelm Dilthey's Research and the Current Struggle for a Historical Worldview," in *Becoming Heidegger*, 235–274).

*Boehlau the elder*

Johannes Boehlau (1861–1941) was a classical archaeologist. In 1891, he accepted a position as assistant-director at the Fridericianum Museum in Kassel. In 1902, he became director and oversaw the departments of prehistory, early-history, antiquity, numismatics, and plaster-castings. In an effort to offer further support for the arts and sciences in Kassel, he founded the Museum Association in 1903, reorganized the Kassel Art Society in 1908, and contributed to the founding of The Kurhessen Society for Art and Science in 1912.

*Boehlau (the younger)*

The son of Johannes Boehlau.

*Husserl will be lecturing on phenomenological psychology*

Edmund Husserl, *Phänomenologische Psychologie*. Summer semester lectures, 1925, edited by Walter Biemel (*Husserliana*, Volume IX) (Netherlands: Den Haag, 1962). The first two sections relate to Dilthey.

*Dr. König*

Josef König (1893–1974) attended Heidegger's lectures in 1925/1926. In 1946, he became a professor of philosophy at the University of Hamburg, and from 1953 until 1963, he was a philosophy professor at the University of Göttingen.

*Misch*

Georg Misch (1878–1965) was a student of Wilhelm Dilthey and a proponent of *Lebensphilosophie* ("life-philosophy"). He was a professor of philosophy at the University of Göttingen from 1919 until 1935, and in 1939 he emigrated to Great Britain. His most important philosophical work was *Lebensphilosophie und Phänomenologie: Eine Auseinandersetzung der Diltheyschen Richtung mit Heidegger und Husserl* (Leipzig: B. G. Teubner, 1930).

*Philosophischer Anzeiger, edited by Plessner*

Helmuth Plessner (1892–1985) emigrated to Istanbul in 1933, and then on to the Netherlands, where he taught as a professor of sociology and philosophy (with an interruption between the years 1943 and 1946). He is one of the more significant proponents of philosophical anthropology.

*I will review it in the Deutsche Literatur-Zeitung*

The review appears in the *Deutsche Literaturzeitung* (Berlin), 49:5 (1928), pages 1000–1012. It can also be found in GA 3, 255–270 (Martin Heidegger, *Kant and the Problem of Metaphysics*, translated by Richard Taft [Bloomington: Indiana University Press, 1990]).

*Vol. III, on art, will now follow*

The third volume, published in 1929, bore the subtitle *Phänomenologie der Erkenntnis*.

*Have you finished the work on personalism?*

It could not be determined to which work this refers.

**68. M.H. to K.L., August 24, 1925, Letter (copy)**

*In the winter I will lecture on logic*

GA 21 (*Logic: The Question of Truth*, 2016).

*In the advanced seminar I will be working on Hegel's Logic, Book 1*

Martin Heidegger: "Phänomenologische Übungen für Fortgeschrittene (Hegel, *Logik* I)" ["Advanced Phenomenological Tutorials: Hegel's *Logic* I"].

*a lecture given by Heitmüller*

Wilhelm Heitmüller (1869–1926) was an evangelical theologian. He was Ordinarius Professor of the New Testament at the University of Marburg from 1908 until 1920, when he moved to the University of Bonn and later (in 1924) to the University of Tübingen. He published, among other things,

*Taufe und Abendmahl im Urchristentum* (Tübingen: J. C. B. Mohr, 1911) and *Jesus* (Tübingen: J. C. B. Mohr, 1913). He delivered a lecture to the Marburg Theological Society on July 20, 1925.

*An article on Yorck–Dilthey*

Helmuth Stadie, "Die Stellung des Briefwechsels zwischen Dilthey und dem Grafen Yorck in der Geistesgeschichte," in *Philosophischer Anzeiger*, edited by Helmuth Plessner, first half-volume (1925), 146–200.

*there now also exists Symposion*

*Symposion: Philosophische Zeitschrift für Forschung und Aussprache* was published in Erlangen from 1925 to 1927.

*Logos*

*Logos: Zeitschrift für systematische Philosophie*, edited by Bruno Bauch, Julius Binder, Ernst Cassirer, Edmund Husserl, Friedrich Meinecke, Rudolf Otto, Heinrich Rickert, Eduard Spranger, Otto Vossler, and Heinrich Wölfflin, was published in Tübingen beginning in 1911 (by J. C. B. Mohr).

*"Ethos"*

*Ethos: Zweimonatsschrift für Soziologie, Geschichts- und Kulturphilosophie*, edited by D. Koigen, W. F. Hilker, and F. Schneersohn.

*Jacob Burckhardt*

Jacob Burckhardt (1818–1897) was a Swiss cultural-historian whom both Heidegger and Löwith held in high regard. He corresponded for a time with Friedrich Nietzsche. In 1858, he accepted a chair in history and cultural-history at the University of Basel, which he occupied until 1893. His most important works are *Die Cultur der Renaissance in Italien: Ein Versuch* (Basel: Schweighauser, 1860); *Griechische Culturgeschichte* (four Volumes), edited by Jacob Oeri (Berlin/Stuttgart: Spemann, 1898–1902); and *Weltgeschichtliche Betrachtungen*, edited by Jacob Oeri (Berlin/Stuttgart: Spemann, 1905). See also LSS 7.

*Wiesemann has showed up in Marburg*

Gustav Wiesemann became a constant participant in Heidegger's seminars beginning in 1921.

**69. K.L. to M.H., August 22/29, 1925, Letter**

*the land of the Cimmerians*

According to legend, the Cimmerians lived on the western coast of Italy between Pozzuoli and Baja, dwelling in perpetual fog.

*ohimè*

"Woe is me."

*Goethe's diaries of his journey through Italy*

Johann Wolfgang von Goethe, *Tagebuch der italienischen Reise*, with an afterword and annotations, edited by Heinrich Schmidt (Leipzig: Alfred Kröner, 1925).

*the last Winckelmann letters*

Johann Joachim Winckelmann, *Briefe an seine Freunde*, with supplements and annotations, edited by Karl Wilhelm Dassdorf, two parts in one volume (Dresden: Waltherische Buchhandlung, 1777–1780).

*Gregorovius*

Ferdinand Gregorovius, *Wanderjahre in Italien*, five volumes (Stuttgart: F. A. Brockhaus, 1856–1877).

*Hehn*

Victor Hehn, *Italien: Ansichten und Streiflichter*, third revised and augmented edition (Berlin: Bornträger, 1887).

*at the Zeppelin commemoration*

The memorial celebration took place at the monument for Count Zeppelin in Constance on August 23, 1925.

*Scheler's Formen des Wissens und der Bildung*

> Max Scheler, *Die Formen des Wissens und der Bildung* (Bonn: Friedrich Cohen, 1925). Based on a speech held at the ten-year celebration of the founding of the *Lessing-Akademie* in Berlin.

*but not his good Psyche*

> Carl Gustav Carus, *Psyche: Zur Entwicklungsgeschichte der Seele*, second improved and augmented edition (Stuttgart: Scheitlin, 1851).

*his Symbolik*

> Carl Gustav Carus, *Symbolik der menschlichen Gestalt: Ein Handbuch zur Menschenkenntnis*. Newly revised and expanded by Theodor Lessing (Celle: Kampmann, 1925).

*a book on philology by Vossler*

> Karl Vossler, *Geist und Kultur in der Sprache* (Heidelberg: Carl Winter Verlag, 1925).

*Pirandello*

> The author Luigi Pirandello (1867–1936) was a writer, and one of the most important dramatists of the twentieth-century. He received the Nobel Prize for literature in 1934.

*a parable—"Così è, se vi pare"*

> Luigi Pirandello, *Così è (se vi pare)*—Parabola in tre atti, 1917. *Così è (se vi pare)* means: "Things are as they seem to you."

*Chiedendo notizie ed informazioni*

> "Asking for news and information."

*Scheel's beautiful biography of Luther*

> Otto Scheel, *Martin Luther*, two volumes (Tübingen: J. C. B. Mohr, 1916/1917).

*his Konstantin, the Basel lectures, and some of his correspondences*

Jacob Burckhardt, *Die Zeit Constantins des Großen* (Leipzig: Seemann, 1853). "The Basel lectures" refers to *Die Culturgeschichte der Griechen* and *Die Weltgeschichtliche Betrachtungen*. By 1925, the following correspondences involving Burkhardt had been published: *Friedrich Nietzsches Briefwechsel mit Fr. Ritschl, J. Burckhardt, H. Taine, G. Keller, Freiherrn von Stein und G. Brandes* (Berlin: Schuster & Löffler, 1904); *Jacob Burckhardt, Briefe an einen Architekten 1870–1889* (Munich: Müller und Rentsch, 1913); *Jacob Burckhardts Briefe an seinen Schüler Albert Brenner* (Basel: Schwabe & Co., 1918); *Briefe Jakob Burckhardts an Gottfried und Johanna Kinkel*, edited by Rudolf Meyer-Kraemer (Basel: Schwabe & Co., 1921); *Jacob Burckhardts Briefe an seinen Freund Friedrich von Preen: 1864–1893* (Stuttgart/Berlin: Deutsche Verlag-Anstalt, 1922); and *Briefe und Gedichte an die Brüder Schauenburg* (Basel: Schwabe & Co., 1923).

**70.** M.H. to K.L., August 31, 1925, Postcard (copy)

*Krüger*

Gerhard Krüger (1902–1972) was friends with Löwith and Hans-Georg Gadamer. His habilitation (in 1929) was supervised by Heidegger, and his habilitation thesis—*Philosophie und Moral in der kantischen Kritik*—was published in 1931 (Tübingen: J. C. B. Mohr). He became Extraordinarius Professor at the University of Marburg in 1938, and Ordinarius Professor of philosophy at the University of Münster in 1940. In 1946, he accepted an appointment at the University of Tübingen, and in 1952 he became Gadamer's successor in Frankfurt. His most notable publications are *Einsicht und Leidenschaft: Das Wesen des platonischen Denkens* (Frankfurt am Main: Vittorio Klostermann, 1939); *Grundfragen der Philosophie: Geschichte, Wahrheit, Wissen* (Frankfurt am Main: Vittorio Klostermann, 1958); and *Freiheit und Weltverwaltung: Aufsätze zur Philosophie der Geschichte* (Freiburg/Munich: Verlag Karl Alber, 1958).

**71.** K.L. to M.H., March 16, 1926, Letter (privately held)

*I am sending you the Dilthey along with this letter*

Löwith's habilitation thesis had four main themes: (1) "L. Feuerbach and the End of Classical German Philosophy" (later published in LSS 5, 1–26); (2) "Burckhardt's Position with Respect to Hegel's Philosophy of Spirit" (later published in LSS 7, 9–38); (3) "Dialectic and Dialogical Thinking"; and (4)

"Dilthey's Foundation for the Humanities." On June 23, 1928, Löwith delivered a lecture on Burkhardt. The mention of "Dilthey" here refers to the expansion of the fourth section.

*a Shrovetide sermon by Brunner*

Emil Brunner (1889–1966) was a reformed Swiss theologian who, along with Karl Barth, co-founded dialectical theology. Brunner and Barth later became rivals.

*Barth's Zwischen den Zeiten*

The journal *Zwischen den Zeiten* was the voice of "dialectical theology" in which Barth, Gogarten, Thurneysen, and Bultmann published many essays between 1923 and 1933. Barth published some forty contributions. Between 1923 and 1927, he published the following: "Not und Verheißung der christlichen Verkündigung," in *Zwischen den Zeiten* 1 (1923), 3–25; "Das Problem der Ethik in der Gegenwart," in 1/2 (1923), 30–57; "Reformierte Lehre, ihr Wesen und ihre Aufgabe," in 2/1 (1924), 8–39; "Brunners Schleiermacherbuch," in 2/1 (1924), 49–64; "Zur Kenntnisnahme," in 2/1 (1924), 79–80; "Barmherzigkeit," in 3/1, 3–11; "Schleiermachers 'Weihnachtsfeier'" in 3/1 (1925), 38–61; *"Sunt certi denique fines*: Eine Mitteilung," in 3/1 (1925), 113–116; "Menschenwort und Gotteswort in der christlichen Predigt," in 3/2 (1925), 119–140; "Das Schriftprinzip der reformierten Kirche," in 3/3 (1925), 215–245; "Die dogmatischen Prinzipienlehre bei Wilhelm Hermann," in 3/3 (1925), 246–280; "Wunschbarkeit und Möglichkeit eines allgemeinen reformierten Glaubensbekenntnisses," in 3/4 (1925), 311–333; "Kirche und Theologie," in 4/1 (1926), 18–40; "Die Frage der 'dialektischen' Theologie," in 4/1 (1926), 40–59; "Vorwort zur fünften Auflage des 'Römerbriefs'," in 4/2 (1926), 99–101; "Vom heiligen Geist," in 4/4 (1926), 275–279; "Bemerkungen," in 4/4 (1926), 356; and "Die Kirche und die Kultur," in 4/5 (1926), 363–384.

*I had agreed with Plessner to keep it around one sheet*

This was for the journal *Philosophischer Anzeiger*, which was edited by Plessner. Löwith's manuscript "Dilthey und die Grundlegung der Geisteswissenschaften" ("Dilthey and the Foundation of the Humanities") was never published.

*a big pile of trash by Nicolai Hartmann*

Nicolai Hartmann, *Ethik* (Berlin/Leipzig: de Gruyter, 1926).

*witty platitudes by Troeltsch*

This perhaps refers to Ernst Troeltsch, *Deutscher Geist und Westeuropa: Gesammelte kulturphilosophische Aufsätze und Reden*, edited by Hans Baron (Tübingen: J. C. B. Mohr, 1925).

*"a Catholic Nietzsche"*

This perhaps refers to August Vetter, *Nietzsche* (Munich; Reinhardt, 1926).

*Do you still want the Görres?*

This may refer to the four-volume work *Die christliche Mystik* by Joseph Görres.

**72. M.H. to K.L., March 17, 1927, Letter (copy)**

*Clauss' impertinence*

Ludwig Ferdinand Clauss, *Rasse und Seele: Eine Einführung in die Gegenwart* (Munich: J. F. Lehmann, 1926).

**73. K.L. to M.H., May 1, 1927, Letter**

*the lecture*

GA 24 (*The Basic Problems of Phenomenology*, translated by Albert Hofstadter [Bloomington: Indiana University Press, 1982]).

*and seminar*

Martin Heidegger, "Seminar für Fortgeschrittene: Die Ontologie des Aristoteles und Hegels Logik" ("Advanced Seminar: The Ontology of Aristotle and Hegel's *Logic*"); now under the title "Aristoteles-Hegel-Seminar," in GA 86 (*On Hegel's Philosophy of Right: The 1934-35 Seminar and Interpretive Essays*, translated by Andrew Mitchell [London: Bloomsbury, 2014]).

*the third systematic part of your work*

In his lecture "Die Grundprobleme der Phänomenologie" ("The Fundamental Problems of Phenomenology"), Heidegger deals with the issue of the third, unpublished division of *Being and Time* entitled "Zeit und Sein" ("Time and Being"). Available as GA 24 (*The Basic Problems of Phenomenology*, translated by Albert Hofstadter [Bloomington: Indiana University Press, 1982]). Löwith must have learned further details regarding the content of the lecture from Heidegger.

*for leaving me a copy*

I.e., a copy of Martin Heidegger, *Sein und Zeit* (*Being and Time*).

*Feuerbach*

Ludwig Andreas Feuerbach (1804–1872) habilitated in 1828 at the University of Erlangen. Between 1829 and 1837 he gave lectures there concerning logic, metaphysics, and the history of philosophy. In 1830, he anonymously published his work *Gedanken über Tod und Unsterblichkeit* (Nürnberg: Johann Adam Stein). His major work, *Das Wesen des Christenthums*, appeared in 1831 (Leipzig: Wigand). Feuerbach was an independent scholar.

## 74. K.L. to M.H., August 2, 1927, Letter

*Dr. Freiling*

Heinrich Freiling was a psychologist who completed his habilitation under the supervision of Erich Rudolf Jaensch. He completed his dissertation, *Über die räumlichen Wahrnehmungen der Jugendlichen in der eidetischen Entwicklungsphase* (Leipzig: Barth, 1923), at the University of Marburg in 1923. He published two articles in collaboration with Jaensch: "Der Aufbau der räumlichen Wahrnehmung" and "Das Kovariantenphänomen, mit Bezug auf die allgemeinen Struktur- und Entwicklungsfragen der räumlichen Wahrnehmungen," both of which appeared in Erich Rudolf Jaensch's *Über den Aufbau der Wahrnehmungswelt und ihre Struktur im Jugendalter: Eine Untersuchung über Grundlagen und Ausgangspunkte unseres Weltbildes, durchgeführt mit den Forschungsmitteln der Jugendpsychologie, angewandt auf erkenntnistheoretische, naturphilosophische und pädagogische Fragen* (Leipzig: Barth, 1923), 245–266 and 273–294.

*Beck and Schmidt-Ott*

Friedrich Gustav Adolf Eduard Ludwig Schmitt-Ott (1860–1956) was a lawyer who served as Prussian Minister of Culture from 1917 to 1918. In 1920, he became the first president of The Emergency Association for the Promotion of German Science. Beck was presumably a co-worker of Schmitt-Ott's.

*the honorable and imposing figure of Goebel*

Karl von Goebel (1855–1932) was Ordinarius Professor of botany at the University of Munich (*Organik der Pflanzen*, 1928) and, prior to that, in Freiburg, where Löwith studied with him.

*Elwert and Ebel's*

A bookstore in Marburg.

*"fesieggiare"*

"To celebrate."

*My godchild*

Jutta Gadamer

*my critique of Klages*

Karl Löwith, "Nietzsche im Lichte der Philosophie Ludwig Klages," in Erich Rothacker (ed.), *Probleme der Weltanschauungslehre* (Darmstadt: Reichl, 1927), 258–348. Also available in LSS 6, 7–52. This probably refers to the *Kölnische Volkszeitung*.

*Frau Förster-Nietzsche*

Elisabeth Nietzsche (1846–1935) was Friedrich Nietzsche's sister. From 1885 until 1889, she was married to the political agitator Bernhard Förster (1843–1889). She founded the Nietzsche Archive, which was initially located in Nietzsche's birth city of Naumburg, and then later relocated to the "Villa Silberblick" in Weimar. Friedrich Nietzsche lived in the villa until his death in 1900. Elisabeth was the sole proprietor of the Nietzsche Archive and estate.

*Nietzsche's biography by Frau Förster-Nietzsche*

Elisabeth Förster-Nietzsche, *Das Leben Friedrich Nietzsche's*, three volumes (Leipzig: Naumann, 1895, 1897, 1904). The letter referenced here is included as Supplement 1.

*le mieux est l'ennemi du bien*

"The better is the enemy of the good."

**75. K.L. to M.H., August 10, 1927, Postcard**

*could this be Plessner?*

It appears Löwith's presumption was incorrect.

*Spitta*

Theodor Spitta (1873–1969) was a politician, mayor, and senator in Bremen. Regarding Spitta, see also Heinrich Wiegand Petzet, *Auf einen Stern zugehen: Begegnungen und Gespräche mit Martin Heidegger 1929–1976* (Frankfurt am Main: Societäts-Verlag, 1983), 46 and 62.

*Knittermeyer*

Hinrich Knittermeyer (1891–1958) became editor of the Marburg based journal *Christliche Welt* in 1922. However, the review to which Löwith is referring did not appear in *Christliche Welt*, but rather in *Theologische Literaturzeitung* 53 (1928), 481–493.

**76. K.L. to M.H., August 17, 1927, Letter**

*in philosophical terms: that search is too expansive (from 1921)*

See the letter from April 22, 1921 (i.e., document 23).

*completely untouched by "today"*

See the letter from March 26, 1924 (i.e., document 57).

*Herr Seidemann*

Alfred Seidemann (1895–1976) studied with Heidegger in Marburg in 1926/1927. He completed his dissertation, *Bergsons Stellung zu Kant* (Endingen, 1937), at the University of Freiburg in 1937.

*your opinion about my habilitation thesis*

On December 15, 1927, Löwith submitted his habilitation thesis to the philosophical faculty of the University of Marburg under the title *Phänomenologische Grundlegung der ethischen Probleme* [*The Phenomenological Foundation of Ethical Problems*]. (The revised version appeared a year later under the title *Das Individuum in der Rolle des Mitmenschen* [*The Individual in the Roll of Fellow Human Being*] (Leipzig: Drei Masken Verlag, 1928); now also in LSS 1, 9–197. Heidegger had advised Löwith to change the title to *Beiträge zur anthropologischen Grundlegung der ethischen Probleme* [*Contributions to the Anthropological Foundation of Ethical Problems*] for the sake of securing him a lectureship in social philosophy (which he actually obtained three years later).

*the Schelling seminar*

Martin Heidegger, "Phänomenologische Übungen für Fortgeschrittene: Schelling, Über das Wesen der menschlichen Freiheit" ("Advanced Phenomenological Tutorials: Schelling, *On the Essence of Human Freedom*"), in GA 86, 49–54; 529–549.

**77.** M.H. to K.L., August 20, 1927, Letter (copy)

*the help of Mahnke*

Dietrich Friedrich Hermann Mahnke (1884–1939) completed his dissertation, *Leibnizens Synthese von Universalmathematik und Individualmetaphysik* (Halle an der Saale: Max Niemeyer, 1925), under the direction of Edmund Husserl. In 1927, he became a professor of philosophy at the University of Marburg.

*sit venia verbo*

"May what is said be forgiven."

*a scene of such ass-kissing*

Carl Heinrich Becker (1876–1933) was an orientalist and a politician. He was the Prussian Minister of Culture from 1925 until 1930.

*my Duns Scotus*

Martin Heidegger's habilitation thesis from 1915, *Die Kategorien- und Bedeutungslehre des Duns Scotus*, was published in 1916 (Tübingen: J. C. B. Mohr). It is now available in Martin Heidegger, *Frühe Schriften*, 131–353.

**78.** M.H. to K.L., October 6, 1927, Postcard (copy)

*Many thanks for the birthday greeting*

The birthday greeting is not in the possession of the estate.

**79.** K.L. to M.H., December 29, 1927, Postcard

*Number 2 by Segantini*

Giovanni Segantini (1858–1899) was an Italian painter who specialized in mountain landscapes.

*Kaehler's "Humboldt"*

Siegfried A. Kaehler, *Wilhelm von Humboldt und der Staat: Ein Beitrag zur Geschichte deutscher Lebensgestaltung um 1800* (Munich/Berlin: Oldenbourg, 1927). Löwith reviewed this book in *Logos* 17 (1928), 361–367; it is also available in LSS 1, 1981, 208–215.

**80.** K.L. to M.H., January 16, 1928, Letter

*Klemperer's lecture*

Victor Klemperer (1881–1961) was a romance philologist, and was a professor of romance studies at the Dresden Technical University. He was released in 1935. After 1945, he worked at the University of Greifswald, the University of Halle, and the University of Berlin. His major work is *Die französische Literatur von Napoleon bis zur Gegenwart*, four volumes (Leipzig/Berlin: G. B. Teubner, 1925–1931). His most famous works are his journals: *Leben sammeln, nicht fragen wozu und warum – Tagebücher 1919–1932*, edited by Walter Nowojski (Berlin: Aufbau Verlag, 1996); "Ich will Zeugnis ablegen bis zum letzten": *Tagebücher 1933–1945* (Volumes I–VIII), edited by Walter Nowojski (Berlin: Aufbau Verlag, 1995); *Und So ist alles schwankend - Tagebücher Juni-Dezember 1945*, edited by Walter Nowojski (Berlin: Aufbau Verlag, 1996); *So ich sitze zwischen allen Stuhlen*, Volume 1 (1945–1949) and Volume 2 (1950–1959), edited by Walter Nowojski (Berlin: Aufbau Verlag, 1999); and *LTI [Lingua Tertii Imperii]: Notizbuch eines Philologen* (Aufbau Verlag, Berlin 1947).

*Spitzer*

Leo Spitzer (1886–1960) was a professor of romance linguistics at the University of Marburg beginning in 1925, and then at the University of

Cologne beginning in 1930. In 1933, he emigrated to Istanbul, and in 1935, he became professor of Romance Studies at the Johns Hopkins University in Baltimore.

## Deutschbein

Max Deutschbein (1876–1949) was a Germanist and professor at the University of Marburg beginning in 1919.

## Hamann

Richard Hamann (1879–1961) was a professor of art history at the University of Marburg from 1913 until 1949.

## Wechsler's book

This probably refers to Eduard Wechsler, *Esprit und Geist: Versuch einer Wesenskunde des Deutschen und des Franzosen* (Bielefeld/Leipzig: Velhagen & Klasing, 1927).

## Café Markees

This café (which no longer exists) was on *Reitgasse*, a street in Marburg.

## My well-behaved and disciplined Turazza

No further information could be obtained regarding "Turazza."

## he is the polar opposite of Grassi

Ernesto Grassi (1902–1991) taught philosophy at Italian and German universities. He began studying with Heidegger in 1928. After World War II, he became a professor of the philosophy of humanism at the University of Munich. In 1942, Heidegger published his essay "Platons Lehre von der Wahrheit" ("Plato's Doctrine of Truth") in the journal *Geistige Überlieferung: Das zweite Jahrbuch* (Berlin: A. Francke, 1942, 96–124), for which Grassi was the editor. (Now available in GA 9, 203–238 [*Pathmarks*, 155–182].) See also Wilhelm Büttemeyer, *Ernesto Grassi—Humanismus zwischen Faschismus und Nationalsozialismus* (Freiburg im Breisgau: Karl Alber, 2010).

**82.** M.H. to K.L., February 7th, 1928, Letter (copy)

*I had to go into debt and go hungry*

> Heidegger experienced extreme financial hardship in the summer of 1911 following the discontinuation of his theological studies, as his stipend had been contingent upon them.

**83.** M.H. to K.L., February 21st, 1928, Letter (copy)

*you could inquire in Munich about the publication of your book*

> This refers to *Drei Masken*, a publisher in Munich.

*Schmalenbach's Leibniz book*

> Herman Schmalenbach, *Leibniz* (Munich: Drei Masken Verlag, 1921).

**85.** M.H. to K.L., March 20th, 1928, Postcard (copy)

*It is still uncertain when I will go to Berlin*

> This is presumably owing to his appointment as Husserl's successor at the University of Freiburg.

**86.** M.H. to K.L., April 29th, 1928, Letter (copy)

*to study your book*

> The "book" in question is the printed text of Löwith's habilitation thesis, *Das Individuum in der Rolle des Mitmenschen* (*The Individual in the Role of Fellow Human Being*).

**87.** M.H. to K.L., Summer 1928, Postcard (copy)

*much better than Fahrner's*

> Rudolf Fahrner (1903-1988) was a Germanist. Following his habilitation, he was professor of Germanism in Marburg, Heidelberg, Athens, Ankara, and, after 1958, Karlsruhe. Other than Otto John, Fahrner was the only member of the Stauffenberg plot to survive the events of July 20th, 1944.

**88.** M.H. to K.L., End of Summer, 1928, Postcard (copy)

*I wish you much joy and a wonderful time in Copenhagen*

> Löwith was invited to give a lecture. It could not be determined which lecture he gave.

**89.** M.H. to K.L., September 28th, 1928, Postcard (copy)

*Thank you so much for the birthday wishes*

> The birthday postcard is not in the possession of the estate.

*Jacobsthal*

> Paul Jacobsthal (1880-1957) was professor of archeology at the University of Marburg beginning in 1912. He was forced to give up his professorship in 1935, after which he emigrated to England. He began lecturing at Christ Church College in Oxford in 1937.

**91.** M.H. to K.L., October 22nd, 1928, Letter (copy)

*the appointment*

> I.e., the appointment of Heidegger's successor.

*Many thanks for the essay*

> Karl Löwith, "Burckhardts Stellung zu Hegels Geschichtsphilosophie," in *Deutsche Vierteljahrsschrift für Literaturwissenschaft und Geistesgeschichte* 6 (1928), 702-741. Also in LSS 7, 9-38. It contains the revised edition of Löwith's inaugural lecture, which he had given in Marburg during the summer of 1928.

**92.** M.H. to K.L., October 24th, 1928, Letter (copy)

*Becker is taking the news very calmly*

> Oskar Becker had hopes of being Heidegger's successor.

**93.** M.H. to K.L., February 23rd, 1929, Letter (copy)

*[Freiburg] 23.II.29*

The document itself says "II.23.28." However, this cannot be true, owing to the fact that Löwith first began holding lectures in the winter semester of 1928/29. A mistake such as writing "II" instead of "XII" can be presumed, as Heidegger wished Löwith a quiet Christmas holiday.

*Many thanks for your two letters*

The letters are not in the possession of the estate.

*Schröer*

Arnold Schröer (1857-1935) became a professor of English language and literature at the University of Cologne in 1919. Heidegger's brother Fritz (1894-1980), like Martin himself, attended the *Gymnasium* in Constance. Regarding Martin and Fritz Heidegger, see Hans Dieter Zimmermann, *Martin und Fritz Heidegger: Philosophie und Fastnacht.* (Munich: C. H. Beck, 2005)

**94.** M.H. to K.L., April 21st, 1929, Letter (copy)

*Thank you for your card*

The postcard is not in the possession of the estate.

*Niemeyer is quite stingy with offprints*

Martin Heidegger, "Vom Wesen des Grundes," in *Jahrbuch für Philosophie und phänomenologische Forschung*, supplementary volume, *Festschrift für Edmund Husserl zum 70 Geburtstag* (1929, 71-100) (*Pathmarks*, 97-135). As alluded to below, it also appeared at the same time as a special edition.

*Davos*

This refers to the Davos University Conferences (which took place between March 17th and April 6th, 1929), during the course of which Heidegger and Ernst Cassirer held their now famous lectures and conversed with one another. "Davoser Disputation zwischen Ernst Cassirer und Martin Heidegger"—seminar in the context of the second of Davos' University Weeks, from March 17th until April 6th, 1929. A protocol of the seminar was compiled by O.F. Bollnow and J. Ritter, and published for the first time in Guido Schneeberger, *Ergänzungen zu einer Heidegger-Bibliographie*, with four supplements and one illustration (Bern 1960, 17-27). (The fourth supplement appears in Martin Heidegger, *Kant und das Problem der Metaphysik* (1973), 246-268, and in GA 3, 274-296 (*Kant and the Problem of Metaphysics*, 193-207.) Martin Heidegger, "Kritik der reinen Vernunft und die Aufgabe einer Grundlegung der Metaphysik"—three lectures from the second of the Davos University Conferences. First published (as a summary provided by Heidegger) in *Davoser Revue* (4):7, April 15th, 1929, 194-196. Included in Martin Heidegger, *Kant und das Problem der Metaphysik*, 243-245, and GA 3, 271-273 (*Kant and the Problem of Metaphysics*, 191-192).

**95. K.L. to M.H., May 9th, 1929, Letter**

*Mommsen*

Wilhelm Mommsen (1892-1966) accepted an appointment (created specifically for him) for Medieval and contemporary history at the University of Marburg in 1929. He was the director of the history department there.

*A. Messer's commentary on Kant*

August Messer, *Kommentar zu Kants 'Kritik der reinen Vernunft'* (Stuttgart: Strecker & Schröder, 1923).

*the abundantly confused senior Jacoby*

No additional information could be obtained regarding Jacoby.

*some other members from the A.V.*

This apparently refers to members of the academic association.

*Dostoevsky's Notes from the Underground*

Fyodor Dostoevsky, *Aus dem Dunkel der Großstadt: Acht Novellen*.

*The Dream of a Ridiculous Man*

Fyodor Dostoyevsky, *Traum eines lächerlichen Menschen*. It could not be determined exactly which edition is being referenced.

*Nötzel*

Karl Nötzel (1870-1945) was most known for his translations of the work of Russian authors such as Dostoyevsky and Gogol.

*Stephun*

Fedor Stephun (1884-1965) earned his doctorate in 1910 under the direction of Wilhelm Windelband. He was co-founder, along with Max Weber and Georg Simmel, of the journal *Logos*. He was a professor of sociology at the Dresden Technical University beginning in 1926; he was dismissed in 1937. From 1946 on he was honorary professor of Russian intellectual history at the University of Munich.

*Koch*

Hans Koch (1894-1959) was a theologian and a specialist in Eastern European history.

*the Huizinga*

Johan Huizinga, *Herbst des Mittelalters: Studien über Lebens- und Geistesformen des 14. und 15. Jahrhunderts in Frankreich und in den Niederlanden*, translated by T. Jolles Mönckeberg (Munich: Drei Masken, 1924).

**96.** M.H. to K.L., September 3rd, 1929, Letter (copy)

*To you and your bride*

Elisabeth Adelheid (Ada) Löwith (1900-1989) was the daughter of Dr. Professor Martin Kremmer, director of the Berlin *Arndt-Gymnasium*. Karl Löwith became engaged to Ada (who was three years younger than he) in 1929, and they married a short time later in Berlin-Dahlem. Ada supported Karl over the decades. After his death, she oversaw the publication of his autobiography. Regarding Ada Löwith, see also Löwith, *Mein Leben in Deutschland,* 66 (*My life In Germany*, 68).

*The concluding remark of your postcard*

The postcard is not in the possession of the estate.

*differed from the published essay*

This refers to the revised edition of Löwith's inaugural lecture, "Burckhardts Stellung zu Hegels Geschichtsphilosophie" ["Burkhardt's Position Regarding Hegel's Philosophy of History"], which he gave in Marburg in the summer of 1928. Now also in LSS 7, 9-38.

**97. M.H. to K.L., November 17th, 1929, Letter (copy)**

*Thank you so much for your letter*

The letter is not in the possession of the estate.

*the theme of your essays for the theological review*

Karl Löwith, "Grundzüge der Entwickelung der Phänomenologie zur Philosophie und ihr Verhältnis zur protestantischen Theologie" ("Fundamentals for the Development of a Phenomenology of Philosophy and its Relation to Protestant Theology"), in *Theologische Rundschau* 2 (1930), 26-64, 333-361. Reprinted in LSS 3, 33-95.

*"Philosophische Weltschauung"*

Max Scheler, *Philosophische Weltanschauung* (Bonn: Friedrich Cohen, 1929).

*my inaugural lecture, "What is Metaphysics"*

Heidegger gave his inaugural lecture "Was ist Metaphysik" ["What is Metaphysics"] on the 24th of July, 1929. It was published in 1929 by Friedrich Cohen Publishing (Bonn). Now also in: Martin Heidegger, *Wegmarken* (Frankfurt am Main: Vittorio Klostermann), 1967, 3-19, and in GA 9, 103-122 (*Pathmarks*, 82-96).

**98. K.L. to M.H., December 22nd, 1929, Letter**

*J. Conrad's wonderful story "The Shadow Line"*

Joseph Conrad, *Die Schattenlinie: Eine Beichte von Joseph Conrad*, with a Foreword by Jakob Wassermann (Berlin: S. Fischer, 1926).

*the final chapter of your Kant book*

Martin Heidegger, *Kant und das Problem der Metaphysik*, 3 (*Kant and the Problem of Metaphysics*, 2).

*I will make up for it in part two*

> Contrary to the plan expressed in this letter, Löwith did not refer to Heidegger's "What is Metaphysics" in the second part of the essay.

*P. Hofmann*

> Paul Hofmann, *Metaphysik oder verstehende Sinn-Wissenschaft? Gedanken zur Neugründung der Philosophie im Hinblick auf Heideggers 'Sein und Zeit'* (Berlin: Pan Verlag Kurt Metzner, 1929).

*H. Barth*

> Heinrich Barth, "Ontologie und Idealismus: Eine Auseinandersetzung mit Martin Heidegger," in *Zwischen den Zeiten* 7 (1929), Issue 6, 511-540.

*what Misch has written*

> Georg Misch, "Lebensphilosophie und Phänomenologie," in *Philosophischer Anzeiger* 3 (1929), 267-368 and 405-475. A final installment appeared in Volume 4 (1930), 181-330. In 1930, Misch published the essays as a book under the title *Lebensphilosophie und Phänomenologie: Eine Auseinandersetzung der Diltheyschen Richtung mit Heidegger und Husserl* (Leipzig/Berlin: B. G. Teubner, 1930).

*Jaensch tells me that he has an article in press*

> Cf. Erich Rudolf Jaensch, *Die Eidetik und die typologische Forschungsmethode: In ihrer Bedeutung für die Jugendpsychologie und Pädagogik, für die allgemeine Psychologie und die Psychophysiologie der menschlichen Persönlichkeit; Mit besonderer Berücksichtigung der grundlegenden Fragen und der Untersuchungsmethodik* (Leipzig: Quelle & Meyer, 1927).

*My wife, who heard you lecture while earning her degree in Frankfurt at the time*

> This probably refers to Heidegger's lecture "Philosophische Anthropologie und Metaphysik des Daseins" ("Philosophical Anthropology and the Metaphysics of *Dasein*"), which he gave (on invitation) to the Frankfurt Kant Society on January 24th, 1929 (GA 80).

**99.** K.L. to M.H., April 2nd, 1930, Letter

*The press announces the news of your appointment*

Heidegger was offered an appointment at the University of Berlin, which he denied. See his two letters to Minister Grimme in GA 16, 61-65.

*Spranger and Maier*

Eduard Spranger (1882-1963) was a philosopher, pedagogue, and psychologist. He was one of the principal representatives of humanistic pedagogy. His main works are *Lebensformen: Geisteswissenschaftliche Psychologie und Ethik der Persönlichkeit*, second totally revised edition (Halle an der Saale: Max Niemeyer, 1921), and *Psychologie des Jugendalters* (Berlin: Quelle & Meyer, 1924).

Heinrich Maier (1867-1933) was a philosopher. His major work, *Philosophie der Wirklichkeit*, appeared in three volumes: I. *Wahrheit und Wirklichkeit* (Tübingen: J. C. B. Mohr, 1926); II. *Die physische Wirklichkeit* (Tübingen: J. C. B. Mohr, 1934), and III. *Die psychisch-geistige Wirklichkeit* (Tübingen: J. C. B. Mohr, 1935). Because they were teaching as professors at the University of Berlin at the time, they were both considered as possible successors to Ernst Troeltsch.

*Herr von den Driesch*

Johannes von den Driesch (1880-1967) was a colleague of Carl Heinrich Becker, the Prussian Cultural Minister in Berlin. He was professor of pedagogy at the Catholic Pedagogical Academy in Bonn from 1931 to 1937.

*Herr "Court-Photographer" Mauss*

Court photographer Wilhelm Mauss documented, among other things, the 400-year anniversary of the University of Marburg.

**100.** K.L. to M.H., July 17th, 1930, Letter

*We were invited to the Jaceks yesterday evening*

No additional information could be determined regarding Jaceks.

*the magnificent fresco by Tiepolo on the ceiling above the grand staircase*

The Würzburg royal house is a baroque residential building on the edge of the inner-city of Würzburg, and was built between the years of 1719 and 1744. The building's interior was completed in 1781. Giovanni Battista Tiepolo (1696-1770), one of the most important Venetian painters, was involved (between 1750 and 1753) with decorating the stairwell (with the world's largest interconnected ceiling fresco), the emperor's hall, and the court church.

*Herder's treatise concerning the "origin of language"*

Johann Gottfried von Herder, *Abhandlung über die Ursprung der Sprache* (Berlin: Voss, 1772).

*Hamann's critique*

Johann Georg Hamann, *Des Ritters v. Rosencreuz letzte Willensmeynung über den göttlichen und menschlichen Ursprung der Sprache* (1772), and *Metakritik über den Purismus der Vernunft* (1784).

*J. Grimm's treatise*

Jacob Grimm, *Über den Ursprung der Sprache* (Berlin: Dümmler, 1851).

*the big collected works of Marx-Engels*

Karl Marx, "Zur Kritik der Hegelschen Rechtsphilosophie: Kritik des Hegelschen Staatsrechts" (§§261-313), and "Zur Kritik der Hegelschen Rechtsphilosophie: Einleitung." In Karl Marx and Friedrich Engels, *Historisch-kritische Gesamtausgabe*, Volume 1.1, Marx: *Werke und Schriften bis Anfang 1844 nebst Briefen und Dokumenten*, edited by D. Rajzanov and V. Adoratsjki (Frankfurt am Main: Marx-Engels-Institut Verlag, 1927), 201-333 and 378-391.

*Klages' text "Ausdruckslehre und Charakterkunde"*

Ludwig Klages, *Zur Ausdruckslehre und Charakterkunde: Gesammelte Abhandlungen* (Heidelberg: Kampmann, 1926).

*The second part of the phenomenology / theology essay*

This refers to Löwith's essay, "Phänomenologische Ontologie und protestantische Theologie" ("Phenomenological Ontology and Protestant Theology") in *Zeitschrift für Theologie und Kirche*, 11 (1930), 365-399, now also in LSS 3, 1-32. Bultmann wrote the following in a letter to Heidegger from August 24th, 1930 (*Heidegger-Bultmann Briefwechsel 1925-1975*, 132): "My Tübingen lecture, 'Die Geschichtlichkeit des Daseins und der Glaube,' is now at press; it will appear, along with Heim's 'Ontologie und Theologie' and Löwith's

'Phänomenologische Ontologie und protestantische Theologie,' in the October edition of *Zeitschrift für Theologie und Kirche*. Löwith's essay was originally the second part of his review for the theological journal, but was not ultimately suitable for this, since it is less a research report and more of an independent argument. He situates himself essentially apart from you concerning the relationship of ontology to ontic *Dasein*. Even though I am also of the opinion that he does not ultimately understand you, I still find the essay to be valuable, and hope that you can respond to it."

*the Liszt edition*

The *Carl Alexander Edition* of the works of Franz Liszt, which appeared during the years of 1907 to 1936.

*Father Rochlow*

No further information could be found regarding Father Rochlow or the lecture series.

**101.** M.H. to K.L., December 4th, 1930, Postcard (copy)

*Thank you so much for your card*

The postcard is not in the possession of the estate.

*after the lecture*

On the 5th of December, 1930, Heidegger delivered a lecture under the title "Philosophieren und Glauben: Das Wesen der Wahrheit" ("Philosophizing and Faith: The Essence of Truth") to the Protestant Theological Association in Marburg.

**102.** K.L. to M.H., April 18th, 1932, Letter

*Prof. Gabetti*

Guiseppe Gabetti (1886-1948) was founder and director of the *Instituto italiano di studi germanici* (Italian Institute of German Studies) in the Villa Sciarra, where Heidegger was invited to deliver his lecture "Hölderlin und das Wesen der Dichtung" ("Hölderlin and the Essence of Poetry") on April 2nd, 1936. Later that year, the text of the lecture appeared in the journal *Das Innere Reich: Zeitschrift für Dichtung, Kunst und deutsches Leben*, and was published by the National Socialist publisher Albert Langen / Georg Müller in Munich.

Heidegger's 1937 book *Hölderlin und das Wesen der Dichtung* was published through this same publisher. Also available in GA 4, 33-48 (*Elucidations of Hölderlin's Poetry*, trans. Keith Hoeller [Amherst, N. Y.: Humanity Books, 2000], 51-65).

*Gentile*

Giovanni Gentile (1875-1944) was an Italian philosopher and politician. He was a professor of the history of philosophy in Palermo, Pisa, and Rome; he was also a proponent of Neo-Idealism. From 1932-1943, he was the director of the *Scuola Normale Superiore* in Pisa. From 1922 to 1924, he was the Minister of Education in Mussolini's cabinet, and he remained committed to fascism until his death. His works include *Der aktuale Idealismus* (Tübingen: J. C. B. Mohr, 1931.) (The Italian edition consists of 60 volumes.)

*Weber and Marx*

Karl Löwith, "Max Weber und Karl Marx," in *Archiv für Sozialwissenschaft und Sozialpolitik* 67 (1932), 53-99, 175-214. A slightly altered edition appears in *Gesammelte Abhandlungen: Zur Kritik der geschichtlichen Existenz* (Stuttgart: Kohlhammer, 1960), 1-67, and also in LSS 5, 324-407 (*Max Weber and Karl Marx*, trans. Hans Fantel [New York: Routledge, 1993]).

*Herr Dr. Brock*

Werner Gottfried Brock (1901-1974) was a Privatdozent, and was Heidegger's assistant from 1931 until 1933. He was initially let go, but then returned to his position under Heidegger's rectorship and remained there the entire summer semester of 1933. Owing to his Jewish heritage, he emigrated to England in 1935, where he became a lecturer of German philosophy at Cambridge University. He began teaching at the University of Freiburg in 1949. His publications include: *An Introduction to Contemporary German Philosophy* (London: Cambridge University Press, 1935), and also an anthology of Heidegger's works entitled *Existence and Being* (London: Henry Regnery Co., 1949), for which Brock provided a 200-page introduction.

**103.** M.H. to K.L., April 19th, 1932, Letter (copy)

*I find the "Theology" far-fetched*

Karl Löwith, "Grundzüge der Entwicklung der Phänomenologie zur Philosophie und ihr Verhältnis zur protestantischen Theologie" ("The Essential Features of the Development of Phenomenology to Philosophy and its Relation to

Protestant Theology") in *Theologische Rundschau*, second new edition (1930); also in LSS 3, 33-95.

*my lecture "Phänomenologie und Theologie"*

Martin Heidegger, *Phänomenologie und Theologie* (Frankfurt am Main: Vittorio Klostermann, 1970) (*Pathmarks*, 39-62).

Barth

Heinrich Barth (1890-1965) was professor of philosophy at the University of Basel. He developed a Christian existential philosophy.

Przywara

The Jesuit Erich Przywara (1889-1972) worked on the editorial staff of the journal *Stimmen der Zeit* from 1922 until 1941. In 1932, he published an essay on Heidegger's thought entitled "Sein im Scheitern—Sein im Aufgang" (in *Stimmen der Zeit*, 123 (1932), 152-161).

**104.** M.H. to K.L., December 6th, 1932, Letter (copy)

*the loss of your father*

Regarding the death of Löwith's father, see Löwith, *Mein Leben in Deutschland*, 67 ff. (*My Life in Germany*, 69 ff.).

Groethuysen

Bernhard Groethuysen (1880-1946) was a philosopher and historian. His publications include *Die Entstehung der bürgerlichen Welt- und Lebensanschauung in Frankreich* (Halle an der Saale: Max Niemeyer, 1927 and 1930).

*your review of Jaspers*

The review of the book *Die geistige Situation der Zeit* (Göschen Collection, Volume 1000; Berlin: Springer, 1931) appeared in *Neue Jahrbücher für Wissenschaft und Jugendbildung* 9 (1933), 1-10. Also in Karl Löwith, *Heidegger—Denker in dürftiger Zeit: Zur Stellung der Philosophie im 20. Jahrhundert* [LSS 8], edited by Bernd Lutz (Stuttgart: J.B. Metzler, 1984, 19-31) ("Heidegger: Thinker in a Destitute Time," trans. by Gary Steiner, in

*Martin Heidegger and European Nihilism*, edited by Richard Wolin, New York: Colombia University Press, 1995).

*the "great" work*

Karl Jaspers, *Philosophie*: Volume 1, *Weltorientierung*; Volume 2, *Existenzerhellung*; and Volume 3, *Metaphysik* (Berlin: Springer, 1932).

**105.** M.H. to K.L., January 14th, 1933, Postcard (copy)

*Thank you for your letter*

The letter is not in the possession of the estate.

**106.** M.H. to K.L., February 20th, 1933, Telegram

*advise unconditionally to accept*

I.e., acceptance of the Rockefeller Scholarship.

**107.** M.H. to K.L., May 22$^{nd}$, 1933, Letter (typewritten)

*Thank you for your two letters*

The letters are not in the possession of the estate.

*I currently have neither the time nor the quiet*

On the 21st of April, 1933, Heidegger was elected rector of the University of Freiburg. On the 3rd of May, 1933, he joined the NSDAP; on April 23rd, 1934, he resigned as rector. On the 27th of May, 1933, he delivered his so-called "rectorship address," "Die Selbstbehauptung der deutschen Universität" (published in Breslau in 1933 by Wilh. Gottl. Korn; also in GA 16, 107-117) ("The Self-Assertion of the German University," trans. Karsten Harries, in *Martin Heidegger: Philosophical and Political Writings* [New York: Continuum Publishing, 2003], 2-11). Regarding Heidegger's relationship to National Socialism, see Holger Zaborowski, "Eine Frage von Irren und Schuld": *Martin Heidegger und der Nationalsozialismus* (Frankfurt am Main: S. Fischer, 2010), and *Heidegger-Jahrbuch* 4 and 5 (2009).

*My pairing with Jaensch in Frankfurt was made without my foreknowledge and against my will*

This refers to the establishing of the KADH—the "Kulturpolitische Arbeitsgemeinschaft Deutscher Hochschullehrer" ("Cultural-Political Consortium of German University Professors"), initiated by Ernst Krieck (1882-1947), who was a pedagogue and leading thinker of national socialist politics of education. In 1928, he was appointed to the Pedagogical Academy in Frankfurt. He joined the NSDAP in 1932, and in 1933 became rector of the University of Frankfurt. Regarding Krieck, see Ernst Hojer, *Nationalsozialismus und Pädagogik: Umfeld und Entwicklung der Pädagogik Ernst Kriecks* (Würzburg: Königshausen und Neumann, 1997). See also the journal *Volk im Werden* (edited by Krieck in 1933), and especially *Nationalpolitische Erziehung* (Leipzig: Armanen-Verlag, 1932). (24 editions of this appeared between 1932 and 1941.) See also "Die Erneuerung der Universität," in Ernst Krieck and Friedrich Klausing (editors), *Die deutsche Hochschule* 1 (Marburg, 1933) (Frankfurt am Main: as a monograph published by Bechold in 1933). See also his book *Wissenschaft, Weltanschauung, Hochschulreform* (Leipzig: Armanen-Verlag, 1934), which contains a collection of Krieck's essays regarding higher-education. Heidegger was among the founding members of the KADH. Ernst Jaensch was also present at the inaugural meeting, and on Heidegger's wishes. On this, see Heidegger's letter to Elfride from the 19th of March, 1933, in *Mein liebes Seelchen*, 186 (*Letters to His Wife*, 141-142). The KADH sought to replace the hallowed "Verband der deutschen Hochschulen" (VDH) ("Association of German Universities"). See also Heidegger's letter to Kurt Bauch from the 14th of March, 1933, in *Martin Heidegger / Kurt Bauch: Briefwechsel, 1932-1975*, edited with commentary by Almuth Heidegger (Freiburg/Munich: Karl Alber, 2010), 13. On June 8th, 1933, at the Berlin Rector's Conference, there was a dispute between those wishing to revise the academic tradition and those wishing to maintain and protect it. Heidegger hoped that the Rector's Conference speakership would be moved from Halle to Freiburg. Freiburg University, which had championed forced coordination, would (Heidegger hoped) also take a leading institutional role. However, the conservative powers carried the day. Only the universities of Frankfurt, Freiburg, Göttingen, Greifswald, and Kiel voted for the dissolution of the VDH. After their initial collaboration, Heidegger and Krieck later became enemies. See Holger Zaborowski, "Eine Frage von Irren und Schuld," 220-222 and 561-563, as well as Lutz Hachmeister, *Heideggers Testament*, 256-282. Heidegger's judgment concerning Krieck can be found in a letter to his wife from June 9th, 1932: "Krieck is an upstart elementary schoolteacher full of resentment" (*Mein liebes Seelchen*, 175) (*Letters to his Wife*, 133). See also Victor Farías, *Heidegger und der Nationalsozialismus* (Frankfurt am Main: S. Fischer, 1989), 210-218.

*Davis*

Davis was probably an employee for the Rockefeller Foundation.

**108. M.H. to K.L., June 12th, 1933, Letter (copy)**

*I politely ask that you refrain from dedicating the book to me*

The only independent publication of Löwith's at this time that he could have dedicated to Heidegger is the booklet *Kierkegaard und Nietzsche oder philosophische und theologische Überwindung des Nihilismus* [*Kierkegaard and Nietzsche, or the Philosophical and Theological Overcoming of Nihilism*] (Frankfurt am Main: Vittorio Klostermann, 1933). A slightly modified version appears under the title "Kierkegaard und Nietzsche" in *Aufsätze und Vorträge 1930-1970* (Stuttgart: Kohlhammer, 1971), 41-63; also in LSS 6, 53-74.

*with an eye toward possible situations*

With his mention of "situations," Heidegger is probably referring to the possibility of an appraisal of Löwith with regard to a grant or a position abroad.

*Rectorate Address*

Martin Heidegger, "Die Selbstbehauptung der deutschen Universität" ["The Self-Assertion of the German University"] (*Martin Heidegger: Philosophical and Political Writings*, 2-11).

**109. M.H. to K.L., July 29th, 1933, Letter (copy)**

*my short stay in Marburg*

On the 14th of July in Kiel, Heidegger presented the lecture "Die Universität im Neuen Reich" that he had already given in Heidelberg on June 30th. See GA 16, 764-755 ("The University Under the New Reich," in *The Heidegger Controversy: A Critical Reader*, edited by Richard Wolin, Cambridge: MIT Press, 1992, 43-45). He came to Marburg on Wednesday and left again on Friday morning. (See his letter to Rudolf Bultmann from July 12th, 1933, in *Bultmann-Heidegger Briefwechsel*, 197.) Because he had met up with Bultmann (and perhaps also Jaensch), he did actually not have time for a meeting with Löwith.

## 110. M.H. to K.L., June/July 1936, Letter

*[in Löwith's handwriting] June/July, 1936*

In the beginning of April, 1936, Heidegger spent ten days in Rome, where he gave the lecture "Hölderlin und das Wesen der Dichtung" ("Hölderlin and the Essence of Poetry") to the Italian-German Cultural Institute. He also used this occasion to spend more time with Löwith. Cf. *Mein Leben in Deutschland*, 57-60) (*My Life in Germany*, 59-61), as well as the extract from Löwith's diary that is included in this volume as Supplement 3. The fact that Heidegger used this occasion to spend more time with Löwith—and the fact that Löwith wanted to spend time with him—demonstrates that the Jewish ancestry of Löwith (who was himself Protestant) did not play a role in their personal relationship. In the spring of 1935, Löwith was unlawfully deprived of his teaching position. It was owing to the curator and the dean that Löwith continued to have 200 Marks transferred to him in Italy for another six-months. Because he had been granted the scholarship from the Rockefeller Foundation, he could continue to live and work in Rome. Cf. Karl Löwith, *Mein Leben in Deutschland*, 104-110 (*My Life in Germany*, 109-116).

*you represent an entirely different compliment to Reichenbach*

Hans Reichenbach taught philosophy in Istanbul. Under the leadership of Alexander Rüstow, the German professors of the university there attempted to establish a second philosophy position that would be (in contrast to Reichenbach) more oriented toward intellectual history. However, because only scholars who were already professors in Germany could be appointed to the position in Istanbul, there was a plan to present Löwith with a one-year position.

*Regarding Jaspers' book*

Karl Jaspers, *Nietzsche: Einführung in das Verständnis seines Philosophierens* (Berlin: Walter de Gruyter, 1936).

*Nietzsche-Registry by Oehler*

Friedrich Oehler, *Nietzsche-Register—alphabetisch-systematische Übersicht zu Nietzsches Werken* (Leipzig: Naumann, 1926).

*Herr Dr. Antoni*

Carlo Antoni (1896-1959) was an Italian philosopher who was friends with Löwith. At the time, he worked at the *Istituto di studi germanici* in Rome. He also translated Heidegger's "Hölderlin und das Wesen der Dichtung" into Italian.

**111.** M.H. to K.L., July 18th, 1937, Letter (copy)

*Thank you for your letter*

The letter is not in the possession of the estate.

*a Japanese translation*

This refers to the Japanese translation of "Hölderlin und das Wesen der Dichtung." It appeared in Tokyo in 1938 under the title "Herudârin to Shi no Honshitsu."

*a French translation*

Martin Heidegger, "Hölderlin et l'essence de la poésie," in *Qu'est-ce que la métaphysique?, suivi d'extraits sur l'être et le temps et d'une conférence sur Hölderlin*. Translated from the German with a Foreword and notes by Henry Corbin (*Les Essais* III) (Paris: Gallimard, 1938).

*the published Italian translation*

Martin Heidegger, *Hölderlin e l'essenza della poesia*, trans. C. Antoni (Florence: Sansoni, 1937).

*your books*

Karl Löwith, *Nietzsches Philosophie der ewigen Wiederkehr des Gleichen* (Berlin: Verlag Die Runde, 1935) (*Nietzsche's Philosophy of the Eternal Recurrence of the Same*, trans. J. Harvey Lomax [Berkley: University of California Press, 1997]); also in LSS 6, 101-384; and *Jacob Burckhardt: Der Mensch inmitten der Geschichte* (Lucerne: Vita Nova Verlag, 1936); also in LSS 7, 39-362.

276                           *Annotations*

*you have found a stable and worthwhile appointment*

The end of the letter is not in the possession of the estate. In *Mein Leben in Deutschland* (59) (*My Life In Germany*, 61), Löwith alleges that Heidegger never responded to his sending of books or to his answer to Heidegger's questions about translations. Either Löwith suppressed some paltry answer that he had given, or it had arrived late. Löwith probably never received the lengthy letter than Heidegger had mentioned.

**113. K.L. to M.H., July 26th, 1958, Postcard (privately held)**

*academic conferences are not conducive to conversation*

On the 26th of July, 1958, Heidegger gave his second version of the lecture "Hegel und die Griechen" ("Hegel and the Greeks") to the entire assembly of the Heidelberg Academy of Sciences. The lecture was published in *Die Gegenwart der Griechen im neueren Denken: Festschrift für Hans-Georg Gadamer zum 60. Geburtstag* (Tübingen: J. C. B. Mohr, 1967), 255-272. It is also in Martin Heidegger, *Wegmarken* (GA 9), 427-444 (*Pathmarks*, 323-336), and includes the handwritten remarks of the author.

*you will be speaking at the Bavarian Academy in November about "language"*

As part of a series called "Die Sprache," arranged by the Bavarian Academy of Fine Art, Heidegger gave a lecture entitled "Der Weg zur Sprache" ["The Way to Langauge"] in the University of Munich's auditorium on January 23rd, 1959. The lecture is published in Martin Heidegger, *Unterwegs zur Sprache* (Pfullingen: Verlag Günther Neske, 1959), 239-268 (*On the Way to Language*, trans. Peter D. Hertz and Joan Stambaugh [New York: Harper and Row, 1971], 111-138).

*Herr Tsujimura*

Kôichi Tsujimura (1922-2010) studied philosophy with Tanabe and Nishitani, and Zen with Hisamatsu. He studied with Heidegger at the University of Freiburg from 1956 until 1958. He came to occupy the chair that had once been held by Nishida and Tanabe in the Philosophy Department at the University of Kyoto. He is a representative of the third generation of the Kyoto School.

*the Shintoist*

Löwith probably means Shinichi Hisamatsu (1889-1980), who in the summer of 1958 participated with Heidegger at a colloquium in Germany on the theme "Die Kunst und das Denken" ("Art and Thinking"). One may find the protocol for this colloquium in *Heidegger Jahrbuch* 7 (2013), *Heidegger und das Ostasiatische Denken*, 51-55.

*sun-goddess Amaterasu*

Amaterasu Omikami, "The Luminous Heavenly One," is the sun-goddess of the Japanese Shinto religion. She is a beautiful, smiling goddess who brightens the world with her inner radiance and watches over it. She is the goddess of agriculture, showing human beings how to grow silk and also how to spin it. She also protects women from violence committed against them. Her symbols are the silkworm, an eight-sided mirror (which sits in her temple), as well as the rising sun (which can still be found as a sign of the goddess on the Japanese flag).

*volume 3 of Schlecta's Nietzsche edition*

Friedrich Nietzsche, *Werke*, Volume 3, edited by Karl Schlechta (Munich: Hanser Verlag, 1956).

*it will be published in the Merkur*

Karl Löwith, "Zu Schlechtas neuer Nietzsche-Legende" ["On Schechta's New Nietzsche Legend"] in *Merkur* 12 (1958), 781-784; also in Karl Löwith, *Nietzsche* (LSS 6), 513-517.

**115. K.L. to M.H., June 17th, 1967, Postcard**

*a colloquium being held by the Herder Foundation*

In 1967, The Hermann-Herder Foundation organized a series of global colloquies. Löwith took part in the fifth colloquium, on the theme of "Modern Atheism and Morality." His contribution, "Atheismus als philosophisches Problem" ("Atheism as a Philosophical Problem"), was published in the conference proceedings: *Moderner Atheismus und Moral*, edited by the Arbeitsgemeinschaft Weltgespräch (Freiburg: Herder Verlag, 1967), 9-21; also in Karl Löwith, *Wissen, Glaube und Skepsis* (LSS 3), 331-347.

*in the seminar by Marx*

Werner Marx (1910-1994) studied jurisprudence in Freiburg, Berlin, and Bonn. He graduated in 1933. Following his dismissal from civil-service in 1933, he emigrated to Great Britain, then on to Palestine in 1934, and finally to the United States in 1938. From 1949 on he taught at the New School for Social Research in New York City. In 1962, he became the Fulbright Professor in Heidelberg, and in 1964 he became Heidegger's successor at the University of Freiburg. His publications include *Heidegger und die Tradition* (Stuttgart: Kohlhammer, 1961), and *Gibt es auf Erden ein Maß? Grundbestimmungen einer nichtmetaphysischen Ethik* (Hamburg: Felix Meiner, 1983).

**116.** M.H. to K.L., June 18th, 1967, Letter

*the card*

The postcard is not in the possession of the estate.

*your new book*

Karl Löwith, *Gott, Mensch und Welt in der Metaphysik von Descartes zu Nietzsche* (Göttingen: Vandenhoeck & Ruprecht, 1967); also in Karl Löwith, *Gott, Mensch und Welt* (LSS 9), 1-194.

*I will be coming to your lecture tomorrow*

This refers to Löwith's lecture "Atheismus als philosophisches Problem" ("Atheism as a Philosophical Problem").

**118.** M.H. to K.L., July 28th, 1970, Letter

*your masterful presentation of the "Hegel-Renaissance"*

Karl Löwith, "Hegel-Renaissance?," in *Frankfurter Allgemeine Zeitung*, July 11th, 1970, Number 157; also in Karl Löwith, *Hegel und die Aufhebung der Philosophie im 19. Jahrhundert* (LSS 5), 239-248.

**120.** M.H. to K.L., February 25th, 1972, Letter

*the only text of Nishitani's that I possess*

This refers to Keiji Nishitani, "Preliminary Remarks (to Heideggers zwei Ansprachen in Meßkirch)," in *The Eastern Buddhist* 1, 2 (1966), 55-67.

*the subject of Mallarmé-Valéry*

During his visit to Freiburg, Löwith had evidently given Heidegger his 1971 book *Paul Valéry: Grundzüge seines philosophischen Denkens* (Göttingen:

Vandenhoeck & Ruprecht, 1971); the second chapter ("Gadanken Zur Sprache" ["Thoughts on Language"]) deals with the relation between Valéry and Mallarmé. Also in Karl Löwith, *Gott, Mensch und Menschenwelt – G. B. Vico – Paul Valéry* (LSS 9), edited by Henning Ritter (Stuttgart: J. B. Metzler, 1986), 229-400.

*My "Schelling"*

Martin Heidegger, *Schelling: Vom Wesen der menschlichen Freiheit* (Tübingen: Max Niemeyer, 1971). Also in Martin Heidegger, *Schelling: Vom Wesen der menschlichen Freiheit*, edited by Ingrid Schüssler (GA 42) (Frankfurt am Main: Vittorio Klostermann, 1988) (*Schelling's Treatise on the Essence of Human Freedom*, trans. Joan Stambaugh [Athens: Ohio University Press, 1985]).

**122.** M.H. to K.L., May 5th, 1973, Letter

*Gadamer wrote to me regarding your illness*

Karl Löwith died three weeks later in Heidelberg.

*it belongs to a series of "Thoughts"*

Martin Heidegger, "Gedachtes: Für René Char in freundschaftlichen Gedenken," German with French translation by Jean Beaufret and François Fédier in Dominique Fourcade (editor), *Les Cahiers de l'Herne (15). Hommage René Char* (Paris, 1971), 169-187. Included in Martin Heidegger, *Aus der Erfahrung des Denkens*, edited by Hermann Heidegger (GA 13) (Frankfurt am Main: Vittorio Klostermann, 1983), 221-224 ("Thoughts," trans. by Keith Hoeller, in *Philosophy Today* 20:4 (1976)). The published version deviates from this version.

**123.** M.H. to A.L., June 4th, 1973, Letter

*the mercifulness of your husband's death*

Karl Löwith died on the 26th of May, 1973. Martin Heidegger died three years later, also on the 26th of May.

# Annotations to the Supplements

**1.** *Letter from Elisabeth Förster-Nietzsche to Karl Löwith*

*The final volume of the Musarion Edition*

> Between 1920 and 1929, Musarion Publishing in Munich released an edited 23-volume edition of Nietzsche's works.

*Musarion is releasing two volumes of additional autobiographical material*

> Elisabeth Förster-Nietzsche (editor), *Der werdende Nietzsche: Autobiographische Aufzeichnungen* (Munich: Musarion Verlag, 1924). The second volume was never published.

*Ebner*

> Ferdinand Ebner (1882–1931) is, after Martin Buber, the most important representative of dialogical thinking. His work is oriented around the I–You relation. Heidegger was already aware of him at the beginning of the 1920s, owing to his essays in *Der Brenner*, in which Georg Trakl also published his poetry.

**2.** *Martin Heidegger's Assessment of Karl Löwith's Habilitation Thesis (1928)*

*Assessment of Karl Löwith's Habilitation Thesis (1928)*

> Heidegger's assessment refers to the typewritten version from 1927, which differs from the published version in many important ways. The assessment appears in LSS 1, 470–473 (edited by Klaus Stichweh).

*Stirner's concept of "the only person"*

Max Stirner, *Der Einzige und sein Eigentum* (Leipzig: Otto Wigand, 1845).

**3. Excerpt from Karl Löwith's Italian Diary (1934–1936)**

*Karl Löwith's Italian Diary (1934–1936)*

Karl Löwith, "From An Unpublished Diary." The original can be found in Löwith's estate in the German Literary Archive (in Marbach). Ulrich von Bülow has published, and has presented as facsimiles, many passages from this diary, including the segment presented here. Ulrich von Bülow, "Reise um die Erde in 18 Jahren: Karl Löwiths Exil," in *Offener Horizont: Jahrbuch der Karl Jaspers-Gesellschaft* I (2014), 197–211.

*Husserl's publisher (Niemeyer)*

Husserl published his works with the publisher Max Niemeyer, who also published *Jahrbuch für Philosophie und phänomenologische Forschung*.

*Scheler's publisher (Cohen)*

Max Scheler published the majority of his writings with Cohen Verlag.

*the rectoral address with the Nazi publisher (Korn)*

I.e., Heidegger's rectorate address, "Die Selbstbehauptung der deutschen Universität" ("The Self-Assertion of the German University"). The publishing house, which published works by authors such as Arthur Möller van den Bruck and Harald von Königswald, published a number of *völkisch*/nationalistic writings.

*Hölderlin*

Heidegger's lecture in Rome, "Hölderlin und das Wesen der Dichtung" ("Hölderlin and the Essence of Poetry").

*the polemic in the newspaper about his Zurich lecture*

Heidegger presented his lecture "Der Ursprung des Kunstwerkes" ("The Origin of the Work of Art") on January 17, 1936, at the invitation of the student body in Zurich. Hans Barth published a review of the event entitled "Vom Ursprung des Kunstwerks: Vortrag von Martin Heidegger ["On the Origin of the Work of

Art: A Lecture by Martin Heidegger"] (*Neue Zürcher Zeitung* 157, n. 105). For the present purposes, the important passage is as follows: "Obviously, we must take credit for the fact that Heidegger takes the floor in a democratic political system, since he was regarded—at least for a time—as one of the philosophical spokesmen for the new Germany. But we also must remember that Heidegger dedicated his *Being and Time* to the Jew Husserl 'in veneration and friendship,' and forever associated his Kant interpretation with the memory of the half-Jew Max Scheler. (The first, in 1927, the second in 1929.) As a rule, people are not heroes—and neither are philosophers, with a few exceptions. It can therefore hardly be demanded that one ought to swim against the stream; only a certain obligation toward its own past heightens the reputation of philosophy, which is not only knowledge, but was indeed once wisdom." Emil Staiger submitted a letter to the editor, entitled "Noch einmal Heidegger," which was published along with a reaction from Barth (*Neue Zürcher Zeitung* 157, n. 125, from January 23, 1936). Staiger wrote: "A criticism such as Barth has given of Heidegger's lecture cannot remain unchallenged. Its prejudicial character is immediately visible; Barth issues a political missive in advance of his actual critique, which guarantees him the public's approval; he finds fault with Heidegger's language, and ultimately throws together some sentences which he wrote down during the lecture [. . . .] But it is absolutely absurd to place Heidegger's political outlook so prominently in the foreground, as Barth has seen fit to do—indeed, just as absurd as if one were to begin a review of *The Critique of Pure Reason* with a remark about Kant's position on the French Revolution [. . . .] Moreover, Heidegger is not on the same level as Oskar Sprenger or Tillich, to name just two philosophers from opposing camps; rather, Martin Heidegger stands next to Hegel, Kant, Aristotle, and Heraclitus." Barth answered laconically with the following: "Herr Staiger alleges a lack of objectivity on the part of the commentator, owing to the fact that he has issued a 'political missive' in advance. That was done purposefully—for it is not possible to separate, as with an abyss, the philosophical and the human, thinking and being. Herr Staiger alleges that an adequate treatment of such a lecture cannot be accomplished 'journalistically.' However, the question of whether or not it is an excessively 'journalistic' judgment to place Heidegger in immediate proximity to Hegel, Kant, Aristotle, and Heraclitus, as Herr Staiger has done in all seriousness, is a question that I would like to leave up to interested readers and experts to decide. I happily leave the decision of the legitimacy of this downright gargantuan estimation of Heidegger to the literary historian." The reports are published in their entirety in *Heidegger-Jahrbuch 4, Heidegger und der Nationalsozialismus, Dokumente*, (2009), 197–201.

## *He has once again withdrawn entirely from university politics*

This is not entirely true. Heidegger always still remained a member of the Committee for the Philosophy of Law at the Academy for German Law.

## Becker's reviews written from the racial perspective

Oskar Becker published the following essays in *Rasse: Monatsschrift der nordischen Bewegung* (between 1934 and 1936): "Nordische Metaphysik", in *Rasse* (1), Issue 5, 81–92 (1934); "Philosophie und Weltanschauung," in *Rasse* (2), Issue 1, 32–35 (1935); "Philosophie und Weltanschauung," in *Rasse* (2), Issue 12, 493–498 (1935); and a review of B. Bavink's *Über Rasse und Kultur*, in *Rasse* (3), Issue 12, 474–476 (1936).

## Jaspers' Nietzsche

Karl Jaspers. *Nietzsche: Einführung in das Verständnis seines Philosophierens.*

## Heyse

Hans Heyse (1891–1976) became a Privatdozent at the University of Breslau in 1925. In 1932, he was given the Kant Chair at the University of Königsberg. In 1933, he joined the Nazi Party. In 1935, he was named successor to Georg Misch at the University of Göttingen. In the same year, he became a member of the academic committee of the historical/critical collected works of Nietzsche at the Nietzsche Archive in Weimar. Heidegger also became a member of the academic committee in 1935; he resigned in 1942. Regarding this, Löwith writes: "In an analogous fashion, Heidegger also sat on the academic committee of the Nietzsche Archive together with a Nietzsche 'scholar' like Richard Oehler—again probably to prevent 'much worse,' while in reality he covers up the bad with his good name" (Karl Löwith, *Mein Leben in Deutschland*, 160) (*My Life in Germany*, 151–153). On this, see also Marion Heinz and Theodore Kisiel, "Heideggers Beziehungen zum Nietzsche Archiv im Dritten Reich," in Hermann Schäfer (editor), *Annäherungen an Martin Heidegger: Festschrift für Hugo Ott* (Frankfurt am Main/New York: Campus, 1996, 103–136).

## Through his book

Hans Heyse. *Idee und Existenz* (Hamburg: Hanseatische Verlagsanstalt, 1935).

## Baeumler

Alfred Baeumler (1887–1968) earned his doctorate in 1914 on the basis of his work *Das Problem der Allgemeingültigkeit in Kants Ästhetik* (Munich, 1915). Following his military service from 1914 to 1918, he worked as a freelance writer and published a work on Nietzsche. In 1924, he habilitated at the Dresden

Technical University on the basis of his work *Das Irrationalismusproblem in der Ästhetik und Logik des 18 Jahrhunderts bis zur Kritik der Urteilskraft* (Halle an der Saale: Max Niemeyer, 1923). He was Extraordinarius Professor until 1929, after which he became Ordinarius Professor of theoretical pedagogy and philosophy. Following his entry into the Nazi Party in 1933, he received the newly created chair for political pedagogy at the University of Berlin. From 1934 on, he was director of the Office of Science (and then later of the main office) in the Amt Rosenberg. In 1941, he became head of the Nazi Party's "advanced school." His publications include: *Bachofen und Nietzsche* (Zurich: Neue Schweizer Rundschau, 1929) and *Nietzsche: der Philosoph und Politiker* (Leipzig: Reclam, 1931). Heidegger and Baeumler maintained a personal relationship from 1932 on and remained connected to one another until the war's end. See, for example, Heidegger's letter to Elfride from June 9, 1932: "Baeumler has disappointed me to the extent that philosophically he is really quite weak—good as a historian—excellently informed in the latest movements. According to his reliable sources, the Nazis are still very narrow-minded in all cultural–spiritual matters—technical college and school of character—this formula is meant to solve everything and of course means ruin" (*Mein liebes Seelchen*, 175) (*Letters to His Wife*, 133). In his letter to his wife from April 12, 1943, Heidegger again mentions Baeumler: "I'm enclosing a copy of the letter from Baeumler. He's presumably basing his form of address on party membership. I wonder if this is now the sign of retraction" (*Mein liebes Seelchen*, 218) (*Letters to His Wife*, 173).

*the scholarly committee of the Nietzsche Archives*

See Marion Heinz and Theodore Kisiel, "Heideggers Beziehungen zum Nietzsche Archiv im Dritten Reich," 103–136.

*the Academy for German Law*

The Academy for German Law was created on the initiative of Hans Frank, the Reichskommissar for the Enforced Coordination of the Judiciary. The aim of the Academy was to restructure German laws in accordance with the national socialist worldview. However, this aim was not successful, owing to the fact that the ministerial bureaucracy successfully asserted its jurisdiction. Along with Heidegger, Carl Emge, Carl Schmitt, Hans Freyer, Erich Rothacker, and Hans Naumann were also founding members of the Committee on the Philosophy of Academic Law, which was established in May of 1934. Heidegger was active on this committee, which Julius Streicher had meanwhile joined, until at least 1936. On this, see Victor Farías, *Heidegger und der Nationalsozialismus*, 277–280, and Herlinde Pauer-Studer, *Die Normativität des Rechts* (Frankfurt am Main: Suhrkamp, 2013).

## Streicher

Julius Streicher (1885–1946) was a Nazi politician. He was founder, owner, and editor of the anti-Semitic political pamphlet "Der Stürmer." He was one of the 24 major war criminals accused in the Nuremberg proceedings. In 1946, he was sentenced to death and executed for crimes against humanity.

## É un bambino

"He is a child."

## lecture of Naumann's

Hans Naumann (1886–1951) was a professor of ancient German and Folklore at the University of Frankfurt am Main from 1921 to 1932 and, subsequently, at the University of Bonn. He joined the Nazi Party in 1933 and was one of the principal players behind the book burning that took place in Bonn on May 10, 1933. His publications include *Deutsche Nation in Gefahr* (Stuttgart: J. B. Metzler, 1932); "Sorge und Bereitschaft (Der Mythos und die Lehre Heideggers)," in *Germanischer Schicksalsglaube* (Jena: Diedrichs, 1934, 68–88), reprinted in *Heidegger-Jahrbuch* 4, *Heidegger und der Nationalsozialismus, Dokumente* (2009), 178–193 (see also Krieck's review in *Volk im Werden* 2 [1934], 247–249, now also in *Heidegger-Jahrbuch* 4 [2009], 193–195); and *Der deutsche Mensch* (Stuttgart: Deutsche Verlags-Anstalt, 1935). For an in-depth treatment of Naumann, see Thomas Schirrmacher, *"Der göttliche Volkstumsbegriff" und "der Glaube an Deutschlands Größe und heilige Sendung": Hans Naumann als Volkskundler und Germanist unter dem Nationalsozialismus*, two volumes (Bonn: Verlag für Kultur und Wissenschaft, 1992).

## his freshly baked book

Hans Naumann. *Wandlung und Erfüllung: Reden und Aufsätze zur germanisch-deutschen Geistesgeschichte* (Stuttgart: J. B. Metzler, 1933).

# Editor's Afterword

As the second volume of the second part of *The Collected Letters of Martin Heidegger*, this volume presents the correspondence between Martin Heidegger and Karl Löwith.

The correspondence presented here contains 124 letters and postcards. Of these, seventy-six are authored by Martin Heidegger, and forty-eight by Karl Löwith. The correspondence between them has not been preserved in its entirety. What has been preserved is in the possession of the German Literary Archive in Marbach, Germany, as well as in the private possession of the Heidegger family. With the exception of Heidegger's telegram from February 20, 1933, his letter from May 22, 1933, and Löwith's letter from March 22, 1972, all documents are handwritten.

Karl Löwith (1897–1973) was among Heidegger's most important pupils, and was one of only five philosophers whose habilitation was overseen by Heidegger. Not only was Löwith personally close to Heidegger; he was also a significant thinker in his own right. After receiving his Ph.D. (in 1923) under Moritz Geiger, Löwith—who had studied with Heidegger and Husserl in Freiburg from 1919 to 1922—followed Heidegger to Marburg. In 1928, he successfully habilitated with his work *Das Individuum in der Rolle des Mitmenschen* {*The Individual in the Role of Fellow Human Being*}—a work which, though it arose from out of Heidegger's thinking, nevertheless took this thinking in a new direction. Löwith adopted Heidegger's determination of the being of the human as being-with-others {*Mitsein*}: human *Dasein* also entails being with other humans. Because Heidegger had neither given the idea of being-with-others nor the ethical dimension of human existence much attention in *Being and Time*, Löwith's text provided both an important interpretation, and an enduringly worthwhile critique, of Heidegger's major early work. Unlike Heidegger, Löwith provides a contribution to the foundation of ethics through his interpretation of the I–You relationship as the grounding phenomenon of human *Dasein*.

The course of Löwith's life reflected, in a distinctive way, the history of the twentieth century:

> 1933 did not require me to make a personal decision. It was forced upon me by the now forgotten Nuremburg Laws which were made possible in 1935 and immediately enforced. Emigration led me through a series of lucky coincidences, which one likes to call fate, via Rome to a Japanese University. After the German pact with Japan, and under pressure of National Socialist foreign propaganda, my position became insecure. At that time Paul Tillich and Reinhold Niebuhr helped me—six months before Pearl Harbor—to obtain a teaching post at an American theological seminary (1941), were I received the offer of a chair at the New School for Social Research in 1949. After eighteen years' absence (1952) I returned to Germany, where I found the conditions of the university oddly unchanged, despite everything that had happened in the interim.[1]

Löwith, who had classified himself as a philosopher within the tradition of skepticism, primarily concerned himself with existential philosophy (i.e., Heidegger and Jaspers) and the philosophy of the nineteenth century (i.e., Hegel, Nietzsche, Marx).

The letters represent four phases in the relationship between Heidegger and Löwith. The first phase began in 1919 and lasted until Löwith's first sojourn to Italy (in 1924–1925). It is surprising how open and critical Heidegger and Löwith are in their philosophical engagement with one another. It is also worth noting how critical Heidegger and, even more so Löwith, are of Husserl. For example, in his letter from February 26, 1921, Löwith writes the following: "You will remember how already during my second semester I often expressed to you my vehement resistance to his philosophical cast of mind. Today it is absolutely clear to me that Husserl, on the deepest level, is not a great philosopher, and that it is a massive delusion to put him on the same pedestal as Kant; his whole disposition is infinitely far removed from reality—it is without life and is doctrinally logical. It would be a waste of time and energy if I were to penetrate into his way of thinking, all from out of a misguided intellectual conscience." One sees such criticism also in Heidegger's letter from September 20, 1922: "During those eight days I was able to breathe freely; with Jaspers there is that sort of philosophical existence that Husserl does not even remotely possess." The letters in this first phase also deal with economic and professional uncertainties.

---

[1] From Karl Löwith, "Curriculum Vitae (1959)," in Karl Löwith, *Mein Leben in Deutschland*, 185f. (*My Life in Germany*, 162).

In the second phase, which runs from 1925 to 1929, the relationship grows somewhat distant. After his time with Löwith, Heidegger changed as a teacher. He was no longer a *primus inter pares* {first among equals} who thought alongside and along with his students, as he had during his time as a Privatdozent. He had now become a proper professor and presented himself as such. Löwith's upcoming habilitation is at the core of this period of exchange. Beginning in the 1930s, contact between them diminishes; in this third phase, and even while serving as rector of the University of Freiburg (in 1933), Heidegger supported Löwith. However, at the same time, he refused the dedication of one of Löwith's writings. Heidegger's meeting with Löwith in Rome in 1936 was their last encounter until the 1950s. The fourth phase begins with Löwith's congratulatory telegram from 1949, which signifies a *de facto* resumption of their correspondence. Heidegger was very concerned about Löwith's critique in his writing *Heidegger—Denker in dürftiger Zeit* (1953) and felt betrayed, as is evidenced from Heidegger's letter to his friend Elisabeth Blochmann:

> Löwith is extraordinarily well-read, as well as gifted in his multitudinous use of citations. However, he really has no clue about Greek philosophy, since he lacks the proper tools. He has a certain talent for phenomenological description, and he could indeed perform legitimate tasks within this field. But, for a long time now he's been living beyond his means. He simply has no fitness for *thinking*—indeed, perhaps he even hates it. I have never met a human being who lives *so* exclusively from out of resentment and the 'anti.' When he was habilitating in Marburg, he was the reddest Marxist. He considered *Being and Time* to be 'theology in disguise.' Later, this same book was 'pure atheism.' Why shouldn't one turn from Feuerbach to Augustine? But if one does, then that same person shouldn't go around explaining to others a 'turn' that he himself has not yet understood. I would like to remain silent about the nastier things he has done, despite me helping him along in Italy and Japan with good assessments. Ebbinghaus also has his hands full with Löwith, with whom he worked robustly with the communists. It would be enough if even one 'anti-Heidegger' ('enemy' would be too high of an estimation) becomes his successor. With regard to Claus Reich,[2] perhaps there could be a swap with Heidelberg, since Gadamer has already had enough of his friend, and his 'effect' is going to push him away.[3]

---

[2] Heidegger probably means Klaus Reich (1906–1996), who habilitated under Ebbinghaus in 1946. From 1947 on, he was a professor of philosophy in Marburg. Klaus Reich, *Gesammelte Schriften*, with an introduction and annotations, edited by Manfred Baum (Hamburg: Felix Meiner, 2001).

[3] Martin Heidegger/Elisabeth Blochmann, *Briefwechsel 1918–1969*, 102 f. Heidegger wanted to prevent Löwith from being appointed to the University of Marburg. He expresses a similar criticism in a letter to Rudolf Bultmann: "Löwith is a tremendously well-read and versatile person, but

The last letters document the reconciliation between Heidegger and Löwith, which came about during the end of the 1950s.

The letters are reproduced here unabridged and without omissions. Dates, greetings, and salutations remain unaltered and appear in their original form to the greatest extent possible, in order that the personal character of the letters might be better preserved. Idiosyncrasies in use of upper-and-lower case letters, compound spellings, and use of "ß" v. "s" (as well as "hab" or "seh" instead of "habe" or "sehe") have also been preserved. The punctuation, however, was standardized. The new orthographic reform was not used in presenting the documents. Corrections made by the authors themselves in the forms of insertions were adopted, and strikethroughs were omitted. Underlined words have been placed in italics. Because Heidegger's letters from 1919 to 1937 exist only as copies, and the origin of the underlining cannot be determined, no italics were used in reprinting the letters here. "[???]" has been used to denote an illegible word, while "[?]" indicates an uncertain rendering. Necessary editorial additions appear in square brackets, while obvious errors were corrected without notice. In the annotations section, information about the document in question is provided under the respective document number. Subsequent to this, information germane to the letter's content is provided. Concepts and thoughts were not annotated, as this would have significantly increased the size of the present volume.

In addition to the letters, six supplements have been included: two letters (a letter from Elisabeth Förster-Nietzsche to Karl Löwith, and a letter from Ada Löwith to Elfride Heidegger), an entry into the Heidegger family guest book at the hut, a list of Heidegger's courses in which Löwith took part, Heidegger's assessment of Löwith's habilitation thesis, and an excerpt from the diary Löwith kept while in Italy. These last two documents are of particular interest.

I owe special thanks to Herr Dr. Hermann Heidegger and his wife Jutta Heidegger, as well as Herr Arnulf Heidegger and Frau Adelheid Krautter, who have very carefully collated and corrected the transcribed correspondence. Their numerous tips and suggestions have been of enormous help and have supported this work to a great extent.

I extend my heartfelt gratitude to Herr Ulrich von Bülow of the German Literary Archive in Marbach, as well as his co-workers, for their help, especially with photocopying.

I offer thanks, too, to Herr Professor Holger Zaborowski, who supported my application for a grant and the editorial work.

---

he cannot think; and he always says 'no!' on principle, where it is valid to pursue a matter: he is a skeptic to the bone, and manages even to use Christianity to that end" (Martin Heidegger/Rudolf Bultmann, *Briefwechsel 1925–1975*, 207 f.).

I want to give special thanks to the Gerda Henkel Foundation, which supported my editorial work by means of an award of a fourteen-month research grant.

For their careful copyediting and critical commentary, I also thank Frau Professor Marion Heinz and Herr Dr. Matthias Flatscher.

Many thanks, finally, to Herr Lukas Traber at the publisher Karl Alber for supporting the volume.

Vallendar, Germany—November 2016                               Alfred Denker

# Abbreviations

A.L. = Ada Löwith
DLA = *Deutsches Literaturarchiv Marbach* [German Literary Archive in Marbach]
E.H. = Elfride Heidegger
GA = Martin Heidegger, *Gesamtausgabe* (Frankfurt am Main: Vittorio Klostermann)
K.L. = Karl Löwith
M.H. = Martin Heidegger
LSS = Karl Löwith, *Sämtliche Schriften* (Stuttgart: J.B. Metzler)

# Biographies

## MARTIN HEIDEGGER

| | |
|---|---|
| 1889 | Born on the 26th of September in Messkirch / Baden as the son of the master cooper and sexton Friedrich Heidegger and Johanna Heidegger (Kempf). |
| 1903–1906 | Attends *Gymnasium* in Constance |
| 1906–1909 | Attends *Gymnasium* in Freiburg |
| 1909–1911 | Studies theology and philosophy in Freiburg |
| 1911 | Cessation of theological studies |
| 1911–1913 | Studies philosophy, humanities, and natural science in Freiburg |
| 1913 | Doctorate overseen by Arthur Schneider |
| 1915 | Habilitation overseen by Heinrich Rickert |
| 1915–1918 | Military service (postal surveillance in Freiburg and weather station at the front) |
| 1917 | Marries Elfride Petri |
| 1919–1923 | Privatdozent and assistant to Edmund Husserl at the University of Freiburg |
| 1919 | Birth of son Jörg |
| 1920 | Birth of son Hermann |
| 1922 | Purchases hut in Todtnauberg / Black Forest |
| 1923–1928 | Professor at the University of Marburg |
| 1928 | Appointment in Freiburg to Chair of Philosophy |
| 1933 | Founding member of the Cultural-Political Consortium of German University Professors (KADH); on April 21st, elected rector of the University of Freiburg |
| 1934 | Resigns from rectorate |

| | |
|---|---|
| 1934–1937 | Member of the Committee for the Philosophy of Law in the Academy for German Law |
| 1935–1942 | Member of the Scientific Committee of the Historical-Critical Edition of the Work of Friedrich Nietzsche, through the Nietzsche Archive in Weimar |
| 1944 | November: drafted into the *Volkssturm* ("people's militia") |
| 1946–1949 | Banned from teaching |
| 1949 | Delivers Bremen lectures |
| 1950 | Retires |
| 1950–1953 | Lectures actively in Bühlerhöhe and at the Bavarian Academy of Fine Art |
| 1951 | Attains emeritus status |
| 1955 | Takes first trip to France; meets with Jacques Lacan, among others; holds Seminar in Cérisy-la-Salle |
| 1957 | Admitted into the Heidelberg Academy of Sciences and into the Berlin Academy of the Arts |
| 1959 | Awarded status of Citizen of Honor in the city of Messkirch. Begins the Zollikon Seminars with Medard Boss |
| 1960 | Awarded the Hebel Prize |
| 1962 | Takes trip to Greece |
| 1966 | Holds first seminar at Le Thor (continued in 1968, 1969, and 1973 at Zähringen) |
| 1969 | Admitted into the Bavarian Academy of the Fine Arts |
| 1975 | Publication of the first volume of the *Gesamtausgabe* |
| 1976 | Dies on May 26th in Freiburg; buried on May 28th in Messkirch |

## KARL LÖWITH

| | |
|---|---|
| 1897 | Born on January 9th in Munich, the son of the painter Wilhelm Löwith and his wife Margerete Löwith (Hauser). Löwith's parents were Jewish |
| 1914 | Early graduation (owing to the war) at the *Realgymnasium* in Munich, after which he freely enlists for military service |
| 1915 | Is severely injured and is sent to an Italian prisoner-of-war camp |
| 1917 | Released from the Italian prisoner-of-war camp |
| 1917–1919 | Studies biology and philosophy at the University of Munich |

| | |
|---|---|
| 1919–1922 | Studies philosophy and biology at the University of Freiburg with Spemann, Husserl, and Heidegger |
| 1920–1921 | Tutors in Baden-Baden |
| 1922 | Returns to Munich |
| 1923 | Tutors in Kogel. Dissertation is overseen by Moritz Geiger |
| 1924–1925 | Resides in Italy |
| 1928 | Habilitation overseen by Martin Heidegger |
| 1928–1933 | Privatdozent in Marburg |
| 1929 | Marries Elisabeth Adelheid (Ada) Kremmer |
| 1934–1936 | Resides in Rome |
| 1936–1941 | Teaches at the University of Sendai (Japan) |
| 1941–1949 | Teaches at the Hartford Seminary in Connecticut (USA) |
| 1949–1952 | Teaches at the New School for Social Research in New York, NY (USA) |
| 1952–1964 | Works as Ordinarius Professor in Heidelberg |
| 1965 | Foreign member of the Italian Academy of Sciences in Rome |
| 1966 | Foreign member of the National Academy of Moral and Political Science in Naples |
| 1969 | Receives honorary doctorate from the University of Bologna, and honorary professorship at the Institute for European Knowledge in Urbino |
| 1973 | Dies on May 26th in Heidelberg |

# Selected Writings of Karl Löwith

## KARL LÖWITH

Karl Löwith, *Sämtliche Schriften* (Stuttgart: J. B. Metzler). (Abbreviated as LSS.)

Volume 1: *Mensch und Menschenwelt: Beiträge zur Anthropologie*, edited by Klaus Stichweh, 1981.

Volume 2: *Weltgeschichte und Heilsgeschehen*, edited by Bernd Lutz, 1983. (Portions translated into English as: Karl Löwith, *Martin Heidegger and European Nihilism*. Translated by Gary Steiner, edited by Richard Wolin. New York: Columbia University Press, 1995.)

Volume 3: *Wissen, Glauben, Skepsis: Zur Kritik von Religion und Theologie*, edited by Bernd Lutz, 1985.

Volume 4: *Von Hegel zu Nietzsche*, edited by Bernd Lutz, 1988. (Karl Löwith, *From Hegel To Nietzsche: The Revolution in Nineteenth-Century Thought*. Trans. David E. Green. New York: Columbia University Press, 1964.)

Volume 5: *Hegel und die Aufhebung der Philosophie im 19. Jahrhundert – Max Weber*, edited by Bernd Lutz, 1988.

Volume 6: *Nietzsche*, edited by Bernd Lutz, 1987.

Volume 7: *Jacob Burckhardt*, edited by Henning Ritter, 1984.

Volume 8: *Heidegger – Denker in dürftiger Zeit. Zur Stellung der Philosophie im 20. Jahrhundert*, edited by Bernd Lutz, 1984. [Portions translated into English as: Karl Löwith, *Martin Heidegger and European Nihilism*. Trans. Gary Steiner, edited by Richard Wolin. New York: Columbia University Press, 1995.]

Volume 9: *Gott, Mensch und Welt – G. B. Vico – Paul Valéry*, edited by Henning Ritter, 1986.

## KARL LÖWITH'S WORKS CITED IN THE CORRESPONDENCE

*Auslegung von Nietzsches Selbst-Interpretation und von Nietzsche Interpretationen* (München, 1922) [unpublished dissertation].

"Nietzsche im Lichte der Philosophie von Ludwig Klages," in Erich Rothacker (editor), *Probleme der Weltanschauungslehre*, in Darstellungen von B. Groethuysen u. a., Darmstadt, Otto Reichl, 1927, 285–338. Now also available in: LSS 6, 7–52.

Review: L. F. Clauss, *Rasse und Seele: Eine Einführung in die Gegenwart* (München: J. F. Lehmann 1926), in *Zeitschrift für Menschenkunde* 2 (1926/27), 18–26. Now also available in: LSS 1, 198–208.

"Burckhardts Stellung zu Hegels Geschichtsphilosophie," in *Deutsche Vierteljahresschrift für Literaturwissenschaft und Geistesgeschichte* 6 (1928), 702–741. Now also available in: LSS 7, 9–38.

*Das Individuum in der Rolle des Mitmenschen: Ein Beitrag zur anthropologischen Grundlegung der ethischen Probleme* (München: Drei-Masken-Verlag, 1928). Now also available in: LSS 1, 9–197.

"L. Feuerbach und der Ausgang der klassischen deutschen Philosophie," in *Logos* 17 (1928), 323–347. Now also available in: LSS 5, 1–26.

Review: Siegfried A. Kaehler, *Wilhelm von Humboldt und der Staat: Ein Beitrag zur Geschichte deutscher Lebensgestaltung um 1800* (München/Berlin: Oldenbourg, 1927), in *Logos* 17 (1928), 361–367. Now also available in: LSS 1, 208–215.

"Grundzüge der Entwicklung der Phänomenologie zur Philosophie und ihr Verhältnis zur protestantischen Theologie," in *Theologische Rundschau*, Neue Folge 2 (1930), 26–64, 333–361. Now also available in: LSS 3, 33–95.

"Phänomenologische Ontologie und protestantische Theologe," in *Zeitschrift für Theologie und Kirche*, NF 11 (1930), 365–399. Now also available in: LSS 3, 1–32.

"Max Weber und Karl Marx," in *Archiv für Sozialwissenschaft und Sozialpolitik* 66 (1932), 53–99, 175–214. Now also available in: LSS 5, 324–407. [Translated as: Karl Löwith, *Max Weber and Karl Marx*. Translated by Hans Fantel, and edited by Tom Bottomore and William Outhwaite. London: Routledge, 2003.]

Review: Karl Jaspers, *Die geistige Situation der Zeit* (Sammlung Göschen, volume 1000, Berlin: Springer 1931), in *Neue Jahrbücher für Wissenschaft und Jugendbildung* 9 (1933), 1–10. Now also available in: LSS 8, 19–31.

*Kierkegaard und Nietzsche oder philosophische und theologische Überwindung des Nihilismus* (Frankfurt am Main: Vittorio Klostermann, 1933). Now also available in: LSS 6, 53–74.

*Nietzsches Philosophie der ewigen Wiederkehr des Gleichen* (Berlin: Verlag Die Runde, 1935). Now also available in: LSS 6, 101–384. (*Nietzsche's Philosophy of the Eternal Recurrence of the Same*. Trans. J. Harvey Lomax. Berkeley: University of California Press, 1997.)

*Jacob Burckhardt. Der Mensch inmitten der Geschichte* (Luzern: Vita Nova Verlag, 1936). Now also available in: LSS 9, 1–194.

*Gott, Mensch und Welt in der Metaphysik von Descartes zu Nietzsche* (Göttingen: Vandenhoeck & Ruprecht, 1967). Now also available in: LSS 9, 1–194.

"Atheismus als philosophisches Problem," in *Arbeitsgemeinschaft Weltgespräch* (editor), *Moderner Atheismus und Moral* (Freiburg: Herder Verlag, 1967), 9–21. Now also available in: LSS 3, 331–347.

"Hegel-Renaissance?," in *Frankfurter Allgemeine Zeitung*, July 11th, 1970, number 157. Now also available in: LSS 5, 239–248.

*Paul Valéry: Grundzüge seines philosophischen Denkens* (Göttingen: Vandenhoeck & Ruprecht, 1971). Now also available in: LSS 9, 229–400.

*Mein Leben in Deutschland vor und nach 1933: Ein Bericht*, with a foreword by Reinhart Koselleck and an afterword by Ada Löwith, newly edited by Frank-Rutger Hausman (Stuttgart/Weimar: J. B. Metzler, 2007). (*My Life in Germany Before and After 1933*. Trans. Elizabeth King. Oxford: Athlone Press, 1994.)

# List of Documents

Unless otherwise indicated, the documents are housed in the German Literary Archive in Marbach, Germany.

1.  M. H. to K. L., 8/22/1919, Postcard (copy)
2.  K. L. to M. H., 9/8/1919, Postcard
3.  M. H. to K. L., 9/10/1919, Postcard (copy)
4.  M. H. to K. L., 12/14/1919, Postcard (copy)
5.  M. H. to K. L., 1/24/1920, Postcard (copy)
6.  M. H. to K. L., 2/15/1920, Postcard (copy)
7.  M. H. to K. L., 3/23/1920, Letter (copy)
8.  M. H. to K. L., 9/1/1920, Postcard (copy)
9.  M. H. to K. L., 9/13/1920, Postcard (copy)
10. M. H. to K. L., 9/19/1920, Postcard (copy)
11. M. H. to K. L., 10/9/1920, Postcard (copy)
12. M. H. to K. L., 10/20/1920, Postcard (copy)
13. K. L. to M. H., 1920, Postcard
14. K. L. to M. H., 11/29/1920, Letter
15. M. H. to K. L., 12/17/1920, Postcard (copy)
16. K. L. to M. H., 1/22/1921, Letter
17. M. H. to K. L., 1/25/1921, Postcard
18. K. L. to M. H., 2/18/1921, Postcard
19. M. H. to K. L., Winter 1921, Postcard (copy)
20. K. L. to M. H., 2/26/1921, Letter
21. K. L. to M. H., 3/19/1921, Postcard
22. M. H. to K. L., 4/2/1921, Postcard (copy)
23. K. L. to M. H., 8/15/1921, Postcard
24. K. L. to M. H., 8/17/1921, Letter

25. M. H. to K. L., 8/19/21, Letter (copy)
26. K. L. to M. H., 10/1/1921, Postcard
27. M. H. to K. L., 10/3/1921, Postcard (copy)
28. K. L. to M. H., 10/17/1921, Letter
29. K. L. to M. H., 8/17/1922, Letter
30. M. H. to K. L., before September 1922, Postcard (copy)
31. M. H. to K. L., 9/20/1922, Letter (copy)
32. K. L. to M. H., 9/22/1922, Letter
33. K. L. to M. H., 9/22/1922, Postcard
34. K. L. to M. H., 9/30/1922, Postcard
35. K. L. to M. H., 11/20/1922, Letter
36. M. H. to K. L., 11/22/1922, Letter (copy)
37. K. L. to M. H., 12/7/1922, Letter
38. M. H. to K. L., 12/9/1922, Postcard (copy)
39. K. L. to M. H., December 1922, Postcard
40. K. L. to M. H., 2/15/1923, Letter
41. M. H. to K. L., 2/20/1923, Letter (copy)
42. M. H. to K. L., 4/21/1923, Letter (copy)
43. M. H. to K. L., 5/8/1923, Letter (copy)
44. K. L. to M. H., 5/10/1923, Letter
45. K. L. to M. H., June 1923, Postcard
46. M. H. to K. L., 6/18/1923, Postcard (copy)
47. K. L. to M. H., 6/21/1923, Postcard
48. K. L. to M. H., 7/9/1923, Postcard
49. K. L. to M. H., 7/27/1923, Postcard
50. M. H. to K. L., 7/30/1923, Postcard (copy)
51. K. L. to M. H., 8/6/1923, Letter
52. M. H. to K. L., 8/23/1923, Letter (copy)
53. M. H. to K. L., 9/27/1923, Postcard (copy)
54. M. H. to K. L., 10/1/1923, Postcard (copy)
55. M. H. to K. L., 3/19/1924, Postcard (copy)
56. M. H. to K. L., 3/26/1924, Letter (copy)
57. K. L. to M. H., 8/17/1924, Letter
58. M. H. to K. L., 8/21/1924, Letter (copy)
59. K. L. to M. H., 9/13/1924, Postcard
60. K. L. to M. H., 9/22/1924, Postcard
61. K. L. to M. H., 10/18/1924, Postcard
62. K. L. to M. H., 10/28/1924, Letter (privately held)
63. M. H. to K. L., 11/6/1924, Letter (copy)
64. M. H. to K. L., 12/17/1924, Postcard (copy)
65. M. H. to K. L., 3/27/1925, Postcard (copy)
66. M. H. to K. L., 6/30/1925, Letter (copy)

67. K. L. to M. H., 8/17/1925, Postcard
68. M. H. to K. L., 8/24/1925, Letter (copy)
69. K. L. to M. H., 8/22 or 8/29/1925, Letter
70. M. H. to K. L., 8/31/1925, Postcard (copy)
71. K. L. to M. H., 3/16/1926, Letter (privately held)
72. M. H. to K. L., 3/17/1927, Letter (copy)
73. K. L. to M. H., 5/1/1927, Letter
74. K. L. to M. H., 8/2/1927, Letter
75. K. L. to M. H., 8/10/1927, Postcard
76. K. L. to M. H., 8/17/1927, Letter
77. M. H. to K. L., 8/20/1927, Letter (copy)
78. M. H. to K. L., 10/6/1927, Postcard (copy)
79. K. L. to M. H., 12/29/1927, Postcard
80. K. L. to M. H., 1/16/1928, Letter
81. M. H. to K. L., 1/24/1928, Letter (copy)
82. M. H. to K. L., 2/7/1928, Letter (copy)
83. M. H. to K. L., 2/21/1928, Letter (copy)
84. M. H. to K. L., 3/16/1928, Postcard (copy)
85. M. H. to K. L., 3/20/1928, Postcard (copy)
86. M. H. to K. L., 4/29/1928, Letter (copy)
87. M. H. to K. L., Summer 1928, Postcard (copy)
88. M. H. to K. L., End of Summer 1928, Postcard (copy)
89. M. H. to K. L., 9/28/1928, Postcard (copy)
90. M. H. to K. L., 10/7/1928, Letter (copy)
91. M. H. to K. L., 10/22/1928, Letter (copy)
92. M. H. to K. L., 10/24/1928, Letter (copy)
93. M. H. to K. L., 12/23/1929, Letter (copy)
94. M. H. to K. L., 4/21/1929, Letter (copy)
95. K. L. to M. H., 5/9/1929, Letter
96. M. H. to K. L., 9/3/1929, Letter (copy)
97. M. H. to K. L., 11/17/1929, Letter (copy)
98. K. L. to M. H., 12/22/1929, Letter
99. K. L. to M. H., 4/2/1930, Letter
100. K. L. to M. H., 7/17/1930, Letter
101. M. H. to K. L., 12/4/1930, Postcard (copy)
102. K. L. to M. H., 4/18/1932, Letter
103. M. H. to K. L., 4/19/1932, Letter (copy)
104. M. H. to K. L., 12/6/1932, Letter (copy)
105. M. H. to K. L., 1/14/1933, Postcard (copy)
106. M. H. to K. L., 2/20/1933, Telegram
107. M. H. to K. L., 5/22/1933, Letter (typewritten)
108. M. H. to K. L., 6/12/1933, Letter (copy)

109. M. H. to K. L., 7/29/1933, Letter (copy)
110. M. H. to K. L., June/July 1936, Letter
111. M. H. to K. L., 7/18/1937, Letter (copy)
112. K. L. to M. H., 9/20/1949, Telegram (privately held)
113. K. L. to M. H., 7/26/1958, Postcard (privately held)
114. M. H. to K. L., 3/2/1959, Postcard
115. K. L. to M. H., 6/17/1967, Postcard
116. M. H. to K. L., 6/18/1967, Letter
117. M. H. to K. L., after 6/20/1967, Card
118. M. H. to K. L., 7/28/1970, Letter
119. M. H. to K. L., October 1971 or 1972
120. M. H. to K. L., 2/25/1972, Letter
121. K. L. to M. H., 3/10/1972, Letter (typewritten)
122. M. H. to K. L., 5/5/1973, Letter
123. M. H. to A. L., 6/4/1973, Letter
124. M. H. to A. L., 12/26/1973, Letter

## SUPPLEMENTS

1. Elisabeth Förster-Nietzsche to Karl Löwith, 8/13/1927, Letter
2. Heidegger's Assessment of Löwith's Habilitation Thesis (1928)
3. Excerpt from Karl Löwith's Italian Diary (1934-1936)
4. Ada Löwith to Elfride Heidegger-Petri, 5/30/1976, Letter
5. Entry from Karl Löwith in the Heidegger Family Guestbook at the Hut in Todtnauberg (privately held)
6. List of Heidegger's Courses in which Karl Löwith participated (arranged by the editors by means of the registration lists and seminar books)

# Image Credits

The editors and the publisher are grateful to the following for allowing us to reproduce the images included in this volume:

Karl Löwith
Circa 1950
Photograph
Herder Image Archive

Löwith's Postcard to Heidegger from 9/8/1919
German Literary Archive, Marbach, Germany

Karl Löwith
Circa 1920
Photograph
Herder Image Archive

Martin Heidegger
Circa 1925
Photograph
Martin Heidegger Archive, Messkirch, Germany

Group of six philosophers (Martin Heidegger and Karl Löwith at right)
Circa 1925
Photograph
Martin Heidegger Archive, Messkirch, Germany

Letter from Martin Heidegger to Karl Löwith from June/July 1936
Facsimile
German Literary Archive, Marbach, Germany

Löwith's Entry in the Heidegger Family Guestbook at the Hut, 3/10/1924
Facsimile
In the possession of the Heidegger family

# Index of Names

Alexander of Hales, 242
Alpheus, Karl, 55, 210
Amaterasu, 152, 277
Amelung, Karl, 91–92, 237
Antoni, Carlo, 150, 166, 275
Arendt, Hannah, 190
Aristotle, 8, 16–17, 34, 41, 47, 53, 55–56, 62–68, 72, 73, 81–82, 84, 90, 96, 121, 122, 137, 172, 189, 200, 203, 210, 212, 216, 218–20, 226, 230, 232–34, 236, 252, 283
Augustine, 18, 26, 34–35, 40–43, 53, 57, 74, 76, 77, 79, 82, 84, 90, 98, 137, 171, 180, 189, 194, 195, 198–200, 209, 229, 230, 233, 289

Von Baader, Franz, 50, 206
Baeumker, Clemens, 52, 53, 58, 62, 207, 208
Baeumler, Alfred, 166, 284–85
Barth, Hans, 70, 98, 99, 102, 104, 107, 108, 115, 146, 224, 251, 282–83
Barth, Heinrich, 138, 265, 270
Barth, Karl, 251
Bauer, Bruno, 59–60, 215
Bauer, Walter, 27, 41, 45, 60, 195, 200
Bäumer, Gertrud, 204
Baumgarten, Eduard, 66, 221
Becher, Erich, 52, 53, 207
Becker, Carl Heinrich, 119, 256, 266
Becker, Oskar, 9–13, 16, 18, 24–27, 30–31, 34–45, 52, 54, 55, 65–66, 72–73, 77–78, 83, 86–87, 95–96, 102–4, 107–8, 110, 117, 120–21, 129–36, 166, 181, 184, 189, 211, 240, 260, 284
Bergson, Henri-Louis, 6, 24, 177, 182, 226, 255
Besseler, Heinrich, 5, 6, 11–13, 18, 19, 26, 35, 40, 43, 44, 47, 49, 54, 55, 61, 63, 66, 68, 74, 86, 176
Blüher, Hans, 27, 29, 43, 195, 201
Boehlau, Johannes, 100, 245
Bondi, Elisabeth, 55, 210
Born, Max, 6, 178
Botticelli, Sandro, 92, 237
Brecht, Franz Josef, 93, 238
Brentano, Franz, 53–54, 210
Brock, Werner, 146, 269
Bröcker, Walter, 78, 79, 97, 100, 114, 139, 229
Bruckner, Joseph, 71, 225
Brunner, Emil, 107, 251
Bultmann, Rudolf, 99, 102, 128, 138, 144, 145, 190, 201, 244, 251, 267, 273, 289
Burckhardt, Jacob, 136, 216, 247, 250, 260, 264, 275

Calvin, Johannes, 63, 218
Carus, Carl Gustav, 104, 249
Cassirer, Ernst, 98, 100, 211, 243, 247, 261
Cézanne, Paul, 130
Chaplin, Charlie, 92, 237
Cicero, 50, 206
Clauss, Ludwig, 110, 204, 252
Clemen, Otto, 8, 180
Cohn, Jonas, 53, 57, 175
Conrad, Joseph, 138, 264
Conrad-Martius, Hedwig, 73, 227
Coogan, Jacki, 92, 237
Cousin, Victor, 50, 205
Croce, Benedetto, 17, 189, 190
Curjel, Hans, 5, 176

Descartes, René, 10, 13, 17, 56, 96, 97, 102, 130, 138, 174, 180, 185, 213, 241, 243, 278
Deutschbein, Max, 124, 129, 133, 144, 258
De Wette, Wilhelm, 63, 218
Dilthey, Wilhelm, 5–7, 13, 24, 30, 56, 62, 64, 93, 100, 102, 107–9, 123, 133, 136, 142, 161–62, 175, 185, 203, 213, 219, 226, 242, 245, 247, 250–51, 265
Von Döllinger, Johann, 69, 223
Dostoevsky, Feydor, 23, 29, 30, 134, 195, 262
Driesch, Hans, 16, 77, 93, 188, 238
Von den Driesch, Johannes, 142, 266
Driesch, Margarete, 93, 238
Droysen, Johann Gustav, 172
Duns Scotus, 119, 121, 256
Dürer, Albrecht, 92, 237

Ebbinghaus, Julius, 9, 17, 18, 20, 41, 54, 55, 59, 65, 67, 72, 77, 83, 114, 181, 190, 220, 289
Ebner, Ferdinand, 162, 281
Ehrle, Franz, 89, 235
Einstein, Albert, 6, 178, 187
Elken, Hans, 55, 65, 210
Ephraim, Richard, 57, 214

Fabricius, Ernst, 77, 93, 229
Fahrner, Rudolf, 128, 134, 259
Falckenberg, Richard, 79, 231
Feuerbach, Ludwig, 111–13, 161, 163, 250, 253, 289
Fichte, Johann Gottlieb, 42, 55, 203, 212
Finke, Heinrich, 21, 25, 66, 67, 192, 220, 235
Förster-Nietzsche, Elisabeth, 115, 159–60, 185, 254, 281
Frank, Erich, 96, 130, 132–34, 139–40, 142, 144, 240
Freiling, Heinrich, 114, 119, 253
Freud, Sigmund, 43, 58, 139, 219
Freyer, Hans, 57, 144, 214, 285
Friedländer, Paul, 78, 122, 124, 230
Friedländer, Walter, 93, 211, 238

Gabetti, Guiseppe, 145, 166, 268
Gadamer, Hans-Georg, 77, 80, 84, 86, 91, 95, 107, 115, 126, 130, 134, 139, 154, 155, 167, 203, 211, 212, 222, 232, 250, 276, 279, 289
Gadamer, Jutta, 254
Geiger, Afra, 11, 19, 25, 26, 43, 57–58, 68, 72, 81, 83, 111, 126, 143, 183, 192
Geiger, Moritz, 33, 40, 42, 44, 47, 52–53, 56–58, 73, 198, 202, 212–13, 287
Gentile, Giovanni, 145, 269
George, Stefan, 49, 58–59, 74, 76, 100, 166, 193, 196, 201, 214, 221, 228, 238
Gerling, Elisabeth, 4, 40–42, 103, 106, 174
Geyser, Joseph, 53, 208
Von Goebel, Karl, 114, 254
Goethe, Johann Wolfgang, 23, 59, 103, 145, 176, 185, 199, 206, 215, 248
Gogarten, Friedrich, 70, 98, 102, 115, 224
Göller, Emil, 66, 67, 72, 220
Gothein, Percy, 29, 42, 49, 196
Grabmann, Martin, 96, 242

Grassi, Ernesto, 124, 125, 131, 145, 146, 258
Gratry, Auguste, 50, 204
Gregorovius, Ferdinand, 103, 248
Grimm, Jacob, 143, 267
Groethuysen, Bernhard, 147, 270
Grosser, Charlotte, 72, 78, 83, 87, 89–90, 94, 96, 104, 107, 225
Gründler, Otto, 53, 209, 237
Gundolf, Friedrich, 25, 42–43, 58–59, 93, 123, 194, 200, 214–15, 228, 238
Gurlitt, Wilibald, 11, 45, 48, 183

Haas, Wilhelm, 26, 53, 195, 209
Hagemann, Georg, 53, 208
Hals, Franz, 138
Hamann, Johann Georg, 25, 140, 143, 192, 267
Hamann, Richard, 124, 139, 258
Hamsun, Knut, 30, 196
Van Harnack, Adolf, 53, 57, 69, 209, 236
Von Hartmann, Eduard, 97, 102, 243
Hartmann, Nicolai, 56, 77, 80–82, 88, 99, 109, 119–20, 212, 229, 232, 235, 243, 244, 251
Hegel, Georg Wilhelm Friedrich, 5, 8, 14, 16–18, 23, 30–31, 55, 77, 82, 83, 101, 108–12, 143, 146, 154, 162, 172, 175, 181, 182, 188, 190, 212, 213, 243, 246, 250, 252, 260, 264, 267, 276, 278, 283, 288
Hehn, Victor, 103, 248
Heidegger, Elfride, 167, 189, 204, 272, 285, 290
Heidegger, Friedrich, 83, 233
Heidegger, Hermann, 128, 179, 184, 290
Heidegger, Jörg, 64, 97, 128, 220
Heiler, Friedrich, 69, 224
Heitmüller, Wilhelm, 102, 246
Von Herder, Johann Gottfried, 140, 143, 216, 267
Heymans, Gerardus, 176
Heyse, Hans, 166, 284

Von Hildebrandt, Dietrich, 50, 90, 92, 205
Hisamatsu, Shinichi, 276
Hitler, Adolf, 91, 166, 209, 224
Hofmann, Paul, 138, 265
Hölderlin, Friedrich, 13, 152, 165, 176, 185, 194, 214, 268–69, 274, 275, 282
Holl, Karl, 76, 79, 229, 230
Hönigswald, Richard, 81, 232
Huch, Ricarda, 73, 227
Huizinga, Johan, 134, 137, 263
Von Humboldt, Wilhelm, 86, 122–23, 140, 143, 162, 257
Hume, David, 56, 213
Husserl, Edmund, 7, 9–13, 16, 18, 21–26, 33–34, 38, 41–46, 48, 51, 54, 56–57, 62–68, 73, 74, 76, 77, 79, 85, 87, 98, 100, 111–12, 117–18, 125, 126, 165, 172, 173, 177, 178, 181, 182, 184–86, 188, 190, 191, 196, 199–202, 204, 210–14, 216, 219, 221, 226–28, 233, 243, 245, 247, 256, 259, 261, 265, 282–83, 287–88

Ingarden, Roman, 18, 191

Jacobsthal, Paul, 128, 132, 260
Jaeger, Werner, 73, 96, 98, 226, 241
Jaensch, Erich, 77, 82, 99–100, 114, 119, 120, 125, 130, 133, 139, 144, 148, 229, 253, 265, 272, 273
Jaspers, Karl, 6, 8, 17, 21–24, 27, 30–34, 38, 42, 46–52, 57, 60, 62, 67–68, 73, 77, 79–85, 93, 95, 99, 108, 125, 145–50, 166, 176–77, 183–84, 186, 193, 197–99, 203–4, 211–13, 216, 219, 221, 227, 229, 238, 270, 271, 274, 282, 284, 288
Jonas, Hans, 190

Kaehler, Siegfried, 257
Kahler, Erich von, 9, 22, 180, 193
Kant, Immanuel, 7, 16, 21, 58, 62, 65, 67, 82, 83, 98–100, 109, 110, 112, 123, 133, 138, 139, 146, 147, 161–

63, 165, 175, 176, 182, 194, 197, 212, 220, 230, 232, 243, 246, 250, 255, 262, 264, 265, 283, 284, 288
Karsch, Fritz, 77, 99, 229
Katterbach, Bruno, 89, 91, 235
Kaufmann, Fritz Leopold, 55, 80, 185
Keller, Gottfried, 13, 185, 214, 250
Kerler, Dietrich, 22, 193
Keyserling, Graf Hermann, 22, 27, 43, 192
Kiba, Ryôhon, 66, 67, 221
Kierkegaard, Sören, 8, 13–15, 17, 23, 28–32, 34, 37, 42, 44, 57, 62, 70, 71, 73, 79, 90, 99, 107, 108, 145–47, 163, 183, 185, 194–97, 224, 231, 273
Klages, Ludwig, 53, 59, 114–15, 143, 160, 187, 209, 254, 267
Klein, Jacob, 98, 243
Von Kleist, Heinrich, 59, 60, 215
Klemperer, Victor, 124, 257
Klingner, Friedrich, 78, 230
Knittermeyer, Hinrich, 115, 255
Koch, Hans, 134, 263
König, Josef, 100, 245
Krieck, Ernst, 166, 272, 286
Kroner, Richard, 9, 56, 182
Krüger, Gerhard, 107, 113, 115, 123, 250
Kuki, Shûzô, 226
Külpe, Oswald, 62, 207, 217

Landauer, Gustav, 29, 196
Landsberg, Paul, 98, 243–44
Lask, Emil, 5, 22, 176, 188, 197
Lehmbruck, August Wilhelm, 43, 201
Leibniz, Gottfried Wilhelm, 126, 140, 143, 259
Leyendecker, Herberg, 12, 185
Lietzmann, Hans, 90, 92, 236
Lippert, Peter, 92, 237
Lipps, Theodor, 173
Liszt, Franz, 140, 144, 268
Litt, Theodor, 73, 226, 227, 240
Löwith, Ada, 134, 156, 167, 174, 263, 290

Löwith, Wilhelm, 182
Ludendorff, Erich, 53, 58, 209
Luther, Martin, 8–9, 33, 50, 55, 69–72, 90, 94, 105, 180, 198, 205, 224, 225, 233, 234, 236, 249

Mahnke, Dietrich, 119, 130, 133, 139, 256
Maier, Heinrich, 141, 266
Mallarmé, Stéphane, 154, 278–79
Mann, Thomas, 193, 200
Mannhardt, Johann, 239–40
Marc, Franz, 43, 201
Marseille, Walther, 42–43, 45, 48
Martensen, Hans Lassen, 70, 224
Martin, Gottfried, 96, 240
Marx, Karl, 141–46, 203, 267, 269, 288–89
Marx, Werner, 153, 155, 277
Matthäus von Aquasparta, 96, 242
Mausbach, Joseph, 69, 223
Melanchthon, Philipp, 55
Mercier, Désiré-Joseph, 53, 208
Mertens, Hans, 55, 210
Mertens, Paul, 210
Metzger, Arnold, 10, 11, 14, 18, 79, 85, 182, 231
Miki, Kiyoshi, 87, 89, 96, 226
Misch, Georg, 100, 102, 136, 138, 212, 226, 245, 265, 284
Mommsen, Wilhelm, 133, 187, 262
De Montaigne, Michel, 46
Müller, Johannes, 42, 52, 200
Müller-Blattau, Joseph, 66, 221

Natorp, Paul, 4, 56, 66, 76, 81, 89, 119, 174, 203, 212, 235, 240
Naumann, Hans, 166, 285, 286
Neumann, Friedrich ('Fritz'), 12, 18, 186, 190
Niebuhr, Reinhold, 288
Nietzsche, Friedrich, 13, 14, 22–24, 29–30, 33, 35, 37, 42–45, 53, 58–59, 62, 66, 87, 98, 109, 111, 115, 119, 136–38, 144, 150, 152, 159–60, 166,

185, 193–95, 199, 202, 207, 214–17, 244, 247, 250, 252, 254, 273–75, 277, 278, 281, 284–85, 288, 290
Nishitani, Keiji, 154, 155, 276, 278
Nohl, Hermann, 72, 226
Nötzel, Karl, 134, 263

Oehler, Richard, 150, 274, 284
Oncken, Hermann, 6, 178
Overbeck, Franz, 44–45, 50, 53, 60, 63, 99, 202, 205, 209, 215, 216, 218, 244

Petrarch, Francesco, 62
Pfänder, Alexander, 2, 3, 16, 18, 40, 42, 46, 49, 52, 74, 125, 173, 191, 227
Pfeilschifter, Georg, 69, 223
Pirandello, Luigi, 104–5, 249
Plato, 17, 18, 52, 58, 63, 91, 96, 98, 171, 179, 180, 189, 194, 195, 211, 212, 230, 235, 238, 240–44, 250, 258
Plessner, Helmuth, 100, 109, 114, 115, 120, 246, 247, 251, 255
Plotinus, 8, 180
Pos, Hendrik Josephus, 55, 211
Przywara, Erich, 146, 270

Reich, Claus, 289
Reichenbach, Hans, 149, 274
Reinach, Adolf, 30, 196
Rickert, Heinrich, 12, 15, 30, 56, 176, 177, 182, 185, 187, 196–97, 208, 211, 213, 226, 247
Rieniets, Karl, 35, 83, 199
Rilke, Rainer Maria, 155
Ritschl, Albreht, 46, 202, 250
Rittelmeyer, Friedrich, 62, 217
Rohde, Erwin, 13, 185
Von Rohden, Wilhelm, 43, 48, 51, 54, 56, 59, 65, 68, 73–78, 81, 84, 86, 91, 106, 107, 131, 201
Rothacker, Erich, 20, 63, 66, 97, 192, 219, 242, 254, 285
Russell, Bertrand, 54, 56, 58, 61, 63, 187, 210, 213

Sartre, Jean-Paul, 226
Schapiro, Karl, 16, 189
Scheel, Otto, 105, 249
Scheler, Max, 6, 9, 12, 16, 24, 29, 37, 50, 53, 54, 56, 63, 66, 93, 97, 102, 104, 109, 136, 162–63, 165, 178–79, 181, 188, 205, 238, 242, 243, 249, 264, 282, 283
Schelling, Friedrich Wilhelm, 14, 19, 118, 154, 192, 212, 256, 279
Schilling, Kurt, 96, 240
Schlatter, Adolf, 66, 220
Schlechta, Karl, 152, 277
Schlegel, Friedrich, 11, 50, 206
Schleich, Carl Ludwig, 79, 231
Schleiermacher, Friedrich, 11, 50, 56, 123, 206, 213, 251
Schmalenbach, Herman, 126, 259
Schmidt-Ott, Friedrich, 114, 119, 123, 253
Schmitz-Kallenberg, Ludwig, 21, 192
Schneider, Arhur, 106
Scholz, Heinrich, 16, 188
Schopenhauer, Arthur, 22, 44
Schrempf, Christoph, 62, 217
Schröer, Arnold, 131–32, 261
Schwartz, Eduard, 18, 52, 208
Schwarz, Erich, 191
Schweitzer, Albert, 62, 70, 217
Schweitzer, Pius, 60
Segantini, Giovanni, 122, 257
Seidemann, Alfred, 117, 255
Seidemann, Johann Karl, 233
Seneca, 50, 206
Sextus Empiricus, 50, 205
Shakespeare, William, 59, 105, 215
Simmel, Georg, 7, 24, 73, 163, 179, 182
Slotty, Martin, 79, 231
Söderblom, Nathan, 69–72, 223, 224
Spemann, Hans, 17, 62, 189, 217, 247
Spengler, Oswald, 2, 6, 16, 22, 27, 160, 174, 178, 188
Spitta, Theodor, 115, 225
Spitzer, Leo, 124, 257
Spranger, Eduard, 141, 240, 241, 247, 266
Staiger, Emil, 283

Stein, Edith, 18, 68, 191, 222
Steiner, Rudolf, 59, 215
Stephun, Fedor, 134, 263
Stern, Erich, 6, 18, 178, 190
Stern, Günther, 73, 77, 96, 190, 227
Stern, William, 226
Stirner, Max, 163, 282
Streicher, Julius, 166, 285, 286
Strindberg, August, 69, 104, 231
Stroux, Johannes, 98, 244
Szilasi, Lili, 11, 153, 184, 202
Szilasi, Wilhelm, 7, 11, 48, 179, 202

Tanabe, Hajime, 66, 67, 221, 276
Thomas à Kempis, 94, 239
Thomas Aquinas, 63, 91, 219, 234
Thust, Martin, 11, 16, 27, 29, 116, 183
Tillich, Paul, 90–93, 99, 190, 236, 283, 288
Von Tirpitz, Alfred, 53, 209
Tolstoy, Leo, 114
Troeltsch, Ernst, 53, 67, 93, 109, 142, 210, 222, 228, 252, 266
Tsujimura, Kóichi, 152, 276

Überweg, Friedrich, 84, 233
Unger, Rudolf, 60, 216
Utitz, Emil, 53–54, 210

Vaihinger, Hans, 22, 25, 193, 194
Valéry, Paul, 154, 278–79
Van Gogh, Vincent, 17, 18, 23, 68, 189, 223
Victorius, Käte, 63, 218
Vinet, Alexandre, 50, 205
Vossler, Karl, 96, 104, 240, 249

Walther, Gerda, 2, 4, 20, 26, 42, 45, 66, 67, 72–74, 76, 83, 105, 173, 194, 225, 227, 228
Wasmund, Joseph, 57, 214
Weber, Marianne, 48, 203–4
Weber, Max, 14–15, 30, 48, 52, 143, 145–46, 166, 179, 187, 193, 203–4, 221, 263, 269
Wechsler, Eduard, 124, 258
Wiesemann, Gustav, 55, 103, 107, 210, 248
Wilke, Rudolf, 12, 77, 184
Winckelmann, Johann, 50, 92, 103, 206, 248
Windelband, Wilhelm, 182, 196, 207, 263
Wölfflin, Heinrich, 52, 207, 247
Wolters, Friedrich, 76, 215, 228
Wolzendorff, Kurt, 6, 178
Wyneken, Gustav, 43, 201

www.ingramcontent.com/pod-product-compliance
Lightning Source LLC
Chambersburg PA
CBHW070014010526
44117CB00011B/1562